PRAISE FOR *DEE*

MW00831290

'Once every generation a book comes along that marks the emergence of a powerful new literary voice and shifts our understanding of the nation's past. Billy Griffiths' *Deep Time Dreaming* is one such book. Deeply researched, creatively conceived and beautifully written, it charts the expansion of archaeological knowledge in Australia for the first time. No other book has managed to convey the mystery and intricacy of Indigenous antiquity in quite the same way. Read it: it will change the way you see Australian history.'
MARK MCKENNA

'Deftly weaving together biography, history and literature, an immense variety of Australian landscapes and ecologies with the many and complex strands of archaeology, Griffiths brilliantly charts the history of modern Aboriginal archaeology in Australia. *Deep Time Dreaming* is beautifully written, utterly fluid, with the clarity and feeling of a writer who has mastered both his material and the analytical power of narrative. Rich and absorbing, at times spell-binding.'
GRACE KARSKENS

'A remarkable book, and one destined, I believe, to become a modern classic of Australian history-writing. Written in vivid, evocative prose, this book will grip both the expert and the general reader alike. It tells a story of physical, political and cultural challenge and discovery, where fascinating individuals encounter and decipher awe-inspiring ancient places. Sensitive and scrupulous, the book does full justice to the achievements and concerns of the Indigenous peoples who shaped and inscribed this ancient land, portraying them as living agents rather than static objects of archaeological study. Respectful of the complexities and technical difficulties of archaeological practice, Billy nevertheless manages to convey its soaring excitements and epiphanies. Both ancient and modern Australia have here found a truly worthy historian.'
IAIN MCCALMAN

'A brilliant and reflective history of Australian archaeology in its "Elizabethan age of exploration," when discovery of a continent's deep human past changed a nation's historical imagination.'
MIKE SMITH

'What a revelatory work! If you wish to hear the voice of our continent's history before the written word, *Deep Time Dreaming* is a must-read. The freshest, most important book about our past in years.'
TIM FLANNERY

BILLY GRIFFITHS

Deep Time Dreaming

Uncovering Ancient Australia

Published by Black Inc.,
an imprint of Schwartz Publishing Pty Ltd
Level 1, 221 Drummond Street
Carlton VIC 3053, Australia
enquiries@blackincbooks.com
www.blackincbooks.com

Copyright © Billy Griffiths 2018
Billy Griffiths asserts his right to be known as the author of this work.

ALL RIGHTS RESERVED.
No part of this publication may be reproduced, stored in a retrieval system, or
transmitted in any form by any means electronic, mechanical, photocopying,
recording or otherwise without the prior consent of the publishers.

ISBN 9781760640446 (paperback)
ISBN 9781743820384 (ebook)

 A catalogue record for this
book is available from the
National Library of Australia

Cover design by John Canty
Cover photograph by Crystal Egan / Alamy Stock Photo
Text design and typesetting by Tristan Main

Printed in Australia by McPherson's Printing Group.

In honour of
the original discoverers,
explorers and colonists of Australia

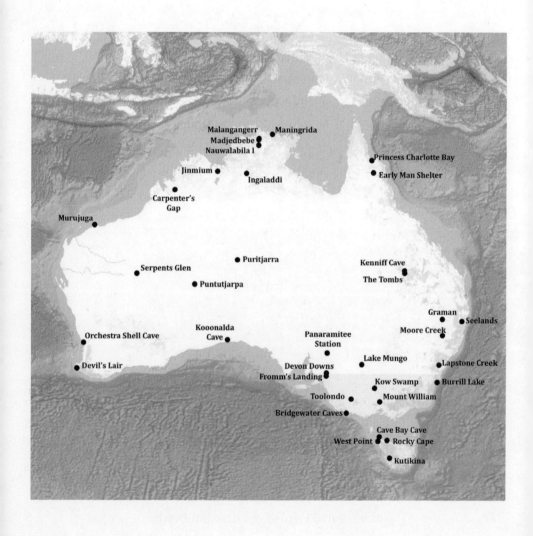

CONTENTS

INTRODUCTION

The Old World

A ustralia's human history began over 60,000 years ago. The continent was discovered by a group of voyagers who travelled across a vast passage of water to a land where no hominid had roamed before. Over millennia, they explored and colonised every region, transforming the terrain as they moved, making the country their own through language, song and story. They harnessed flame to create new ecosystems, dug the earth to encourage crops, and built water controls to extend the natural range of their resources. They thrived in the extreme aridity of the central deserts and hunted in the glacier-filled gorges spreading from the Tasmanian ice cap. They enjoyed times of regional abundance, endured great droughts and adapted to millennia-long floods that saw the sea level rise about 125 metres. They watched territories disappear, lakes dry, volcanoes erupt, dunefields form and species come and go. Theirs is a remarkable story of transformation and resilience. Perhaps a billion people have lived in Australia, historian and archaeologist John Mulvaney estimated to Arrernte filmmaker Rachel Perkins in the early 2000s. 'I remember his eyes twinkling,' Perkins recalls, 'as they observed me grappling with the project to which he had given his life: understanding the depth of Australia's humanity.'[1]

When Mulvaney began his fieldwork on Australian soil in January 1956, excavating a rock shelter at Fromm's Landing (Tungawa) near the mouth of the Murray River, it was widely believed that the first Australians had arrived on this continent only a few thousand years earlier. They were regarded as 'primitive' – a fossilised stage in human evolution – but not necessarily ancient. The expectation, famously expressed by Robert Pulleine, was 'that excavation would be in vain as everything points to the conclusion that [Aboriginal people] were an unchanging people, living in an unchanging environment'.[2] In the decades since, Australian history has been pushed back into the dizzying expanse of deep time. The human presence here has been revealed to be more ancient than that of Europe, which was colonised by *Homo sapiens* some 40,000 years ago, and the Australian landscape, far from being terra nullius, is now recognised to be cultural as much as natural, imprinted with stories and law and shaped by the hands and firesticks of thousands of generations of Indigenous men and women. The New World has become the Old.

Australians tend to have an uneasy relationship with the history of this continent. Of the three strands of our national story – the Indigenous, settler and multicultural pasts – it is the first that we most struggle to comprehend and accommodate. This is partly because Indigenous culture remained for so long outside the national gaze, creating a blindness about both the violence of dispossession and the stories of survival; it is partly because the depth and diversity of Indigenous history has only recently been recognised by anthropologists, archaeologists, historians and linguists; and it is partly because the magnitude of that history – the sheer antiquity of humanity in Australia – is difficult to fathom. 'The human mind may not have evolved enough to be able to comprehend deep time,' American writer John McPhee reflects. 'It may only be able to measure it.'[3]

This book began out of frustration with my own failures of

imagination. I am, in poet Judith Wright's words, 'born of the conquerors'. Australia is a country with which I feel a strong affinity, but to which I am still learning to belong. This is part of the reason I became a historian. I yearned to understand the past and character of the continent I love. Yet the written sources for Australian history are only a few centuries old. They document the voyages of the Macassans in the north, the visits of the Dutch in the west, and the conquest of the British in the east.[4] But this is not where Australian history began. Keenly aware of the limitations of documents, I embarked upon an informal field apprenticeship in the craft of those scholars who deal in deep time.

I earned a place on my first few excavations as the camp manager and cook. By day I would trawl through ancient kitchens, and by night I would cook for a team of hungry archaeologists. The research for this book has taken me to archaeological sites in every state and territory in Australia. I have sieved for weeks on end beside an outcrop of the Arnhem Land escarpment, sorting stones from bones, shell from charcoal; I have excavated in a shelter on a rocky rise in the Western Desert, watching wild camels roam the arid plains below; and I have dug square holes on the urban fringes of Melbourne, Perth and Sydney, uncovering finely worked stone tools under car parks, shopping malls and market gardens. Beneath a thin veneer, the evidence of ancient Australia is everywhere, a pulsing presence.

Archaeology, as with all history and science, is not a simple set of answers: it is an active inquiry.[5] The ideas we have about the past are bound to the attitudes and methods of those who formulated them. My interest in the deep past has grown to include the activities of scholars who, over the past sixty years, have dramatically enlarged Australian history. This book charts the development of the modern discipline of Aboriginal archaeology and the shifting cultural and political climate in which it has emerged. It is a history of some of the people and places that have shaped our understanding of ancient Australia.

Despite my informal apprenticeship, I have sought to maintain an outsider's perspective. This is not a history of archaeology as told from within: it is an assessment from the fringes, steeped in the neighbouring discipline of history.[6] I owe much to the conversations I have had with elders in the field of Australian archaeology, with my fellow fieldworkers and with Indigenous custodians, all of whom have patiently answered my many questions and filled the deep history of Australia with events, trends and people. Every cultural, ecological and climatic insight emerging from these conversations opened a dialogue with Australia's deep past. I hope the following chapters will do the same.

* * *

When Hilary du Cros conducted a survey of Australian archaeologists in the late 1990s, she found that the most common questions they were asked by members of the public were: 'Are there things old enough to be archaeological here?' and 'Have you found any treasure?'[7] Archaeologists in Australia work with a subtle material archive. They read history in landscapes and vegetation, percussion marks and plant residue, sediment and stone arrangements. The grandeur of the past is not to be found in pyramids or pottery, but in changes and connections across millennia. The 'treasure' they seek is neither gold nor silver, as novelist Nicholas Jose observes, 'but time itself'.[8]

In the Western world, the revelation that earth has its own history, separate from humanity, owes much to the work of Scottish naturalist James Hutton and his peers in the late eighteenth century. But it was not until the 'time revolution' of the late nineteenth century – spearheaded by Charles Darwin's *On the Origin of Species* (1859), Charles Lyell's *The Geological Evidences of the Antiquity of Man* (1863) and John Lubbock's *Pre-Historic Times* (1865) – that the chronology of life on earth was firmly wrested from the grip of biblical history and flung into the abyss of deep time. Until then, most geologists, such as Louis Agassiz, worked within the confines of 'sacred history'. Agassiz theorised the existence of ice ages, the movement of glaciers and the crushing power of ice caps with the firm belief, in Shakespeare's words, that 'the poor world is only 6000 years old'. Or, to adopt the scriptural precision of seventeenth-century archbishop James Ussher, the history of the earth began with Creation at sunset on Saturday, 22 October 4004 BC.[9]

There was a reason biblical chronologies were so attractive. Not only did they place people at the centre of the universe, they also provided a genealogy that knitted thousands of years into human generations, thus retaining a sense of time as lived experience. The time revolution within the field of geology was a frightening intellectual breakthrough. In 1981 John McPhee coined the phrase 'deep time' to describe the course of geological events, the formation of glaciers and the movements of tectonic plates: the rifting, crushing, carving forces that slowly sculpt the earth's surface, creating mountains, canyons, seas and continents.[10] Like its twin, 'deep space', the phrase demands that we leave behind the world we thought we knew to confront the limits of our understanding.

In Australia, over the past sixty years, we have had our own time revolution. The human history of Australia is now understood to have spanned three geological epochs: the Pleistocene, the vast period of recurring glaciations in which *Homo sapiens* evolved in Africa and began to spread around the world; the Holocene, the most recent interglacial or warm period that began some 11,700 years ago; and the proposed 'Anthropocene', beginning around 1800, marking the era in which human activity became the dominant influence on climate and the environment.[11] When people discovered geological time, they were themselves becoming a geological force.

This book investigates a twin revolution: the dramatic discovery of Australia's deep history and the reassertion of Aboriginal cultural identity in the second half of the twentieth century. John Mulvaney regarded the latter as 'one of the most significant developments in Australian intellectual history'.[12] It has fundamentally changed the way Australians relate to their continent and their history. 'In my own lifetime,' novelist Tim Winton (born 1960) observed in 2015, 'Australians have come to use the word "country" as Aborigines use it, to describe what my great-great-grandparents would surely have called territory. A familial, relational term has supplanted one more objectifying and acquisitive.'[13]

The title of this book, *Deep Time Dreaming*, seeks to accommodate the two intellectual traditions that inform our understanding of ancient Australia. Although my focus is on uncovering the 'deep time' story, the title is a reminder that history, far from being a 'universal science', is merely one way of thinking about the relationship between past and present. As Jim Bowler, the scholar behind the discoveries at Lake Mungo, observes, 'While I, as a geologist, seek to explain and understand the landscape from within my own cultural framework, my Aboriginal colleagues have an entirely different, and equally fascinating, creation account of those lands. Those perceptions then determine their relationships with the land.'[14]

These connections are often explained through the language of 'the Dreaming', a concept so subtle and pervasive that it eludes Western understandings of 'time', 'history' and 'religion'. Although Indigenous traditions accommodate timing, anthropologist WEH Stanner noted that, 'One cannot "fix" The Dreaming *in* time: it was, and is, everywhen.'[15] This insight is often misinterpreted to suggest that the Dreaming is a realm of myth and legend, where 'time is irrelevant, as in a dream'.[16] With such misunderstandings in mind, the historian Patrick Wolfe criticised the concept as a colonial invention, a 'timeless ever-present' that 'encodes and sustains the subjugation and expropriation of the Koori population'.[17] The term is indeed a colonial artefact, but it was coined by Baldwin Spencer and Frank Gillen at the turn of the twentieth century to foster appreciation of the complexity of Aboriginal society, rather than to force it into existing European categories. 'Far from being an instrument of colonialism,' anthropologist Howard Morphy argues, 'the Dreaming was a challenge to it.'[18]

Today, the phrase 'the oldest continuing cultures in human history' is often invoked to celebrate the depth of achievement of Aboriginal and Torres Strait Islander peoples.[19] It is a statement of cultural pride, as well as a response to the political imperatives of the settler state, which requires expressions of continuity to grant land rights. But such a sentiment implies a false sense of timelessness and suggests a permanent and unchanging way of life. It is a view that merges the 'deep time' story with the 'Dreaming', rather than acknowledging their differences. While I have brought these two traditions together in my title, I do not wish to exaggerate their convergence. Although Indigenous lore contains historical information, and stories of floods and volcanic eruptions can be dated to specific moments in time, the Dreaming is distinct from a scientific approach to the past. It conveys its own truth. This book is concerned with uncovering the *history* of ancient Australia, which is a saga of great change as well as continuity.

* * *

Each of the following chapters explores an individual's relationship with a site or region, beginning with John Mulvaney's excavations on the banks of the Murray River and Isabel McBryde's surveys across New England. I cover the controversy that engulfed Rhys Jones with the release of the film *The Last Tasmanian* and the tragic repercussions of Richard and Betsy Gould's ethno-archaeological work in the Western Desert. I reflect on the place of the Willandra Lakes, Arnhem Land and the Franklin River in the national imagination, and the powerful roles played by Aboriginal leaders such as Alice Kelly, Frank Gurrmanamana and Rosalind Langford in shaping research. I also address the early history of rock art research in Australia, the debates about social change over millennia and the discovery of Pleistocene dates for colonisation. Interspersed throughout are short 'interludes' that analyse the changing nature of archaeology and the rise of the parallel field of Aboriginal history.

By opening this history in the 1950s, soon after the advent of radio-carbon dating, I do not intend to diminish the contributions of earlier scholars, such as Norman Tindale and Frederick McCarthy; rather, I seek to disassociate the discipline of archaeology from the skulduggery of their era. Mulvaney and McBryde both worked hard to change the destructive practices of the stone tool collectors who dominated the field. They were acutely aware of the fragility of the archaeological record, which is under constant threat from wind and water, hooves and burrows, people and policies. They campaigned for the protection of this rich heritage and advocated for Aboriginal voices to be included in decision-making about their land and their history.

There is no denying that archaeology has a murky history in colonialism and social evolutionism.[20] But this book seeks to emphasise the transformative nature of the discipline. An archaeological site is not a monument; it is a history that has been recovered through sweat, science and imagination. Stories that have passed beyond memory and tradition can survive by virtue of archaeology.

The Dreaming describes a varied, contoured and continually transforming tradition. But here I also draw upon the word's more common, vernacular meaning: the archaeologists in this book imaginatively inhabit the deep past; they dream of deep time. The Australian public, with their seemingly insatiable thirst for old sites, are also deep time dreamers.

To dream of deep time is not to dig in search of treasure; it is to seek to understand and revivify the human history of a place from the fragments that have survived the vicissitudes of time. It is an act of wonder – a dilation of the commonplace – that challenges us to infer meaning from the cryptic residue of former worlds. It is a scale of thinking that propels us into a global perspective and allows us to see ourselves as a species. It also asks us to respect the deep past as a living heritage and to recognise the possibilities and responsibilities it generates.

The revelation at the heart of Australian archaeology, as this book demonstrates, is that Indigenous history is ancient, various and ever-changing.

ONE

EXPLORERS IN AN ANCIENT LAND

John Mulvaney at Fromm's Landing

O n Saturday, 19 October 1957, a hot spring morning in the Blue Mountains, Vere Gordon Childe ate his breakfast at the Carrington Hotel in Katoomba, flagged down his regular taxi and made the short journey to Govetts Leap, Blackheath. 'He did not seem to want to talk,' his driver Henry Newstead remembers.[1] Childe instead puffed away at his pipe. On arrival, he pulled his gangly frame out of the car, looked at his watch and then walked off into the bush.

Newstead waited four hours for Childe to return, then became worried and followed his footsteps along the bush track. He found the coat first: a 'blue-green sports coat' on a tree beside the path. Two hundred metres further along, at a point known as Barrow Lookout, he spotted a familiar brown felt hat. The initials VGC were printed inside the brim. Nearby lay Childe's distinctive spectacles, carefully balanced on a rock, and, less than a foot from the cliff edge, his compass. No amount of shouting could muster a reply.[2]

The police view was that 'mislaid spectacles caused Professor V.G. Childe to fall 900 ft to his death at Govett's Leap'.[3] The truth, however, is more sombre. His suicide – like his homecoming – was meticulously planned, a last performance from the world-renowned archaeologist.

Two weeks before his death he wrote to his friend Grahame Clark and vividly described the entrancing sandstone cliffs of the Blue Mountains. He enclosed in the same envelope a personal reflection of his career to be used for obituary purposes at some future stage.[4] In a letter marked '20/10/57', Childe addressed his public from beyond the grave:

> Now I have seen the Australian spring; I have smelt the boronia, watched snakes and lizards, listened to the 'locusts'. There is nothing more I want to do here; nothing I feel I ought and could do. I hate the prospect of the summer, but I hate still more the fogs and snows of a British winter. Life ends best when one is strong and happy.[5]

Childe had left Australia for Britain in 1921, having been denied academic appointments at the universities of Sydney and of Queensland on grounds of his socialist politics. He returned to Sydney on 14 April 1957: his sixty-fifth birthday. In the intervening thirty-six years this reclusive, awkward character rose to world fame. He became the 'great synthesiser' of archaeology, capable of weaving a grand narrative from the disparate material remains of a region or a continent. He championed the role of humanism in a discipline that straddles the border between the arts and the sciences, and he was a firm believer that archaeology was, above all, about people. His wide-ranging work on everything from British prehistory to Australian labour politics made him, at the time, 'probably the most prolific and the most translated Australian author'. And although John Mulvaney compared his 1925 book *The Dawn of European Civilization* – or simply *The Dawn* – with *On the Origin of Species* for the impact it had on his field, little of this fame reached his home continent.[6] In the summer of 1956, Childe retired as director of the Institute of Archaeology in London, packed up his affairs and set sail for Australia. He yearned to return to the country of his youth, to see his sisters and to absorb the sounds and smells of his childhood in the Blue Mountains. He was feeling weary. In the last letter he wrote to his friend WF Grimes, he stated, simply: 'For myself I don't believe I can make further useful contributions to prehistory. I am beginning to forget what I laboriously learned ... New ideas very rarely come my way. I see no prospect of settling the problems that interest me most ... on the available data.'[7]

Childe was deeply disenchanted with the state of Australian society on his return. He saw twentieth-century Australia as a cultural backwater, comparing it on more than one occasion to tenth-century Iceland, and leaving little doubt as to which he preferred.[8] He was particularly affronted by the hopeless neglect of Australian archaeology. As he wrote to his friend Mary Alice Evatt in August 1957, 'I'm sure it's something worth studying and preserving ... particularly the "Aboriginal" rock pictures.' But there 'are only 3 or 4 people working on it at all seriously with rather inadequate training and hopelessly inadequate resources'.[9] Writing to one colleague, OGS Crawford, he described the field as 'all horribly boring unless you're a flint fan', and said he 'could not possibly get interested'.[10] But with others, such as Laila Haglund, a young classics student he befriended in his final days, he was full of plans. Haglund remembers sitting across from his distinctive figure with thick, circular glasses, slicked-back hair and walrus moustache, talking about what had been done in Australian archaeology, who was doing it and the sorts of problems he felt should be tackled. These conversations persuaded Haglund to 'switch over to prehistory'; she went on to become one of the field's first consultant archaeologists. Later she wrote, 'Listening to him at times was rather like hovering over the continent and looking down in a godlike manner.'[11]

In an ABC 'Guest of Honour' radio broadcast on the 13 October, in the final week of his life, Childe urged the Australian public to turn their minds to 'the section of history ... still labelled prehistory – rather absurdly,' he added, 'for it is not a sort of prelude to history but an integral part of history itself'. He railed against the 'old dogma' that Australian history begins in 'the British Isles and Continental Europe, while the Aborigines stagnated in illiterate savagery', and pointed out that 'the archaeological sources for Australia's prehistory are less well studied in 1957 than the sources for European prehistory were in 1857'. As his throaty but sure voice echoed over the airwaves he wondered 'what a systematic investigation of archaeological documents might do for Australian history'.[12]

'Had he lived,' one obituarist mused, 'perhaps Australia would have benefited by a synthesis of Australian prehistory.'[13] In death, the baton passed to the author of those words: John Mulvaney.

Mulvaney was teaching Australia's only university course in Australian and Pacific prehistory when Childe returned in 1957. The two men met briefly in Childe's final month, with Mulvaney managing to convince him to speak to his students at the University of Melbourne, not once but twice.[14] Childe favoured Mulvaney's company over that of his socialist hosts in Melbourne. He was glad to find someone with whom he could *talk prehistory*. The two men passed a pleasant afternoon together in Sherbrooke Forest in the Dandenong Ranges. 'In a vain search for lyre birds,' Mulvaney later recalled, 'we must have walked through the tall timber and clambered over rocks for some two hours. As Childe balanced precariously near a waterfall, I feared that he might lose his balance.'[15]

Their time together was short, but it left an impression. As Childe wrote to Peter Gathercole on 7 October 1957, 'There is an urgent need out here for someone with up to date techniques and notions to make a serious study of South Pacific archaeology. There is much material here some of it rapidly deteriorating but Mulvaney is the only man with first class techniques to tackle it seriously.'[16]

Both men shared a sense that they were standing at the edge of an intellectual precipice in the study of Australian archaeology. They lamented the lack of general interest and specialised research into Australia's Aboriginal past. But by the time Mulvaney met Childe he had already taken the first tentative steps towards an intellectual revolution. The following decade would see Australian history undergo a radical transformation.

* * *

John Mulvaney was a small man, with a quiet smile, large ears, compelling brown eyes and a soft, nasal voice. He was born in the year *The Dawn* first hit the shelves, 1925. He grew up in small towns in Gippsland and the Mallee, wherever his father, a teacher and former Catholic seminarian from Ireland, was posted. It was a 'contented but isolated existence'.[17] He sought escape in historical novels, explorers' journals and boys' weeklies – by the age of ten he even took to writing about the grand days of exploration in Australian history. Over time he would revise his understanding of the first explorers of this ancient land. He pursued his interests in history at high school but knew from a young age what was expected of him: he would follow in his father's footsteps and become a primary school teacher. His only chance of escape lay in the war brewing half a world away. In 1943, in the week following his eighteenth birthday, and after a 'soul destroying' two years as a student teacher, Mulvaney received a call-up to the Air Training Corps: he was to be trained as a navigator in Canada and deployed in England. 'Whatever lay in the future for AC2 438626,' he reflected in his memoirs, 'I knew that I would never return to primary school teaching.'[18]

Mulvaney joined the RAAF a sheltered country lad and returned two years later an adult: mature, determined and alert to his passions. It was not the violence and brutality of the war that influenced him so deeply – the conflict was over before he was needed – it was his time spent in England, a land of cathedrals, castles and hamlets. 'My wartime-as-tourist experiences,' Mulvaney recalled, 'immersed me in a romantic historical mist.'[19] On one long summer evening, as he rode along a narrow Cotswold road, he came upon a weathered stone circle in an overgrown field. The unkempt arrangement, known as the Rollright Stones, was shrouded in mystery and intrigue, redolent of a bygone era. This incidental encounter with the deep past had a profound effect on him.

On his return to Australia, with the aid of the Commonwealth Reconstruction Training Scheme, Mulvaney enrolled in history at the University of Melbourne, specialising in ancient world themes. He was enchanted by the 'majestic' performances of Kathleen Fitzpatrick in British history and Manning Clark's 'breathless' lectures in Australian history, under whose spell 'even banal material sounded profound'.[20] He was especially intrigued by the mention of Aboriginal people in Clark's continental narrative, although they usually appeared as helpless and passive onlookers. As Clark lamented privately towards the end of his life, 'My generation was told the Aborigines were silly children doomed to disappearance in the presence of a vastly superior power.'[21]

Although much is made of Mulvaney's years at Cambridge, Isabel McBryde stresses that the influence of the Melbourne history department 'must not be discounted, as it was then a centre of vigorous and rigorous historical research and teaching'.[22] His time there, under the charismatic head of school Max Crawford, shaped Mulvaney's scholarship.

By 1950 he knew he wanted to be an archaeologist, and, partly due to his lack of Greek or Latin, he was becoming increasingly curious about the prospect of *Australian* archaeology. He had experienced a few 'so-called' archaeological excavations at Melbourne University, which consisted of combing the surface of Phillip Island, 'randomly picking up artefacts' and presenting them to the instigator of the expedition, Leonhard Adam, to adjudicate their worth.[23] He enjoyed this 'daytime indiscipline', but it was John O'Brien's 'unadulterated scholarship' on Roman Britain that stirred his imagination. In these courses he grappled with the writings of archaeological luminaries RG Collingwood, OGS Crawford and Mortimer Wheeler, and boldly disagreed with all three. He pursued these critiques in his master's thesis, which he wrote under O'Brien's guidance. Mulvaney displayed a keen awareness of the ways in which the past is in the present, and the present in the past. Historian Ken Inglis describes the thesis as 'a devastating and gently ironic account ... of how the most eminent English scholars had invented for themselves an ancestral Teutonic people who were responsible for advances in material culture and civilisation hitherto attributed to the alien Romans'.[24] Racial characteristics, Mulvaney concluded, could not be used to determine events in the distant past.

As he was writing this critique in his final year of study, Mulvaney was also reading widely on Aboriginal Australia. He was shocked to find that the only significant archaeological work on the continent had been conducted by three museum curators – Norman Tindale, Frederick McCarthy and Edmund Gill – none of whom had any formal training in archaeology. Otherwise, it seemed, the study of Aboriginal Australia was the domain of stone tool collectors – amateur scientists and humanists, such as Leonhard Adam, who conflated Aboriginal culture with the stone artefacts they left behind. Historian Tom Griffiths unpacks the mentality of these stone tool collectors in his book *Hunters and Collectors: The Antiquarian Imagination in Australia*. Stone tools, he argues, defined – and confined – Indigenous Australia. In a refreshing inversion, Griffiths dubs the intellectual environment of the mid-twentieth century 'the stone age'. He writes of collection as a form of hunting, with stone tool enthusiasts scouring 'collecting grounds' in search of their prey and triumphantly displaying their 'pickings' in home 'cabinets of curiosities'. Aboriginal people, though regarded as primitive, were considered to be relatively recent arrivals, so collection was restricted to surface artefacts. Their culture was seen to be static; their imminent demise was deemed a certainty.[25] Reading a recently published book on the topic – *Stone-Age Craftsman* – Mulvaney was struck by the similarities between the 'dubious' assumptions made about Aboriginal society and those made by the English archaeologists he critiqued in his thesis.[26] Their views said far more about the authors than their subjects.

At the same time as Mulvaney was poring over books in the State Library of Victoria in search of Australian antiquity, American nuclear chemist Willard Libby was refining the technique that would make his quest possible: radiocarbon dating. Libby first realised the dating potential of carbon isotopes while working on the Manhattan Project in 1946. Three years later he and James Arnold published what Rhys Jones described as 'the single most important paper of the 20th century in prehistoric archaeology', outlining how an understanding of decay-ing isotopes could be used as a dating method.[27] Libby got the Nobel Prize for the breakthrough.

Radiocarbon dating relies on carbon: that prime signature of life. While an organism is alive, carbon is constantly flowing through it; when it dies, this exchange stops. No carbon is taken in and the radio-active isotope, carbon-14, gradually decays. The radiocarbon technique measures from this time of death. It compares the decaying isotope, carbon-14, with the steady isotope carbon-12. The rate of decay is the key to getting a date.

'A new time machine has been invented,' Mulvaney declared when he realised the implications of the method.[28] Instead of interpreting abstract signs of age, such as weathering or carbonation, archaeologists could now use the radiocarbon technique to produce a date for a site that was tens of thousands of years old. The curator of fossils at the National Museum of Victoria, Edmund Gill, recognised the signifi-cance of the new technology and ensured that Australian radiocarbon samples were amongst the first tested and published in the world: a midden near Warrnambool was included on the first corrected list of dates Libby published.[29]

In 1951 Mulvaney won a travelling research scholarship and enrolled in 'Stone Age' or 'Palaeolithic' archaeology at Cambridge University, as this was the closest he could come to studying the kinds of tools found in Australia. And, remarkably, he used his PhD scholarship to enrol in a bachelor's degree: 'I needed to learn the rudiments of the discipline.' At Cambridge he studied under the 'charismatic' Glyn Daniel and the 'formidable' Grahame Clark, but it was Charles McBurney's 'directed and enthusiastic' lectures, packed with ideas and possibilities, that most enchanted him. He learnt the tradecraft of archaeology on McBurney's excavations in Libya and throughout Britain and Europe. And it was with the Cambridge model of field archaeology impressed firmly on his mind that he returned to Australia in 1953, eager to apply his newly acquired skills to the Australian continent.[30]

Between his sheltered country upbringing and the intense intellectual world of Melbourne and Cambridge universities, Mulvaney had never knowingly met an Aboriginal person. He viewed Aboriginal prehistory with the same distance as he viewed British prehistory. So his challenge to the idea that Aboriginal society was 'static' was made on intellectual grounds as much as anything else. 'Many eminent Victorians,' Mulvaney wrote in 1958, 'treated Australia as a museum of primeval humanity and a storehouse of fossil culture. In the great dispute between apes and angels, the Aborigines were ranged firmly on the side of the apes.'[31] He could see, even from the limited archaeological work conducted in Australia, that Aboriginal society had changed over time – that Aboriginal people, in other words, had a history. The continent was awaiting further investigation: 'I hankered after the Iron Age but knew I must return to Stone.'[32]

His fellow Cambridge graduate Jack Golson, who established the modern field of New Zealand archaeology in 1954, later reflected on the 'striking similarity of approach we took in our separate situations'.[33] Both scholars followed similar trajectories in the 1950s before coming together

in 1965 to help shape the Research School of Pacific Studies at the
Australian National University (ANU). In New Zealand, Golson used
his fieldwork campaigns to excite and educate students about the possibilities of New Zealand and Pacific archaeology. Within a year of his
arrival he had helped found the New Zealand Archaeological Association
and reviewed the possibilities for dating New Zealand's human past.[34]
In 1961 – on Mulvaney's recommendation – he was appointed to establish a Department of Prehistory at the ANU. Mulvaney also noted their
parallel careers, reflecting: 'I was slower off the mark.'[35]

* * *

It is fitting that the first modern archaeological excavation in Australia
took place on the banks of the Murray River. The rivers and rivulets of
the Murray-Darling system spread like a root pattern across one-seventh
of the continent, collecting the monsoonal rains from Queensland and
the meltwaters from the Australian Alps as the watercourse wends its
way south, then west through the semi-arid interior. Once a wide, cold,
fast-flowing stream, the Murray has developed into a narrow, sinuous,
seasonal river. In the last 13,000 years, the water has slowed and warmed,
forming swamps, low sand dunes and small lakes along the channel,
and seasonal wetlands in the wider riverine plain. Plants, fish and game
thrived in these new conditions and, in turn, so did people. The societies that were drawn to the banks of the Murray wove elaborate nets to
trap fish, ducks and large game; they travelled in canoes cut from the
bark of the mighty river red gums and patrolled short stretches of the
river, rarely straying any further than a skin of water would allow; they
camped, cooked and told stories on the riverbanks and, with great ceremony, they buried their dead in shelters and dunes nearby. Winters
were lean times; droughts were long and bitter. But the almost annual
spring floods ensured seasons of plenty. When the European settlers
arrived, the lower Murray and the lower Darling were perhaps the most

densely populated areas of the continent. In archaeological terms, the Murray River is Australia's Nile.[36]

The sandy banks of the lower Murray had long loomed large in John Mulvaney's imagination. Since his return to Australia in 1953, he had continued to read widely about existing research into Australia's Indigenous past. He published a review of the literature in a seminal two-part article in *Historical Studies*, 'The Australian Aborigines 1606–1929: Opinion and Fieldwork', which ranged from the observations of seventeenth-century Dutch voyagers through to the work of early twentieth-century anthropologists. Archaeologist Denis Byrne has called the article as 'an almost ritualistic cleaning of the slate before "modern" archaeology began'.[37] Historian Greg Dening described it as 'being about the marginal space between prehistory and history', or, as he later named it, 'the ethnographic moment': 'that moment in which confrontation with otherness leads to depiction not only of the other but of self'.[38]

For Mulvaney, however, there was a more pressing purpose to his historical review: he was sifting through the archives in search of sediment to sink his trowel. Where better to apply new field techniques than a site with established archaeological potential? He found what he was looking for at Devon Downs and Tartanga on the Murray River.

In a pioneering excavation conducted in 1929 Herbert Hale and Norman Tindale of the South Australian Museum had uncovered Aboriginal artefacts six metres below the surface on the river banks at Devon Downs and the nearby island of Tartanga. Their report on the excavations documented rich layers of cultural and environmental change – or stratigraphy – and the depth intimated a substantial antiquity.[39] Perhaps this was the dawn of Australian archaeology? Mulvaney certainly believed so, describing Hale and Tindale as 'the founding fathers of Aboriginal prehistory'.[40] It was the first stratigraphic excavation of a rock shelter on the continent. Australian naturalist Charles Barrett was one of the few who enthused about the finds at Devon Downs and

Tartanga. 'This is the opening chapter of the Romance of Excavation in Australia,' he declared in the *Herald*. 'It should stimulate research and may lead to a series of expeditions [in] the quest of prehistoric man in our country.'[41] Yet, with the exception of a handful of 'rough and ready' excavations, mostly conducted for the purpose of collecting artefacts, 'the quest for prehistoric man' stalled. The results of these early stratified excavations were easily forgotten or ignored. Surface collecting prevailed.[42]

It is worth probing the assumptions of these pioneering curators-turned-excavators. Tindale believed that the Devon Downs excavation 'directly contradicted' the contemporary consensus 'that no cultural changes were evident, and that the residence of the Australian Aborigines had not extended far enough back to have affected the ecology of the land'.[43] But despite the emphasis he placed on cultural change, his views remained tangled in the same racial thinking as that of the collectors. He used the artefacts from Devon Downs to help devise a five-stage chronology – or cultural sequence – for Aboriginal Australia, in which each 'culture' (recognisable by artefact types) was of a different racial origin, and in which the succession of 'cultures' – or cultural change – was due to the arrival of the next ethnic group. In other words, Tindale's cultural sequence still considered Aboriginal culture to be essentially static; but instead of one static 'culture', he proposed a series of static cultures. Change, Tindale argued, came only from the succession or intermixture of these cultures, as 'a series of palaeolithic hunting tribal communities' were 'drawn off from the whole seething cauldron of Asia at various intervals of time'.[44] It was a perspective that remained embedded in the prevailing evolutionary framework. Mulvaney, on the other hand, believed cultural change to be the result of the diffusion of ideas and local adaptations, not racial characteristics. Equipped with the new tool of radiocarbon dating, he hoped to find a site that would help clarify these differences.

In early 1955, a chance encounter with the amateur anthropologist Charles Mountford brought Mulvaney news of a promising rock shelter only 10 kilometres from Devon Downs, with a flat, sandy floor beneath tall limestone cliffs. It was known as Fromm's Landing, after the European landholders, the Fromms, who once used the riverbank as a port for the local paddle steamer. It now bears its Ngarrindjeri name, Tungawa. Although Mountford had combed the surface of the site for artefacts in 1951 and geographer Archibald Grenfell Price had led a student 'dig' in one of the shelters in 1952, the deposit remained largely intact.[45] Mulvaney visited the site at the earliest opportunity and was struck by its similarities with Haua Fteah in Libya. The shelter presented a rare opportunity: he relished the possibility of comparing his archaeological findings with those from Tindale and Hale's 1929 excavation. In the early days of 1956, with piecemeal equipment and a motley crew of field assistants, Mulvaney bundled himself into a friend's overcrowded car and drove from Melbourne to the site of Fromm's Landing.

* * *

Just shy of his thirtieth birthday, in 1956, Mulvaney found himself in 'a daunting and lonely position'.[46] The sole university-trained prehistoric archaeologist in the country, with few funds, little field experience and very few people to consult for advice, he faced challenges every way he went. He understood the importance of uncovering the environmental story of the riverbanks, not just the cultural materials, so he tried to persuade an earth scientist and specialists in shell, bone and pollen to join him. He was rebuffed by all but the pollen analyst, Sue Duigan, who had been a fellow student at Cambridge. As for field assistants, he recruited an eclectic team of historians, classicists, scientists and adventurers – five women, nine men – most of whom were affiliated with the history and English departments at the University of Melbourne, where he was teaching Greek and Roman history. The team included Dermot Casey, a skilled photographer and surveyor who had excavated with Mortimer Wheeler on sites in Britain, Vivienne Rae-Ellis, who went on to write the controversial 1976 book *Trucanini: Queen or Traitor?*, and the historians Geoffrey Blainey and Ray Ericksen.[47]

Mulvaney's wife, Jean, was one of the few members of the field team who had any personal experience of Aboriginal culture. She had met John while he was studying in Cambridge, and soon after had completed a mostly solo two-year cycling trip around Australia, funded along the way through work as fruit picker, waitress, fish packer, cook, babysitter, labourer, nurse and pearler, amongst other things. During this trip she had spent time in the Northern Territory with Aboriginal people, shooting crocodiles from a paperbark raft on the Daly River and hunting buffalo from horseback.[48]

In 1956 there was no legislation to define the legal status and owner-ship of artefacts once excavated, no protocols for arranging land access and very few specialist labs to test samples. Mulvaney even faced difficul-ties publishing the results of his excavation – there were so few journals interested in Australian material. He jumped these hurdles one at a time. He received a £200 grant from his head of school, Max Crawford, who became an important champion of Mulvaney's 'unorthodox' archaeo-logical activities. He borrowed cars from friends and charged his field assistants ten shillings for every day on site. He arranged for all the finds from Fromm's Landing to go to the South Australian Museum.[49] And he formed a relationship with the European landholders in order to access the site. It never occurred to him to ask the traditional owners of the land, the Ngarrindjeri people – after all, the Fromms hadn't encountered any Aboriginal people in the lower Murray since they arrived in 1906.[50]

'An archaeological dig', in the words of Greg Dening, one of Mulvaney's field assistants from the 1958 season at Fromm's Landing,

> is a very public and total event. It is not like sitting in a library or archive. It is full of negotiations – with government and local author-ities, with landowners, with sponsors, with those who have special knowledge about the site, with other scientists and disciplines, with

volunteer workers, with students for whom it is a learning experience. There is discomfort, anxiety, camaraderie and small moments of triumph in an archaeological dig.[51]

As Mulvaney negotiated these complexities, he relied heavily on his experience with McBurney in Libya.[52]

The modern era of archaeological investigation in Australia began on Friday 13 January 1956. It was an inauspicious start. 'Our 1st day,' Mulvaney wrote in his field notes. 'Instruction in trowelling, sieving and sorting resulted in slow progress.' The field team camped on the top of the colourful eroded limestone cliffs and each day they clambered down to the shelter below on a track cut into the soft limestone by the site's European namesake. The delays in these opening days were frustrating, but necessary. Mulvaney was determined to distinguish this dig from the amateur excavations that so far constituted Australian archaeological history. He insisted on teaching 'Cambridge methods'. He was dismayed on the third day of the dig when an 'unskilled excavator' found a large grinding stone and removed it from position, rendering it impossible to date.[53] Context is everything in archaeology.

The team used string to divide the surface of the shelter into a neat grid, and two or three excavators worked slowly on one square at a time, purposefully scraping the sand with their trowels. A little distance away, and further along the production line, the sievers tipped buckets through a fine steel mesh, shaking the dust out and sorting through the residue. All finds were recorded according to their location and then packed in white paper bags and labelled. At calculated intervals, Mulvaney would halt proceedings to collect a radiocarbon sample, using a silver spoon to avoid contamination. After negotiating the tricky top levels, which were riddled with rabbit burrows – their tunnels of yellow sand creating a 'honeycomb' of the ashy deposit – they descended into layers of shell middens and hearths and other signs of 'intensive occupation'.[54] At night they returned, tired and dirty, to a fire of chopped Mallee roots, an unexciting meal and the latest chapter of Howard Spring's *Fame Is the Spur*, which Geoffrey Blainey read aloud in serial form.

As they dug, they noticed gradual changes in the deposit and, occasionally, glimpsed a moment in time: a rough scattering of charcoal and bone marked the site of a hearth, a place where people had once prepared and cooked food; a scattering of flakes – stone tool debris – surrounded the spot where a craftsman had once knapped a rock into shape; piles of blackened shells spoke of a feast once held by the riverbank. It took four weeks for them to reach bedrock. In the final days, Mulvaney stood at the base of the five-metre pit, sketching the finely layered sand surrounding him on three sides: an archive of cultural and environmental change. After the relentless heat of the last four weeks, he mused that perhaps the site had been used 'as a shelter from sun, rather than from rain'. Looking at the shells scattered in the lowest layers, he wondered whether the site marked a former shoreline. Sue Duigan sought clues to the vegetation history of the site by attempting to collect pollen samples from the trench wall – to no avail – while others recorded the art and engravings on the rock shelter. They resolved to return to Fromm's Landing the next year and covered the trench with timber.[55]

They had frequent visitors in that first field season. On 23 January 1956, Norman Tindale came and stayed for three days, helping excavate during the day and at night sharing his views on the Devon Downs site and his belief that the artefacts reflected a series of distinct cultures, rather than one society transforming. Mulvaney listened attentively, but cautiously. Since his return to Australia in late 1953, he had been navigating challenging disciplinary terrain. As the sole university-trained archaeologist working on Australia, his peers had become the handful of museum curators interested in Australian prehistory and the notorious stone tool collectors. Mulvaney was often as dismayed by the practices of the so-called professionals as he was by the amateur enthusiasts. One curator 'sieved' his sites by shovelling excavated material onto the metal mesh of a bedstead; another discarded everything except 'finished' stone tools, ignoring food debris, shells and 'waste flakes'. Many of the stone tool collectors considered themselves 'gatekeepers' of Aboriginal sites, refusing to disclose a site's location until they had plundered its contents.[56] But since these were the individuals who claimed possession of Aboriginal sites, Mulvaney worked with them, seeking to learn what he could while educating them about new techniques. He tried to disrupt the 'finders keepers' mentality of the collectors and drew their attention to the science of stratigraphy. 'This was the start of his political activism,' David Frankel observes, 'which was later to become ever more important in his life and to Australian society.'[57] Mulvaney paid tribute to the most rigorous of his predecessors, and although he disagreed with much of what McCarthy and Tindale did, he was a friend to both, and acted as a broker to their professional rivalry.[58] Tindale left Fromm's Landing in 1956 feeling impressed by the 'keenness and attention to detail' of the field team. 'The equipment they are using is new and good and several ideas on excavation aids which they have put into practice should be incorporated into any new equipment we may obtain ourselves,' he wrote back to the South Australian Museum.[59] Tindale also offered plenty of advice to the young team, much of which Mulvaney later 'decided against'.[60]

The biggest flood in recorded history inundated the lower Murray in late 1956. It was devastating for the local communities and the South Australian economy, destroying hundreds of kilometres of crops and flooding whole towns.[61] The river lapped at the edge of the trench and caused Mulvaney to postpone the next field season. But he returned in 1958, and again in 1960 and 1963. Geomorphologists CR Twidale and GH Lawton, with whom he co-authored the 1964 site report, helped to turn Fromm's Landing into an archaeological training ground for students and staff from the University of Adelaide.

Like most archaeological sites, the story of Fromm's Landing emerged slowly, in the aftermath of the dig, through the laborious processes of counting, categorising and testing. It is not the one exciting find that defines a site, but the endless hours of routine recording. Since Australia had no radiocarbon laboratory, Mulvaney drew on an unlikely connection within his field team to decipher a date. The Minister for External Affairs RG Casey (Dermot Casey's brother) helped obtain the first Australian dates from a stratified Aboriginal site. When he next flew to New York for a meeting at the United Nations, he had four radiocarbon samples from Fromm's Landing in his luggage. These precious samples were passed on to a Harvard archaeologist, Hallam Movius, whose results revealed that the site had been occupied since the time of the Pyramids, almost 5000 years ago.[62]

The excavations yielded a jaw of a Tasmanian devil and a tooth of a Tasmania tiger, both of which must have been living on mainland Australia between 3900 and 3300 years ago. The skeleton of a dingo – an introduced species – was found at the 3000-year level at Fromm's Landing, leaving Mulvaney to wonder if the arrival of the dingo caused the mainland extinction of these native carnivores. In later seasons, Twidale uncovered evidence of an enormous flood around 3000 years ago, in which the river had swelled a metre higher than the record-breaking 1956 flood. 'After I delivered a public lecture disclosing this evidence,' Mulvaney later wrote, 'I was deluged (for that is the appropriate term) by people asking if this was Noah's Flood!'[63]

In the excavation report, Mulvaney drew upon documents and material evidence to reconstruct a picture of how people lived on the Murray River over the past 5000 years – what they ate, what technology they used and how they adapted to the changing environment. The artefacts he uncovered at Fromm's Landing underpinned his landmark overview of the field, published in the *Proceedings of the Prehistoric Society* in 1961, in which he reviewed existing research and posed the large, continental questions that would dominate the next decade of archaeological investigation.[64] As Rhys Jones wrote: 'Mulvaney's 1961 paper, steeped as it was in the concepts and controversies of the previous forty years, can in some ways be seen as the last major contribution of the older style, and yet in terms of its critical approach ... it heralded a new tradition in Australian studies, which it itself did much to stimulate.'[65] Australian archaeology was beginning to emerge, Mulvaney reflected, 'from the byways of antiquarianism and the haphazard fringes of lunacy, into a vigorous and exciting discipline'.[66]

＊＊＊

After the first season at Fromm's Landing, Mulvaney led a range of excavations in his home state of Victoria. With Dermot Casey by his side, he surveyed the Glenelg River for stratified cave deposits, searched the small shelters at Glen Aire on the Otway coast and assessed the archaeological potential of the basalt plains of western Victoria.[67] But he yearned to travel further afield. 'One of the essential requirements for an objective prehistory,' he stressed, 'was the excavation of stratified sequences in other regions.'[68] He was eager to gain a broad outline of the chronology and cultural sequence of ancient Australia: how long had people been here? Where did they come from and where did they first settle? How fast did they colonise the continent and what routes did they take on their journeys? In 1960 these questions led him to the Carnarvon Range in western Queensland, almost 2000 kilometres north of Fromm's Landing but part of the same great river system. It takes three months for water to flow from the tributaries around this rugged plateau to the mouth of the Murray.[69]

As Mulvaney roamed the Carnarvon Range periodically over four years, recording and mapping its archaeological archive, he became increasingly aware that he was walking through inscribed country. The land held stories he could not understand. It was on his first field trip to Queensland, in 1960, that he finally knowingly met an Aboriginal person. It was an incidental encounter in a pub in the remote town of Mitchell – he would not work closely with Aboriginal people until three years later at Yirrkala in Arnhem Land. 'I felt like an explorer in this ancient landscape,' he wrote in his memoirs; but he longed to learn more about its *original* explorers.[70]

One cold morning in August 1960, while his colleagues were on a supply run, Mulvaney made his way alone across a sandy flat in the Carnarvon Range towards a weathered sandstone outcrop. He was aiming for a shadow in the wall: a vast concavity in the rock. In the distance he could hear the meandering flow of Marlong Creek. As he approached, he saw a sea of hands stencilled on the white, flaking sandstone: red and yellow ochre forcefully blown onto flesh. Fingers reaching out across time. The stencils followed him into the cavern, where he came face to face with a 'striking' figure: a five-foot-nine person, vividly outlined in red ochre, arms outstretched, 'guarding the entrance' to the shelter. 'In the eerie silence of the dark and frigid cave,' Mulvaney later wrote, 'I felt a strange sensation, for surely this was a ceremonial site of profound significance. It was not a place in which to be alone'.[71] He made his way around the shelter slowly, systematically photographing the art, allowing himself to become absorbed in the task. He counted at least 181 stencilled hands, and carefully recorded the red figure, 'three-dimensional in the shadows'. In his blue-lined exercise book, he also made notes about the more recent 'European scrawlings' over the surface of the stencil, casual graffiti defacing 'this undoubted sacred place'.[72]

The shelter had been abused in other ways, too. Local Europeans knew it as the Tombs, for it had once been a burial chamber. Over many generations the ancestors of the Bidjara people had come here to farewell their dead. The bodies, wrapped in bark, bound with hides and decorated with ochre, were carefully placed in the natural tunnels in the rock. But by the time Mulvaney visited in 1960, little evidence remained of this elaborate mortuary culture. The graves had been plundered, the bodies souvenired or sold. Archaeologists, with trowels in hand and eyes on the earth, are often accused of such destructive activities. But archaeology, Mulvaney believed, is a fundamentally creative exercise. Through a careful and systematic program of recording and excavation, he hoped to piece together the history of those who had lived in this region before the arrival of the British.

He had been drawn to the Carnarvon Range after looking at some photographs sent to him in late 1959 by Reg Orr, a radio operator for the Royal Flying Doctor Service who spent his free time searching the mountainous region for Aboriginal art. As Mulvaney rifled through the box of photos at the University of Melbourne, his eyes were drawn to a shelter with level sandy floors and ornately decorated walls. 'Chance, linked with a hunch, would not constitute a respectable research design today,' he reflected in 1984, 'yet that combination sufficed to discover a major site which both solved and posed problems of continental application.'[73] The site he referred to was Kenniff Cave, a 90-metre-long deep depression in a quartzite sandstone ridge near Meteor Creek, with hand stencils on the walls and bat guano plastered on the grey, gritty floor. It was named after the 'gun-toting cattle-duffers' Patrick and James Kenniff, who supposedly used it as a hide-out after murdering a policeman and a station-manager in Lethbridge Pocket in 1902. The Kenniffs are to Queensland, Mulvaney explained in his report, 'what the Ned Kelly gang is to Victoria'.[74] But for archaeologists, Kenniff Cave is famous for the deep Indigenous history it preserves. The rich and finely stratified structure of the deposit allowed Mulvaney to advance his new approach to archaeology.

He was re-excavating the site on 27 July 1962 when he heard the radiocarbon results from his first field trip. His wife, Jean, relayed a list of dates over the scratchy Royal Flying Doctor Service radio: sample six dated to 12,300 years ago.[75] At first Mulvaney thought there must have been a transmission error. Surely Jean had accidentally added a zero? Jean tersely informed him she had not. But still Mulvaney had difficulty believing such antiquity. There was no other evidence to suggest that the first Australians had an Ice Age past. This date eclipsed the oldest known site – Tindale's 8700-year-old site at Cape Martin in South Australia – by several millennia. On his return to Melbourne he sent a letter formally questioning the lab about the date. The response was apologetic: the site was actually 12,600 years old. 'I thought it rash to claim 12,300 [years] for the age of Aboriginal occupation in Australia,' Mulvaney wrote back excitedly. 'Now I am delighted to find that it is pushed back a further 300 years.'[76]

When the site report was published in 1965, samples from the second season of excavation pushed the date back to 16,000 years ago, which was recalibrated in 1971 to 19,000 years ago. These variations reflect the rate at which the radiocarbon technique was being refined in the 1960s, as well as the enduring challenges of translating radiocarbon years (which are a direct measure of isotopic decay) into 'calendar years' (which need to be calibrated to factor in the changing proportion of carbon in the atmosphere over time). Mulvaney was exhilarated to learn that the first Australians had a Pleistocene past and called the ABC, thinking it might become a big news story. He was told it would be of 'no interest' to the general public.[77]

Mulvaney was also excited about the technological story he had uncovered at Kenniff Cave. The depth of the site and the variety of stone tools it contained allowed him to identify 'a dramatic change' in technology over the past 5000–6000 years. The upper (younger) layers were rich with delicately made small stone tools: tiny points and backed blades, which appeared to have once been hafted to a wooden grip or handle. The lower (older) layers, on the other hand, were dominated by a range of larger, chunkier 'non-hafted' artefacts.[78] Mulvaney resisted the practice of naming each layer as if it was evidence of a distinct culture and instead published the results with statistical tables and illustrations to document the changing composition of the toolkit. He later drew together his finds in Queensland, Victoria and South Australia with other emerging archaeological work to suggest that the stone tool technology of Australia could be divided into three broad phases: an older tradition of large hand-held tools that began in the Pleistocene and continued throughout the Holocene; a younger tradition or 'Inventive Phase', emerging around 5000 years ago and characterised by smaller, hafted tools; and a recent 'Adaptive Phase', appearing around 1500 years ago, featuring a new range of small mounted artefacts.[79] The conceptual scheme filled a void and was immediately used, critiqued and elaborated upon by Mulvaney's growing number of colleagues. American archaeologist Richard Gould recognised that innovation, not hafting, was the main technological marker in this scheme, and in 1969 he dubbed the two younger toolkits 'The Australian Small Tool Tradition'.[80] In 1970 archaeologists Harry Allen and Rhys Jones revised and relabelled the older toolkit as 'The Australian Core Tool and Scraper Tradition'.[81]

Archaeologists today tend to emphasise the distinctive regional character of Aboriginal technology, rather than referring to these continental schemes. But the simplicity of Mulvaney's model, and the transparency of the published results, made it invaluable at the time. It set a new standard for stone tool analysis and gave fieldworkers a practical means to infer the rough age of a site from its technology alone. It also raised new questions about the history of ancient Australia. What had caused the dramatic changes in technology over recent millennia? What might they tell us about other transformations in Aboriginal society?

Mulvaney outlined this technological story in his landmark 1969 continental synthesis, *The Prehistory of Australia*. The book revolutionised the conventional narrative of Australian history by painting a rich picture of Aboriginal occupation prior to European settlement and asserting, repeatedly, that Aboriginal people were the 'first Australians'. Its triumphant opening sentence declared: 'The discoverers, explorers and colonists of the three million square miles which are Australia, were its Aborigines.'[82] The immense significance of this sentence, and the dramatic shift in perspective it inspired, is the subject of this book.

Mulvaney published three editions of *The Prehistory of Australia*. From 1965 he conducted this work alongside Jack Golson at the Research School of Pacific Studies at the ANU. They divided the region between them, with Mulvaney leading and supervising much of the research in Australia and Golson managing archaeological investigations in the South Pacific and New Guinea.[83] After more than a decade pioneering field archaeology in Australia, Mulvaney began to shift his attention to the institutions and legislation that had formed around him. As a public advocate for Indigenous heritage, he sought to protect and preserve sites like Fromm's Landing, the Tombs and Kenniff Cave. 'John was now moving into the role of tribal elder,' David Frankel reflects, 'affecting and directing, even while observing.'[84]

In 2012, in his late eighties, Mulvaney described his role in Australian archaeology as that of an organiser rather than an expert.[85] The distinction speaks volumes for how much Australian archaeology has transformed over the past sixty years, from a historical enterprise into a specialised craft. It also reflects Mulvaney's earnest, practical style, which allowed him to lay the foundations of the modern discipline. He introduced rigorous excavation techniques and a historical vision to a field that was languishing in the hands of amateurs and at the mercy of archaic evolutionary assumptions. And like Childe, his breakthroughs were with the pen as much as the trowel.[86] He sought to understand the human drama of ancient Australia, using his disciplined imagination to bring past societies to life, and drawing their stories together into a powerful – and empowering – continental narrative.

TWO

HAUNTED COUNTRY

Isabel McBryde in New England

Mist billows up the cliff face, merging with the low cloud and shrouding the valley in a thick white blanket. This is often the view from Point Lookout, a high spur of the New England tableland, north-east of Armidale, near the headwaters of the Styx and Serpentine rivers. On a clear day, the view stretches over the high country in the west and eastwards out to sea, and sharp rays of light pierce the canopy of the rainforest below, setting the wet understorey of moss and ferns and staghorns aglow. Today, as the clouds heave across the granite escarpment, the snowgums become lost in the white.

I am here on the trail of the archaeologist Isabel McBryde, who roamed the landscape of northern New South Wales in the 1960s in search of rock art and ceremonial grounds, scarred trees and surface scatters, middens and massacre sites, rock shelters and quarries. 'We aim at a complete, systematic and objective record of all archaeological features in an area,' McBryde wrote of her survey team in 1962, 'not only the most spectacular.'[1] Her study area extended from the high plateau country of the tablelands, which slopes gently to the black soil plains of the Darling Basin, to the broad rivers of the subtropical coastal valleys in northern New South Wales. Sites on the escarpment, such as Point

Lookout, marked the divide between these dramatically different environmental zones. Through her survey, she sought to discern the cultural implications of these varying climates and environments: she yearned to understand 'the personality of New England'.[2]

But as I make my way through the undergrowth on this cool, damp May morning, I am haunted by the words of the great Australian poet Judith Wright, who came here often as a child. She lived on the tablelands and camped at Point Lookout with her father, as he had with his mother. She remembered being mesmerised by the splendour of the cliffs, the mystery of the thickly forested valley and the 'the great blue sweep of the view from the Point to the sea'.[3] But she saw a darkness here, too. To the north of Point Lookout, jutting out from the plateau and dropping in sheer cliffs into the thick rainforest below is a place once known as Darkie Point. Wright's father told her the story of how it got its name: how, 'long ago', a group of Aboriginal people were driven over those cliffs by white settlers as reprisal for spearing cattle. Their sickening plunge was inscribed with Gothic flair in one of Wright's early poems, 'Nigger's Leap, New England' (1945). The story was later revealed to be an 'abstracted and a-historicised' account of a documented event.[4]

Through her poetry, and especially in her later histories, Wright sought to confront the violence in Australian settler history and to reimagine it through the eyes of the first Australians. Her words breathed sorrow and compassion into the early encounters between settlers and Indigenous people, evoking the tragedy of the Australian frontier. Her love of the New England highlands was bound to a creeping uneasiness about its past. She lived in 'haunted country'. In another early poem, 'Bora Ring' (1946), she mourned the passing of a dynamic world:

> *The hunter is gone; the spear*
> *is splintered underground; the painted bodies*

a dream the world breathed sleeping and forgot.
The nomad feet are still.[5]

In seeking out such stories, Wright was fighting against what
anthropologist WEH Stanner described in 1938 as 'a mass of solid indifference' in Australian culture to Indigenous Australia.[6] In his 1968 ABC
Boyer Lectures, Stanner coined the phrase 'the great Australian silence'
to describe the phenomenon, which could not be explained by mere
'absent-mindedness':

> It is a structural matter, a view from a window which has been care-
> fully placed to exclude a whole quadrant of the landscape. What
> may have begun as a simple forgetting of other possible views turned
> into habit and over time into something like a cult of forgetfulness
> on a national scale.[7]

The silence to which he referred was largely a phenomenon of the twentieth century, rather than colonial Australia.[8] And its mist was clearing
by the time he spoke those words. Despite a tempestuous and harrowing history, Aboriginal people had survived the invasion, and they were
making their voices heard. The fog was lifting from Darkie Point.

When Isabel McBryde came to New England in 1960, she expected
to encounter the haunted landscape of Wright's early poems: a land
stripped from its first inhabitants, their culture and tradition 'splin-
tered underground'. She had been led to believe that her study would
be a 'matter of archaeology and the distant past'.[9] But as she searched
for traces of Aboriginal culture in the landscape of New England, her
views began to change. She found a series of stone arrangements to the
south-west of Point Lookout, near the Serpentine River, and recorded
the cairns, walls and standing stones that protruded from the steadily
encroaching bush. Across the tablelands she found carved trees and surface scatters; she mapped axe quarries on the ridgelines and excavated

campsites under towering granite boulders; she recorded ancient middens on the coastal plains and wandered through old bora grounds
in the river valleys. She formed relationships with locals, absorbing
their intimate knowledge of the history and traditions of the country,
and worked with landholders, teachers, historians, field naturalists and
Indigenous people. And as she surveyed this vast region, and imbibed
the lore of the land, she stopped thinking of the Aboriginal past as 'a
dream the world breathed sleeping and forgot' and started seeing it as
a living heritage, maintained through powerful connections to country, 'preserved faithfully by a small community' and 'now the focus of
a revival of interest in traditional culture and values'.[10]

This quiet revelation, experienced by many researchers throughout
the 1960s, would forever alter the course of Australian Aboriginal archaeology. As McBryde reflected in 2004, 'It gave a whole new dimension
[to the field] and also made new demands' – no longer were academic
priorities the only priorities. Archaeologists were compelled to be cultural scholars as well as researchers, and they were faced with a conflict
of obligations: 'your obligation to investigate and record and your obligation to respect the wishes of the members of the creating culture'.[11]
The story of Australian archaeology – and Isabel McBryde's career – is
inextricably entwined with that seismic shift in Australian historical
consciousness.

* * *

Isabel McBryde is an enigmatic character in Australian archaeology. She
is at once conservative and radical, gentle and passionate, modest and
visionary. She has quietly, patiently transformed the way we relate to the
Aboriginal history of Australia. One of her students, Sharon Sullivan,
described her as 'a real lady': 'kind', 'courteous' and 'thorough', with a
'powerful intellect' and a 'steel-edged, or should I say stone-edged view,
of what is "proper".'[12] Her conservative demeanour belied her innovative

and often subversive ideas and practices. The significance of her early contributions to Australian archaeology remains understated. If John Mulvaney is the so-called father of Australian archaeology (a term with which he was uncomfortable), then McBryde is undoubtedly its mother.

McBryde had no direct contact with Aboriginal people as a child. She grew up in a seafaring family and moved constantly, living in Fremantle, Adelaide, Sydney and Melbourne before the age of nine. She was used to her father, a merchant seaman from Scotland, being away at sea, and she took great comfort in his steady stream of letters. She and her older sister were cared for by their mother, who had worked as a secretary before her marriage. Occasionally her mother talked of the Aboriginal people she had known when she lived in Kalgoorlie, but, for the most part, the not-too-distant past was obscured. 'Why,' McBryde reflected in her seventies, 'didn't I pick up that dissonance in the reporting of Australian history?'[13] Her experience of growing up in white, middle-class Australia in the 1930s and '40s speaks to the heart of 'the great Australian silence' that Stanner described in 1968. Even the most socially aware Australians were subject to the structures that marginalised Indigenous Australians.

McBryde recalled a childhood of writing and reading poetry, practising the violin and 'devouring' books on the train as she commuted to school. She developed a fascination with the classical world at an early age, especially ancient Rome, and when she matriculated in 1952, she enrolled in Latin and history at Melbourne University. Like Mulvaney, she envisaged a career in school teaching and, also like Mulvaney, her first glimpse of another career path came under the tutelage of the historian John O'Brien. In his lectures on the classical world, delivered in a precise, even style, he urged his students to query accepted wisdom – to return to the primary sources and develop their own interpretations of the past. It was an empowering approach and it encouraged an inquisitive eye and a broad understanding of the range of historical evidence available. McBryde wrote her honours thesis on the Roman poet Lucan, who raised questions of liberty and power in his epic on civil war before falling foul of his friend, the mad emperor Nero; she pursued similar themes in her master's thesis on expressions of resistance to the Roman government at the end of the first century. Spurred on by her passion for the ancient world and the encouragement of her teachers, McBryde decided to pursue a career in the academy.[14]

When she graduated in 1957, the possibility of a career in archaeology seemed no more than a dream. As curator Frederick McCarthy put it drily in 1959, archaeology remained 'a non-career course' in Australia: there were no jobs in the universities, no funds to finance excavations and no institutional support for the lone researcher.[15] But McBryde had heard of Mulvaney's work at Fromm's Landing in South Australia, and as enamoured as she was with the classical world, she could see the importance of his pursuit of Australia's ancient past. Australian archaeology, she decided, would be 'more worthwhile and realistic than classical archaeology'.[16] But the only way to study prehistoric archaeology was to travel abroad, and all the scholarships of the day were designated for 'young men'. She would have to pay her own way. She lectured in ancient history at the University of New England for six months in 1958 and then, with the support of her parents, sailed to the United Kingdom.

Cambridge University seemed an obvious choice. It had a strong archaeology department under the guidance of Grahame Clark, and postgraduates had the privilege of small classes, fieldwork opportunities and ready access to leading intellectuals. Clark's interest in *world* prehistory made Cambridge especially attractive. His desire to fill in the gaps of global knowledge – to gain an outline of the diverse 'cultural endowment of mankind' – led him to encourage and facilitate research abroad and to equip his students with the expertise necessary to pioneer a new field. In his office he had a map of the world covered in colourful pins, a physical manifestation of his vision for Cambridge's international role. Each pin represented an archaeologist from the Cambridge diaspora, from Louis Leakey's groundbreaking excavations in Kenya and the Rift Valley to Jack Golson's pioneering efforts in New Zealand.[17] When McBryde arrived in 1958, a lone pin pierced the heart of Melbourne, representing John Mulvaney's Australian contribution to the 'Cambridge archaeological empire'.[18]

The archaeology and anthropology department was located in a gloomy Edwardian building in Downing Street that also housed the Museum of Archaeology and Ethnology. Lectures were held in an uncomfortable theatre alongside cabinets filled with antiquities from all parts of the world. But the department had a 'compelling atmosphere' and McBryde found her time there to be 'intellectually, very, very stimulating'.[19] These were the heady postwar years and she recalls feeling an exciting sense of possibility about what could be achieved. Many of the major discoveries in European and British prehistory had been made in McBryde's lifetime. As Golson reflected, 'The discipline to which we had apprenticed ourselves was young and the opportunities it offered seemed limitless.'[20] And the value of archaeology at Cambridge was undisputed. Clark described it as being 'as necessary to civilized man as bread itself'.[21]

The Cambridge model of archaeology was dominated by the methods and principles of Mortimer Wheeler, who emphasised the importance of systematic, stratified excavation, while other forms of archaeology were considered to be, in McBryde's words, 'the province of the non-digging amateur'.[22] McBryde was initiated into this tradition during excavations at an Iron Age farmstead and two Roman forts on Hadrian's Wall. But she was also drawn to another strain of archaeological thought. She found Clark's ecological approach, which combined documentary and environmental evidence, 'eminently translatable' to the Australian context. And she was intrigued by the work of OGS Crawford and Cyril Fox, who viewed an entire landscape as an archaeological site: 'The history of the part', Crawford argued, 'cannot be divorced entirely from the history of the whole.'[23]

By studying a region, not simply a site, and by focusing on interactions between people and land, Crawford was able to read the English countryside in a new light, finding Roman roads and Celtic fields, barrows and quern quarries, megalithic monuments and medieval castle mounds. 'The surface of England is a palimpsest,' he wrote in 1953, 'a document that has been written on and erased over and over again; and it is the business of the field archaeologist to decipher it.' His method was to look for patterns in the landscape, to study maps and aerial photography, paying particular attention to topography, and then to walk the country, searching for the cultural in the natural. This was his primary source. Secondary sources, such as local histories or seeking out 'the old-time local antiquary' were useful, but walking, he believed, was 'preferable to talking'.[24] Cyril Fox took a similar approach. He sought to understand the 'personality of Britain': how the nature of the landscape had affected 'the distribution and fates of her inhabitants and her invaders'.[25]

McBryde gained firsthand experience with these geographically oriented methods in the last few months of 1959, when she took a scholarship to work in the British School of Archaeology in Athens. There she studied sites across a whole landscape, asking why they were where they were, what connections they had with other sites, and exploring the relationships between history and landscape. It was a fusion of two of her longest-held passions, classics and geography. It was also her introduction to understanding the sacred and the mythic in landscape.

* * *

Isabel McBryde's return to Australia in 1959, after a year abroad, doubled the number of professionally trained Australian archaeologists.

She dived immediately into fieldwork, joining John Mulvaney in excavating rock shelters at Glen Aire, Cape Otway, in January 1960. By that stage, Mulvaney already had a vision of the key questions in Australian archaeology. The best way to approach them, he believed, was though careful, systematic excavation of deep stratified sites: 'The cornerstone of prehistory is stratigraphy, and in this pioneering phase of Australian research, precedence must be given to the spade (or preferably the trowel).'[26]

In her new role as lecturer in prehistory and ancient history at the University of New England, McBryde began to articulate a different vision. Echoing Crawford, she argued that regional field surveys, in combination with stratigraphic excavation, should form the backbone of any archaeological program. Her head of department, historian Mick Williams, shared her regional vision and had already established connections with local historical societies and field naturalists.[27] McBryde was the first female lecturer in the Department of History, and she was alone amongst her colleagues in using material culture as a historical source. When introduced as an 'archaeologist', she was often asked by those outside the university: 'What is there for you to do here?' She sensed the same question on the lips of her colleagues. Due to the lack of awareness of Indigenous history, she devoted much of her time to community outreach. She advertised the potential of the field, giving public talks at schools and regional societies across northern New South Wales and introducing concepts such as 'antiquity' and 'cultural change' to lay understandings of Aboriginal Australia.[28] Through these talks, and in an early film on archaeological techniques, she joined Mulvaney's attempts to rein in the persistent culture of surface collecting and educate the broader public on the importance of protecting Aboriginal sites: 'Occupation sites in Australia (middens, rock shelters and open stations) are not so numerous that we can afford to be prodigal with them, to allow them to be destroyed ... to be dug carelessly by treasure-hunters whose sole interest is the collection of curious rel-ics for the family mantelpiece.'[29]

These public meetings also allowed her to conduct valuable research. Unlike Crawford, McBryde prioritised talking, alongside walking. She sought out and interviewed members of the local Aboriginal commu-nities on the tablelands and the coastal plains, and fostered interest and involvement amongst locals with the belief that a conversation over a cup of tea could yield as much historical insight as a week in the field. In the Clarence Valley especially, McBryde formed connections with Bundjalung people who maintained a strong sense of cultural conti-nuity despite the ravages of dispossession.[30] Over time, her views on site protection became more inclusive: 'If we argue for conservation of sites, for protective legislation, and acknowledge the very real con-cerns of the Aboriginal people, then we should also argue for Aboriginal involvement in decisions of site management, on conservation policy and on research.'[31] If the deep past was a living heritage, then engaging with Indigenous communities, and making the insights of archaeology accessible to them, seemed to be fundamental to any research program:

> Unless archaeology, in the present, addresses social questions, unless it is 'peopled' archaeology, its representations will lack dimensions of meaning as pasts, as history. If it fails to interact with other groups within society, it is not accessible to their poetics, it denies to them aspects of their past.[32]

The landscape of northern New South Wales lent itself to field survey. The thin soils of the tablelands meant that deep, layered sites were few and far between, while the coastal plains were dominated by recent shell middens: the cultural artefacts, in archaeologist Sandra Bowdler's words, of 'the unremitting efforts of woman the gatherer.'[33] But McBryde was also eager to establish a regional chronology and she searched for older, stratified sites, where evidence of human occupation had built up over millennia. On her initial survey in February 1960 she came across a series of overhangs in a low outcrop overlooking the Clarence River at Seelands near Grafton. The sandstone walls bore clusters of cryptic engravings, the roof of the main shelter was stained by smoke and animal bones, shell fragments and debris from tool-making lay scattered on the sloping sandy floor. She returned to Seelands to excavate in August, and again the next year, uncovering a dynamic history of occupation over the past 6000 years. She also continued to survey the surrounding area, finding axe-grinding grooves and rock art nearby, and collecting the stories and stone tools amassed by the landowner, Mr O'Grady, during his time in the area.

In this slow, thorough way she progressed across the coastal plains, excavating middens, recording rock art, and mapping stone working sites at Evans Head, Station Creek and Moonee, before taking the survey onto the tablelands and western slopes, where she dug sites at Bendemeer, Graman and Moore Creek. She could be ambitious about the scope of the study as she intended it to be an open-ended, collaborative departmental program. A year in she took it on as her PhD under the supervision of John Mulvaney and Russel Ward.[34]

Excavation and survey work took place during university vacations and on weekends. McBryde relied on her students and her colleagues (especially Mary Neeley) as field assistants, and marvelled at their intellectual and physical ability: 'They could drive trucks, mend fences and dissuade curious bulls from exploring the trenches ... All this, of course, provided there was a transistor radio between the sieves and the trenches so no one missed an episode of [American soap opera] "Portia faces life"'.[35] McBryde gained a reputation amongst her students for her warmth and kindness, as well as her 'nerve and nous'. She was hands-on and hardworking, with the uncanny ability to emerge from a day in a dusty trench, in Sharon Sullivan's words, 'clean, well groomed, with lippy in place and radiating energy and goodwill'.[36] Her field notebooks are similarly immaculate, with detailed observations and ideas executed in impeccable handwriting. She was organised, precise and thorough, and she understood that good food was essential to the success of any fieldwork. She purchased a Rice Bros horse float and refitted it as a mobile field lab with a sink, a stove, a cupboard, a drawing board, water tanks and material to transform it into a darkroom for developing photos. It became known as 'the soup kitchen' and she towed it along the small, winding New England roads behind her Land Rover, 'Telemachus'. She called on a colleague, Professor Ian Turner, to look up the rations for the British Army in Mesopotamia in World War I, and used that as a catering guide for fieldwork.[37]

Alongside the field survey, McBryde and her students pored over regional historical records, analysed early photographs and trawled through word lists for insights into Aboriginal culture and traditions. She was haunted by the collision of cultures captured in the colonial archive and later wrote about some of the witnesses to this transformative period, such as early anthropologist Mary Bundock and photographers John William Lindt and Thomas Dick. As she reflected in 1978, 'It seemed unwise when attempting to reconstruct culture history to ignore the evidence of observers of tribal life at the time of its passing, in the last few decades of its prehistory.'[38] While she found such documentary sources illuminating, she also acknowledged their limitations as a lens through which to view the deep past: 'The ethnographic present may always haunt the archaeologist in this continent, both inspiring and constraining interpretation.'[39]

What emerged from her study was a clear, cultural distinction between the societies that lived in the coastal river valleys and those that roamed the tablelands and western slopes over the last 9000 years. The differences in rock art, ethnography and artefact groupings – or 'assemblages' – underlined the isolation of the two cultural groups, with the steep escarpment of the plateau and the poor high country of the tablelands acting as a 'barrier' between them.[40] It showed that while Australia may be a continent, it is made up of many countries.

Yet despite this barrier, McBryde found some rare raw materials – such as axes made from andesitic greywacke – scattered across the whole region. Along with geologist Ray Binns, she investigated the origin, distribution and composition – or petrology – of these stone axes, and together they unravelled a remarkable map of how people had moved and traded across the landscape over several thousands of years. They were able to trace, for example, greywacke stone axes found in excavations at Graman in northern New South Wales to a large axe quarry 200 kilometres away on Mount Daruka, Moore Creek, where greywacke lies cracked in heaps along the ridgeline in sight of Tamworth. McBryde's breakthrough was to view these trade routes as more than 'purely mechanisms for the distribution of raw rare materials'. By considering the social and ceremonial aspects of the stone axe trade, and the 'ritual cycles of exchange', she could glimpse webs of connections and interactions, past social affinities and mythology. She had found the shadow of a complex system of exchange that was intimately entwined with the symbolic construction of the landscape.[41]

'Nobody,' Mulvaney reflected in 2005, 'had previously traced and explained the dynamics and social determinants of exchange networks using science, linguistics, anthropology and ethnohistory.'[42] It was groundbreaking international work, coming alongside Colin Renfrew's famous study of obsidian networks in the Aegean, and it emphasised the magnitude of the insights that could emerge from the minutiae of local, regional research. McBryde later continued her work with axes at Mount William quarry in Victoria, where she mapped a great network of exchange that saw greenstone axes travelling over 1000 kilometres across south-eastern Australia.[43]

The significance of such vast, sprawling 'chains of connection' cannot be overstated. 'In theory,' Mulvaney mused, 'it was possible for a man who had brought pituri from the Mulligan River and ochre from Parachilna to own a Cloncurry axe, a Boulia boomerang and wear shell pendants from Carpentaria and Kimberley.'[44] These exchange networks brought to the fore the intimate knowledge Aboriginal people have of the land and its resources, and the interconnectedness of their societies across the continent. They also provided an archaeological signature for an oral phenomenon: the travels of ancestral beings in the Dreaming, and the epic songs they left in their wake.[45]

* * *

By the time McBryde finished her thesis in 1966, archaeological investigations were being carried out in every Australian state and Aboriginal archaeology was being taught as a university subject in Melbourne, Armidale, Sydney and Brisbane. 'Miss McBryde's vigorous one-woman band' was gradually gaining the attention of this growing archaeological community.[46] As Mulvaney announced in 1964: 'I feel that the model for us to follow is provided by Miss McBryde's patient survey and record of all aspects of New England prehistory.'[47]

But although Mulvaney and Jack Golson fostered a strong program of regional research at the ANU, McBryde lamented that most archaeology in Australia continued to be 'based on the evidence of a small number of excavated sites, widely separated in both space and time'.[48] Why, we must wonder, did large-scale regional surveys not take on in Australia, considering the insights into land use that McBryde had demonstrated with her work on New England? The changing political landscape of the 1960s and 1970s had a part to play. With the dramatic shift in control that followed the rise of the Aboriginal land rights movement, archaeologists faced new challenges negotiating access to sites on Aboriginal land, let alone surveying large swathes of country.

Gender was also undoubtedly a factor. Although men also mapped landscapes and women led grand stratified excavations, these activities carried gendered assumptions, attitudes and behaviours, which changed the way they were valued.[49] There was little prestige in survey work, while the search for the oldest and most spectacular finds was caught up in the machismo of 'cowboy archaeology'.[50] Sylvia Hallam, another pioneer of the regional model, raised this point in 1982 when reviewing Josephine Flood's survey of the south-eastern highlands. 'Are only women sufficiently tough, conscientious and foolhardy to collect and analyse such a mass of trivia, and hammer it into meaning and shape?' she wryly asked.[51]

In 1974 McBryde moved to the ANU, where she became increasingly concerned with promoting an inclusive approach to Indigenous heritage. She saw an urgent need to empower Aboriginal people to tell their own stories and to create mechanisms through which they could control their own heritage. Through her roles on the Australian Heritage Commission, the World Heritage Committee and the UNESCO advisory body, she argued for legislation that recognised the significance of whole landscapes, the inseparability of natural and cultural heritage and the intangible values of connections to country. This advocacy has had a profound role in shaping Australian and world heritage conservation practice. McBryde's proudest achievement, however, is the number of Aboriginal students she has helped become archaeologists.[52]

* * *

In 1991 McBryde returned to New England and walked the land as she once had done. She revisited familiar places on the tablelands and across the coastal plains, and met and talked with residents, both Indigenous and non-Indigenous. As she moved across the landscape, wandering through rich subtropical valleys and densely forested steep terrain, she was followed by a story. Helpful locals told her of a woman who had come to look at the archaeology in the region long, long ago, 'maybe last century'.[53] She gradually identified the woman as herself. Her work had merged in local memory with that of another pioneer: nineteenth-century anthropologist Mary Bundock. She had entered the lore of the land.

McBryde first encountered Bundock's name in 1968 while trawling through the Australian ethnographic collection at the Rijksmuseum voor Volkenkunde in Leiden: 'With intense excitement I began to realise, working through registers and cabinets, that its collection included a comprehensive regional group of artefacts from my own research area of north-eastern New South Wales.' The carefully documented artefacts, donated to the museum between 1885 and 1892, led her to their collector, the little-known Mary Bundock. Information about Bundock's life was sparse, yet McBryde was intrigued by one surviving fragment of her writing: an eleven-page document titled 'Notes on the Richmond River Blacks'. Bundock's ethnographic notes bore the stamp of someone who had formed close bonds with the Indigenous community on the upper Richmond River and had a knowledge of the local dialect of Bandjalang. 'The Aborigines in her account are people,' McBryde noted, 'not exemplars of a stage of human existence long past in the civilised European world.' She also detected in the modest, non-judgemental observations what she has described as 'an inheritance of concern': 'a response to the challenges of living on the pastoral frontier, of facing the responsibility of being dispossessors'.[54] That same inheritance has shaped McBryde's life and values; it underwrites the inclusive, social approach to archaeology she has advocated since the 1960s. Her routes across the landscape linger today, sustained in fragments of text and memory, casting light upon the shadows of a haunted country.

Before it is too late, 1961

ON A COOL MORNING ON MONDAY, 15 MAY 1961, AN UNUSUAL convergence of scholars met at University House in Canberra. The eclectic group of anthropologists, linguists, archaeologists, ethnomusicologists, physical anthropologists, historians and curators had gathered from all corners of the continent to discuss the culture and heritage of the first Australians. This was the first time many of the attendees had met their direct colleagues, let alone those in other disciplines. The organiser of the event, anthropologist WEH Stanner, had brought them together with the belief that 'fields of study are not cut off from one another but mingle, just as people do'.[1]

The gathering signalled a new era for the study of Indigenous Australia. Many archaeologists look back at 1961 as 'the Dreamtime year for Prehistory', 'the *annus mirabilis* of Australian archaeology'.[2] There were, of course, deeply rooted underlying causes for the explosion of archaeological research at this time, such as the discovery of radiocarbon dating in 1949, the expansion of universities and the arrival of Cambridge-trained archaeologists. But at the heart of this new wave of research was a shift in thinking about Indigenous history and culture, which was manifested in the foundation of the Australian Institute for Aboriginal Studies (AIAS).[3]

Amongst the fifty-five researchers who huddled in University House on that May morning was Isabel McBryde, representing 'prehistory' while John Mulvaney was away in London working at the Institute of Archaeology. It was her first conference, and she recalled being 'quite daunted' by the experience. There was a great sense of occasion: it was a grand coming together of people and ideas. At the conference dinner on 17 May McBryde found herself sitting between the eminent anthropologists Charles Mountford and Donald Thompson. 'They talked very nicely over my head,' she recalled.[4]

The conference, in McBryde's words, was a 'salvage job'.[5] It was inspired by a submission Liberal Minister WC Wentworth had made to the commonwealth government in 1959 proposing an urgent redirection of funds to research on Indigenous Australia. His nine-page paper, titled 'An Australian Institute for Aboriginal Studies', agitated for an institute with a keen awareness of 'the development of interest in coloured peoples throughout the world, and the significance this can have for Australia's treatment of its own coloured people'.[6]

His enthusiasm for Indigenous cultures was tinged with archaic thinking about confronting the primordial – 'studying man and man's nature' – but he also believed that a record of their history and traditions would be 'one of the priceless treasures of mankind'. There was a powerful sense of urgency to his proposal. Like many others at the conference, he espoused the colonial belief that traditional culture was 'dying out', not transforming. 'Within ten years there will be nothing but a fraction of a fraction left,' he wrote. 'It must be recorded now, or it will go unrecorded for ever.'[7] He also emphasised the importance of Indigenous people to Australia's standing internationally: 'If Australia were to allow the Aboriginal culture to evaporate unrecorded, she would run the risk of incurring the perpetual reproach of the world of scholarship.'[8] Anthropologist Nicolas Peterson highlights the explicit nationalism of Wentworth's proposal: 'He perceived that

Aboriginal people and their cultures were a crucial icon of an independent Australian identity.'[9]

Acting Prime Minister John McEwen saw the utility of such a
conference, and gave it reserved encouragement: 'A thorough study [of
Aboriginal culture and heritage] could have some practical significance
for our domestic policy and for some aspects of our international relations. Viewed thus, it can be regarded as a national responsibility.'[10] It
was with such a brief that Stanner, as convenor and chairman, invited
his colleagues 'to assess the state of scientific knowledge' in their fields,
'to appraise the gaps', and to suggest 'concrete' proposals to fill those
gaps with future research. He, too, regarded the study of Indigenous
Australia to be an important aspect of 'our duty to posterity' and 'to scientific understanding'. And he hoped the development of a specialised
research institute would contribute 'to the sympathetic understanding of the aborigines and their culture by the community as a whole'.
'Archaeological research,' Stanner wrote in the report on the conference,
'not only throws light on the origins and past history of these people,
but also contributes to the understanding of the contemporary status
of the aboriginal population and the problems of its assimilation.'[11]

As an afterthought, in 1962, Wentworth suggested that when establishing the permanent council for the Australian Institute of Aboriginal
Studies 'consideration should be given to adding one or two aborigines as members'.[12] But here Wentworth was ahead of council thinking.
There were no Aboriginal people present at the 1961 conference, and in
the years that followed enthusiasm for the institute waned. Wentworth's
original scheme, which envisaged the AIAS as a research hub as well
as a coordinating body, was deemed 'too elaborate'.[13] Although Prime
Minister Robert Menzies 'accepted the argument that aboriginal studies deserve some special encouragement, particularly because of rapidly
vanishing source material', he felt it was also a 'limited' field and that
funding should be kept 'in proportion'. The institute, he decided,

'should be primarily a co-ordinating and sponsoring body'.[14] It was with this scope that the Interim Council of the AIAS was made permanent on 2 June 1964 through an act of parliament, with Frederick McCarthy as its first principal. Kim Beazley (Snr), who co-sponsored the bill with Wentworth, celebrated that: 'For the first time officially in Commonwealth history the Commonwealth is recording its appreciation of aboriginal life, and of the aboriginal people.'[15]

The impact of the AIAS on archaeological research was instantaneous. Archaeologists harnessed the institute's resources to build the foundations of their discipline. It became, in Vincent Megaw's words, 'our Federal fairy godmother'.[16] One of the first acts of the AIAS was to fund a radiocarbon laboratory at the ANU and the first round of grants in 1962 supported John Mulvaney, Isabel McBryde and Rhys Jones to conduct fieldwork in, respectively, Kenniff Cave, New England and Rocky Cape. Despite ongoing conflicts over the purpose and function of the AIAS, archaeologists seized upon it as an organising body, using the institute's conferences, general meetings and newsletters to discuss the concerns and development of their field.[17]

The institute 'revolutionized research' in the field, in McCarthy's words, creating 'a great body of information, about the Aborigines and their culture, of which Aboriginal people should be proud'.[18] The unforeseen impact of Wentworth's proposal, and the development of the institute, was to create a space in which, over time, Aboriginal and Torres Strait Islander peoples could develop a powerful political voice.[19]

THREE

THE FIRST TASMANIANS

Rhys Jones at Rocky Cape

There is a photo of the archaeologist Rhys Jones sitting alone on the ridge behind Sisters Beach in north-western Tasmania, surrounded by quartzite boulders, native grasses and banksia serrata. It was taken in the early 1960s and Jones is boyish and bearded, with his Dai cap tipped to the side and big black boots emerging from the undergrowth. But it is his gaze that dominates the image. He leans back on the rock with his hands folded in front of him and his head raised, staring intensely across the choppy waters of Bass Strait in the far distance. He is posing, yes, performing for the camera, but I also imagine that he is dreaming: travelling through time in his mind's eye, as he so often did, and watching the sea before him recede, the torrid waters give way to a low land bridge, the landscape return to its form at the end of the last Ice Age, when the polar ice caps bulged and Tasmania was still attached to the Australian mainland as part of the greater continent of 'Sahul'.

Jones had the imaginative capacity for time travel. He spent so much of his time dreaming of the deep past that he believed he had 'in a sense absorbed into my skin a feeling of what it was like to live in Tasmanian society' through time.[1] He used this intuitive understanding to conjure an image of the past that he could then study: 'It is only a still photograph and it rapidly fades, but in the meantime we can count the people, observe their social groups, analyse their economic activities.'[2] Over three archaeological field seasons along the northern coast of Tasmania he camped behind the ridge in this photo. At night he would walk along the beach, sometimes alone, sometimes with others, admiring the glow of the moon on the inky black water of Bass Strait. 'At that time,' Jones reflected, 'we weren't sure how old anything was.' Bass Strait provided the climatic key to Australia's Ice Age past. The land bridge between Tasmania and the mainland had been sundered at the end of the last Ice Age, around 12,000 years ago. Had the first Tasmanians voyaged to an island? Or had they watched from the peninsula as the tide encroached and the land bridge was drowned, isolating them for millennia? These were the questions that loomed in Jones' mind as he wandered Sisters Beach gazing out across the stormy strait. To the west he could make out the jagged, saw-tipped edge of the Rocky Cape peninsula, where he sought answers in his archaeological excavations. To the east, sea cliffs stood sentry over the strait, evoking the Ice Age landscapes of the north African coast and La Cotte de St Brelade off Normandy: 'It was a classic Paleolithic terrain.'[3]

In 1978, after fifteen years of working in the state, Jones was commissioned by the publishing house Thomas Nelson to write a popular book on Tasmanian history and archaeology. It was supposed to tie in with a film he had made with director Tom Haydon, *The Last Tasmanian: A Story of Genocide*, and Jones hoped to capture that filmic quality in his prose. He wanted to write of the past as if he were there relaying his observations like 'a radio correspondent', conveying intimate, sensuous details 'that could draw the reader in, so that in his guts he has a feeling of what this life was like'. Writing to his publisher Bob Sessions on 21 October 1980, he outlined a series of 'scenes' he and Haydon envisaged for the book: the formation of the 'Gondwana Supercontinent and the southern rain forest'; the first human crossing of the swept Bassian Plain towards the ice cap of the Tasmanian peninsula; the smells and sounds of camp life at Sundown Creek in 1800; 'the deck of Baudin's ship in the summer of 1802 going up D'Entrecasteaux Channel'; François Péron's experiences with 'the Tasmanian girl he fancied', Ouré Ouré; the climate of fear in 'a shepherd's hut on the upper Clyde River c. 1826'; 'the Black Line' spreading across Tasmania in 1830; 'the decimation of the Pieman River band due to disease'; and the 'rounding up' of survivors to be shipped off to the Bass Strait islands. In the penultimate scene he envisaged an image of Truganini, the so-called 'last Tasmanian', whose skeleton was 'strung up' and displayed in 'a dusty museum' for a century. But his final scene was reserved for a more positive – and rather heroic – story: 'the new archaeology and discovery of the Tasmanian past – ie my first expedition'.[4]

The book was never written. *The Last Tasmanian* and its creators became embroiled in controversy almost as soon as the publishing contract was signed. The film confronted the violence and tragedy in Tasmania's past, marketing itself as 'more than a film … an historic document of major importance'.[5] It delved deep inside what art historian Bernard Smith would call 'the locked cupboard of our history' and made an early argument for the forcible dispossession of Tasmanian Aboriginal people to be understood as genocide.[6] It was a critical and commercial success in Australia and around the world, and for many Australians it came as a grim and disturbing revelation about their all-too-recent past. Yet, with its very title, Haydon and Jones were accused of undermining those who had survived this harrowing history. A resurgent Tasmanian Aboriginal community, led by those who had lived for years on the Bass Strait islands, attacked the film and the flamboyant archaeologist at its centre for denying their political existence and perpetuating a nineteenth-century 'dying race' myth. *The Last Tasmanian* was painted as part of the legacy it was trying to overturn.

The uproar surrounding the film delayed the writing process; but the book was also bedevilled by Jones' intellectual restlessness. He found the writing slow and struggled to convey 'the Tasmanian Aborigines as themselves ... and not as some cyphers of cardboard cut-out caricatures of humanity in the explorers' note books'.[7] There are a few fragments of the manuscript buried away in his personal archive. They are raw, 'totally and utterly uncorrected', and were obviously committed to the page in bursts, with sentences written and rewritten as Jones played with rhythm, poetry and imagery. The rough pages of the discarded manuscript have been typed and retyped, edited in scrawls of blue and black pen, with long passages of handwriting between typed pages. It is messy, but vivid and imaginative. He takes us 'in our mind's eye' to an Aboriginal camp on the west coast of Tasmania beside steep dunes and with majestic views, and then we are propelled on a journey up the Gordon River through the ancient southern forests where 'dark squalls of rain and low cloud sweep in from the south west ocean, and mist hangs in skeins around the tree tops and river-side rocky bluffs'.[8]

Jones loved the rigour and precision of archaeology. He had a mathematical mind and was at home working through masses of quantitative data. But he also sought to create images that could carry his ideas. As much as he was an archaeologist or a scientist, he was also a poet. He yearned to reanimate the past and capture the texture of a lost world, rather than reduce it to a tendentious list. As he wrote to his increasingly exasperated publisher, 'These are the small episodes, the minutiae of history, but they exemplify great events, like a personal human life is both intimate and is the product of and in some way affects the great currents of history.'[9]

Jones also found himself swept up in the great currents of history. John Mulvaney readily cedes him the title of 'the most significant archaeologist to work in Australia' and he had a unique impact on the field of Australian archaeology. He was irrepressible: restless and romantic, boastful and brilliant. He courted controversy and provoked debate. 'Although he never wrote a book,' Mulvaney reflected, 'several of his articles throw up more ideas than many volumes.'[11] His breathless manner and penchant for performance made him a gift to journalists seeking to understand the emerging story of ancient Australia. Novelists thinly fictionalised his rugged, larrikin persona; *Australian Playboy* devoted a seven-page feature to his vision of ancient Australia; and he was heralded in the press as 'Australiana Jones', the 'prehistory cowboy' and, due to his diminutive stature, the 'Welsh Leprechaun'.[12] As I sift through his papers in the National Library of Australia, his larger-than-life character overflows from every page, from the witty asides buried amongst his conference notes, evidently intended for another distracted audience member, to his personal file on '*L'Homme Sauvage*', in which he documented, tongue-in-cheek, the 'savage' within us all. He pioneered the study of Tasmania's Aboriginal past, challenging expectations and preconceptions of Indigenous people across the continent, and yet found himself frequently associated with the archaic views he sought to upend. As historian Rebe Taylor shows in her series of articles on the restless Welshman, 'Jones's ability to give poetic power to academic ideas left him vulnerable to being misread.'[13]

* * *

From a young age Rhys Jones was drawn to the mysterious relationship between geography and history. He was born into a Welsh-speaking family during World War II on 26 February 1941 and grew up with an acute sense of being in an ethnic minority – even within Wales. His middle name – Maengwyn – evokes the standing stones of Ynys y Maengwyn, which rise from hard ground in the coastal wetlands in south-west Meirion. When his ancestors moved from rural Meirionnydd and Maldwyn into the industrial slate-quarry towns of northern Wales they carried their traditions and language with them, naming their children after totemic sites of their own *bro* or country. Maengwyn translates literally as 'Island of the white, shining or magical stone'. Rhys shared the name with his father, Griffith Maengwyn Jones, and he wore it, and the lineage it symbolised, with pride. 'Not every archaeologist has the good fortune to be named after a megalith.'[14]

These deep historical resonances are a key to his character. It was no coincidence, Jones believed, that Welsh society began and ended on the fringes of the upland zone. 'As a Welshman myself, I feel a loss that my country has suffered, in its marginal place on the edge of a dominant England.'[15] Jones was proud to call himself an indigenous Briton. As his colleague Carmel Schrire reflected in 2001,

> He understood what it felt like to look out across a grey sea, whether from Bangor or Burnie, and feel your back pressing against the wall of what you thought was your own land … It was a measure of his genius that he converted this personal sense of loss into a universal sense of suffering, that transformed not only the way people thought about Tasmania, but the way they understand their own deep past.[16]

Jones enjoyed hamming up his Welsh heritage in the field, often smearing his face with dirt to achieve the look of a Welsh miner – an occupation his grandfather had pursued as a teenager. And he continued to speak and write Welsh throughout his life, publishing his Tasmanian research in Welsh academic journals and even narrating a Welsh-language version of *The Last Tasmanian* for BBC Wales – the first Welsh feature film, according to the Guinness World Records.[17]

As a child Jones moved often, staying in towns of stone and slate, following the work of his father, a physicist. In 1949 they settled in Blaenau Ffestiniog in northern Wales, Jones' father's ancestral town. It was this 'great, grey, cold and wet place' surrounded by 'a wall of rugged peaks clothed, almost always, in mist' that became home.[18] And it was the ancient landscape that surrounded Blaenau Ffestiniog that ignited Jones' archaeological imagination. Stone-paved Roman roads traversed the country behind his backyard at 'Bryn Offeren'; megalithic monuments (stone arrangements) were scattered throughout the damp, green fields; and mournful Norman castles lined the nearby ridgelines, telling in their ruin stories of glorious defeat.[19] These ancient monuments became Jones' 'fantasy world', and it was in their shadows that he kindled a lasting passion for historical re-enactment. He built Neolithic turf huts and a pit house in his overgrown garden at 'Bryn Offeren' and made makeshift armour and bows and arrows with his friends, reliving the bloody conflicts between the Welsh and the Normans, the Celts and the Romans. In the evenings, he listened intently to his family's stories of the Druids in Welsh history and watched the popular BBC television show *Animal, Vegetable, Mineral*, on which the archaeological luminaries Glyn Daniel, Mortimer Wheeler and Gordon Childe appeared. 'All my early childhood memories,' he reflected in 1991, 'are in a sense archaeological.'[20]

In 1954, his father died suddenly from a brain tumour. Rhys was twelve years old. His mother, Enid Watkin Jones, moved the family to Cardiff to be closer to her parents, and Rhys was enrolled in Whitchurch Grammar School along with his two cousins. The three of them found themselves speaking 'Welsh in a sea of English.'[21] Enid taught French in Cardiff and during the summers took Rhys and his sister across the channel to Brittany, where they learnt French and snippets of the Celtic Breton. A school assignment from this time survives in his personal archive. He filled a neat exercise book titled 'Geography: Form III A' with colourful maps of Australian geography and brief historical summaries of the states. 'Tasmania,' he wrote in 1954, '. . . is a mountainous island about 3 times the size of Wales.'[22]

The decision to become an archaeologist came naturally to Jones. His father's influence ensured that he pursued physics, maths and chemistry at school, but it was the ancient landscape of his youth that drew him in: 'My deep core interests were still that landscape history, but I saw in archaeology a way in which you could use the physical methods to create history, so that these two actually welded together.'[23] In 1958 he met Hubert Savory, Keeper of Archaeology at the National Museum of Wales, and was fortunate enough to be involved in excavating a Bronze Age barrow at Sant-y-Nyll in the Vale – eventually dated to 1500 BCE. As a sixteen-year-old, he rode out to the site every day on his bicycle to help with the excavation. As the summer wore on, other volunteers dropped off and Jones often worked on the site alone, under the direction of Savory. They dug a big trench across the barrow and followed the layers of the site down, uncovering human cremations and postholes at the base. His report on the excavation caught the eye of the host of *Animal, Vegetable, Mineral*, Glyn Daniel, and won him the Trevelyan Scholarship to Emmanuel College at Cambridge University.

* * *

Jones studied natural sciences at Cambridge University for two years before seeking to enrol in archaeology and anthropology. Within a fortnight of his application, on 26 May 1961, he received a personal note from the Disney Professor of Archaeology, Grahame Clark, who enthusiastically accepted his enrolment and apologised profusely for the slightly delayed response. 'I wonder if you are free by any chance about 9.30 on Monday morning … We are always very keen to get people with Natural Science background to read archaeology.'[24]

Clark's eagerness to recruit Jones is telling of the changes the discipline had been undergoing since John Mulvaney finished his studies in 1953. A 'new wave' of archaeologists, as Jack Golson has described them, had begun challenging the 'old guard'.[25] Traditional modes of archaeology, which centred on artefacts, cultures and landscapes, were being incorporated into complex and interwoven questions about subsistence strategies, ecological adaptations and settlement patterns. In America, these ideas found expression in the work of scholars such as Lewis Binford, Gordon Willey and Philip Phillips: self-described 'new archaeologists' or 'processual archaeologists', who advocated a more anthropological and scientific approach.[26] In Britain, the central focus of these 'new waves' was on the interactions between people and their environments: between 'man and his resource base'. With a growing array of evidence and techniques becoming available to archaeologists, the discipline was urgently in need of science-literate recruits. As Don Brothwell and Eric Higgs argued in 1963, 'It becomes clear that not to use the scientific methods now available to archaeology, is to commit the worst of archaeological crimes, to ignore available evidence or during excavation to destroy it.'[27]

Rhys Jones kept a semi-regular diary during his years at Cambridge. It was a heady time, full of social and intellectual adventures. Most entries were bracketed with an exuberant 'Wake!' and an exhausted 'Bed'.[28] He was surrounded by fierce intellects who would later join him in Australia, such as Peter White and Carmel Schrire, with whom he developed an 'aggressive and somewhat acerbic mode of "discussion"'.[29] Jones was already full of self-belief. His experience at Sant-y-Nyll had given him a taste for excavation, and he threw himself into the available fieldwork opportunities, joining Charles McBurney at La Cotte de St Brelade in Jersey in 1962 and Ogof Coygan in Wales in 1963, travelling to the Caspian Sea and north-east Iran and accompanying Eric Higgs on his first Palaeolithic expedition to north-west Greece 'as the official geologist'. 'Clearly I was educated in a global tradition,' he later reflected, acknowledging the influence of Clark's 'world history' approach. In particular, he was drawn to the world of the last Ice Age – the Palaeolithic – and the movements and activities of *Homo sapiens*, who he referred to in shorthand simply as 'hunters'. He was fascinated by the common humanity of hunters across the globe. 'In deep prehistory,' he wrote in 1989,

> there is no place for racial or ethnic pride. The salient fact that emerges from a global perspective is how similar were the lives, the artefactual remains, the casual by-products of human actions of all of us humans on all continents. Perhaps this is the greatest

contribution that prehistory can make to the modern human condition. If this were not to be the case, that we were to revert to palaeo-tribalism, then I would give up the game.[30]

Much to his mother's chagrin, Britain was covered in ice 40,000 years ago and thus held few prospects in Palaeolithic archaeology: Jones would have to pursue his career abroad. The question of where seemed a moot point, so long as he could study the ancient hunting way of life. He simultaneously applied for work in Nova Scotia, the Upper Volta and Australia, resolving to take the first job he was offered. On 12 March 1963, his fate was decided: 'Got letter from Richard Wright offering me a job in Sidney. Feel highly chuffed.'[31] The job seemed like a wild adventure to the 23-year-old; he knew little about Australia outside of explorers' stories and school geography. 'I didn't even know how to spell Sydney in those days.'[32]

Jones' acceptance of a teaching fellowship at the University of Sydney marked the arrival of the 'new waves' of archaeology on Australian shores. Jack Golson has described the almost simultaneous impact of 'new archaeology' on Australia and New Zealand as a 'radical, indeed revolutionary change of paradigm'.[33] But perhaps 'evolution' is a more fitting term. The new mode of practice that emerged in Australian archaeology in the 1960s enlarged, rather than replaced, the existing work of Mulvaney, Golson and McBryde. It enriched and complicated an established tradition with new questions and technologies. And it is difficult to classify the changes that took place in Australian archaeological practices as 'new archaeology', considering they grew out of the distinctive geological and environmental histories of Australia as much as international influences. It was a tradition that remained fieldwork-oriented, rather than theory-bound.

The shift towards a distinctive Australian archaeological tradition was driven by many individuals, but, as Golson wrote in 1986, 'The locus of change ... can be readily identified as the seminar room of the

Department of Anthropology at the University of Sydney. The dominant figure was Rhys Jones.'[34] That seminar room also included staff
such as anthropologists Les Hiatt and Mervyn Meggitt and archaeologists Vincent Megaw and Richard Wright. It became a testing room
for the ideas of a group of students who would come to shape the
Australian archaeological tradition, including Harry Allen, Jim Allen,
Annie Bickford, Sandra Bowdler, Emily Coleman, Ian Glover, Johan
Kamminga, Harry Lourandos, Leslie Maynard, Betty Meehan and
Alan Thorne. Each of these researchers would play major roles in what
Jones and Jim Allen have described as the 'cowboy' phase of Australian
archaeology.[35]

* * *

Jones arrived in Australia on a warm, clear day in late August 1963. The
light was 'bright and brazen' and as he descended from the plane he was
immediately 'struck by the smell of gum'. His new colleague Richard
Wright, with whom he would share a teaching load, met him at the
airport in an old pink Peugeot: 'He had desert boots, khaki trousers
and an open-necked shirt, and I thought "this is great".' They got off
to a good start when Wright offered him the choice of going to sleep
or visiting a nearby excavation. 'Naturally,' Jones said, 'I wanted to see
the excavation.' Within an hour or so of landing in Australia, he was
investigating a shell midden on the shores of Botany Bay, near where
Captain Cook had moored in 1770. The site was unlike anything he
had seen before. He recalled being overwhelmed by the knowledge that
'Hunters lived in this landscape until yesterday'.[36]

The excavation, run by Vincent Megaw at Curracurrang rock shelter in the Royal National Park, was where many of his colleagues and
students at the University of Sydney cut their archaeological teeth. And
as a shell midden, not a traditional stratified deposit, it presented completely different challenges to the sites Jones had worked on during his

time at Cambridge. Instead of a series of layers, the archaeologist had to decipher a complex stratigraphy of interleaving lenses of shell, ash and sand, in which a meal lasting a few minutes could sit beside another separated by a thousand years. Within a few months he would become intimately familiar with the sculptural structure of a midden, working his way across 'a complex of practically continuous midden' along the northern Tasmanian coastline.[37]

Alongside his teaching duties, Jones' new position required that he enrol to do a PhD. Today, a PhD topic in archaeology might consist of the analysis of a specific aspect of a site, such as the faunal remains or the shells. In 1963, Jones was invited to write his PhD on the history and archaeology of an entire state. 'There were political reasons why the next person to arrive would need to do Tasmania,' Jones later reflected.[38] Little was known of the archaeology of the region and John Mulvaney had been growing increasingly concerned about the 'finders keepers' mentality that prevailed on the island state. On a visit to Mount Cameron West in May 1962, he had been shocked to find an iconic Aboriginal carving site severely damaged and surrounded by crumbling debris: the carvings had been sawn off the rock face to make a display in the Hobart Museum. The AIAS resolved to cease all funding for research in the state until a trained archaeologist was able to do a survey of existing Aboriginal sites.[39]

Jones, excited by the sheer lack of archaeological research on the island, was happy to fill the role. The AIAS provided him with funds and a Land Rover to carry out a reconnaissance expedition during the summer of 1963–1964. He was keen to find out how long people had been in Tasmania and whether they had arrived there before the sundering of Bass Strait. He also hoped to excavate a variety of sites in order to ask questions about subsistence patterns, seasonal movements and the ways in which the archaeology can be interpreted in light of the ethnographic evidence, 'flimsy though it is'.[40] He assembled a team of

young men from the archaeology department at the Sydney University
to accompany him: Jim Allen, Ian Glover, Ron Wild and Bob Reece.
Campbell McKnight from the ANU joined the team in January 1964,
bringing with him the dramatic news of Mulvaney's Kenniff Cave date:
the first Australians had a Pleistocene past. 'That night,' Allen recalled,
'as we gazed northwards over Bass Strait, we knew the answer to Flinders'
conundrum, although the final proof would require years more research
to demonstrate. People had walked, dry-shod, to Tasmania, at a time
when lowered sea levels exposed dry land, at a minimum, more than
8000 years ago.'[41]

In advance of the expedition, Jones had sought advice from colleagues in geology at the University of Tasmania. He was warned about
the paucity of deep stratified archaeological sites on the island. 'Search
might produce something,' wrote JL Davies on the eve of Jones' depar-
ture, 'but don't build any hopes too high in this direction.'[42] The warning
underlined how little was known about the island's archaeology. 'The
major problem in Tasmania,' Jones soon discovered on arrival, 'was not
how to find a site, but how out of hundreds, to choose one or two on
which to concentrate.'[43]

One of the few sites Jones knew about before his arrival in Tasmania
was Rocky Cape (pinmatik), and it was a site he was determined *not*
to dig on this first expedition. Rocky Cape was a familiar name to
archaeologists around the world. It had long been regarded as 'the key
to Tasmanian prehistory', as well as holding answers to evolutionary
questions about the Tasmanians' origins.[44] The South Cave had been
dug dozens of times in the twentieth century by treasure-seekers, amateurs and well-meaning curators. It was even looted between Jones' brief
visits in January and March 1964. 'The site looked a shambles,' Jones
reported back to the AIAS. 'Collapsing holes, disturbed deposit, tin
cans, beer bottles, and other non Aboriginal artefacts attest to enthusiastic though somewhat less scientific interest.'[45] He took a charcoal

sample from one of the exposed pits to find out how long people had lived there, but resolved not to add to the destruction of the cave site in that first field season. Instead, he decided to test his methods 'and perhaps make my initial mistakes' at a similar coastal cave site 10 kilometres west of Rocky Cape. 'There was a feeling that before we could tackle, or even comment on the established Australian controversies, we had to learn the archaeological alphabet in Australia.'[46]

On 21 December 1963 Jones followed a steep track behind Sisters Beach to the low, wide mouth of 'Blackman's Cave', which was perched high above sea level in the side of a Pre-Cambrian quartzite cliff. His notes on the day were brief: 'Looked at cave at Sister's Creek – Beauty!'[47] He was especially excited because the cave had preserved a rich variety of animal bones, which would allow him to answer questions about what people were hunting and gathering, cooking and eating: to apply 'the economic approach to prehistory'. He started excavation on 1 January 1964, exposing a nine-metre long section and gaining a glimpse of an ancient society: 'people sitting in the mouth of the cave, chipping and using their tools, and then dumping their shells and animal bones further inside'.[48]

To put the site 'into some sort of archaeological perspective', the team embarked on a survey of sites along the north coast. They struggled through a contemporary midden at an abandoned oyster cannery at St Helens, explored eroding middens in the sand dunes of Ansons Bay, and in the Bay of Fires excavated a stone arrangement, exposing another stone arrangement in the same spot, 30 centimetres below the surface: a powerful demonstration of deep ceremonial connections to place.[49] They investigated the inland sandstone country, recording more than thirty rock shelters in Murderer's Gully, and at Trial Harbour on the west coast found dozens of clay pipes mixed in with Aboriginal artefacts buried deep within a sand dune. The weather was 'bloody awful', Jones wrote in his distinctive scrawl, but the sites were 'bloody rich!'[50]

The most promising site they came across was a large, exposed, grassed-over midden on the low rocky shore near West Point lighthouse. A sample pit turned up thousands of animal bones and artefacts amidst the cracked and blackened shells, as well as a human molar. This single tooth became a crucial piece of evidence back in Sydney: it was all physical anthropologists Alan Thorne and Neil 'Black Mac' Macintosh needed to overturn the nineteenth-century belief that the Tasmanians were a separate race to continental Aboriginal people.[51] It demonstrated that the first Tasmanians and the first Australians shared a common ancestry in the Pleistocene past.

The stories from this first expedition have entered archaeological folklore. As Jones' wife, Betty Meehan, later reflected, 'He took a seedy-looking bunch of males on his first expedition and received quite a bit of flak for not including any women!'[52] Most locals regarded the group of twenty-something, bearded academics with some contempt, not least because 'we were dealing with the Aboriginal question'. 'We were seen as a kid expedition and we didn't look right. We were dirty and got drunk and ran around with women and things like that.' On more than one occasion the expedition was stopped by the police, who suspected them of stealing the Z-plated Land Rover they had received from the AIAS. They camped in army tents, worked long hours in wet, windy conditions, and drank late into the night at the local pubs. The atmosphere in the group was often tense, with the 'big, burly and rather gruff' Jim Allen playing Fletcher Christian to Jones' Captain Bligh: 'I had lots of mutinies and stuff, partly because I was a Captain Bligh and I didn't tolerate mutinies.'[53] The only visible Aboriginal presence Jones encountered on this first expedition was at the 1964 Burnie Show, when he and Allen were invited to 'come up and punch a Darkie' outside Jimmy Sharman's boxing tent.[54] (They declined.)

Jones returned in December 1964 with a more gender-balanced excavation team, as well as more focused questions about the geology, ecology and zoology of the region. His tattered field journals, caked in dirt, are full of complex equations, rough geological sketches and lists of vegetation with notes on the taste of local nuts, leaves and flowers. He saw in the West Point site an opportunity to understand the structure of a midden, not only stratigraphically, layer by layer, but spatially across a living floor: How was the mound formed? Where did people cook? Where did they work? Where did they sleep? He decided to excavate the site as if it were a Bronze Age barrow, driving two large trenches through the middle of the mound in the form of a cross. Over six weeks they dug, sieved and sorted through 60 tons of deposit, uncovering the material remains of a society with a high-protein diet of seals and whales, wombats and wallabies, shellfish and mutton-birds.[55] In the middle of the mound, they found stone flakes, cooking hearths and burnt bones, surrounded on the edges by piles of abalone shells. Thirty years later, Jones lamented his large-scale approach: 'I had this lust: that I wanted "it", whatever "it" was ... I had more material than I could possibly ever analyse.' It was a 'euphoric experience' to work on such a rich site, but in retrospect, he reflected, 'West Point was discovered too early'.[56] He would not make the same mistakes at Rocky Cape.

* * *

The field season at Rocky Cape was comparatively short. Jones started work at the South Cave in February 1965 with a reduced team. The chamber was narrow and deep, with a rough, sloping roof. The vandalism of the site – the many holes that riddled the cave floor – gave Jones a rare three-dimensional view of the deposit: he was able to read the exposed stratigraphy from the side, while trowelling his way from the top down. It was a process Jones described as 'a kind of sculpture in reverse'.[57] Winifred Mumford's published illustrations of these 'interleaved and intercut elliptical hearths and shell lenses' are stunning works of art.[58] While Jones drew stratigraphy in the South Cave, Annie

Bickford, Harry Lourandos and Don Miller began excavating in the North Cave on the opposite side of the peninsula. It quickly became apparent that they were working on two distinct sites.[59]

Although only separated by a seven-minute walk, there were dramatic differences in the diet, technology and trading patterns of the societies that lived in the two caves. The difference, Jones realised as they dug deeper, was chronological: combined, the two cave sites provided a continuous record of occupation. After four weeks of excavation, on 1 March 1965, the perplexed team packed the finds into orange cases to be taken back to Sydney for analysis.[60] Six months later Jones returned to Tasmania to announce a tentative history of the region at the 1965 ANZAAS congress in Hobart.

The first Tasmanians, he argued, walked across the Bassian Plain from mainland Australia sometime during the last Ice Age.[61] As the ice caps melted and the sea levels rose, Rocky Cape was transformed from an inland ridge to a coastal cave; heath and sedgeland replaced the surrounding moorlands and rainforest. Almost as soon as the seashore lapped at the base of Rocky Cape around 8000 years ago, people started to occupy the caves, leaving behind them thousands of shells, fishbones and stone tools. They hunted fur and elephant seals, killing and butchering them away from the caves, and harvested vegetables from the surrounding coastal heath, softening them with stone and cooking them in small kitchen fires. Around 5000 years ago new raw materials began to appear on the living floor, reflecting an expansion of trade patterns and regional movements along the north coast: 'an enlargement of the ecological space of the Aborigines'.[62] The South Cave, where Jones had begun excavating, gradually began to fill up and, around 3500 years ago, was abandoned. At the same time a dramatic change occurred in the society living at Rocky Cape: scale fish seemed to suddenly and completely disappear from their diet. 'In archaeological terms,' Jones wrote in his thesis, 'this was an instantaneous event and in actual historic terms, the time period referred to, could not have been more than the order of a hundred years.'[63] Bone tools and some variants of stone technology also appeared to drop out of use; simple spears, throwing sticks and unhafted and unground stone tools were all that remained. People continued to use the North Cave into recent times, living off wallabies, seals, shellfish and vegetables. But fish did not return to the diet of the Tasmanians living at Rocky Cape.

— Why did the Tasmanians stop eating fish? The abrupt change of diet and technology, Jones argued, could not be explained by a trans-forming ecology or climate; it was part of a broader cultural shift: an internal change within a single society.[64] At first he characterised the simplification of technology as 'a gradually improving exploitation of an environment', a trend towards efficiency by a highly agile society.[65] In later papers he imagined the Tasmanians as castaways, stranded from the cultural dynamism of mainland Australia, in social disarray and economic stagnation. The cessation of fish eating became evidence of 'devolution': an 'economic maladaptation'. He argued that the sunder-ing of the Bassian Plain, and the resulting millennia-long isolation, had forced a slow cultural decline. 'Like a blow above the heart,' he wrote in 1977 in heightened prose, 'it took a long time to take effect, but slowly but surely there was a simplification of the tool kit, a diminution in the range of foods eaten, perhaps a squeezing of intellectuality. The world's longest isolation, the world's simplest technology.'[66]

While few disputed the archaeological findings, Jones' devolution thesis sparked one of the longest and most heated debates in Australian archaeology. It was the first argument for cultural degeneration in the world.[67] Jones' colleagues and students searched for alternative expla-nations. Sandra Bowdler disputed the representative nature of Rocky Cape and argued that fish had never been a staple of the Tasmanian diet. Harry Allen tackled Jones' thesis with an optimal foraging argu-ment: why eat fish when you can harvest higher-energy foods such as seals? Harry Lourandos suggested the changes and expanded territories were triggered by a drier, cooler climate. Ron Vanderwal and David Horton argued for the shift to be understood as 'adaptation' rather than 'degeneration'. And, more recently, historian Rebe Taylor uncovered oral and written evidence that challenged the very assumption that the Tasmanians stopped eating scale-fish. The charged nature of debate brought an exasperated Richard Wright to exclaim in 1982 that 'Any journal editor who sees a title which includes the words "Tasmania" and "Fish" should reach for a gun.'[68]

* * *

The 1965 conference, where Jones gave his first version of the Rocky Cape sequence, proved to be especially influential for another reason. It was there that Jones and Betty Meehan (then Hiatt) gained access to an advance copy of NJB (Brian) Plomley's transcription of George Augustus Robinson's journals, which offered by far the richest account of Aboriginal life in Tasmania at the point of contact. Meehan drew heavily upon the new transcriptions for her honours thesis on Aboriginal diets and subsistence in Tasmania, while Jones searched the journals for insights into the Tasmanians' sudden 'ichthyophobia'.[69] Jones empathised with Robinson, who must have felt the 'cruel irony ... that his efforts in conciliating the Aborigines probably hastened their final extinction', but he also developed a deep admiration for the ways in which Aboriginal people had responded to the turbulent moment of contact, seamlessly incorporating dogs (new arrivals from the mainland) into their hunts, learning to handle and maintain guns, knapping glass and ceramics for tools, painting with rust instead of ochre. 'It would be wrong to see the Tasmanians as passive observers at their own funeral,' he wrote in 1971. 'A society which had retained its fundamental integrity since at least early postglacial times, managed to adapt rapidly to new conditions.'[70]

Jones was especially intrigued by Robinson's observations of deliber-
ate burning and Tasmanian 'fire sticks'. 'The Tasmanian Aborigines are
dead,' Jones concluded in 1967, '. . . however, [they] have left their own
mark on the Tasmanian landscape.'[71] Robinson's journals, and those of
other early colonists, were rich with stories of Aboriginal burning and
vivid descriptions of grasslands and open-canopy woodlands that were
now being closed in by rainforest. Since the 1965 ANZAAS Congress,
Jones had been fascinated by the idea of Aboriginal people as ecological agents. In an influential paper, the botanist Bill Jackson had drawn
attention to how 'a long history of firing by the Tasmanian natives' had
fundamentally altered the coastal vegetation; he attributed recent ecological changes to 'the lower incidence of fire in the regions following
the extinction of the aboriginals'.[72] If the sedgeland surrounding Rocky
Cape was 'pyropytic in origin', Jones wondered, then how deliberately,
how systematically had the first Australians manipulated the natural
environment?[73] In 1966, on a short visit to Jim Allen's excavation at
Port Essington in the Northern Territory, Jones gained his first glimpse
through a plane window of Aboriginal fires moving across a landscape:
'smoke from fires extending over fronts of scores of miles'.[74] He contrasted the mosaic ecological patchwork in Arnhem Land with the
'empty' landscape of Tasmania, where traditional burning had stopped
more than a century earlier, and he began to think of the Australian
landscape 'as a human artefact, in the same way that a cleared field is
one'.[75] 'Perhaps', he suggested provocatively in 1969, 'we should call
what the Aborigines did "fire-stick farming"?'[76]

Jones was not alone in drawing attention to Indigenous 'pyro-
management', but he was the first in Australia to conjure an image and
a phrase that ignited academic debate. It was a theme taken up immediately by historians such as Noel Butlin and Keith Hancock, and fully
developed by Sylvia Hallam in her masterful study of Aboriginal society
on the Swan River, *Fire and Hearth*.[77] Jones' ideas about fire evolved

further when he and Betty Meehan lived for a year in Arnhem Land in 1972–1973, where they learnt the Gidjingarli tongue and recorded the burning and subsistence practices of the Anbarra people of the Blyth River (see Chapter 6). On these expeditions, Jones aspired to be a 'mini Robinson': 'not the evangelism, nor the enormous courage of that man, but still as an observer'. He hoped, like Robinson had been in his time, to be a 'floating eye ball', noting in his journal the mundane details that were 'so obvious that nobody else bothered to record' them. In this spirit, on his preliminary field trip in May 1970, he made an inventory of his belongings, documenting 'the artefacts of mid 20th C technological man'.[78]

The friendships he formed during his time living with the Anbarra people, and the cultural insights they afforded him, gave him a more integrated understanding of the subtleties and complexities of Aboriginal life. 'Up until then, I'd played the fool a bit. It was like a Boy's Own story. But when you learn an Aboriginal language, you see the landscape quite differently. You see it through their eyes. You have to try to cross the boundary.'[79] Although he still regarded the first Australians as 'hunters' of the Ice Age world, his time living with the Anbarra allowed him to appreciate the immutable links in their society between land and people, language and ecology, the natural and the supernatural. Seasonal burning, he was taught, was a vital part of the natural and spiritual management of the land. He observed firsthand the routine of anthropogenic fire, timed to biological and climatic cycles and staggered geographically so that the burned mixed with the unburned. He was in awe of the complex system that had been developed over hundreds of generations by 'hunting gardeners'.[80]

But despite his intimate understanding of Aboriginal uses of fire, Jones relied too heavily on one interpretation offered by the editor of Robinson's journal, Plomley: that the Tasmanians could not make fire. There are no eyewitness accounts of Aboriginal people actively making fire in Tasmania before the 1840s, leading Plomley and, in turn, Jones to conclude that, 'Fire was carried ... in smouldering slow burning fire-sticks, but the Tasmanians did not know how to make it.'[81] This supposition fitted neatly into Jones' argument for cultural devolution – and surely must have encouraged it – but it was another provocative statement that would come to haunt him. As ethnobotanist Beth Gott points out, absence of evidence is not evidence of absence. 'Fire-making was difficult in the damp Tasmanian climate,' Gott argued, 'and the preference was to carry fire from place to place, but the Tasmanians did know how to make fire.'[82]

Jones synthesised his archaeological insights in his 1971 PhD thesis, 'Rocky Cape and the Problem of the Tasmanians', which he finished in a ten-week writing surge from his new position at the ANU. The 'problem' in his title alluded to the long-running debates over the Tasmanians' origins and their 'place within the evolutionary sequence of human societies'. But Jones also set out two new 'problems': the effects of isolation on Tasmanian Aboriginal culture, which he addressed with his 'regression' argument, and the horrific violence and 'deep guilt' attached to Tasmanian colonial history, which he would explore more fully in the 1978 film *The Last Tasmanian*. 'Within their terrible lifetime,' Jones wrote in his introduction, 'an entire people with a distinctive history going back to the end of the Ice Age, was snuffed out. For the Australian nation, and perhaps for humanity, this will be the problem of the Tasmanians.'[83]

Jones felt the need, as 'a global citizen', to confront this colonial crime, and, as a Welshman, he empathised, in Schrire's words, 'with what it is like to be on the receiving end of cultural drowning, and cultural loss'.[84] As Rebe Taylor has argued, the idea of extinction shaped the way in which Jones approached and analysed sources about the Tasmanian past.[85] The culmination of his immersion in Robinson's journals was his contribution to Norman Tindale's *Aboriginal Tribes of Australia* (1974), in which he drew all the available ethnographic information into a masterful and mournful synthesis of Aboriginal society in Tasmania at the point of contact.[86] This book, along with the accompanying map of tribal territories, is still used today, often by Indigenous Australians, to illustrate the diversity and complexity of Aboriginal society.

Jones was profoundly affected by the violence he read about in Robinson's journals and in his thesis he drew comparisons between Tasmania's colonial history and the atrocities of Buchenwald and My Lai:

> One's gorge rises at this sorry tale – of psychopathic sadism, of punitive parties and concentration camps, of Sunday afternoon man hunts, of sexual mutilation, of cutting flesh off living bodies and feeding it to dogs, of burying a baby up to its neck in sand and kicking its head off in front of its mother, of tying the severed head of a husband around the neck of the raped spouse. Floating above this, was the cynical hypocrisy of officialdom, the simpering of apologists, the great covering up of truth. Torn diaries and documents in the archives, witness a deep guilt that has yet to be expiated from the cool Georgian landscape of old Tasmania.[87]

That terrible history and those Georgian landscapes, along with Jones' archaeological ideas, were brought to life in Tom Haydon's ambitious and controversial documentary *The Last Tasmanian*.[88]

The idea for the film grew out of a conversation in a Sydney pub, when a fellow drinker turned to Haydon and asked, 'Tell me, Tom, what *did* happen to the Tasmanian Aborigines?' Haydon felt that the history of Tasmania had been 'deliberately hidden from people' and he recruited Jones to co-write a film about 'the life and death of the Tasmanian Aborigines'.[89] The 'infectiously enthusiastic' Jones, now older and stouter than he was when we met him on Sisters Beach, stars in the film as explorer and explainer. In one scene he and Jim Allen build a bark hut beside the water, cook abalone on the beach and talk about the simple technology and delicious diet of the first Tasmanians. In another, Jones whittles a spear with a stone tool and then uses it to stalk Allen, who shelters fearfully in a shepherd's hut. In yet another, Jones lands heroically on the shore of Cape Barren Island, his face wet from sea spray, and goes mutton-birding with the Aboriginal Tasmanians who live there. His breathless performances are interspersed with sweeping vistas of the Tasmanian landscape and solemn statements by the narrator, Leo McKern: 'By 1876, when Truganini died, Tasmania was empty of Aborigines. It's the swiftest and most complete case of genocide on record.'

The poetic tension of the film came from the collision of the archaeological story, of a gradually simplifying society, with the dramatic 'extinction' of the Aboriginal Tasmanians 'within a generation'. In this stylistic rendering of the story, Jones' arguments for a slow cultural decline over thousands of years were all too easily conflated with the devastating impact of European settlement. 'Even if Abel Tasman had not sailed the winds of the Roaring Forties in 1642,' Jones wondered in 1977, 'were they in fact doomed – doomed to a slow strangulation of the mind?'[90] Jones couldn't resist the lyricism of this phrase: the dramatic convergence of archaeology and history and the terrible fate of Tasmanian Aboriginal society. He couldn't anticipate the grief these words would cause. In his rush to romantic realisation he had made himself a glaring target.

The film was applauded in the press as 'a remarkable and haunting documentary', 'a rare achievement' that was 'likely to severely jolt the national conscience'. Many critics wrote of tearful audiences in 'silent mourning', lingering in the cinema long after the film had ended.[91] Jones gave over 120 interviews on radio, television and in the press to generate public interest in the film and its subject. But even while *The Last Tasmanian* was in production it was targeted by a resurgent Aboriginal community, who accused Jones and Haydon of 'dancing on the graves of Aboriginal people'.[92] Soon after the film's release, promotional posters around the country were plastered with a bright blue banner, declaring: 'Racist! This film denies Tasmanian Aborigines their LAND RIGHTS.' 'The name of the film alone,' wrote Aboriginal activist Michael Mansell, 'leaves us with a sick taste in our mouths. At a time when Aboriginal people in Tasmania are fighting to maintain their existence in a racist white society, this film really attempts to undermine us.'[93] The criticism was sharpened by the fact that the filmmakers had sought advice and information from the Tasmanian Aboriginal Community. 'We trusted and were betrayed,' Aboriginal leader Rosalind Langford later said. 'We weren't consulted, our stories were edited, a particular line was advanced, and we helped portray the story which denied our existence.'[94]

The backlash from the Aboriginal community found support amongst some of Jones' colleagues. Archaeologists such as Annie Bickford and Sandra Bowdler, who had worked with Jones in Tasmania, condemned the film for perpetuating archaic racist ideologies; Bickford even helped make the 'Racist!' banners that were plastered over the film posters.[95] There was a feminist element to these critiques: a denunciation of Jones' cowboy bravado and the film's all-male archaeological cast. Both Bowdler and Bickford associated him with the tarnished and interlinking ideas of imperialism, machismo and racism. In her review, 'The Last Tasmanian: Superb Documentary or Racist Fantasy?', Bickford especially attacked Jones' devolution thesis and his heightened prose: 'We learn in the film that the Tasmanians were already on the way to extinction long before their conquest. The doom of the Tasmanians was merely consummated by the coming of the Europeans.'[96] This was certainly how Keith Windschuttle chose to interpret Jones' work when writing his 2002 polemic, *The Fabrication of Aboriginal History*.[97] Haydon responded to the criticism in sheer disbelief: 'How can a film be damned as "racist" when its main burden is an indictment of the whites for what they did to the Tasmanian blacks?'[98] While the film exposed long-suppressed colonial crimes, its extinction narrative did not allow space for survivors to speak for their own cultures and histories.

The irony of *The Last Tasmanian* is that it features the survivors: the descendants of the Aboriginal people who were rounded up on Tasmania and forced to live on islands in Bass Strait. 'I'm not an Aboriginal. I'm only the descendent of one,' says Annette Mansell, a Palawa woman representing the Cape Barren Island community in the film. 'There's no tradition in Tasmania with the Aboriginals.'[99] And yet, as she says these words, she is plucking the feathers from a mutton-bird, an evocative display of cultural continuity. This was the dramatic image Haydon hoped to conjure: 'The people looked and acted like Aborigines, yet what they said had within it ambiguity and doubt.'[100] As Taylor reflects, 'Haydon manipulated the contemporary Aboriginal voices in his film not to absolve white guilt but to shock; a story of survival would have dulled the impact.'[101] Haydon and Jones were aware of the treacherous semantic terrain they were treading in calling the film *The Last Tasmanian*, and Meehan, who had worked closely with Aboriginal communities, urged them to adopt a different title. In early correspondence with Jones, Haydon keeps the crucial word – 'last' – in inverted commas. They also discussed the best terminology to refer to the Aboriginal people on Cape Barren Island, dismissing names such as 'part-Aboriginal' or 'half-caste' and eventually settling on 'islanders', 'descendants' and 'Straitsmen'. Jones later lamented the lack of a question mark in the title.[102]

Despite Jones' injudicious words about a 'doomed' society and the uproar that surrounded the title, the hostility towards *The Last Tasmanian* can only be understood in its unique social-political context. After over a century in which their identity was suppressed, Aboriginal Tasmanians were experiencing a cultural renaissance in the 1970s. In the wake of the *Aboriginal Land Rights (Northern Territory) Act* in 1976, long-running debates over social identity moved into questions of ownership and control. A land rights march – the first of its kind in Tasmania – filled the streets of Launceston in November 1976. When the Queen visited Hobart in early 1977 she was confronted by Aboriginal activists waving a land rights petition. Historian Lyndall Ryan documented this transformative period in her book *The Aboriginal Tasmanians*. Over ten years she sought out Aboriginal communities, recorded oral histories and dredged the colonial archives to weave together a story of resistance: 'The Tasmanian Aborigines,' she wrote in 1981, 'have survived.'[103]

The Last Tasmanian was written by two progressive intellectuals who sympathised with this movement and wanted to expose the atrocities of the colonial past. Instead, the film became a rallying point around which Tasmanian Aboriginal people could assert their collective identity. 'Sadly,' John Mulvaney lamented in 2000, 'their invective was directed against the person who did more than any other non-indigenous person to demonstrate the antiquity, cultural significance and humanity of their ancestors.'[104] Jones felt wounded by this vilification; he wrestled with it, as Tim Flannery wrote in his obituary in 2001, like 'a puzzle he simply could not solve'.[105] From the 1980s he was effectively barred from conducting field research in Tasmania.

In his 2014 Quarterly Essay *A Rightful Place*, Aboriginal lawyer and activist Noel Pearson returned to the tragedy of Truganini. He recalled learning Truganini's name at primary school in the 1970s 'and the awful meaning of her distinction': 'it was one of those salient facts that every child absorbed' and it filled him with 'emotional convulsions of identification and memory'. He wonders whether it is harder today 'to face the question of Truganini's moral legacy': 'I don't know if they teach Truganini today … Maybe the scale of the horror diminished as the country accepted the fact of the continued survival of Tasmania's Aboriginal community.'[106]

Pearson struggles with these questions in the essay, both 'as an Aboriginal and an Australian'. And while he urges Australians to confront the story of the 'last' Tasmanian, he is also cautious about the implications of this narrative:

> The fact that a descendant community survived this history does not negate or reduce the profundity of the loss ... I mean not to return to the mind-frame of racialist eugenics that has so tangled the history that I wish untangled. I just do not want to deny or diminish the tragedy of Truganini and the old people of Tasmania.

They were people, he adds, drawing on a phase of archaeological work Jones initiated, who 'had occupied that land for more than 35,000 years'.[107]

* * *

Over the Christmas holidays of 1966, four children were scrambling up the ragged side of Rocky Cape when one of them noticed an opening in the rock.[108] Rhys Jones had marked it on his 1964 field sketch of the South Cave and dismissed it as a 'badger hole': 'a naive reference to wombats which were still novelties to me then'.[109] The children resolved to investigate. One of the boys, Seamus Campbell, squeezed into the opening while his sister, Theresa, held his feet. The hole turned into a low tunnel that continued over two metres into the rock before opening out into a cavern, nine metres long and almost four metres wide at its widest part. The air in the hidden chamber was still and warm. The cave floor was covered in bones and shells and ash that had been coated in a fine white powder, a lacework of calcium carbonate crystals. In one corner, a grinding stone had been left in position on its bed stone, like a mortar and pestle, to await use on the next visit. The children reported their find to their father and eventually it drew the attention of the new archaeologist at the Tasmanian Museum, Harry Lourandos, who recognised its significance and sealed the narrow entrance with a large rock until it could be properly studied.

By the time Rhys Jones arrived on the scene, the rock seal had been broken, the cave entered, and several bones had been removed. But, for the most part, the hidden chamber remained untouched. It was a remarkable find: here was an ancient campsite – a time capsule – that had been preserved for 6700 years. The discovery made the front page of the local papers and the *Canberra Times*. Jones excavated the site from May to August 1967, with hundreds of locals visiting for 'impromptu "seminars" at the cave mouth'. He regarded the hidden chamber as a once-in-a-generation find, and was determined to keep it intact: 'If you walked on it you destroyed it.'[110] He elaborately cantilevered planks into the confined space to make a platform on which the team could stand. They were digging 'across space' inside the hidden chamber, and 'through time' with a small trench outside the cave mouth.

After carefully sampling the inner cave and arranging for students to study the stone tools, faunal remains and coprolites – fossilised turds of Tasmanian Devils that were feeding off the remains of the camp – Jones resealed the chamber 'for future scientific work'. Inside, he left the best bottle of port he could afford, one glass and a note wrapped in tinfoil: a message through time. In resealing the hidden cave, Jones was highlighting the destructive nature of archaeology as well as its creative potential.

Since Jones' initial Tasmanian reconnaissance, new archaeological excavations have increased our understanding of the history of the Tasmanians. Sandra Bowdler's discovery of human occupation on Hunter Island 23,000 years ago confirmed in 1974 what Jones and Allen had intimated in 1963: that the first Tasmanians had a Pleistocene past.[111] This insight into the Ice Age world was consolidated in the 1980s and 1990s by archaeological work in the southern forests and the dramatic finds on the Franklin River, which extended the length of occupation in Tasmania to over 40,000 years. That story – and Rhys Jones' contribution – will be explored in Chapter 8.

The debate continues over the effect of isolation on the first Tasmanians. The main change, as archaeologist Richard Cosgrove observes, has been a shift of emphasis: from a narrative of loss to one of replacement and transformation.[112] Most archaeologists suggest that Aboriginal society became more expansive, dynamic and innovative over the last 3000 years, with the development of new trade networks, the introduction of rock engravings along the west coast and the emergence of new social practices (including a prohibition on fish). But there remain some scholars who have returned to Jones' thesis of an isolation-induced cultural devolution. 'The simple survival of the Tasmanians through such an extraordinary exile,' wrote Tim Flannery in 1994, 'is testimony to their ingenuity and durability.'[113] For the most part, new discoveries have enlarged, rather than eclipsed, the interpretation Jones first gave voice to in 1965. This is a testament to his ability to create meaning out of the complex structure of a shell midden, to identify changes and to find beginnings and endings in a mass of archaeological data.

Archaeological knowledge, as Greg Dening reminds us, 'is hard won, full of claims and counter claims, zigzagging through a dozen disciplines. It is never static. There are no short cuts. It is a brilliant experience to be out there on the frontiers of knowledge. But it is a dangerous place to be.'[114] In the wake of *The Last Tasmanian*, Jones turned his mind to northern Australia and a two-decade long search for the oldest archaeological sites on the continent (Chapter 10). He paid a high price for living on the frontiers of knowledge and dreaming of deep time. But for the self-described 'cowboy archaeologist', there was nowhere else he wanted to be.

FOUR

TRACKS IN THE DESERT

Richard and Betsy Gould at Puntutjarpa

*'Yiwara' is the word used by the Gibson Desert Aborigines to mean 'track'...
it means the track left by an animal across the sand ... the tracks left by
people ... the track of a mythical totemic being in the 'dreamtime', when
such beings are believed by the Aborigines to have transformed themselves
into present landmarks of the desert. And, finally, yiwara has come to mean
the white man's road or track into the desert, with all the implications this
has for change.*

Richard Gould, *Yiwara*, 1969[1]

From above, the ranges twist across the arid zone, thin
dry riverbeds reach for water, and dunes, endless dunes,
corrugate the landscape. I gaze through my small plane
window at a shifting mosaic of stones and saltpans, scrub
and sand: a desiccated palette of purples, whites, oranges and reds.
Australia's deserts are diverse. The texture of each landscape speaks of
a unique history of wind and water, basin and range.

Australia's deserts are ancient, but they took their current shape
during the Holocene – the last 11,700 years. People have lived here far
longer. Mike Smith's archaeological excavations at Puritjarra, a cav-
ernous rock shelter in the west of central Australia, give us a glimpse

of this deep past. There are hints – a few flakes, a core and some red ochre – of early, fleeting visits around 45,000 years ago, but the rock shelter came into heavy use 35,000 years ago as the global climate cooled and fresh water became scarce. It was the beginning of an age of extreme aridity. The Australian coastline expanded as the sea level fell by tens of metres. Ephemeral lakes dried, sealed by salt crusts. Strong winds caused huge sand dunes in central Australia to move across the interior. The sand ridges that stripe the Simpson Desert, over which we fly, align with the dominant wind patterns at the peak of the Last Glacial Maximum, around 21,000 years ago. At that time, rainfall in the interior was half what it is today. Global temperatures were cooler by six to ten degrees Celsius. But at Puritjarra, as in many parts of the arid zone, people remained, stepping out across the desert hinterland from soak to spring, adapting to the changing climate. The first Australians didn't colonise today's deserts; as Peter Hiscock and Lynley Wallis reflect, in many important ways the modern arid zone formed around them.[2]

Today, the desert interior spreads across nearly 70 per cent of the Australian landmass. The Gibson Desert, where we are bound, makes up part of the 'Western Desert', a cultural region stretching from the Nullarbor in the south to the Kimberley in the north, and from the lands of Martu in the west through to Pintupi country in the east. Far from 'timeless' or 'empty', these arid landscapes are better understood, in Smith's words, 'as a palimpsest of different deserts, stratified in time, stacked one above another, each with its climates, physical landscapes and environments; each with its social landscapes and people'.[3] A rich history of cultural and climatic change is inscribed in the earth.

I am on my way to the Gibson Desert to help re-excavate Puntutjarpa, a small rock shelter embedded in the Brown Range near Warburton, surrounded by spinifex and sandhills. Puntutjarpa was the first archae-ological site to be dug in Australia's deserts and for many years it has provided the interpretative framework for Western Desert archaeology. It is still the largest dig ever undertaken in a desert rock shelter, one of the most remote sites in Australia and one of the best reported. But there remain questions about the chronology and sedimentary history of the site. And until these are resolved, Puntutjarpa will remain the *bête noire* of Australian archaeology.[4] Our team is returning to the site to recover a small sample of the deposit in order to clarify what Puntutjarpa tells us about ancient Australia. But my interest extends beyond the archive of the earth. I am curious about the people who first dug Puntutjarpa in 1966–1967 and again in 1969–1970.

American anthropologist-archaeologist Richard 'Dick' Gould and his wife and collaborator, Betsy (Elizabeth, neé Barber), lived in the Western Desert with Ngaanyatjarra people for almost two years. They revelled in the experience and developed a profound scholarly and personal appreciation of the land and its people. But the Goulds' story is marked by controversy and tragedy. Their time in the Western Desert has become a parable of the changing notions of consent and the shifting climate of Aboriginal politics in the 1960s and '70s. A year after his work at Puntutjarpa was completed, Richard Gould was forbidden to return to the region. When he attended a conference in Alice Springs in 1974, a spearing party drove 1500 kilometres from Laverton in the Western Desert to meet him. They missed each other by a matter of days. Gould came very close to being the first archaeologist in Australia to get speared.[5] The same floodtide that would surge around Rhys Jones with *The Last Tasmanian* engulfed Gould a decade earlier.

As the seatbelt sign comes on and we make our final approach to Alice Springs, a new colour comes to define the landscape below. The recent rain has turned the red centre a lush green. It is May 2014, and last week the wide sandy bed of the Todd River flowed. The town is abuzz with the news. Water still defines life in the arid interior.

Our small team, led by Alan Williams and June Ross, and under the remote guidance of Mike Smith, pack our gear in Alice Springs, pick up a Toyota from the Ngaanyatjarra Council, and drive west into the desert.

* * *

Betsy Gould was accustomed to travelling for her husband's work. She had accompanied him around the north-west Californian coast over vacations, summers and weekends throughout his PhD research into the history of Tolowa people. As a team, between February 1963 and April 1965, they gathered oral testimony from the living Tolowa, Tututni and Yurok Indians in the belief that indigenous knowledge and oral traditions, 'if carefully checked for accuracy and detail', could dramatically enlarge historical knowledge.[6] Their interviews, when paired with archaeological evidence, told the story of a thriving coastal settlement that had been abruptly ravaged by an epidemic, most likely cholera, in the mid-nineteenth century, as well as a series of violent episodes with the white usurpers. Gould used the testimony to ask questions about cultural continuity and change in the archaeological record.

Gould had learnt the craft of archaeology under the tutelage of the celebrated American archaeologist Jessie Jennings. During 1961 and 1962 he joined a team recording and excavating sites along the Colorado River in advance of the construction of Glen Canyon Dam.[7] His work with Jennings instilled in him an appreciation of the science and intellectual rigour of archaeology, while his experience with the Tolowa people opened his eyes to how indigenous testimony could shape his research. Although the Tolawa had never lived in the area he was studying, they immediately guided him to the richest occupation sites and helped him understand the stone tools he excavated. It made him wonder what it would be like to live amongst a people who were still occupying their traditional sites and how their knowledge might inform his archaeological eye. He brought up the topic with anthropologists Catherine and Ronald Berndt when they visited the University of California in April 1964 and they encouraged him to pursue work in Australia.[8]

In 1965, at the age of twenty-six and with Betsy at his side, Gould left for the Western Desert. At a time when archaeological activity hugged the coast, Gould chose the most remote part of Australia for his area of study. He was guided to the Gibson Desert by Ronald Berndt's 1963 article 'Groups with Minimal European Associations'.[9] It was here, in the heart of the arid zone, that he hoped to find a 'living archaeological experience'.

Although the Goulds were embarked on an exercise in extreme cultural immersion, the insights they sought were of a universal flavour. In the wake of World War II, anthropologists turned away from questions of race and difference to adopt a language of unity and universality. It was a shift from long-standing evolutionary theories about 'types' towards complex questions about people and their social organisation, diets and mobility. This search for shared human attributes led to a surging academic interest in 'surviving hunter-gatherer societies'. The deep past, like the ethnographic present, was ransacked for insights into the human condition. This burgeoning period of biological humanism culminated in the landmark symposium 'Man the Hunter', which took place in Chicago while Gould was in Australia in April 1966.[10]

The conference brought together scholars from around the world to discuss the geographic and biological expertise of hunter-gatherer societies. The emphasis on universality was both a vision of promise and threat. There was a powerful sense amongst those who attended that a way of life that had existed for most of human history was rapidly fading away. And if 'man' was a hunter, would he cope in the nuclear age?[11] 'Of the estimated 80,000,000,000 men who have ever lived out a life span on earth,' wrote Richard B Lee and Irven DeVore, the conference organisers, over 90 per cent have lived as hunters and gatherers; about 6 per cent have lived by agriculture and the remaining few per cent have lived in industrial societies ... It is still an open question whether man will be able to survive the exceedingly complex and unstable ecological conditions he has created for himself.[12]

The conference came at a time of agitation and unrest in the United States. Protests against the Vietnam War and the burgeoning civil rights movement were both readily invoked by attendees. Another flourishing movement, feminism, critiqued the masculinist nature of the proceedings and responded with another conference: 'Woman the Gatherer'.[13] The sense of political and cultural upheaval seeped into the proceedings and fuelled more romantic notions about the simpler, 'essential' nature of hunter-gatherer life and what it might reveal about the human condition. But the organisers insisted that such an inquiry was merely a 'logical exercise', and that 'there is no assumption that living hunter-gatherers are somehow living relics of the Pleistocene'.[14]

Although the conference title suggests rather narrow concerns, the papers ranged from gender dynamics in foraging societies to overturning the lingering idea, propagated by many nineteenth-century social-evolutionary thinkers, that the hunter-gatherer lifestyle was, by its very essence, dictated by the economics of scarcity. But the central theme of 'Man the Hunter', to which Gould reacted directly, was the importance of collaboration between anthropology and archaeology. Lewis Binford was the most vocal on this point, calling on his colleagues to harness ethnographic observation to help interpret archaeological evidence.[15]

In Australia, Norman Tindale offered a similar challenge to archaeologists at the 1965 ANZAAS Congress in Hobart. He derided them as 'emus with their heads in the spinifex' and urged them to come out 'from their cave holes to study at first hand the data provided by living peoples'. Gould called such a practice 'living archaeology'.[16]

Gould received support from his institution, the American Museum of Natural History, to live in the Western Desert, but this was a personal as much as a professional undertaking. He yearned 'to experience the tempo and detail of the hunting and foraging way of life'.[17] And, as he wrote in his research proposal, he wanted to approach this very anthropological task 'from the point of view of an archaeologist'.[18] He was keen to observe contemporary hunting and butchering activities and develop a systematic understanding of stone technology, to study camp layouts and living floors and compare these with their ancient counterparts, to live with a society still painting and singing and dancing as they had for generations, and to record these activities in photos, records and film. He would look for a 'patterning' to their archaeological remains that reflected 'basic rules of behaviour within the culture'.[19]

On their way to Australia, the Goulds passed through England and made the pilgrimage to the ancient standing stones of Stonehenge. The visit aroused mixed feelings of excitement and apprehension. In the shadow of this enigmatic monument, Gould wondered openly about what lay in store for him in the Australian deserts, now that he was 'irrevocably committed' to his project. Would he arrive in Australia to see such stone arrangements still in use? 'Would it be possible to see Aborigine artists making rock paintings? Or would the monuments and paintings of these Aborigines keep their mysteries as Stonehenge and the European cave paintings have done?'[20]

At the heart of his expedition was the idea that what he learnt in fieldwork had meaning beyond that immediate moment and place. He hoped to gain insight into the human story of the deep past.

* * *

When Richard Gould came to Warburton in 1966 he recalls a Ngaanyatjarra man, Tommy Simms, buying one of the first cars in the region, a three-and-a-half ton Bedford truck that made long trips across the desert overloaded with relatives and with tyres stuffed full of spinifex. Such cars had 'short, hard lives' and quickly expired on the rough bush tracks around the mission. 'On our last trip out in the Land-Rover,' Gould wrote in 1969, 'we counted four of these hulks abandoned along the road between Warburton and Laverton.'[21] In our short time in the Western Desert in 2014, we encountered hundreds of such wrecks. The road to Warburton is lined on both sides by old cars, upturned, gutted and torched, their rusted hulks in the grip of scrub and sand. Writer and artist Kim Mahood has compared these abandoned vehicles to the steady stream of whitefellas (*kartiya*) who come to work in remote Indigenous communities. 'Kartiya are like Toyotas,' she records a woman from another part of the Western Desert remarking. 'When they break down we get another one.'[22]

We veer off the main road near the rubbish dump and loop back through the mulga towards the sandy spinifex country. Thick red dust billows and hangs in our wake. We are taking the long way out to the site in order to avoid culturally sensitive areas of country. Every feature in this landscape is imprinted with meaning and law. The earth, rock, sky and scrub pulse with the life force of the *Tjukurpa* (the Dreaming). The circuitous route to work each day reminds us of the power of these associations. Our quarters in the old police station sit on a Kangaroo Dreaming.[23] And the rock shelter we have come to work on, Puntutjarpa, nestles into the Brown Range, which evokes the muscular body of the ancestral perentie lizard, *Ngintaka*. Country is story.

We first visited Puntutjarpa with senior traditional owner Mr Cyril Simms, Warburton elder Mr Phillip West and anthropologist David Brooks. (There is a naming convention in the Western Desert that confers formal titles on senior Indigenous individuals, giving conversations about local happenings the tenor of a Jane Austen novel.) The rock shelter sits on a slight slope, commanding a spectacular view across the valley towards the Warburton township. Over the coming days, June Ross insists we eat our lunch with this view in the shade of the shelter: the archaeologist can learn a lot from quietly absorbing a landscape.

Mr Simms and Mr West amble up the sandy slope ahead of us to inspect the small overhang. They are quick to point out the lacework of perentie (*ngintaka*) tracks on the shelter floor – 'he's been here' – and a small patch of light-grey ash further along the range: the archaeological signature of Mike Smith, who visited the site in July 2013 to consult with the community in advance of this visit. 'We left him and he camped here, made himself a cup of tea,' Mr West explains. Later, when more of the community visit us at the site, they laugh at 'that other one doctor's' choice of firewood.

The surface of the site is scattered with artefacts from the earlier excavations. I fumble over some rusted tins, a gas wheel and an old pot pie left here by Gould. Mr West worked on the original excavation of Puntutjarpa in the late 1960s and remembered 'Dr Gould' well. He asked after him. This is only the second time Mr West has visited the rock shelter since that time. (The first was with Smith last year.)

We struggle to locate Gould's original trench beneath the spinifex and introduced buffel grass, and have to refer to old photographs and stylised site drawings. The site is almost unrecognisable in the photos: a gaping hole with a rugged rocky base, sieves hanging from the escarpment and a small white sign with the American and Australian flags sticking out of the spoil heap.

Even the rock wall is different. In 1967 Gould photographed Aboriginal artists using charcoal, dung and emu fat to adorn the shelter with paintings of snakes and emu tracks and the ancestral perentie. These have almost completely disappeared. Over the coming days, June Ross and Samantha Keats painstakingly record these and other images along the range, while Alan Williams and I descend into the earth, carefully trowelling our way through time. We are acutely aware

that our presence marks the first archaeological excavations in the
Warburton region since Gould departed in 1970. We, too, are casting
tracks in the desert.

* * *

Since the late nineteenth century, intermittent intrusions by explorers, surveyors, prospectors, pastoralists, doggers and missionaries had
established a white presence in the Western Desert. But the pace of contact quickened with the construction of the Woomera Rocket Range
in 1946. Germany's bombardment of London with V1 pilotless flying
bombs and V2 rockets during World War II stirred fear and disbelief
throughout the commonwealth. 'It was the harbinger of a new kind of
warfare,' writes military historian Peter Morton, 'a war of technicians,
not soldiers; a war where an aggressor could sit snugly at home and
point his finger of force against another country.'[24] The British needed
to develop their own rocket program and they turned to Australia, with
its wide 'unpopulated' space, for help. The task of finding a stretch of
desert in Australia even 1600 kilometres long did not seem onerous
in comparison to testing rockets in the British Isles. But the Anglo-
Australian Joint Project needed first to ensure the land was uninhabited.
From 1958 to 1963 missile recovery roads were graded out across the
Western Desert and government patrols were regularly sent to locate
people living in the estimated impact zones, and then to resettle them
on missions and reserves.

As these patrols infiltrated the desert, many of the Indigenous inhabitants were moving in the opposite direction. In an extraordinary series
of migrations in the mid-twentieth century, Aboriginal people 'cleared
out' of the Western Desert and moved into settled areas. In many ways
these migrations resembled historic population movements, coinciding
as they did with drought periods – the late '20s, early '40s, mid-'50s,
early '60s and into the mid-'80s. But this mass 'exodus' was far from

a passive drift. The people of the Western Desert were adjusting their movements to include new sources of food and trade, and, as historian Shannyn Palmer shows, they quickly made the European settlements their own.[25] When Gould arrived in 1966 most of the Aboriginal people he encountered lived on or near reserves and missions, such as the one Will Wade set up in Warburton in 1932. The people at the Warburton Mission would speak to him of the desert where they once lived as being 'too lonely'. Gould described the Gibson Desert as 'the loneliest place on earth', for 'what can be lonelier than a place where people have lived their lives and then left forever?'[26]

Richard and Betsy Gould encountered a society in flux. They moved through the desert communities in Laverton, Tika Tika and Clutterbuck Hills before settling in the Warburton region, where they remained for almost a year living with the Ngaanyatjarra community. Ngaanyatjarra country lay directly under the flight path of the Blue Streak (non-atomic) missiles, and on a few occasions Gould joined the patrols that searched the desert for families still living a traditional way of life. Once, he came across the fresh footprints and campsite of a group of eleven Tjilanatjara-speaking people, but he did not meet them until he returned to Warburton in November 1969. Another patrol encountered a group of 'Ngatjara-speaking Aborigines' in the Mt Madley region and Gould spent a week with them in April 1970. 'They were extremely pleasant to be with,' he wrote to John Mulvaney from Warburton. 'Betsy was the first white woman they had seen, and they were fascinated by her.'[27]

It was an exciting, but also melancholy time for Gould. He found that he was able 'almost simultaneously' to satisfy his curiosity about the hunter-gatherer way of life 'and to observe the essential changes being brought about by white contact'.[28] He became fluent in the local language and was regularly invited to ceremonies, where he took notes on social structures, kinship relations, law and spiritual life. He struggled 'with the haunting problem of how to do justice to the richness and complexity' of Ngaanyatjarra society, and he was reflective about his own role in colonisation.[29] He recognised the 'sharp irony' that the same Western technology and specialisation that had 'invaded' and transformed this remote part of the world had also produced anthropologists and archaeologists and enabled them to learn about the traditions and histories of the people who lived there.

Gould became a chronicler of this immense collision of cultures, and he recorded contact artefacts with fascination: blunted steel rods taken from abandoned windmills and used as digging sticks, old petrol tins and hubcaps carefully hammered into bowls, and worn chisel-blades that had been hafted with kangaroo or emu sinew onto wooden handles. Despite the changes of material, Gould reasoned, 'the functions and motor-patterns associated with their use have remained basically unchanged'.[30] They were evidence of entangled cultures and of traditions transforming. 'Having brushed against both cultures,' writes historian Philip Jones of such objects that span the frontier, 'they wear a double patina, of ochre and rust.'[31]

Over the course of his fieldwork, Gould developed a profound respect for the Ngaanyatjarra people and their culture. He had not come to Australia with any 'built-in sympathies' or quixotic notions of 'the noble savage', but he left with a deep appreciation for the Ngaanyatjarra peoples' 'rewarding and satisfying' approach to life. He made strong friendships, formed deep connections and was quick to admit that he had 'misjudged' aspects of the culture:

> Gradually I experienced the central truth of Aboriginal religion: that it is not a thing by itself but an inseparable part of a whole that encompasses every aspect of daily life, every individual, and every time – past, present, and future. It is nothing less than the theme of existence, and as such constitutes one of the most sophisticated and unique religious and philosophical systems known to man.[32]

Gould was absorbed into the existing cultural landscape and became identified as belonging to *panaka*, and his wife, Betsy, necessarily belonged to *tjaruru*.[33] In this way he was 'related' to everyone he worked with and met. He received the name *Mingkultjara* (he who has tobacco), as he was constantly exchanging tobacco for goods, information and favours, such as being allowed to observe a ceremony or being taught a song: 'I was, in fact, the Aborigines' chief source of supply.'[34] Although devoid of spiritual significance, these names gave him certain rights as well as responsibilities to maintain customs and laws.

In August 1966 Gould was led out to a small overhang set in the quartzite ridge of the Brown Range. This 'minor sacred site', he learnt, was known as 'Puntutjarpa'. The shelter surface showed the signs of recent activity and, he judged, could provide the archaeological ballast for his ethnographic work. He returned in 1967 with a party of men 'affiliated with this sacred tradition' to seek permission to excavate. These men would return on other visits 'both while excavations were in progress and afterward, to satisfy themselves that no sacred landmarks were being violated'.[35]

The preliminary excavation at Puntutjarpa was conducted in 1967 by Richard and Betsy Gould with the assistance of Aboriginal people such as Mr West. Gould was excited by the site because the ceiling of the rock shelter had collapsed on numerous occasions, potentially 'sealing' the deposit – preserving a series of ancient living surfaces in time. The deposit was littered with the refuse of daily camp life: stone tools, red ochre, hearths and scraps of butchered bone. The rock walls were decorated with paintings, 'some of which were put there during our stay'.[36] He found a well in the western cave, and he learnt from his Ngaanyatjarra guides that in recent times the site had been used as a hunting trap, with hunters using fire to drive kangaroos and wallabies off the cliff above.

Gould excavated 707.6 cubic feet of fill from this exploratory trench, none of which was sieved. He proceeded by arbitrary six-inch levels and used a sledgehammer to remove the rock fall. When published, these methods incurred the wrath of the Australian archaeological community. Ian Glover and Ron Lampert led the charge, accusing Gould of destroying the site simply to 'satisfy his curiosity'. 'If time and labour are limited,' they implored, 'dig a small hole carefully rather than a big hole quickly; if you cannot screen the deposit from a cave site, do not dig it.'[37] Gould was also attacked for his identification of 'microliths' (small stone tools), his dating techniques and his use of ethnography to interpret the archaeological evidence. Some of the hostility derived from the fact that he was an American and that he had imported the theories and terminology he was familiar with, rather than anchoring his research in Australian debates.

Gould returned to Puntutjarpa in 1969–1970 to conduct a systematic large-scale excavation of the site and defend his preliminary results. He found some resistance to his attendance at ceremonial activities on this second field season, so he focused on the archaeological work. His core team of seven worked full-time for nine weeks, exposing an enormous area of the shelter. Gould read continuity and conservatism in the archaeological record at Puntutjarpa. He argued that a 'distinctive' society emerged 10,000 years ago with 'the onset and persistence' of harsh arid conditions, and, remarkably, that it had maintained a stable cultural and economic system through to the present day. He proposed the term 'Australian Desert Culture' for this 'resourceful' society, with its hallmarks of high mobility, 'risk minimising opportunism' and a mobile toolkit. Their successful adaptation, he believed, 'must surely stand as one of the most dramatic cases of cultural conservatism on record'.[38]

These were bold ideas to come out of a pioneering exploratory dig, and in many ways they paralleled the contemporary interpretations of his mentor, Jesse Jennings, at Danger Cave in Utah. But the concept of a stable, conservative 'desert culture' never gained support in Australia. Further work on the Puntutjarpa collections undermined the claims of a consistent technology throughout the deposit, while later studies on climatic change suggested that aridity ameliorated, not intensified, at the start of the Holocene.[39] Our 2014 excavations at Puntutjarpa revealed a more nuanced story, with three distinct phases of occupation over the past 12,000 years, as opposed to a single, static culture.[40]

'The project was successful beyond our expectations,' Gould wrote in his fieldwork report in 1970. 'It was a rewarding fieldtrip, both personally and scientifically.'[41] In his final months in the region, he gained access to a plane (a Cessna 182), which he piloted accompanied by his Aboriginal guides. He conducted aerial surveys within a 320-kilometre radius of Warburton, identifying sacred sites, rock alignments and rock shelters, all of which he was eager to revisit and investigate. But this would be his last time in the Gibson Desert.

* * *

Throughout the course of his fieldwork, Gould was aware of a major ethnographic filmmaking project commissioned by the AIAS. Working in the 'before it is too late' documentary mode, a genre with which Gould was familiar, a film unit recorded a range of ethnographic activities in the Western and Central Deserts from 1964–1969, including stone knapping, burning regimes and restricted men's business. The resulting films, *People of the Western Desert* and *Desert People*, remain influential.[42] The Aboriginal participants allowed filming to continue with the firm assurance that the images would not return to the community. Gould made a similar verbal contract with the Ngaanyatjarra people.[43]

It was in this climate that Gould wrote *Yiwara: Foragers of the Australian Desert*, a popular account of his 1966–1967 field trip. *Yiwara*, Gould explained, roughly translates as 'track': 'This book is itself a track of the Aborigines' destiny from the nomadic existence of the desert to the more settled and westernized existence on reserves and missions.'[44] In lucid, mournful prose he wrote of his observations and experiences

in the Western Desert. The book included fifty-two photographs, eleven
of which showed restricted ceremonial places, objects and activities. The
accompanying text allowed the identification of some of the people from
whom he obtained this 'secret-sacred' material. It was an unwise and
even rash decision to include these images in the book, given he intimately understood their restricted nature. But such practices were still
common in his field. The promise that images would not return to the
community relied on a separation between the world of the subject and
the professional world of academia, yet, as anthropologist Fred Myers
reflects, the divide between 'us' and 'them' was shrinking.[45] The changes
Gould had been documenting were catching up with him.

On 16 May 1971 a Ngaanyatjarra schoolgirl returned to her home in
Laverton with a copy of *Yiwara*. She had bought the book on a recent
trip to Perth after recognising the woman on the front cover as a close
relative. She showed the book to many women, but when her father
saw it he became very angry. The book revealed information that was
restricted to initiated men. By having it in her possession, there was
concern the schoolgirl had breached customary law, and that she would
be ritually speared for the transgression. According to some accounts,
the men swore 'they would kill Gould if he ever returned'.[46]

The details of this tragic incident remain sensitive and disputed.
Over time the story has been liberally embellished. In some secondary
accounts, the schoolgirl is killed as punishment for seeing the secret-
sacred material; in others she is speared and 'barred from matrimony'.
Another account suggests it was the woman on the cover and at least
one of the men Gould worked with who were to be punished. I have
condensed and simplified the story for the sake of sensitivity: the schoolgirl was not speared, but the anger the book generated was potent.

Word of the incident quickly spread throughout the desert communities. Four young men found the book, which had been hidden
by the girl's father, and travelled through the night and the next day

to reach Warburton, 565 kilometres away, to spread the news. The district officer of Warburton reported on 24 May 1971: 'Aborigines very upset and angry re Gould's book "Yiwara" ... Elders adamant no further cooperation with anthropologists.'[47]

When anthropologist Noel Wallace visited Amata in the Aṉangu Pitjantjatjara Yankunytjatjara lands in May 1971, he was surprised by the new restrictions placed on his work. For the first time old friends asked him to put away his notebook during certain ceremonies. And he unexpectedly found himself embroiled in tensions between groups: his decision to cancel a field trip so as not to exacerbate the sensitive situation caused great 'distress' for those who relied on his vehicle to visit country. Wallace's report shows the diversity of reactions within desert communities: from general indifference to acute anger at the initiated men who allowed such an exchange to unfold. But he, too, received a message for the AIAS: 'Tell those Canberra fellers they have got to stop other white fellers doing the same as Dr Gould.'[48]

By 23 June 1971 the situation in Warburton remained 'very disturbed'. Attitudes towards outsiders were already tense after the shooting death of an Aboriginal man by a Laverton police officer in 1970 and the theft of some sacred boards from a local cache.[49] Pamela McGrath, in an article with David Brooks, has also highlighted the residual sensitivity about images that lingered after the 1957 'Warburton Ranges controversy'. During a heated public debate about remote Aboriginal health and welfare, politician William Grayden focused national attention on the township through exaggerated reports of Indigenous malnutrition and disease. His documentary film, *Their Darkest Hour*, has had long-lasting local effects, with recent research on the attitudes of Ngaanyatjarra people revealing 'a general distrust of strangers with cameras and considerable anxiety about the viewing of images that may cause others distress'.[50] But despite these local contingencies, there is no doubt, in Ian Crawford's words, that the 'Gould book caused a very great hardening of attitudes'.[51] The situation appears to have been exacerbated by members of the Native Welfare Department showing the book and its sensitive images around the community. In July a journalist from the *Sunday Australian* caught wind of the story and made it front-page news: 'Tribal Threat to Spear School Girl'.[52]

John Mulvaney, then acting principal of the AIAS, first heard of the developments in Canberra and was concerned for the girl's safety and alarmed by the anger the book was generating throughout desert communities. He decided 'as a prudent initial step, to recall all fieldworkers with AIAS grants from the desert region'.[53] He also urged the AIAS to call a major conference to discuss the controversy. The conference, held on 9–10 August 1971 and chaired by Neil 'Black Mac' Macintosh, included deep discussion of permits and Aboriginal consultation, but its largely academic focus was betrayed by the title: 'The Aborigines and the Anthropologists: Problems of Field Access'. The federal minister in charge of Aboriginal affairs, Peter Howson, attended, along with around sixty academics and administrators, almost all white. Mulvaney reflected that, in hindsight, he should have acted more positively to involve Aboriginal people in the proceedings.

The *Yiwara* affair simmered throughout the conference and was variously alluded to as 'the Gould case', 'the schoolgirl incident', 'the episode in the western desert', 'what happened in Warburton' and, simply, 'the hoo-ha'. In this meeting of white intellectuals the story came to represent 'the Aboriginal viewpoint' and 'Aboriginal opinion'. The conference was wide-ranging and occasionally heated. Attendees shared stories about the growing need to seek permission across Australia. Macintosh regarded consultation as a natural part of fieldwork. He recalled getting permission from his guides before excavating in the Northern Territory in 1949: 'They only had one restriction,' he said – not to remove anything from the rock crevices. Ian Crawford described a similar experience in the Kimberley, where 'I was told I was too close to a site of significance and had to stop.'[54] There were some at the conference who expressed frustrations at being restricted from accessing sites, while others, such as Nicolas Peterson, despaired at the 'puritanical hard-line libertarianism' being expounded by some attendees. There is no 'overriding right of scientific enquiry', he said, 'to intrude into a very fragile culture and contribute to its destroying in the name of scientific investigation. We are privileged as anthropologists to be able to go along and work with Aborigines and they accept us.'[55]

Mulvaney later described the meeting as 'a faltering step' towards the positive dialogue fostered at the AIAS under the leadership of Peter Ucko in the 1970s and his push to 'Aboriginalise' the institute.[56] Even before the controversy, the AIAS had changed to a much more restrictive policy on the distribution of ceremonial films made by its film unit. In the wake of the *Yiwara* affair, aware of the damage such films could cause, it announced a recall of all films with secret-sacred material. Amongst the six resolutions that were passed at the conference was the recommendation that 'while recognising the wish of Aborigines to use the permit system to protect their privacy this conference urges a more satisfactory protection of Aboriginal privacy will come from the holding of titles to land by Aborigines'.[57]

In this rather dry statement we see something of the new political landscape that was emerging in the 1960s and '70s. The Aboriginal rights movement, operating in the shadow of contemporary racial movements in Africa and America, was giving urgency to questions of ownership and control, Aboriginality and power.

The *Yiwara* controversy became a flashpoint in this movement – a rare example of an Aboriginal community that was able to regain some control over their cultural information and access to their land. In the wake of the incident, an embargo was placed on permits for all researchers who wanted to work in Western Australian communities. The controversy would ultimately force dramatic changes to the permit system, involving Aboriginal communities for the first time in decisions over who could conduct research on their land.[58] This was a significant shift, as Sharon Sullivan reminds us, because 'whoever controls research into such sites controls, to some extent, the Aboriginal past'.[59]

From America, Gould was shocked and upset by what had happened. He learnt the details of the incident from journalists approaching him for comment and through snippets in his colleagues' letters. He was especially disturbed by reports of outsiders showing the restricted images around the community, inflaming tensions.[60] 'Had I been an Australian citizen and present at the time of the uproar I would have fought these attacks hard, perhaps even in court if necessary,' he wrote to Mulvaney in 1971. 'But being an American and in absentia made it somewhat hard to do that.'[61] He was not invited to attend the AIAS conference.

Gould was also remorseful about the promises he had made to stop secret-sacred material from returning to Warburton. He hoped to visit the communities and apologise for his offence, but the Western Australian authorities refused to sanction his visit. He called on the Australian publishers of *Yiwara*, Collins, to withdraw the book from the Australian market, and requested that his American publisher, Scribner, remove the offending images, but his contract offered him no immediate power over these matters. He shared his correspondence with the publishers with the Department of Native Welfare and asked that they communicate his positive actions to the communities of Laverton and Warburton. He also recorded an interview about the controversy with the ABC and asked for a taped copy to be sent to the Warburton Ranges Mission, so that the Ngaanyatjarra men could hear him explain his actions.[62] Eventually, in 1973, the book was withdrawn and some copies were removed from libraries around the country. Gould has recently expressed a willingness to repatriate the images from his time in the Western Desert.[63]

At the height of the controversy, a book burning (a curiously Western protest) was staged in Warburton, with multiple copies of *Yiwara* set alight in a 44-gallon drum. A similar protest took place in Wingellina in 1979 when Gould's recordings of Western Desert songs, released in 1968, made their way back to the community.[64] In 1972, archaeologists Richard Wright and Peter White warned Gould of the increasing hostility towards anthropologists and 'yourself in particular'. They urged him not to pursue further research in certain areas of the central deserts: 'We are, quite frankly, worried that your life may be in danger.'[65] Gould responded incredulously. He believed the situation had been blown out of proportion and was exasperated by how little control he had over his own fate: 'Spearings are quite common in the Western Desert (I have seen literally hundreds of them take place) and they involve nothing more than a jab in the thigh. A spearing threat is not a threat on one's life.'[66] His frustrated reply intimates a willingness to resolve the matter according to Ngaanyatjarra law. Nevertheless, he heeded his colleagues' advice and restricted his final Australian field-work to a small excavation at Intirtekwerle (James Range East), close to Alice Springs.

Anthropologist Ronald Berndt responded to the incident by removing all sacred photographs from his 1974 edition of *The First Australians*. (Though he included photos of a secret and ceremonial nature in an international publication the same year, along with a special statement entitled 'Readers in Australia Please Note'.)[67] Anthropologist TGH Strehlow adopted a similar policy to Berndt, but was caught out when secret-sacred images published in the German magazine *Stern* made their way back to Australia in 1978 against his will. Historian and poet Barry Hill explored the angst this caused Strehlow in the masterful biography *Broken Song*. Having been born and raised on Hermannsburg Mission, Strehlow considered himself 'the last Aranda man' and believed he had every right to share secret-sacred knowledge. What he failed to realise was that he had been overruled by the culture he had devoted his life to understanding and empowering.[68]

Not all fieldworkers, however, recognised the shifting political landscape. The publication in 1976 of Charles Mountford's *Nomads of the Australian Desert*, which contained images of restricted places, objects and activities taken in the 1930s and '40s, was a blatant breach of Aboriginal customary law. It stirred outrage amongst the Pitjantjatjara community and would ultimately see the *Yiwara* precedent come into law.[69]

Soon after the 1976 *Aboriginal Land Rights (Northern Territory) Act* was introduced, Foster v. Mountford was heard in the Supreme Court of the Northern Territory. Inspired by the withdrawal of *Yiwara* from the market, the Pitjantjatjara people won an injunction to prevent the further publication of Mountford's *Nomads of the Australian Desert*. Justice Muirhead found that the sacred information in the book had 'deep religious and cultural significance' and that the revelation of secrets to the women, children and uninitiated men 'may undermine the social and religious stability of their hard-pressed community'.[70] For the first time, Aboriginal cultural secrets were considered alongside commercial or trade secrets in the eyes of the law. As historian Michael Davis reflects, it was an important 'recognition by the Australian courts of a deep and profound sacredness to Aboriginal peoples' cultural life'.[71]

The irony of the *Yiwara* affair is that Gould was one of the first archaeologists to seek permission and consult with relevant elders about access to sites. Even the name he was given, *Mingkultjara*, tells of the rituals he went through in order to gain information. So while he accepted a degree of responsibility, Gould also believed he had been made a scapegoat at a time when many other researchers were also publishing secret-sacred images.[72] The Ngaanyatjarra took pride in their culture and had gone out of their way to share details about their technology and economy, plants and game, and even aspects of their sacred life.

'On many occasions,' Gould wrote in 1969, 'I was even reprimanded for apparent inattention to something they were showing or telling me, because I was not immediately writing it all down in my notebook.'[73] In 1972, in the wake of the *Yiwara* affair, he wrote an open letter defending his actions: 'Each time I attended a ceremonial event, I did so with the approval of everyone present, with the understanding that I would publish my observations but would keep sacred/secret material from getting back into the area.'[74]

But what did 'publishing' mean to the Ngaanyatjarra people who granted him this permission? Was Gould in a position to promise that material would not return to the region? His characterisation of the exchange of information fails to take into account the highly controlled nature of knowledge in Aboriginal societies. Permission to take the images is not the same as permission to use them. Peterson develops this concept further in his essay 'The Changing Photographic Contract': 'Seeing and knowing about an object or performance does not authorise a person to speak to others about it: the information is only for their own benefit and only those acknowledged as the rightful controllers of knowledge can disseminate it to others.'[75]

Gould tragically misjudged this relationship and overestimated his ability to control the circulation of the images. The expansion of white civilisation had engendered a new reality, for both Aboriginal people and researchers.

* * *

Near the end of the 2014 dig, we photograph the pit, sketch the stratigraphy and then riddle the walls with sample tubes. We have dug a narrow 'telephone booth' shaft into the earth. The pioneering phase of archaeology in Australia relied on excavating such pits. It allows an exhilarating glimpse into a layered landscape: an opportunity to see the refuse of past worlds and evidence of the people who inhabited them.

A well-placed pit is the fundamental ingredient for what Rhys Jones liked to term the 'who was where, when, and what was the weather like?' school of Australian archaeology.[76] Half of our pit overlaps with Gould's earlier trench, the other half cuts through undisturbed deposit. The contrast between the two is stark: on one side is the jumbled rubble and sediment of the backfill of the earlier excavation, on the other a fine-grained, tightly compacted archive of climatic and cultural change: a historical document waiting to be read, once and once only.

Betsy Gould returned from the Western Desert to work as the program director for the New York City Commission to the United Nations.[77] Meanwhile, Richard Gould stepped away from Australian archaeology to work on other fields, first in his mother's homeland of Finland, then to more general interests in underwater archaeology, forensic anthropology and disaster archaeology. In the wake of the September 11 terrorist attacks, he led trial forensic recoveries at the World Trade Center.[78] But he maintained an interest in Australian archaeology over the following decades and made the most of the material he had gathered during his time with the Ngaanyatjarra people. He hoped his work at Puntutjarpa would 'one day be of use' to the Ngaanyatjarra community. In his 1977 site report, he underlined the political dimensions of his work. By demonstrating an ancient and 'continuous' history of occupation, he wrote, 'this report provides support, should it be needed, for future Aboriginal land claims in the courts'.[79] But he also hoped his findings would encourage, amongst Aboriginal and non-Aboriginal people alike, 'an informed appreciation of the nature and success of traditional Aboriginal culture under difficult physical conditions'. He regarded the history he had helped uncover at Puntutjarpa as 'a tribute' to the Aboriginal people who had established and maintained a 'dignified and rewarding way of life under what were perhaps the most rigorous environmental conditions ever encountered by any historic or prehistoric hunters and gatherers'.[80]

It is important not to overstate the significance of Puntutjarpa in the history of Australian archaeology. The site discouraged, as much as encouraged, research into the desert. For many years it remained a lone dot in the centre of the continent, while archaeological research around the coastline flourished.[81] And while Gould wanted his work on Puntutjarpa to speak for the whole of the Western Desert, the next generation of archaeologists have focused on the variety of these arid landscapes, their distinct boom and bust ecologies and the different rhythms of life of their inhabitants. Led by those Gould affectionately described as 'the desert mob' – Peter Veth, Mike Smith, Sue O'Connor and Peter Hiscock – these archaeologists have deepened our under-standing of the arid interior and given us insight into the societies that made these landscapes their own.[82] Desert research has moved away from Gould's reading of cultural 'continuity' over the past 10,000 years to explore complex changes in the archaeological record.

After the extreme aridity of the Last Glacial Maximum, as the sea level stabilised and the deserts took their modern form, desert people experienced the best living conditions in thirty millennia.[83] From 8000 years ago, desert populations boomed; new sites were added to itinerar-ies and old sites were reclaimed. Around 5000 years ago, a rock shelter at Serpents Glen in the Carnarvon Range in the Western Desert was reoccupied after 23,000 years of archaeological silence.[84] But this popu-lation expansion brought new pressures. Desert people lived in a much larger social world. They could no longer always rely on relocating when resources became scarce. The result was a burst of technological and economic change that reverberated across Australia. The emergence, for example, of the specialised seed grinder, which has come to play a central role in desert law, tells us something of the scale of the cultural change at this time. Perhaps this was when the Pama–Nyungan lan-guage family spread through the desert interior.[85] The uniformity of this language family stands in stark contrast to the linguistic mosaic in the north and north-west of the continent. As Mike Smith reflects in *The Archaeology of Australia's Deserts*, a 'new desert society did, in fact, form in the Holocene' as Gould suggested – but much more recently; and this new society represented a distinctive adaptation to arid conditions, 'much as Gould proposed'. But this was only the latest change in a history of occupation and adaptation that stretches across more than forty millennia.[86]

We backfill the pit in the late afternoon and restore the site as best we can, smoothing the sandy shelter floor and resowing clumps of spinifex. We leave it like this. Without the paraphernalia of the dig – buckets, sieves, tape and dumpy – Puntutjarpa resumes its unimposing place in the landscape: a small overhang set into an undulating quartzite range of boulders and hollows.

FIVE

A DESICCATED GARDEN OF EDEN

Jim Bowler at Lake Mungo

We move from the sealed road onto the red Mallee earth without dropping speed. The low blue-grey scrub, cracking clay soils and wide, untrammelled horizon create the impression that we are not moving at all. It is October 2013 and I am making a pilgrimage to the Willandra Lakes, arguably the most iconic archaeological landscape in Australia. It was here in 1968, on the southern shores of Lake Mungo, that geomorphologist Jim Bowler stumbled upon the cremated bundle of human remains that became known as 'Mungo Lady' and, almost six years later, the complete and ceremonially buried skeleton of 'Mungo Man'. These two individuals had lain within 500 metres of each other for over 40,000 years. The discoveries made headlines around the world and announced the coming of age of Australian archaeology. This was the first archaeological site to grip the nation. Indeed, this eerily beautiful chain of dry lakes continues to haunt the Australian imagination. 'It has come to represent,' in the words of historian Kirsty Douglas, 'a fertile site for beginnings, a desiccated Garden of Eden.'[1]

'What kind of effect have the archaeological breakthroughs had on the community here?' I ask my companion, Daryl Pappin, a Mutthi

Mutthi man with a broad smile and a mop of black hair perpetually buried under a Richmond Tigers beanie.

'Good question,' he responds. 'Give me a minute. I know what I'm going to say, but it's like an essay – I need to figure out how to say it.' We listen to the road rumbling beneath us as Daryl chooses his words. Eventually he lifts a hand off the steering wheel and counts down with three fingers. 'It's made people recognise that Australian Aboriginals have a past.' Two fingers. 'It's changed the community, what with the archaeologists and tourists we have now. And I don't mind that.' One finger. 'It's been good, but it's caused all these tensions . . .' He trails off and returns his hand to the steering wheel.

A little later on, trying to prompt him further, I talk about how the discoveries at Mungo pushed the human history of Australia to the limits of radiocarbon dating and presented, for a time, the oldest evidence for modern humans outside of Africa: 'It's amazing how the dating of Aboriginal occupation in Australia went from a few thousand years in the 1950s to 25,000 years in the 1960s, then 40,000 years, and now maybe even 60,000 years.'

'And it's a lot more than that.' Daryl smiles at me. 'It goes up and up and up until forever.'

'Isn't 60,000 years pretty much forever?' I reply. 'I find it hard to even fathom that number.'

Daryl drives silently, as if to say, 'Well, no, 60,000 years isn't forever.'

I gaze out across the vast, flat landscape and make a mental note: I need to start thinking on a different scale.

* * *

The shores of Lake Mungo loomed large in the Australian imagination long before Jim Bowler gave the lake its name. In 1944 artist Russell Drysdale and journalist Keith Newman made a 5000-kilometre trek into inland New South Wales and Victoria to document the 'drought of the century' for the *Sydney Morning Herald*. They were horrified by what they found. The land had been stripped to its very skeleton. The natural rate of erosion had been exacerbated by a combination of long droughts and rabbit plagues, overstocking and inexperience, land clearing and the collapse of Aboriginal burning regimes. Twisted trees teetered on their exposed roots, carcasses of cattle and sheep littered the landscape, and when the wind blew, sediment blocked out the sun. Drysdale's haunting images, spread across the pages of the paper, brought home the tragedy of the drought that was paralysing New South Wales during World War II. They caused a national sensation. His paintings and sketches of isolated structures on barren hills and stoic, solitary figures in an ancient and distressed landscape were etched on the Australian psyche. 'With a few brief exceptions,' Newman reported, 'it has been one long tragedy-track over scorched earth ... Here the wind does not sweep the country – it came down hard on the unshielded land and scrubbed it.'[2]

Some locals know this country as 'the land where the crow flies backwards'. Archaeologist Harry Allen, who used this phrase in the title of his PhD on the Darling Basin, explained that the totemic crow did this 'to keep the dust out of his eyes'. The erosion is relentless. At Lake Mungo, archaeological finds were not excavated, they were revealed. The lakes haven't been full for 18,000 years, yet there are freshwater mussel shells and blackened fishbones scattered throughout the arid landscape, as if they had been cooked and discarded yesterday. In one part of the World Heritage area, a fossilised lakebed has preserved hundreds of human footprints. That most ephemeral of human traces has survived, buried, in this landscape for around 20,000 years. Wind and rain have exposed the trackways of two groups: a family walk across a drying lakebed, while a child scampers through the mud; and, crossing their path, a hunting party, including a one-legged man with a stick, sprint in pursuit of game. When archaeologists called on Indigenous trackers to interpret the footprints, the two Pintupi men had a chuckle at a spear mark made by an ancient hunter: 'He missed.'[3]

One night in mid-December 1944, Drysdale's party camped on the Mungo pastoral station on the sandhills of the 'Walls of China', a remarkable landform possibly named after the Chinese labourers who built the nearby Mungo woolshed in 1869. 'Sitting by the fire on a brilliant moonlit night,' Drysdale's biographer wrote,

> he found it one of the most extraordinary places in the world ... This revealed another reality and a new way of looking at the Australian landscape ... in terms of endless time, of geological activity and the presence of immense forces of nature which have shaped the land over millions of years.[4]

The party recognised the parched landscape as an ancient lakebed once fed by a mighty river. Newman was especially struck by the sculpted remnant dunes or 'residuals' for which Lake Mungo has since become famous: 'pillars of rich soil up to 12ft high among the sand, held in place by the skeletons of great trees which died on guard duty against the desert.'[5] The party was in awe of the geological story encrypted in the landscape, but they were also aware of the human history buried in the dunes. As Newman reported back for the *Sydney Morning Herald*, 'Erosion is disturbing the dead as well as menacing the living. The wind's giant hand has scooped away the earth from aboriginal burial grounds, to reveal skeletons of long dead men. How long, nobody knows. ... the anthropologists will have to hurry.' Ancient bones were coming to light and turning to dust.

Newman urged Australians not to be indifferent to the erosion that was devastating the inland. There was an 'urgent need for scientific assault' to salvage the ancient landscape that was disappearing into the wind: 'For, however far from the great cities, this land was part of our heritage and our future.'[6]

* * *

It would be more than two decades before major research was carried out in the desiccated lakes system. On a flight from Broken Hill to Sydney in the mid-1960s, geomorphologist Joe Jennings spotted a series of curved ridges through his aeroplane window. Back at the ANU, he traced the flight line and identified the features in aerial photographs as an interconnected chain of basins: a fossil remnant of an ancient flow from the Lachlan River. He reported the find to his student and colleague Jim Bowler, who was studying inland closed lake systems as if they were rain gauges: sensitive indicators of major climatic change.

Bowler had spent his life studying the land, first as a potato farmer, then mustering cattle through the Snowy Mountains, and finally as a geologist and geomorphologist (someone who studies landscapes and the processes by which they form). He is a philosopher and a dreamer, and from a young age was drawn to big questions about humanity, landscapes and the cosmos. He became restless growing up on a farm in the small country town of Leongatha, where his great-grandfather had emigrated from the west coast of Ireland in the late nineteenth century. 'There's a big wide world out there,' he exclaims to me in 2015, 'and I'm stuck here with these bloody cows!'[7] As a fifteen-year-old he turned his back on farming life and entered the seminary at Corpus Christi. It was an intensely intellectual time of learning and self-reflection. His reading moved beyond theology into the fields of evolution and, in the wake of Hiroshima, nuclear energy. He recalls being scolded at the seminary for possessing a clandestine essay on Charles Darwin. While he remains an Irish Catholic, his search for origins and understanding ultimately led him to geology. Deep time became the scale on which he viewed the world, and he quickly realised that water was the key to unlocking its secrets.

'A history of Australia,' Bowler wrote in 1988, 'could well centre on water resources. The environmental historian can read these landscapes as other scholars read documents in archives, finding new understanding of the continent both before people inhabited it and in its early stages of human occupation.'[8] Bowler's career has been shaped by water. As a junior lecturer at Melbourne University in the early 1960s, his first geological investigations were into the climatic history of Port Phillip Bay. In his scuba gear, sitting on the sea floor below a scallop boat with a winch, Bowler collected fifty cores across the bay by hammering cylindrical tubes into the mud, creating columns of sedimentary history. As recently as 6000 years ago, this sea floor had been a fertile hunting plain and the Yarra River had flowed out through the heads of Portsea and Queenscliff onto the Bassian Plain. Through coring, Bowler hoped to find out how Port Phillip Bay had filled up. It was a 'dangerous and murky exercise', particularly when working near the shipping channel, and Bowler was happy to move on to other climatic archives. His work on the active lakes of western Victoria – Colac, Purrumbete, Bullen Merri and, in particular, the volcanic crater lake of Keilambete – allowed him to map past shorelines, to see when the lakes shrank or overflowed and to compare the sandy sediment that lapped onto the slopes of the craters with the clay that gathered on the lakebed. He wanted to find out how changing water levels in south-eastern Australia tied into global climatic events. This was pioneering work. Bowler's careful reconstruction of lake levels filled in vast gaps in knowledge about climatic change and helped write the hydrological history of ancient Australia. But, as his colleague RW Galloway wrote in 1969, it was still 'painfully clear that we know very little'.[9]

When Bowler learnt of the Willandra Lakes, he was a PhD student in the Research School of Pacific Studies at the ANU and he saw it as an opportunity to study an ancient water system on a more manageable scale. The erosion of the lakes system would allow him to 'see inside' the landscape. As Bowler explains, mainland Australia has a peculiarly stable geological history: 'There's been no ice sheets, no mountain building. This landscape, right across southern and inland Australia, in many places has not changed much over the last million years.' This has allowed remnants of the deep past, which in other continents have been carved out by glaciers, to survive through to the present day. When major erosion creates gullies and residuals out of this deep time record, there is no need for excavation or coring: a skilled eye can read its history in the exposed walls of sediment and soil.

Following Jennings' advice, Bowler made his first visit to the Willandra Lakes in early 1967 with Roger Houston. It was hot and they were grateful for the hospitality of the pastoralist Len Carroll, who allowed them to stay a few nights in the shearers' quarters at Gol Gol Station. This was Bowler's first encounter with the massive lunettes of the Willandra Lakes: low, curving lines of sandy hills that arc around the shores of shallow lake basins, named because they resemble a crescent moon. It was also his first experience of the erosion that is weathering the landscape away. During a survey of Lake Mulurulu he and Houston were engulfed by a dust storm and their camp was buried under drifting sand. They took shelter in their Land Rover, listening to the wind and the wireless.

He returned alone a few months later, travelling across the low ridgelines and nested dunes on a flat-tyred motorbike, studying the landscape during the day and retreating to his quarters on the Mungo pastoral station in the evenings. He was fascinated by this dry place that had been shaped by water, a landscape that could be read like scripture. In late 1967 Bowler first explored a basin further south where there had been major erosion on the margin, exposing freshwater shells and gravel beaches: signals of periods when the lake had been full. 'You could actually put your spade on the point,' he marvelled. 'This is where the water was when that beach was formed.' As he worked, his mind turned over the climatic change he was observing. Was it cyclic? And how had this landscape formed over time?

Bowler felt at home amongst the dunes. As his daughter Jenny writes, 'The breadth and depth of isolated places resonated with him.'

He was 'rough and ready, he played his classical music loud and cooked a good hot curry'.[10] His hosts at the Mungo pastoral station, Albert and Venda Barnes, accommodated his eccentric interest in their sheep paddocks. They had not known they lived on a fossil lakebed. Indeed, at that stage the lakes had no cartographic name. Having mapped the basins, Bowler was charged with that responsibility and chose to name them after the sheep stations. The origins of the name 'Mungo', which has become so iconic of Aboriginal Australia, are disputed. Some claim it derives from the Ngyiampaa word for canoe – *mangar*; others trace it back to the sixth-century Scottish apostle Saint Mungo. When Alex and Albert Barnes bought Mungo pastoral station in 1934 from Ewan and Angus Cameron, they found a photo of the St Mungo cathedral in Glasgow on the dining room wall.[11]

Bowler's great contribution was to understand the anatomy of the lunettes, to unpack the great cycles of change, the drying of the lakes and the building of the big dunes.[12] It was only gradually that he realised that there were human actors on this environmental stage. The lunette at Lake Mungo curves for over 30 kilometres around the basin and towers over this flat landscape at some 24 metres high and 200 metres wide. The Lake Garnpung lunette, to the north, is the largest clay lunette in the world, rising to 30 metres high. Building on the earlier findings of geologist Edwin Sherbon Hills, Bowler found that the lunettes were mostly composed of fine clay, which had formed on the damp lake floor before being clumped into fluffy pellets by salt and blown by the wind up onto the lakeshore, where the clay gradually built up, layer by layer. When the lake basins held water, the wind was the agent that built the lunettes; but with no moisture or salt to create clay, it is now blowing them away and, in the process, exposing long-buried shorelines. By understanding their formation, and identifying distinct phases of climatic change and soil development, Bowler had revealed the structure of the landscape.[13]

When the first Australians arrived on the continent some 65,000 years ago, Lake Mungo had been dry for over 50,000 years. As the climate cooled, glaciers formed in the mountains and the melting ice enlarged the rivers. From around 60,000 to 50,000 years ago, the Lachlan River supplied the Willandra Creek with enough water from the snowfields on the Snowy Mountains to maintain a system of thirteen lakes with over 200 kilometres of shoreline. 'In the Willandra system alone,' Bowler writes, 'more than 1000 km² of open water was introduced to a region where no permanent water existed previously.'[14] Lake Mungo was an overflow lake, fed by the nearby Lake Leaghur. As the climate became more arid, the mountain snowfields shrank, the rivers changed shape and the lakes became salty and ephemeral, before a drying trend set in leading up to the Last Glacial Maximum at 21,000 years ago. By around 14,500 years ago the lakes were defunct.

The first intimations that people were a part of these great climatic events were the freshwater shells that Bowler found beyond the natural shorelines. They appeared to have been carried there. He reported the burnt shells, along with scattered hearths and flaked stones back to his colleagues at the ANU, but was greeted with scepticism. His interpretation of the landscape structure suggested that this evidence for human activity was associated with the lake-full periods of 30,000–40,000 years ago: almost double the oldest dates for human occupation in Australia at the time. 'I was sort of politely told, "Look you're a geologist, you stick with your stones and we'll look after the archaeology."'[15]

* * *

Bowler first presented his research on the Willandra Lakes as part of a seminar series at the ANU between October and December 1968. The papers from this forum were later collected in the landmark volume *Aboriginal Man and Environment in Australia* (1971). The editors, John Mulvaney and Jack Golson, were keenly aware of the importance of interdisciplinary research and encouraged collaboration between archaeology and the earth sciences. 'Human history,' geologist George Seddon reminds us, 'is not complete without environmental history. It is not enough to detail the actions of the actors; the stage is equally important.'[16]

In some ways, the seminar series can be seen as a response to the challenge Rhys Jones had issued to the field in a provocative editorial for *Mankind* in June 1968. Jones urged his fellow Australian archaeologists to take stock of the recent discoveries, to synthesise the mass of raw data about ancient Australia, and to take a global view of their research. 'The honeymoon is over,' he declared. 'The new wave of Australian archaeology is settling down comfortably to a premature middle age.' He was searching for a 'glimmer of independent archaeological thinking which could grow into a viable and recognizable Australian school':

> Let us not confuse the accumulation of raw data with improved quality of thought. Simple-minded archaeology is still simple minded, be it conceived over a continent or over a parish ... In terms of the 'main stream of history', Australia is a peripheral eddy. If we are content merely to document this local sequence, we consign our work to a footnote of world prehistory.[17]

Jim Bowler's seminar paper on human activity at Lake Mungo pulled Australian archaeology from a footnote onto the front page of world prehistory. 'Immediately afterwards the situation changed,' Bowler reflected in 2015. 'Peter White [from the University of Sydney] collared me as we came out and said "I'd love to go out there. When can we go out there?" I was then subsequently clobbered by Rhys Jones [from the ANU], "Don't have anything to do with Sydney! Wait until we're ready!"'[18]

The main cause of the excitement was a chance discovery Bowler had made during a geomorphological survey of the lunettes. On 5 July

1968, he noticed 'some strange bone fragments' eroding from the south-ern shores of Lake Mungo on the Joulni sheep station. The context of the bones told him immediately that they had lain there since the last Ice Age. It looked to him like the remains of a meal 'burnt by early man'. Perhaps the bones belonged to one of the giant extinct marsupials that once roamed this lakeshore? He marked the site with a red iron peg – 'about twenty metres away so that sheep wouldn't come and scratch against it' – and postponed further investigation until the arrival of archaeologists, 'the ordained members of the intellectual clergy' whose hands are 'anointed' to work on such things.[19]

The earliest he was able to draw a party to look at the find was the following March, when he led a group of geologists, soil scientists and archaeologists around the Willandra Lakes. They stayed in the shearers' sheds at Lake Mungo, explored the dunes during the day and debated ideas at night over lamb chops and flagons of wine. The archaeologists, Harry Allen, Rhys Jones, Con Key and John Mulvaney, were tantalised by the suggested association of giant marsupials and artefacts and they excitedly followed Bowler to Joulni to investigate the charred bones. But the find was even more dramatic than they imagined. As they care-fully investigated the shattered bundle of bones, out dropped a piece of human jawbone. Geologist Keith Crook recalls Jones dancing as he held aloft the diagnostic evidence. In an instant, the scale of Australian his-tory changed. 'We were confronted,' in Bowler's words, 'not only with human activity but by the very presence of humanity itself.'[20]

'We had not come prepared for an excavation,' Jones and Allen later wrote, 'and yet here before us was a feature which could contain the old-est human bones so far discovered in Australia.'[21] And it was turning to dust before their eyes. While Bowler was explaining the lunette struc-ture to his geomorphologist colleagues on a neighbouring dune, Jones, Allen and Mulvaney photographed and drew the features of the burial and collected the loose bones. They then made the decision to remove the bones. 'It was a very dramatic moment,' Mulvaney later reflected: 'It was more dramatic because there were sheep all around and they were walking all over it.'[22] A thunderstorm was brewing and they were acutely aware that one downpour could sweep the bones away. They carefully cut and removed the disintegrating calcrete blocks in which the bones were set and packed them in the only vessel available: John Mulvaney's suitcase. Some of Mulvaney's clothes were returned as padding. That suitcase is now in the National Museum of Australia.

'The discussion that night,' Harry Allen recalled, 'was one largely of shock. The archaeologists were in shock. It was a monumental discovery, a monumental shift in the way the Aboriginal past – the Australian past in human terms – was understood.'[23] Bowler described the feeling of the group as 'elation'. They took the remains back to Canberra the following day, and that evening zoologist John Calaby confirmed they were human. While physical anthropologist Alan Thorne began the painstaking task of excavating, cleaning and reconstructing the shattered skull, Allen, Jones and Bowler returned to the site to look for other archaeological evidence. They pitched their tent near the Walls of China as thunder clouds rolled across the vast horizon and an 'enormous storm broke'. 'The ground in seconds became white with pelting water,' Jones wrote in his diary. 'That night we saw my first Aurora Australis.'[24] They awoke to find another layer of the lunette stripped away, and a wide variety of stone tools scattered across a Pleistocene beach. The artefacts they collected on that return visit formed the kernel of their argument for a pan-continental, Pleistocene 'Australian Core Tool and Scraper Tradition', which was an important elaboration of the oldest phase in Mulvaney's technological scheme.

In Canberra, it took Thorne over six months to excavate and reconstruct the hundreds of bone fragments, many the size of postage stamps, contained in the calcrete blocks. They were found to belong to a young adult female of slender build and small stature who had been burnt on a pyre by the lakeshore between 25,000 and 32,000 years ago – later revised to over 40,000 years ago. What was groundbreaking was that the remains were unequivocally human, making them at the time the oldest evidence of *Homo sapiens* outside of Africa.[25] Here was the skeleton of 'a young woman who lived a long, long, long time ago,' Thorne reflected, 'and she was just like us.'[26]

The discovery challenged interpretations of other skeletal evidence in Australia and shattered the lingering nineteenth-century assumption that Aboriginal people had evolved from an earlier race of hominids. Thorne, who had studied a markedly different group of burials at the nearby site of Kow Swamp, devised an evolutionary model that could accommodate the co-existence of the 'gracile' Mungo skeleton and the more 'robust' Kow Swamp remains, suggesting two distinct waves of Pleistocene colonisation. But the palaeoanthropological community has since refuted this hypothesis, attributing the anatomical differences to genetic diversity, environmental variation and an ethnographically observed cultural practice of 'head pressing', whereby a mother gently rubs and shapes her newborn's head over several months. What was once described as 'the mark of ancient Java' might instead be explained by a caring mother's hands.[27]

The skeleton – or Mungo I – became affectionately known as Mungo Lady. Her cremated remains had been buried in a small round hole on a sandy beach a few metres from the water's edge. There she had remained for 40,000 years, as the lake system dried and the camp was abandoned, as her descendants moved to other parts of their country, and as the rabbits and goats and farmers arrived. If Jim Bowler hadn't stumbled across her remains in July 1968, all evidence of her life and death would have eroded into the wind within a year. The fortuitous nature of her preservation, and the influence of her discovery on the Australian public, has led traditional owners such as Dorothy Lawson to declare that, 'She surfaced for a reason.'[28] As Mutthi Mutthi elder – and

Daryl's mother – Mary Pappin wrote, 'I believe that the Mungo Lady came to walk with our people to help us with our struggle and to tell the rest of the world about our cultural identity with that land.'[29] The resurrection of Mungo Lady changed the face of Australian archaeology. As Bowler reflected in 2015, 'I stumbled across these bones and blundered into an archaeological and cultural minefield!'[30]

* * *

Little has been written about the Aboriginal history of the Willandra region. The turbulent post-contact history of the Paakantji, Mutthi Mutthi and Ngyiampaa people is marked by loss and pain, struggle and survival. The traditional owners of Mungo were forced off their land to live in fringe camps in the surrounding towns and settlements of Balranald, Wentworth, Wilcannia and Mildura. In these camps and missions it was illegal to practise aspects of their traditional culture and they were forbidden to speak their language. Up until 1969, the Aborigines Welfare Board (previously the Aborigines Protection Board) was still forcibly removing Aboriginal people, in particular Aboriginal children, to reserves and managed stations. Mutthi Mutthi woman Tanya Charles remembers the panic that arose when they heard 'welfare coming' and how she would hide in the bush waiting for an all-clear whistle.[31] Paakantji elder Dorothy Lawson lamented the cultural upheaval in her lifetime: 'It hurts me ... that I have lost the way of speaking in my ... native tongue.'[32] Even the landscape has changed through European settlement. Many of the plants and animals upon which Indigenous people traditionally depended have become locally extinct through overgrazing, drought and the invasion of ferals. As Paakantji elder Ronnie Mitchell recalled: 'When we was a child ... you could go out and pick up things, yams, stones and find things to eat. Now we can't find anything out in the bush ... Because they brought cattle and sheep and that out and cleaned up everything.'[33]

When the archaeologist Harry Allen began his large-scale regional survey of the Darling Basin in 1969, he hoped 'to interview the few old Aborigines of the area who had lived in the bush' to see how their traditional knowledge could inform the archaeological story. He had been a part of the student scene at the University of Sydney during the Freedom Rides and was interested in connecting contemporary Indigenous affairs with stories of the deep past. But he faced difficulties tracking down traditional owners, let alone interviewing them. His attempts to cross the cultural divide were met with suspicion. He later reflected, wryly: 'I'd been picked up by the police because I wanted to talk to Aboriginal people'.[34] It was with 'some regrets' that he decided to restrict his ethnographic study to the written record.

Allen found only snippets of information about cultural and economic practices in the documentary record, and most of this was tied to the main rivers, which the early European explorers followed closely in their searches for an inland sea. He opened his thesis with 'a history of the Aboriginal peoples of the Darling Basin and of the destruction of their society by the Europeans'. He recorded the devastating impact of disease on Indigenous populations as well as the conflict and bloodshed that stained the Darling and the Murray. As pastoral leases spread across Australia in the mid-nineteenth century, Aboriginal people became seen as 'trespassers' on their own country, 'aliens in their own land'. Without access to their traditional hunting grounds, Aboriginal people speared the intruders – cattle – which far too often, wrote nineteenth-century anthropologist Alfred Howitt, 'led to the tribe being, in the euphemistic phrase of the frontier, "dispersed"'.[35] 'They rounded them up like kangaroos, my people,' Mutthi Mutthi elder Alice Kelly mourned in 1990, 'women and children too. They drove them on foot from horseback, with whips cracking over their heads. They shot them and the sands covered them over ... Barbarians. Saxon barbarians. They showed us no mercy.'[36]

The traditional owners had little choice but to leave their home-lands and attempt to find food and safety on the fringes of the new homesteads dotting the country. Some worked as shepherds and on homesteads, playing an important role in the pastoral industry, but homestead accounts document a rapid decline in Aboriginal populations in the late nineteenth century and fears that they would soon become extinct. Then came the protection-era policies, which were still in place when Allen was writing his thesis. The surviving inhabitants of the upper Willandra Creek were rounded up and relocated to Balranald Mission; some were forced onto paddle steamers and shipped down the Murray to missions at Goolwa.[37]

Harry Allen's method of regional survey combined with ethnography was similar to Isabel McBryde's approach in New England, but he was also influenced by what Betty Meehan and Rhys Jones have characterised as the 'Sydney School'.[38] He was interested in using ecological and economic analyses to understand the seasonal nature of archaeological remains – an approach that attracted criticism for projecting recent accounts of Aboriginal culture onto the deep past.[39] But the sheer scale of his PhD research is virtually unmatched in Australian archaeology. He documented details of twelve sites across the wider Darling Basin, mapped hundreds of square metres of middens and systematically collected and excavated artefacts from the eroding shorelines of Lakes Leaghur, Garnpung, Arumpo, Mungo and Mulurulu in the Willandra region. The climate was harsh and he often worked alone, travelling across vast distances on a small motorbike. His study extended from remote open sites in the rocky uplands to shelters on pastoral stations, from middens on the lunettes to the Mildura fish 'n' chips shop, where he compared the ear bones of golden perch with their ancient counterparts.

It was a challenging and unfamiliar environment for archaeologists, and Allen relied heavily on Bowler's interpretations of the landscape structure to put the ancient surface finds into context. He was particularly interested in possible associations between humans and extinct megafauna, hoping to 'throw some light on whether or not the Aborigines had caused the extinction of the giant marsupials'.[40] He had no luck solving this vexed question. Amidst the thousands of faunal remains recorded across the Willandra region over the past four decades, there have been remarkably few belonging to extinct megafauna, and none have been found in Aboriginal campsites.

Allen speculated that Aboriginal occupation of the Willandra was largely dependent on freshwater phases of the lakes, with societies retreating to the river systems when the water turned saline or dried up. When the lakes were full, the inhabitants hunted kangaroos and bettongs on the sand dunes and plains; they foraged for emu eggs and trapped small birds in the scrub; they caught Murray cod and golden perch with nets in the deep lake waters and dug into the muddy shoreline for shellfish; 'they came together in large semi-sedentary groups living in village-like encampments of substantial grass huts' to feast and fight, to trade and conduct business.[41] He interpreted the introduction of the grindstone around 15,000 years ago – and the accompanying practices of harvesting and storing grain – as a response to the drying phase of the lakes. But his overall interpretation, much like Richard Gould's findings at Puntutjarpa two years earlier, was 'one of a single continuous cultural tradition': 'Changes took place in this tradition during man's 32,000 year history in the area, but these were not so great as to destroy the impression of continuity.'[42]

Allen was also struck by the continuity of faunal remains in the area: the same animals had been hunted and collected over 30,000 years without any apparent population changes. He read this stability as evidence that people had developed a remarkably sustainable system of interaction with their environment. 'This longstanding relationship,' he added ruefully, reflecting on recent extinctions, 'was destroyed with the introduction of sheep, cattle, foxes and rabbits in the area by Europeans.'[43]

In 1998, with the benefit of Jane Balme's research in the wider Darling River region, Allen revisited his original survey material. 'In 1972, I sought to question Aboriginal subsistence in terms of either continuity *or* change and the search was restricted to matters of technology.' But Balme had demonstrated that profound social and economic change could accompany technological continuity. Considering that culture is a dynamic process, not something fixed in time, Allen moved away from his interpretation of stability to emphasise the immense adaptability of the people who have called this region home.[44]

* * *

The discovery of Mungo Lady was a watershed. 'Something remarkable is taking place in a field of Australian science that once seemed as dry as dust,' journalist Gavin Souter wrote at the time.[45] Of Mungo Lady, another journalist wrote:

> She rises up from the very dawn of prehistory, this eternal woman, to unlock the mind of early man. With this and other finds, Australia – virtually ignored by prehistorians until the late 1960s as a tedious archaeological backwater – is now the focus of the quest to unravel the prehistory of mankind.[46]

The excitement was heightened by the international significance of the finds. 'As old as anything in America at the present time, and as old as any other modern-man finds in the world,' wrote Jacqueline Rees, 'the discoveries indicate the rapidity of the development of Australian research in recent years.'[47] The *Sydney Morning Herald* published a colourful two-page poster pull-out on 'The Aborigines', as well as a series of articles on Aboriginal society, past and present: 'The 601 Tribes of Australia', 'Subtle Complexities of Tribal Society', 'Why Does a Boomerang Return?' and features on contemporary Indigenous art and dance.[48] A stream of international archaeological greats such as François Bordes, Lewis Binford and Glynn Isaac made the pilgrimage to Lake Mungo. The quiet work of Australian archaeologists suddenly began to be recognised.

And research in the Willandra was only beginning. Archaeologists such as John Mulvaney and Isabel McBryde were eager to investigate this transient fossil landscape and they advocated for its protection. Their campaigns to conserve the Willandra culminated in the acquisition of Mungo Station from Albert and Venda Barnes for the creation of Lake Mungo National Park in 1978 and, three years later, the registration of the Willandra Lakes as a UNESCO World Heritage landscape. It was listed at the same time as the Great Barrier Reef and Kakadu National Park and, significantly, it was recognised for its natural *and* cultural heritage. It was a celebration of Lake Mungo as 'one of the world's great open-air museums': Australia's Rift Valley.[49] Bowler pays tribute to the role of the Barnes family in this process, who 'forfeited their heritage, Mungo Station, to permit the investment of that region's scientific treasures in the national interest'.[50]

The initial expedition to excavate Mungo Lady in 1969 (including fuel, meals and accommodation for three people) had cost the ANU a meagre $94: 'a remarkably productive investment,' Mulvaney noted, 'that ensured the Willandra Lakes a World Heritage registration by 1981'.[51] The 1973 research agenda, on the other hand, was the first exercise in 'big archaeology' in Australia. 'This project is the most ambitious collaborative effort between environmental scientists and prehistorians to have been attempted in Australia,' wrote Mulvaney in his grant application.[52] Alongside a systematic regional survey, they sought to undertake a large-scale excavation at Lake Mungo to help place eroded finds in context. The AIAS approved funds for a geological technician, a bright yellow tractor with a backhoe, a bespoke set of pneumatic sieves, the chartering of a light plane for aerial photography, and a field and lab technician in the form of John Magee. A recent survey of Willandra Lakes, led by Rainer Grün in 2006, harnessed satellites, lasers, aircraft, deep physics, geomorphology and traditional knowledge in its pursuit of the deep past.

By the early 1970s we also see the emergent legislative landscape archaeologists had to navigate. For the first time, they needed permits from the NSW National Parks and Wildlife Service (NPWS) to conduct fieldwork. Permission to excavate was granted in three- or twelve-month increments, and was accompanied by conditions to backfill trenches, lodge findings with museums and complete ongoing paperwork such as environmental impact statements. It was the kind of heritage protection Mulvaney had long campaigned for, but when his permit arrived in the mail the director of the NPWS apologised for what might appear to be a 'tirelessly bureaucratic' and 'unnecessarily restricting' process.[53]

In 1973 Mulvaney dug a three-metre trench in the southern end of the Mungo lunette into a series of beach gravels, while Isabel McBryde, Peter Bellwood and Wilfred Shawcross systematically mapped artefacts over a large area of the western end. Mulvaney's large, tiered trench, which had 'an architectural grandeur', produced the widely quoted date of 'greater than 40,000 years'. Aboriginal leader Marcia Langton, who studied archaeology as an undergraduate at the ANU, recalls the significance of this work in the student movement for Aboriginal rights: 'I learnt about that as a young student ... It not only changed the way other people saw Aboriginal people but it was enormous news for Aboriginal people to have an actual date.'[54] Shawcross took over direction from Mulvaney in the three subsequent seasons. McBryde's interest in the region grew in 1974 as she focused on systematically collecting, measuring and dating shell middens, hearths and artefact scatters on the Outer Lake Arumpo lunette. Meanwhile Bowler continued his geological survey, investigating the anatomy of the landscape and trying to understand this 'dramatic panorama of environmental change'.[55]

On 26 February 1974, Bowler was 'confined to the barracks' at Mungo Station most of the day by heavy rains. In the late afternoon, as the skies cleared and the mud dried, he 'hastened' to the Joulni lunette, where he had found Mungo Lady almost six years earlier, 'eager to explore surfaces refreshed by cleansing rains':

> While I was following a distinctive soil horizon, one that had already yielded many artefacts, the late afternoon sun highlighted a tiny patch of something white shining through a cover of expansive sand mantle. An immediate examination revealed what was obviously the domal part of a human skull. I brushed away sand to reveal that the jawbone was intact. This was part of an emerging body.[56]

He reported the find to the ANU by phone from a nearby homestead and two days later a team arrived to investigate. As always, the threat of heavy rain imposed a sense of urgency: the site was ephemeral. On 28 February the team removed the covering sands to reveal a burial. Thorne identified it immediately as a man, lying in an outstretched position, hands over the groin, in a carefully prepared grave dug 80–100 centimetres deep.[57] There were several areas of 'collapsed and crumbling bone', probably due to the wandering hooves of the stock that had grazed in this area, but the body was remarkably intact. The initial age estimate was 28,000–32,000 years. This was later revised to 40,000–42,000.[58] 'With each delicate removal of sand,' Bowler later reflected, 'a new chapter of Australian history was unfolding before us.'[59] The curious feature of the burial was the presence of 'a strange brownish-red zone around the upper part of the body' and a 'pink staining' around the grave margins. While examining a small pellet, Bowler realised that he was looking at ochre: an incredibly rare resource in the Willandra area that must have been traded and transported there from over 200 kilometres away. The body had been painted or sprinkled with over two kilograms of this sacred resource: a ritual practice unfathomable to the researchers at that time.

Bone analysis by Alan Thorne and Steve Webb gives us some insight into this individual who walked the lakeshores of the Willandra region before humans had penetrated the icy heart of Europe. Mungo Man was around the age of fifty when he died. He was missing both canine teeth, which may have been extracted during an initiation ritual in his teenage years. His lower molar teeth were worn down in a way that suggests they had been used to strip fibre off long leaves 'so that it could be teased into string for making nets to use in the lakes'. He suffered from serious osteoarthritis of the right elbow, possibly the result of a lifetime's use of the spearthrower or woomera. Webb, who painstakingly studied the remains at the ANU, finds it 'easy to picture him sitting, slowly rubbing the aching elbow in front of his fire on a cold ice age night'.[60] Indigenous custodians such as Tanya Charles find the evidence of the ancient past just as vivid: 'It's like yesterday that our people were still walking across this country. I can't go back and say hundreds and thousands of years because everything's like yesterday to me, especially when you've still got the spirits around and you can feel the presence of them.'[61]

Studies of the health, DNA and isotopic bone and teeth structures of Mungo Man have given us an insight into life in ancient Australia. But it is the ritual nature of his burial, Bowler stresses, that 'has changed our understanding of the time-depth and complexity of Aboriginal culture'.[62] The central nature of rare ceremonial ochre, which had been imported from distant sources, the careful arrangement of the body in the grave and the presence of a nearby hearth 'presented one of the dramatic mysteries of ancient human cultural development'.[63] The evidence also resonated with contemporary Aboriginal connections to country. 'There is great dignity here in that people–land relationship,' Bowler wrote in 2016. 'Exemplified today in the Dreaming, song lines and creation stories, they remain of central importance in helping define traditional people's identity with and connection to the place they call home. White Australians have something important to learn from our Aboriginal cousins.'[64] But, as Shawcross reflected of the archaeologists in the area, 'We, and that includes me, had not remotely considered that the Aboriginal people would be concerned about what we were doing ... I suppose we felt rather righteous – I felt rather righteous – that here we were rediscovering their past. Shouldn't they be grateful?'[65]

* * *

In 1973, on learning of the archaeological activities at Lake Mungo, one of the traditional owners of the region , Mutthi Mutthi elder Alice Kelly, wrote a letter to the NPWS expressing concern. She wanted to know why she hadn't been consulted about the work that was being under-taken on her land. She was particularly concerned by the removal of Aboriginal bones: it conjured painful memories of the skulduggery of grave robbers along the Murray River throughout the nineteenth and early twentieth century, such as the farmer and collector George Murray Black, who exhumed 'two truckloads of skeletons' for the Department of Anatomy at Melbourne University.[66] Human remains were not sci-entific evidence, they were relatives, ancestors, spirits. 'Please withdraw any further excavation of skeletons from the Walls of China, New South Wales, about 70 miles north-east of Mildura,' she wrote. 'They are our tribal people ... The point is they would not like the same thing done to their people.'[67]

Sharon Sullivan, the NPWS's first archaeologist, received the letter and together with Isabel McBryde, who was on the committee, made the case for the traditional owners to be consulted and involved in field-work. The committee's recommendation was to 'contact Mrs Kelly and discuss the excavation with her, perhaps taking her out to see work in progress'. 'Mrs Kelly,' McBryde added in a letter to Mulvaney, 'is appar-ently a serious and concerned lady, quite sophisticated, and acting on her own initiative not as [a] tool for outside activists.'[68]

Alice Kelly was born in 1919 near the banks of the Murrumbidgee River, where as a child she had watched her father cut his own bark canoe. At the age of fifteen she married a drover, Alf Kelly, and started a family in nearby Balranald. She was proud of her heritage, and soon after the creation of the Aboriginal flag in 1971 she adorned the windows of her house with the bold red, yellow and black symbol.[69] As Bowler wrote in the wake of her death in 2003, 'She remembered language, observed traditional laws and above all, developed a passionate love of the land to which her people were intimately attached.'[70] Jean Charles, one of her eleven children, stressed the importance she placed on words. She took a dictionary everywhere she went and 'wrote everything down': 'She put dates on those papers too, whether it was on a piece of card-board, a Weet-Bix box, butchers paper, whatever.'[71] When linguist Luise Hercus interviewed her in the mid-1960s, she was impressed to find that Kelly was already collecting her own word-lists of Aboriginal languages. Her passionate advocacy for Aboriginal rights, and the discipline and determination with which she conducted her affairs, made her for many years the voice for Aboriginal people in the area. And in Isabel McBryde, Kelly found a good friend and sympathetic ear.[72]

The resurgence of the local Aboriginal community and the increas-ingly vocal national calls for land rights had major implications for archaeological research in the region, as they had for Rhys Jones in Tasmania and Richard and Betsy Gould in the Western Desert. Over the following decade a rift formed between the traditional owners and the researchers. Isabel McBryde ceded control to Alice Kelly and others: 'I felt that the only way I could show I was genuine was to say, "If you are unhappy about what I am doing, I will not go on."'[73] Many of her colleagues, on the other hand, remained concerned about the ongoing destruction of the Willandra landscape and the natural and cultural heritage that was being lost through erosion. Mulvaney defended the work of scientists in the region, arguing that they had a duty to protect these sites for the sake of posterity. At stake were fundamental questions of ownership and identity. As British archaeologist Christopher Chippindale reflected, 'Does the history of humans in Australia ... belong to the ethnic descendants of those first inhabitants? ... Or is there some wider claim, of science and common human concern, to rights of access to relics of the past?'[74] In 1988, the Western Regional Land Council placed an embargo on archaeological excavation at Lake Mungo.

The complex layers of bureaucracy in the Willandra region compounded the tension between researchers and the traditional owners. As a World Heritage landscape, the lakes system comes under federal supervision and requires a management plan to protect its natural and cultural heritage. As a national park it also falls under the jurisdiction of the state government, which in turn has legislation to empower the views of the traditional owners – in this case the three Aboriginal land councils of the Paakantji, Mutthi Mutthi and Ngyiampaa people – as well as a responsibility to accommodate the interests of pastoral leaseholders. The High Court rulings on native title (*Mabo* in 1992 and *Wik* in 1996) have added further complications to this mix. Alice Kelly represented local Aboriginal interests on boards and committees at every level of this bureaucracy and played a key part in negotiating a management plan for the World Heritage area. In 1988 the National NAIDOC Committee awarded her the title of Aboriginal of the Year.[75]

In June 1989, following the embargo on research, a three-day seminar was held at Mungo, bringing together scientists, conservation managers, landholders and local Aboriginal people. The lengthy discussions about conduct of research, control of cultural heritage, park management and the return of human remains paved the way for a new era of research, anchored in collaboration and dialogue. 'It was decided,' the resulting statement read, 'to embark on a course of reconciliation between archaeologists and Aborigines. It was recognised that

Aboriginal people must have the final say whether research was done and what it might be.'[76] The resolution was in tune with the national zeitgeist, with federal parliament establishing the Council for Aboriginal Reconciliation with cross-party support two years later.[77] At the heart of the reconciliation in the Willandra region was a symbolic act: the return of Mungo Lady to a 'Keeping Place' on the site where she had been buried.

In a moving ceremony on the shores of Lake Mungo on 11 January 1992, Alan Thorne handed over the remains of Mungo Lady to thirteen elders. Over 200 people, mostly Aboriginal, watched as the remains were officially welcomed home by Alice Kelly. At the end of the ceremony, the crowd had a chance to view the fossil skeleton and pay their respects. Mungo Lady now rests in a locked, decorated safe underground in Mungo National Park. 'There are two keys to this lock,' Senior Ranger Badger Bates announced at the ceremony. 'One key is held by Aborigines and one key is held by scientists. Only when both keys are turned together will the safe be open.'[78]

Since that powerful moment, a fragile partnership has formed between researchers and traditional owners. There remains some bewilderment about the scientific study of ancient Australia, as voiced by an exasperated Lottie Williams in the film *Message from Mungo*. 'What were they trying to prove?' she asked. 'When me and all the rest of us know we were here all the time, so that wasn't news to us.'[79] But there is also a growing accommodation of scientific practices, and many custodians, such as my guide Daryl, are involved in uncovering the archaeological story of the Willandra Lakes.[80] Junette Mitchell, an elder of the Paakantji people, recently gave a DNA sample to a geneticist studying the evolutionary history of Aboriginal people because she 'wanted to see how close we were to Mungo Lady'. She took pride in the international recognition of her homeland: 'It's a big breakthrough now to prove that Aboriginal people was in Australia before anyone had 'em here. That's what Mungo Lady showed.'[81] In her welcoming address to the Mungo youth festival in 2006, Mary Pappin also paid tribute to 'our ancestor, our mother, who came up out of the ground, who was accidentally found, who was then taken away'. 'It all comes about because of that Mungo Lady,' she said.[82] Since 2009, the Paakantji, Mutthi Mutthi and Ngyiampaa people have been joint managers of the national park in partnership with the NSW government.

While Alice Kelly saw Mungo Lady and Mungo Man as a fundamental part of her own culture and identity, she also invited others to share in their story. 'Mungo,' she declared, 'is for all Australians, black and white, it can embrace us all in its spirituality and draw us closer to the land.'[83] Her words speak to the idea of Lake Mungo as a site of national reconciliation. While no landscape is inherently culturally or environmentally valuable, some places are made so through research, art, literature and legislation. After all, historian Simon Schama observes, national identity would lose much of its 'ferocious enchantment' without the mystique of a landscape tradition: 'its topography mapped, elaborated, and enriched as homeland'.[84] The role of the Willandra Lakes in the Australian imagination remains undefined, as does the deep history that has been preserved in its lakeshores. But in the years since Jim Bowler first rumbled across the lunettes on his flat-tyred motorbike, Lake Mungo has emerged as a national landscape, representing the ancient past of a young nation and the symbolic Eden of its Indigenous population.[85]

* * *

The man who made the discoveries at Lake Mungo has been haunted by the finds ever since. Although Jim Bowler did not meet any Aboriginal people until the 1970s, he grew up aware of the people who had lived in Leongatha before him. Two ground-edged axes, recovered from the onion patch, took pride of place on the mantelpiece in the family kitchen, and his father treasured a copy of anthropologist AP Elkin's 1938 tome, *The Australian Aborigines: How to Understand Them*. The later editions of that book included a final chapter titled 'The Aborigines on the March', documenting 'the slow building up and expression of Aboriginal opinion and the stirring of Aboriginal feelings'. In the 1974 edition, the year Mungo Man emerged, Elkin reflected on the dramatic cultural and political changes afoot in Indigenous affairs: 'They are still on the march, but now within the threshold ... They are now, as it were, advancing into and occupying the promised land of independent citizenship on an Australia-wide front, with their own leaders and spokesmen.'[86] Within his lifetime, Bowler has witnessed a dramatic social transformation, and through his work at Lake Mungo, he found himself at the centre of discussions about cultural identity. 'He was bound by his fate,' his daughter Jenny reflected. 'These discoveries of such cultural and international significance swept Jim Bowler into other-worldly realms.'[87]

Jim has been working on his magnum opus on Mungo for decades. The process of writing has always burdened him, but the struggle he faces with the Mungo book is twofold. He wants to write the scientific story of a fossil landscape that can be read like scripture to understand life in ancient Australia. But he is also driven by a more philosophical impulse. He sees Mungo, and the ritual burial of Mungo Man, as representing a bridge between cultures: 'Mungo Man crosses many boundaries, boundaries between science and traditional cultures, between past and present, between black and white, between life and death.'[88] Inspired by the work of theologian Teilhard de Chardin, he seeks to understand the human and spiritual significance of the discovery of Mungo Man.[89] He views the ritual anointing of Mungo Man's body with ochre as a powerful and universal expression of connection to country: something that all people once had, and that Aboriginal people have managed to retain. As he wrote in the *Guardian* in 2014,

In my pursuit of rational science, those lakeshore sands, originally solely of geological interest, have been transformed into sacred grounds. My eyes have been opened to glimpse and share in some small way that inner view long entrusted to Mungo Man's Aboriginal descendants, a deep connection to country, to their ancestral spirit-charged lands.[90]

The magnitude of this insight weighs him down as it lifts him up. Jim meditates on the significance of the 'people-land conjunction' as he labours on his Mungo book in his 'monastic retreat' in Foster, with its distant view of the Bassian Plain, and when he is out in the arid landscape he knows so well. Jenny has witnessed her father's struggle her whole life. She has 'come to terms with the painful realisation that his extraordinary spirit is not found in these moments [at home]. It's out there, exploring the rhythms of the land and listening to the echoes of an ancient culture.'[91]

✳ ✳ ✳

In November 2015 Mungo Man made his first steps back towards the desiccated shores whence he came. There was a great sense of occasion in the Great Hall at University House at the ANU, where scientists gathered with traditional owners who had travelled from Mildura and Swan Hill and surrounds to attend. Mary Pappin spoke about the learning and the heartache at Willandra over the past forty years, of the 'old women' led by Alice Kelly, who had fought for their cultural heritage:

They stood up, them girls, and said, 'What are you doing with our culture?' … They knew to make sure that our ancient people taken out of the ground there, and taken to the ANU, had a story to tell … They knew that Aboriginal Australians would come to their country to learn about the past … Our cultural heritage is all we have now, because our landscape, even our sky, is changed.[92]

Isabel McBryde, in her eighties, attended the meeting and was lauded for her role as a listener on the lunettes. Archaeologist Nicola Stern spoke of the new generation of research and the relationship of 'mutual trust and collaboration' that has formed over the past thirty years. Steve Webb outlined a vision for Willandra's future, including plans for the much-delayed Cultural Centre and Keeping Place. His advice was: 'Involve the world: the world is interested.' Finally, Jim Bowler gave an impassioned speech about the injustices of the past and the possibilities for understanding contained in Lake Mungo's epic story: 'We took away the kids, we took away the land, and gravest of all, we took away dignity. We need to give back. We hand back, in humility, the deep scientific story and how to communicate it.' He ended on a personal note, reflecting on 'forty-two years of living with Mungo Man', from the discovery 'in the cathedral of Lake Mungo's shores' through to the elevation of this ancient individual to the status of a national icon: 'I owe a great debt to Mungo Man. He has changed me, and he is capable of changing everyone else.'[93]

Eaglehawk and Crow, 1974

IN THE WAKE OF THE MUNGO DISCOVERIES, IN 1974, PRIME Minister Gough Whitlam celebrated Indigenous culture as 'one of the oldest and most remarkable in the world': 'It has been developed over 30,000 years; it is expressed in a wealth of art and song. I want the rest of the world to experience and understand it.'[1] He considered Aboriginal people to be 'our true link with our region' and connected Indigenous affairs with Australia's international responsibilities. 'Australia's treatment of Aboriginal people,' he announced in his policy speech on 13 November 1972, 'will be the thing upon which the rest of the world will judge Australia and Australians – not just now, but in the greater perspective of history.'[2] His government introduced a raft of policies to facilitate Aboriginal self-determination, including setting up the Aboriginal Land Rights Commission, creating the Department for Aboriginal Affairs and expanding the Aboriginal Study Grants Scheme. Whitlam also sought to enliven public appreciation of Indigenous culture by supporting the establishment of the Australia Council's Aboriginal Arts Board and dramatically increasing the funding for the Australian Institute of Aboriginal Studies. In his first year in office he tripled its annual grant, from $512,000 in 1972/73 to $1.5 million in 1973/74.[3]

The recently appointed principal of the AIAS, archaeologist Peter Ucko, harnessed the new funds to organise a major international conference on Aboriginal Australia. He invited scholars from across the world, such as Lewis Binford and François Bordes, to meet in Canberra for a seventeen-day conference on Indigenous art, prehistory, linguistics, anthropology, psychology and human biology. Echoing the ambition of the 1961 conference, the 1974 event lay at the heart of his push to change the culture of the institute. Although the institute had some Aboriginal council members, Ucko had been confronted, on appointment, by the 'untenable situation' whereby 'whites gave out money to whites, through white committees, to study the blacks'.[4] As principal, he sought to 'Aboriginalise' the institute and involve Aboriginal people in decision-making at every level.[5]

During Ucko's tenure, the Australian archaeological community began to depend less on the AIAS as an organising body and to develop their own institutional infrastructure. In August 1973, after an ANZAAS meeting in Perth, around a dozen people met in the back room of a pub to launch the Australian Archaeological Association (AAA). At that time, Ron Lampert reflected, archaeologists were still 'thin on the ground, a species of scientist largely unknown to administrators, developers and others with whom we interact today as a matter of routine; legislation to protect archaeological sites was still under formulation; the concept of "public archaeology" in Australia only just emerging.'[6] The AAA was established as an inclusive organisation, with membership open to all, regardless of qualification. (An organisation for 'professional' archaeologists was developed in 1979.[7]) The first issue of the AAA 'newsletter', *Australian Archaeology*, was published in 1974 and distributed to its seventy-four members. Lampert, the inaugural editor, hoped it would play a vital role in overcoming misunderstandings and establishing dialogue with Aboriginal people 'by publishing opinions and comments both from archaeologists and Aborigines'.[8] The new president of the AAA, Western Australian curator Ian Crawford, hoped the association would help educate the public about Aboriginal history and bring an end to remarks such as: 'I don't suppose there is any archaeology in Australia!'[9]

In the months before the much-awaited 1974 AIAS conference, a Sydney-based group called 'Eaglehawk and Crow' launched an attack on the academic study of Aboriginal society, and in particular on the AIAS. Their name echoed the title of anthropologist John Mathew's 1899 'study of the Australian aborigines', while acknowledging the forces of the ancestral beings *Bunjil* (Eaglehawk) and *Waa* (Crow).[10] Their open letter to the AIAS and its members questioned the purpose of the institute and accused it of ignoring the concerns of Aboriginal people in favour of 'doubtfully relevant studies' and an expensive international conference: 'Money and other resources are in short supply for Aboriginal control of their livelihood, but not, it seems, for discussing it.'[11]

Although Ucko was seeking to 'Aboriginalise' the institute, Jacquie Lambert notes in her history of the AIAS that his focus on 'traditional' culture reinforced the alienation felt by those who lived in cities and no longer spoke their own languages.[12] Of the six signatories of the Eaglehawk and Crow letter – Terry Widders, Gary Williams, Lyn Thompson, Bob Bellear, Len Watson and Peter Thompson – only the latter was non-Indigenous. They urged the institute to take a public stand on issues that were important to the Aboriginal community, such as land rights.

The letter dominated the 1974 conference, and shocked many Australian archaeologists into action. They had long campaigned for heritage legislation to protect Aboriginal sites and to promote understanding of Indigenous history and culture within settler communities; now, it seemed, they had to communicate the nature and value of archaeology to the Indigenous public as well. The public role of the Australian Archaeological Association seemed clear. 'We are now at a

most crucial stage in archaeological development in Australia,' curator David R Moore declared, 'which might well be characterised as the
"Publicize or Pack Up" interstadial.'[13]

In January 1975 John Mulvaney and Isabel McBryde invited a number of Aboriginal critics, including Charles Perkins, to discuss the nature
of archaeological research in Canberra. It was, in Mulvaney's words, 'the
first major dialogue between prehistorians and the people whose past
they studied'.[14] Jack Golson spoke of the value of archaeological research
for both Aboriginal Australians and settler Australians: 'Co-citizens as
they are, it can help to foster a joint pride in the unique past of the
particular part of the world where both now live.'[15] Ray Kelly, the first
Aboriginal person employed by the NSW National Parks and Wildlife
Service, agreed: 'I feel we need to get all our people to become knowl-
edgeable about Aboriginal history and culture – things that only a few
of us seem to be interested in at present.'[16] But the symposium made it
clear that further research into the Aboriginal past hinged on dialogue
and respect. As Sandra Onus, a Gunditjmara woman and land rights
campaigner, wrote in *Australian Archaeology*:

> It has been and still is the feeling amongst my people that archaeol-
> ogists are a bloody nuisance only good for sticking their noses and
> tools where they are not wanted 'just like most white men' ... I am
> just as interested in knowing about the age and past habits of my peo-
> ple, but not to the point where it interferes with our tribal laws and
> customs that were laid down by my ancestors thousands of years ago.[17]

The 'Eaglehawk and Crow' letter served to accelerate Ucko's agenda
for change at the AIAS. In the years that followed, he oversaw the establishment of an Aboriginal Advisory Committee in 1975; the institute
created grants for Aboriginal people to receive training and conduct
research, as well as funds for Aboriginal-requested research; and, in a
reversal of its previous position, the AIAS council threw its support

behind the repatriation of Truganini's remains.[18] Many more Indigenous people were also employed as staff and cultural practitioners. One of Wiradjuri journalist Stan Grant's first jobs was to deliver the internal mail at the AIAS in Canberra in the 1970s. In his 2016 memoir, *Talking to My Country*, Grant reflected on the opportunities afforded by the re-energised organisation:

> At the Institute I reconnected with the kinship I had lost when we moved to the city. There was a subterranean black community lurking below this bland bush city ... At the Institute there were people like me – Aboriginal people – studying, writing and wrestling with new ideas. These people worked as film and sound archivists and anthropologists and historians. Black people did this? I could barely believe it. [19]

In between his mail rounds, Grant searched through the archives, learning more about his family history: 'It was a magical place where I could touch my past.'[20] It was in the AIAS corridors that he met Marcia Langton, a bibliographer in the institute library and already a strong intellectual presence in Aboriginal affairs, who encouraged him to enter journalism. Langton, too, recognised the value of the institute as a place of learning and understanding. 'There cannot be any doubt that teaching and research about Aboriginal society adds dignity to humankind as a whole,' she wrote in 1996. 'It is an essential means of leading other Australians to greater tolerance and understanding.'[21]

With the decline of the biennial AIAS meetings in the late 1970s, the Australian Archaeological Association took over as the central organ of the discipline, with its own conferences, a research-oriented academic journal and a growing membership. Peter Ucko, meanwhile, resigned his position at the AIAS in 1981 and made way for its first Aboriginal principal, Eric Willmot. The institute, now known as the Australian Institute of Aboriginal and Torres Strait Islander Studies (AIATSIS), became the first Indigenous-controlled national research centre in Australia.

SIX

LANDSCAPES OF THE MIND

Carmel Schrire and Betty Meehan
in Arnhem Land

Arnhem Land lies at the tip of the Top End, jutting out between the Timor Sea and the Gulf of Carpentaria.[1] It is a land of contrasts. The stony, faulted plateau – home to some of the oldest surface rocks on earth – is also one of the world's most flammable landscapes, yet in the cool depths of chasms and gorges, remnants of rainforest survive, protected from fire for millennia. The great cliffs of the escarpment divide the rugged plateau from the sweeping plains below. In the wet, the plains shimmer with fresh water and birdlife, fed by rivers flowing from the stone massif above. In the early dry, small leads of smoke streak the lowland plains, as the country is worked and cleaned by Aboriginal burning. This dramatic landscape is where many archaeologists came to 'discover' Aboriginal Australia, for the first time working alongside and observing individuals who had been born into a foraging way of life. To archaeologists, Arnhem Land is 'one of the world's most important storehouses of information about prehistory and the art of hunting and gathering man'.[2] To the first Australians, it is an inscribed landscape, shaped by the movements of totemic beings and pulsing with the life force of the Dreaming.

Despite many attempts, Australia's northern coast was never conquered, nor systematically settled, by white colonists. As late as 1933 journalist Ernestine Hill described Arnhem Land as being 'the only corner of Australia that has persistently baffled, and even frightened, the white pioneer ... For 100 years Arnhem Land, by the sheer ferocity of its natives, has defied colonisation'.[3] Rhys Jones and Betty Meehan believe the key to the resilience of the people of Arnhem Land is their long history of contact with other cultures.[4] For centuries, Macassan voyagers in search of trepang (also known as sea cucumber) visited the shores of Arnhem Land, growing rice and building stone hearths along the coastline, trading with local communities and even taking Aboriginal people with them back to foreign ports. John Mulvaney surveyed a series of Macassan sites in 1965 to draw attention to what he described as a largely ignored theme of Australian history, and his PhD student Campbell Macknight followed up with the first major research on the Macassan voyages.[5] Macknight argued that trade began sometime between AD 1650 and 1750, and acknowledged oral traditions of visitors known as the Baijini, who came before the Macassan traders.[6] Later scholars such as Darrell Lewis and Anne Clarke suggested that the Macassans started visiting much earlier, around 1000 years ago, and that their influence on Aboriginal culture can be read in changes in archaeology and rock art.[7] The traders introduced new technologies, such as the dug-out canoe, and inspired a shift in diet, from a terrestrial to a more marine economy. Macassan words entered the local languages – and still remain. In the wet season of 1907, the coastal clans of Arnhem Land prepared for the annual trading season as usual, but no Macassan praus arrived.[8] The long history of trade and communication had been formally prohibited by legislation in line with the White Australia Policy.

When the first Europeans voyaged to Australia, long after the Macassan trade had begun, they brought with them a new way of seeing the landscape. Art historian Bernard Smith has explored how the newcomers perceived the unfamiliar terrain through the lens of the familiar. The landscape was prized for its potential: what it could become, what

it could be shaped into.[9] The European colonisation of the Northern
Territory, writes Howard Morphy, 'was a movement inspired by myth
and fantasy, by images of inland lakes, mountains of gold and rich pas-
tures for cattle, all of which were to prove illusory'.[10] The settlement at
Port Essington on the Cobourg Peninsula was one of the many short-
lived, 'forsaken settlements' constructed on the northern coastal rim.
Built in 1838 to foster the long trade relationship with Asia, and to guard
Australia's north coast from invasion, it suffered from limited resources
and a failure to understand the environment. By 1849 this small cluster of houses had been abandoned. The ruins, studied by Jim Allen in
the 1960s, became the subject of Australia's first major excavation in
historical archaeology.[11]

Ironically, it was environmental ignorance and developmental
hubris that ultimately allowed vast areas of northern Australia to remain
relatively unmodified.[12] The spectacular failures of early agricultural and
forestry ventures, which had been devised on an ambitious scale with
limited knowledge, were what enabled Aboriginal people to continue
to live a traditional life on their land well into the twentieth century.
It was perceived to be so marginally productive that only grand visions
and intensive modification of the environment could yield profit. This
view remains popular, as arguments about a 'northern food bowl' attest,
but it clashes with an Aboriginal understanding of country. As Rhys
Jones reminds us, reflecting on the moment of invasion,

> The newcomers struggling through the surf were met on the beaches
> by other men looking at them from the edge of the trees. Thus the
> same landscape perceived by the newcomers as alien, hostile, or hav-
> ing no coherent form, was to the indigenous people their home, a
> familiar place, the inspiration of dreams.[13]

In Arnhem Land, perhaps more than anywhere else, Australian archaeologists began to accommodate this other, more familiar view of country.

Striving to see the landscape through Aboriginal eyes enabled them to understand the ways in which the environment has been modified and used over generations, and how this is reflected in archaeological remains. The first Australians cultivated the land through fire and developed a complex and intimate relationship with the environment that relied upon detailed knowledge of plants, animals and the seasons. The walls of the Arnhem Land escarpment, decorated in reds, yellows, whites and blacks, vividly illustrate this deep cultural knowledge, while the dusty floors at their base preserve an archive of ancient human occupation: the oldest chapter in the history of the first Australians.

'Ever so gradually,' Prime Minister Paul Keating reflected in his iconic 1992 Redfern speech,

> we are learning how to see Australia through Aboriginal eyes, beginning to recognise the wisdom contained in their epic story ... We cannot imagine that the descendants of people whose genius and resilience maintained a culture here through 50,000 years or more, through cataclysmic changes to the climate and environment, and who then survived two centuries of dispossession and abuse, will be denied their place in the modern Australian nation. We cannot imagine that.'[14]

This chapter explores this intellectual transformation against the background of archaeological field research in Arnhem Land. It tells the story of two early scholars, Carmel Schrire and Betty Meehan, who strove to 'see Australia through Aboriginal eyes', and it sets the scene for the archaeological work that delivered the date of '50,000 years or more'.

* * *

When South African–born archaeologist Carmel Schrire (then White) first came to Arnhem Land in 1964, within a few months of arriving in Australia, the Northern Territory seemed like an 'endless outback': 'I was twenty-three years old. I could barely drive, had never run a field trip in my life, and knew almost nothing about Australian archaeology, let alone Arnhem Land.'[15] She drove up from Port Augusta with her supervisor, Jack Golson, and a field supervisor, Ron Lampert, stopping in farms, missions and small towns along the 'tarred ribbon' of the Stuart Highway, where talk in the pubs was mostly 'about women, gins, lubras, bitches, and worse'. Although segregation was not as explicit as it was in apartheid South Africa – there were no signs proclaiming 'Whites Only' – Schrire could not help but notice a customary divide within these remote towns. Her South African accent was greeted with 'conspiratorial nods and nudges'. Whites drank inside while Aboriginal people squatted in the dust outside, 'shooting longing glances towards the hot, beery interiors'.[16] The power to grant entry to Aboriginal reserves rested in the hands of the government, not elders, and required an elaborate formal application, including a chest scan to stop the spread of tuberculosis.

Schrire arrived in the Northern Territory the year Indigenous people graduated from being wards of the state – someone who is unable to act in their own interest – to citizens. They could vote and make decisions about life on their land, even though they were not counted in the census. A year earlier, in 1963, the Yolngu people of north-east Arnhem Land had opposed the federal government's leasing of their land at Yirrkala on the Gove Peninsula and demanded recognition of their rights to country. Their protests saw land rights (as opposed to civil rights) emerge as a national issue.[17] Over the following decade the Northern Territory became a hot spot for Aboriginal activism. In 1966 the Gurindji walked off Wave Hill Station (Jinparak), 600 kilometres south of Darwin, beginning a decade-long campaign for rights to their land.[18] The resounding 90 per cent 'Yes' vote at the 1967 referendum brought Aboriginal people into the census, into civil law and into the commonwealth. Previously, Indigenous affairs had been managed by the states, often through departments that also handled flora, fauna and wildlife.[19]

While the referendum signalled the shifting mood in Australian society, the rejection of the Yolngu's case for land title in April 1971 made it clear that change would have to come from the government rather than the courts. In December 1972 Gough Whitlam was elected prime minister with a land rights platform and in 1976, under Malcolm Fraser's *Aboriginal Land Rights (Northern Territory) Act*, Aboriginal people were able to gain legal title to their country. The scale of this dramatic social, cultural and political transformation was hard to imagine when Schrire first entered the Arnhem Land Reserve.

The choice of Arnhem Land was, for Schrire, a direct outcome of the state of Australian archaeology in 1964.[20] A year earlier, in August 1963, Golson had excavated sites at Sleisbeck and Katherine, 300 kilometres south of Darwin, while John Mulvaney led excavations at the nearby Ingaladdi and Kintore Cave. Schrire was now accompanying Golson on his return trip north to find a region to study for her PhD. Although work had been done in Arnhem Land, the previous excavations were far from systematic and the findings had received little analysis. Anthropologist Donald Thomson had conducted some minor excavations in 1935 and 1937; Neil 'Black Mac' Macintosh had excavated a five-metre trench through Tandandjal cave in 1949; and WEH Stanner had dug a small pit in Yarar shelter in 1958–1959. But the only major excavations in Arnhem Land had been conducted through the 1948 American-Australian Scientific Expedition to Arnhem Land, an extravagant exercise in cultural diplomacy sponsored by a range of governmental agencies and organisations, including the National Geographic Society and the Smithsonian Institution. The nine-month research expedition produced tens of thousands of scientific specimens, hundreds of thousands of words and kilometres of film.[21]

The two archaeologists on that expedition, Frederick McCarthy and Frank M Setzler, excavated Macassan sites on Groote Eylandt and Port Bradshaw, examined middens along the eastern shore of

Melville Bay, found stone points at Yirrkala and recorded art sites on Chasm Island. Their major excavations were at Oenpelli (Gunbalanya), where they worked on two hills flanking the mission, wearing gas masks to cope with the plumes of dust from their sieves. 'The temperature among the rocks was high,' wrote expedition leader Charles Mountford, 'the humidity oppressive and the dust from the sieves so dense that it was sometimes difficult to see the archaeologists.'[22] In their rush 'to determine the origin, or at least the prehistory, of the Australian Aborigines in Arnhem Land', McCarthy and Setzler decided to focus only on large 'finished' stone tools, ignoring food debris, shells and 'waste flakes'.[23] Their method of excavation, Sally K May writes, 'consisted of shoveling all the deposit into sieves and bagging any stone, wood, or shell that remained. Little attention was paid to stratigraphic layering or standard archaeological excavation procedures.'[24] From this selective archive, they recognised five different tool types, which they interpreted as reflecting successive waves of migration into Australia. 'Thus Oenpelli became the Les Eyzies of the Antipodes,' wrote Schrire, 'a cultural meeting place from which colonists spread forth.'[25]

McCarthy and Setzler's report was published twelve years after the expedition, in 1960. Schrire locates it 'at the very roots of modern Australian archaeological theory and practice'.[26] But although the expedition was pioneering in the sense that archaeology was treated as a distinct component of a wider scientific project, I am more inclined to agree with Anne Clarke and Ursula Frederick that it should be seen as 'a relic of an earlier era of research'.[27] In 1964 Jack Golson reviewed the stone tool evidence from the Oenpelli excavations and was shocked by the muddled analysis: 'Two distinct entities', he exclaimed, 'are presented as a single "culture".'[28] In her thesis, Schrire lashed their decision to discard 'waste flakes' and ignore food debris.[29] But what most demarcates their research from the modern era was their role in actively scavenging more than 241 human remains, some quite recent, without the permission and often deliberately behind the backs of their Aboriginal guides. These were then shipped to the Smithsonian Institution in Washington. 'That Aboriginal human remains were fetishised and collected in the name of science, and often taken to institutions in distant lands, is hardly breaking news,' writes historian Martin Thomas. 'But the idea of bone-taking being captured in a National Geographic film production – in colour no less – shocks me even now.'[30] Over the past two decades many of these remains have made the long journey home.

Schrire arrived in Arnhem Land with a different gaze and with a view to working with Aboriginal people as participants, not objects of study. When her party crossed into the reserve, they misjudged the tidal bore of the East Alligator River and drowned their truck at Cahills Crossing. The superintendent of the Church Mission Society settlement at Oenpelli, Alf Wilson, greeted them stonily that evening. As Schrire later wrote, he had 'no interest whatsoever in research, and he felt deeply opposed to having a young white woman, wandering around on her own'.[31] They camped that night on a stony pan beyond the mission under trees laden with raucous cockatoos. They were dirty, tired and covered in insect bites.

In her 1995 book, *Digging Through Darkness*, Schrire imagines what her arrival in the region might have meant to the Aboriginal people with whom she worked. She considers her expedition in the mid-1960s as an extension of the colonial experience, and reflects on its cross-cultural dimensions: 'I have tried to show both sides, invader and native, to let each explain what they were after, as well as letting each reveal the world they thought they knew.'[32] Drawing inspiration from novelist JM Coetzee and historian Greg Dening, she wove fiction with archival sources to reveal 'how fine is the line that separates assumed reality from imagination'.[33] She hoped that her fictional passages would allow her to convey the temper and physicality of her experience in Arnhem

Land, and enable her to make the imaginative leap to the other side of the frontier. 'Possessing the other,' Schrire quotes Dening as saying, 'like possessing the past, is always full of delusions.'[34]

In her chapter on Arnhem Land – if we assume her account hews closer to reality than fiction – her friend, guide and interpreter Frank Gananggu becomes 'Gurrawoy', also known as Fred. Gananggu, like his fictional counterpart, suffered from leprosy and spent many years in the East Arm Leprosarium in Darwin. He grew up in and around Oenpelli and spoke Erre, Gaagudju and, through his time in Darwin, English.[35] Gananggu also knew about archaeology. He had worked on the 1948 expedition through Arnhem Land and one of his first questions to Schrire in 1964 was, 'You with the McCarthy-Mountford mob?'[36]

In her portrait of Gurrawoy, Schrire brings to life the warmth and humour of Gananggu, his struggles with leprosy, the relentless incursion of the white world and his impressions of her 1964–1965 field season in Arnhem Land. She wonders about the cultural implications of having a woman as a boss. What did he make of this 'young, intense' woman 'with a loud voice', who wanted to rummage around old camps on his country?

> The archaeologist habitually wore men's clothes ... Despite her incorporation in their kinship system as Gurrawoy's sister, her gender was indeterminate ... To men whose childhood had been spent hunting possums and spearing fish, she seemed utterly ignorant. Yet you had to hand it to her for sheer persistence, digging away, sunrise to sunset, week after week, with little change to show for it all. A mad person, no doubt, whatever else she might be.[37]

For most of this first season Schrire worked alone with Gananggu and his cousins, whom she paid with cigarettes, food and camp supplies. Golson soon returned to his duties at the ANU, while Lampert departed early after his mandatory TB test delivered him a fatal (though false) prognosis. Schrire's persistence in the field earned her the distinction of being, in Mulvaney's words, Australia's first 'cowgirl' archaeologist – a moniker she quite enjoyed.[38]

Schrire relied heavily on Aboriginal guides and assistants such as Frank Gananggu to lead her to 'old living places'. They were mainly men of more than forty or fifty years old who had lived as hunter-gatherers when they were young. As they walked through the landscape they would tell her of its main features and share some of their immense ecological knowledge.[39] She also worked with women, such as Magdalene, an Edey elder, who was especially forthcoming about the names of shellfish, water plants and animals that were collected for food on the plains. Gananggu constantly advised Schrire to check his information with her: 'My old lady knows.'[40] In the pit, Schrire excavated alone, singing to herself, while the Aboriginal men sieved, sorted and bagged the finds nearby, dividing axes from hammerstones, silcrete from quartz. Their assistance allowed the identification of objects such as the remains of the edible lotus lily, which might otherwise have been discarded. Although Schrire remained sceptical about some of the information she was given – one man attributed the presence of shells in an inland shelter to Noah's Flood – she also acknowledged the influence of indigenous knowledge on her research. Her thesis is dedicated 'to Frank Gananggu of Oenpelli, who told me this story in the first place'.[41]

The first site Schrire excavated was at Malakunanja I – 'a small recess at the base of the escarpment where the cliff met the talus slope'.[42] She excavated in grids using trowels, brushes, paint scrapers, ash pans and circular plastic sieves. After twelve days at this 'hot and uncomfortable site', she abandoned it due to the presence of human remains, some obviously recent. In *Digging Through Darkness* she reflects on this scene: the men standing above the pit while she crouched over the bones, patently human, wrapping them in tissue and foil, packing them into carefully labelled bags.

This was no one they knew; nevertheless, their discomfort grew as they watched her disturb the sacred things ... Gurrawoy stood in silence, his swollen face impassive and shut. Suddenly he wished he had never seen her, the truck, the tins of food, the batteries, even the tape recorder. A wave of shame and hate boiled up at her and her kind.[43]

In this passage, Schrire returns to the theme of her book: 'Colonialism,' she writes, 'is a chronicle of betrayals.'[44] Her intrusion into Gurrawoy's world was simply the latest chapter. She left Malakunanja I behind and moved onto other sites across the plateau and the plains.

* * *

Schrire's views of colonialism and racism drew directly from her experiences growing up in Cape Town during apartheid. As a white, Jewish woman she had a privileged existence in segregated South Africa. She was born in 1941 and lived with her parents and three sisters in a house that clung to the slopes of Table Mountain. She remembers how the atrocities of the Holocaust hung heavily on the shoulders of her father, and the gradual process by which she became aware of a different kind of racial discrimination at home. Her interactions with the family's domestic servants were a daily reminder of state segregation.[45]

Her interest in archaeology stemmed from her parents' membership to the South African Archaeological Society, which held monthly meetings on all things archaeological: from Greek statues and Japanese martial weaponry to early hominids of the Transvaal and the art of the Khoisan people. The meetings were characterised by 'polite applause and desultory questions', followed by tea, hard biscuits 'and subdued good nights'. It was their field trips that drew Schrire into the mysteries and excitement of the ancient world: 'They led us into dank caves and up steep, coastal middens, where millions of shells attested to former meals. I crouched in the dusty holes, wondering how many other children had shivered in the winter rains, thousands of years before.'[46]

She enrolled in African studies at the University of Cape Town in 1958, studying African government and law, Bantu languages, social anthropology, ethnology and archaeology. Archaeology in South Africa, as in Australia, was profoundly influenced by Cambridge University, and Schrire quickly realised that she had unwittingly become an apprentice of the Cambridge archaeological empire. With teachers such as Monica Wilson, John Hilary Goodwin and Glynn Isaac, it was a natural decision for Schrire to follow in their footsteps and pursue archaeology at Cambridge.[47] A private review of her studies, written by Brian Fagan to Ray Inskeep, speaks volumes for the academic culture of her university years: 'Schrire (Carmel, Miss, c.18). A Jewess, and a curvaceous one ... Her interest in archaeology is somewhat superficial – she is at heart a Social Anthropologist. Not interested in the practical side, except perhaps paintings. Works hard. Boy friend (steady) in Jo'burg. Ardent liberal.'[48]

When Schrire arrived in Cambridge in 1960, men outnumbered women ten to one. And while her male peers were afforded special treatment in their colleges, 'women were relegated a subtly lesser role, as helpmeets, rather than protagonists'. Schrire had limited access to tutors and advisors in archaeology and remembers the celebrated archaeologist Eric Higgs refusing to take women into the field 'because they caused nothing but trouble'. Despite these challenges, Schrire thrived in the exciting intellectual environment and formed close connections within her cohort, which included Rhys Jones, Barry Cunliffe, Colin Renfrew and Peter White. During her studies she became engaged to White, who had studied Pacific prehistory under Mulvaney at the University of Melbourne (and who was present when Gordon Childe lectured the class in 1957). Together, at Cambridge, they planned their future careers. In 1963 White was offered a job as an archaeologist in

Peshawar. Schrire, his potential employers suggested, could accompany him and 'teach needlework to the girls'. They resolved to instead 'try our luck in the Antipodes', where Jack Golson was advertising PhD opportunities at the ANU.[49]

It is worth dwelling upon the many obstacles that Schrire faced because of her gender, for they are representative of the experiences of other female scholars at the time.[50] Even so, Isabel McBryde reflects, the field of Australian archaeology has been fundamentally shaped by 'that intrepid yet often shadowy, even invisible, band of women archaeologists'.[51] And since the 1980s, under the leadership of Sandra Bowdler, feminist scholarship and gender archaeology have become dynamic streams in the discipline, culminating in the series of Women in Archaeology conferences that continue today.[52] In 1991, the editors of *Australian Archaeology* drew the attention of their readers 'to the fact that most of the material included in this issue of AA is either written by a woman alone or as a joint author. We did not organise this, it just happened that way!'[53]

* * *

Schrire returned to Arnhem Land for a second season in 1965 with her husband, Peter White, and Edgar Waters, to continue her work with Frank Gananggu's team. While they were in the field, she received the radiocarbon dates from the previous year's excavations. The dates defied belief. Charcoal samples from the lower sands at Malangangerr – a shelter with deep shade near the East Alligator River – came in at over 22,000 years old – then the oldest dates for human occupation in Australia. What was even more baffling was that these dates were associated with ground-edge axes, which she had found in all shapes and sizes – and at considerable depth – at Malangangerr during her first season. For so long, axes had been regarded as a relatively recent invention – a symbol of technological progress and sophistication.

Ground-edge axes were to the 'neolithic' (the era of agriculture) as iron was to the Iron Age. The axes Schrire uncovered undermined this conventional wisdom and revealed the complexity of Aboriginal life during the Pleistocene. At over 20,000 years old, they 'thus appeared to be the oldest in the world'.[54] And by a significant margin: axes in Europe dated to around 8000 years ago.

Schrire returned to Malangangerr to carry out further excavation while a team of geomorphologists visited and checked her stratigraphic interpretations. Their soil samples confirmed the dates, but when she published the find in *Antiquity* in 1967, it was greeted with profound scepticism. Very few archaeologists accepted the dates: you couldn't have the neolithic so early! It put the first Australians at the cutting edge of Pleistocene technology and challenged the widespread assumption that Australia was the last continent to be settled by modern humans.[55] It would take the Mungo discoveries two years later to shake this narrative from its rigid foundations. Australian archaeology continues to deliver surprising and challenging technological evidence. In 2016 a team of archaeologists published the discovery of the world's oldest ground-edge axe: a 44,000–49,000-year-old fragment found in Carpenters Gap in the Kimberley region of northern Australia. In 2017, another team pushed the date back further again, publishing the discovery of ground-edge axes in the lowest levels of a 65,000-year-old site at Madjedbebe, not far from where Schrire worked. A tool that was once linked to the origins of agriculture may have been part of the colonising baggage of the first Australians.[56]

The arrival of the radiocarbon dates at Oenpelli Mission also allowed Schrire to give a timescale to the story she had been reading into the archaeology. Drawing on Gananggu's information and historical sources, she interpreted a distinct cultural divide between the archaeology of the coastal plain and that of the escarpment country. From 20,000 years ago through to 6000–7000 years ago, she argued, one people – 'the old-timers' – roamed across western Arnhem Land with their ground-edge axes. Then around 7000 years ago (after the sea levels had risen dramatically) something changed. The coastal plains became the domain of the 'woodworkers who seldom made or used stone tools', while 'away in the hills lived the stone workers ... with whom the plainsmen traded'.[57] She presented these distinct cultural histories in her 1967 thesis, 'Plateau and Plain'.

Within two years, Schrire had revisited her conclusions and critiqued her own work. With anthropologist Nicolas Peterson, she suggested that instead of two defined groups of people – the wood workers and stone workers – the difference in archaeology could be understood through the seasonal movements of one people between high and low country.[58] But this neat interpretation did not last long either.[59] Ultimately, Schrire settled on a 'less environmentally determined' and more complex story. The differences between the archaeology of the plateau and the plain could not be wholly explained by the changing climate or the seasonal movements of individual groups; they had more to do with 'human decision-making and self-perception as elements operating within the ecosystem'.[60]

This rapid succession of hypotheses is an ongoing part of Schrire's practice; she continues to scrutinise her own work with the same critical eye through which she views others.[61] It also reflects the changing theoretical grounding of the 1970s and '80s and the challenges of combining archaeology and ethnography. Although many of her interpretations would not have been possible without local indigenous knowledge – trying to see the landscape through their eyes – there were limits to how far this cultural information could go. The 'man–land interactions observed at first contact with Europeans', she concluded in 1984, 'could not have existed here for more than the past 1000 years.'[62]

Schrire returned to Arnhem Land in 1968 and 1969 to study diets at Caledon Bay, cultural contact with the Macassans and the different roles of 'Man the Hunter and Woman the Gatherer'.[63] In 1970 she left Australia for North America, where she devoted a decade to teaching and raising children. By the time she returned in 1980, the political landscape in Arnhem Land had changed.

* * *

Another archaeologist, Betty Meehan, gives us a unique view of the transformations in Arnhem Land in the early 1970s. She first worked there as a schoolteacher in 1958 when she accompanied her then husband, anthropologist Les Hiatt, to the small trading post of Maningrida. While Hiatt studied kinship networks, Meehan set up the community's first school, made from corrugated iron and chicken wire. They had met in Bourke, Meehan's hometown, in 1955 and moved to Sydney a few months later as newlyweds. It was a period of 'amazing change' for Meehan, a country girl from a working-class family with Irish and Welsh connections, who had not travelled much further than Bathurst before. She had taught in a primary school in the Sydney suburb of Petersham while Hiatt studied anthropology and worked as a dentist on the side. After he graduated, they made preparations for an extended period of fieldwork in central Arnhem Land, which would form the basis of Hiatt's doctoral research.

Meehan entered Arnhem Land with a very different set of experiences to Schrire: while Schrire grew up with servants in South Africa, Meehan had Aboriginal schoolmates. She and Hiatt also had some linguistic ability thanks to a crash course in Canberra, where she recalls 'struggling with the *ng* sound at the beginning of Aboriginal words and of the soreness this caused to our throats'.[64]

Maningrida had existed for less than a year when they arrived in 1958.[65] It had been set up as a commercial centre in the heart of Arnhem Land, where Aboriginal people could get access to European items such as blankets, tomahawks, sugar, tea and tobacco in exchange for crocodile skins, dingo scalps, pandanus dilly bags, dried trepang and pearls. It was designed to 'stop the drift' of Aboriginal people into Darwin, and it quickly drew people in from the surrounding country. Within a decade it was the fifth-largest town in the Northern Territory. 'Anyone visiting Maningrida at the end of the 1960s would have been overwhelmed by the feeling that all the Aborigines were there to stay,' Meehan later wrote.[66] Ingrid Drysdale, the wife of the first manager and first white woman to live at Maningrida, lamented that the traditional owners were 'at the end of their "dreaming" and at the beginning of a new road unmarked by the spirit ancestors who guided their every step in days gone by'.[67] The Anbarra people, with whom Hiatt worked, lived in public housing in the township; their homelands around the Blyth River region were 'almost deserted'.[68]

But when Meehan returned a decade later as an archaeologist and anthropologist in her own right, she encountered an unexpected phenomenon. In an explicit rejection of attempts at assimilation, Aboriginal people had left the cramped housing in Maningrida and begun moving back onto country. Meehan was shocked by the rapid development of what became known as the outstation movement. Many of the people she had worked with in the town had returned to their homelands. They were hunting and foraging across the rich coastal country surrounding the Blyth River, moving camps according to the seasons and religious needs, and supplementing their diet with food bought from the Maningrida store with money from art sales and pensions. 'Perhaps 20 years of living in a white-dominated European type town was long enough for the Maningrida people,' Meehan and Rhys Jones mused,

> perhaps the glitter of the Balanda [whitefella] culture and its material objects had dulled sufficiently during that time ... There can be no doubt that they desired to avoid the unpleasant by-products of Maningrida culture – alcoholism and associated petrol sniffing,

violence and delinquency – that these were burdens that they no longer wished to bear.[69]

In the early years at Maningrida Aboriginal people had experienced a sedentary lifestyle for the first time – and they had rejected it. They were driven by a responsibility to return to country, tend to sacred sites, and work the land through fire, ceremony, hunting and gathering. Their actions were spurred on by the election of the Labor government in 1972 and the establishment of the Woodward Land Rights Commission. 'Even if the Commission was not a prime cause,' Meehan reflected, 'its existence added grit to the determination of the people who had already taken the plunge.'[70]

Meehan was greeted with smiles and warmth on a reconnaissance trip in August–September 1970, even gathering shellfish with former student Jeannie Maraginyaginya.[71] But as Richard Gould had experienced in the Western Desert, she noticed many cultural changes: 'The Aborigines appear to be much more sensitive about Europeans observing and photographing their ceremonies than they were in 1958 and 1960.' Fortunately, Meehan reflected, 'I am not academically interested in that aspect of the culture.' She and her new partner Rhys Jones hoped to explore 'the relationship between a living culture and the archaeological record'.[72] They were intent on studying the economic practices of the Anbarra people – what foods they collected, what archaeological traces they might leave behind, and how far these cultural practices went back in time. There was a precedent for this kind of study in Arnhem Land. Perhaps the most innovative element of the 1948 American-Australian Scientific Expedition to Arnhem Land was Frederick McCarthy's work with nutritionist Margaret McArthur on subsistence practices at Fish Creek.[73] And as the Anbarra came to appreciate the purpose of Meehan and Jones' presence in the community, they did whatever they could to assist. 'Often we arrived at a hearth to find that the food had been laid out in species ready to be counted, weighed and measured.'[74]

Meehan focused on the role of Aboriginal women as food gatherers, and particularly shellfish collection. For most anthropologists in the past, she observed, 'the collection of molluscs by women would have been an insignificant event compared with the exploits of the active male hunters of the same society'.[75] Although it may seem 'an unspectacular, unobtrusive and humdrum activity', Meehan found that shellfish played a subtle but crucial role in the Anbarra diet. Her focus on middens in particular allowed her to see, and separate, women in the archaeological record.[76] Shellfish contributed no more than one-tenth of their diet, but it was one of the few reliable food sources that could, if necessary, be collected every day of the year. And they perform other social roles. Some shell middens are said to have been made by ancestral beings in the Dreaming, such as the Kula Kula or 'Dog Mounds', which were piled up by the first dog in the country while digging a hole.[77] Far from rubbish heaps, these middens are regarded as sacred monuments. Meehan studied how shellfish were collected for utilitarian, religious and recreational reasons, and wrote of the social history they represent. In her landmark 1982 book, *Shell Bed to Shell Midden*, she argues, 'The ubiquity of shell middens around the coasts of the world may indeed be testimony to the special supportive role of shellfish in coastal economies and be recognised as fitting monuments to yet another unappreciated contribution made by women to the maintenance of human society.'[78]

Although their interests were primarily archaeological, Meehan and Jones revised their research agenda in July 1972 in light of the immense changes accompanying the outstation movement. They extended their stay for a full year and decided to focus on documenting the 'ethnographic situation'. 'I felt that an opportunity to observe people in their own country throughout a yearly cycle should not be missed,' Meehan wrote in her interim report to the AIAS.[79] They hoped their observations over the year would offer 'a vignette in the history of a community' and a portrait 'of an Australian economic tradition that extends back for at least 35,000 years'. The Anbarra welcomed the extension of their stay and 'wished to have their knowledge written down on *djurra* (paper) for some future time when their descendants would all be able to read. They were also keen that *balanda* in "Canberra" should be aware of the subtleties of their ecological knowledge.'[80] Frank Gurrmanana, in whose extended hearth they lived, 'chastised us sometimes for not documenting fully his accounts of the past – "More better you book 'im down straight."'[81]

Meehan and Jones were allowed to camp on the edge of the various settlements, but were left to procure their own food, wood and water. They joined foraging parties during the day, regularly walking 20 kilometres or more and returning exhausted to write notes in their tent. 'I still have vivid and somewhat comical memories of various expeditions,' Meehan later wrote,

> especially those into the jungle areas to get yams, where I, bedecked with cameras, lightmetre, tape, spring balance, notebook and ballpoint pen (not to mention a small haversack containing sunburn cream, mosquito repellent, water and a tin of baked beans), strove to keep up with a group of women on the scent of yams.[82]

Meehan spent most of her time with the women, while Jones roamed the countryside with the men, working closely at times with Les Hiatt. 'Much to my amusement (and a little to my chagrin),' Meehan wrote, 'Gurrmanamana announced to the community that my first husband had given me to his "younger brother", my second husband, and that he himself had acquired a younger wife.'[83] Jones was quickly absorbed into the community and earned the moniker 'wombat' – because he was short, stout and liked to dig.

During the year between July 1972 and July 1973, Meehan and Jones counted thirty species and over 7000 kilograms of shellfish collected by the Anbarra people. In *Shell Bed to Shell Midden*, Meehan identified two kinds of shell middens: the 'base camp', the main area where the community stayed and slept, and the 'dinnertime camp', an ephemeral site where a party of foragers, often women on their own, paused during the day to cook and eat some of the food gathered and hunted. The idea of a dinnertime camp as a symbol of the economic autonomy of women immediately caught on and was used to interpret archaeological sites from Tasmania to the lower Darling, South Australia to the Australian Alps.[84]

Meanwhile, Jones became interested in the religious life of the Anbarra and the 'economic consequences' of the great ceremonies. A restricted men's ceremony, such as *Kunapipi*, brought together around 300 people and required an 'investment of some 400 man weeks': 'This much labour,' Jones reflected, 'might have erected a small hill fort, cleared many acres of ground or written two and a half PhD theses, had these been the aims of the society.'[85] To explain such an expenditure of energy demanded a deeper appreciation of the social, ecological and spiritual roles these ceremonies played in Anbarra life. Jones immersed himself in the language in pursuit of understanding, travelling into the landscapes of the mind, gaining a glimpse of the country in terms of the natural and the supernatural: two realms that 'are but parts of a single concept of reality'. Through these forces, he realised, the land is constantly transforming, dictating the availability of plants and animals and the pattern of religious and social life. But the land is also dependent on people. 'To sing the songs, to paint the designs and to carry out the dances,' Jones wrote, 'is to look after the land, to curate its religious essence.'[86]

Both Meehan and Jones were alert to the wider political transformations of the early 1970s. They explained the electoral process to the community living at Gupanga and helped enrol many adults to vote in the 1972 election, registering their occupations as either a 'hunter' or 'huntress'. 'They took on this role not just for the rights of the Gupanga people,' notes historian Helen Bond-Sharp, 'but as a building block upon which other rights could build.'[87] Meehan and Jones also argued successfully for basic wage payments to be made by the AIAS to their main interlocutors, Frank Gurrmanamana and Nancy Bandiyama.[88] And they were instrumental in assisting Aboriginal people to apply for social security benefits, negotiating the cultural challenges that come with having no birth certificate (and thus not qualifying for the retirement pension) or multiple wives (and being ineligible for the single mothers benefit). 'The importance of this income should not be underestimated,' writes Bond-Sharp, 'Although Aboriginal people in outstations were capable of supporting themselves by hunting and gathering as they had done for thousands of years, they were increasingly aware of the goods and services that other Australians had and aware of their rights as Australian citizens to have access to them.'[89] When news came through of Whitlam's election in 1972, Big Barney, a senior landowner, ran down to the beach-side camp at Gupanga and declared to the two progressive archaeologists, 'You mob bin win.' The election of the Whitlam government, however, was mixed news for the people of Arnhem Land.

* * *

When Carmel Schrire returned to the Alligator Rivers region in 1980, the roads had been sealed, Arnhem Land Reserve had been declared Aboriginal land and, in the heart of the new Kakadu National Park, a mine had been dug. 'Where buffalo guns once blazed,' Schrire wrote, 'geiger counters now crackled, heralding the arrival of Multinational Investors, followed by Supervising Scientists, and Resident Anthropologists.'[90] At the very moment Aboriginal people finally gained legal control over their land, mining companies – and the Australian government – pressured them to give it away in lucrative leases. Schrire joined a project aimed at assessing the effects of uranium mining and royalty payments on formerly isolated communities, many of which had been re-established through the outstation movement.

In the late 1960s, the Alligator Rivers region – or western Arnhem Land – had been found to be home to 70 per cent of Australia's known uranium resources. The Ranger 1 uranium mine was the first of many to be planned, and in 1972 the McMahon government joined with several mining companies to fund dollar-for-dollar a regional fact-finding survey. The mining companies were interested in the region's rich uranium deposits; the Australian government was trying to determine the borders of the proposed Kakadu National Park in the area. Both were keen to establish a body of basic data concerning the land and its resources. Adding to this tense set of interrelationships was the legislation that became the 1976 *Aboriginal Land Rights (Northern Territory) Act*, which acknowledged traditional rights to the land and its minerals.[91]

John Mulvaney quickly recognised the significance of the fact-finding study and lobbied to have archaeology included in the valuations of the cultural and scientific significance of the region. He nominated Harry Allen, who had recently finished his PhD on the Darling Basin, to survey the area and consolidate Carmel Schrire's archaeological work. It was an unusual task at the time – conducting a large-scale survey in a short time frame to satisfy industry and government. Allen and his successor on the project, Johan Kamminga, were amongst the first consultant archaeologists in Australia: an industry that has grown immeasurably over the years and whose fate remains largely entwined with the mining sector. 'It feels a bit lonely here as a contracting archaeologist,' Allen wrote to Mulvaney in 1972, 'as there is no place to which you belong and none who has responsibility for you.'[92] Like Schrire, he was led to sites by Indigenous guides and told which he could and could not excavate. At Mount Brockman, his guides Fred and Peter pointed out where the Rainbow Serpent had emerged from the ground, advising him which caves represented the tail and which the head. 'Both men were adamant that disturbance of either shelter by excavation (after careful explanation of what I wanted to do) would cause the rainbow serpent to come out and could cause the end of the world or at least a major calamity.'[93] Kamminga, Allen's former housemate, continued the regional survey in 1973 after Allen took a job in New Zealand. He, too, faced new challenges getting permission to excavate sites, partly, Mulvaney reflected privately, 'because land rights are such an issue at present'.[94]

Over 1972–1973 Kamminga and Allen independently surveyed and recorded 120 sites, including tool scatters and stone arrangements, bundled burials and wooden weapons, decorated overhangs scarred by quarrying and wet-season stringy bark shelters that still stood on the floodplain. The fact-finding study found western Arnhem Land to be 'one of the most archeologically significant areas in Australia' and helped make the case for the declaration of Kakadu National Park and its subsequent World Heritage listing.[95] But it did not stop the establishment of mining interests in the area. As David Lawrence reflects in his history, *Kakadu*, 'There is little doubt that the Commonwealth, with its 72.5 per cent share of the Ranger mining development, had a conflict of interest during the negotiations.'[96] At a time of high inflation and rising unemployment, Whitlam signed a memorandum of understanding in October 1975 that supported uranium mining in the Alligator Rivers region and bound his successor to comply. On 3 November 1978 the traditional owners signed the Ranger Agreement. It was more of a resignation than an agreement. One of the signatories, Toby Gangale, is reported to have said, 'I've given up. It's been six years now. I'm not fighting anymore.'[97] Historian Justin O'Brien describes the process as a 'failure of Aboriginal land rights legislation to deliver meaningful rights to the recognised traditional owners of the Ranger and Jabiluka project areas, the Mirrar people'.[98]

Aboriginal responses to mining vary across the continent.[99] But to understand the impact of mining on the region and the depth of opposition that continues in many communities today demands an Aboriginal understanding of country. Aside from health and land management concerns, there are profound spiritual matters at hand. Archaeologist Mike Smith put it well in a recent interview: 'It's not just that people are losing control over the sites or losing access to lands; the actual land is being shipped off to China. I mean, there goes the Dreaming! There goes the body of the ancestral beings!'[100]

* * *

After almost three years monitoring the impact of uranium mining on traditional societies, Schrire decided to return to South Africa in 1983. She felt increasingly drawn to the archaeology of contact in her own country. 'I began to feel what it was like to witness, and perhaps, to preside over the transformations of indigenous societies,' she reflected. 'The longer I watched, the more the desire grew to explore the concrete expression of such change. I wanted to taste dispossession in the material elements of invasion, the clay pipes, stone flasks, and bottles.'[101] Although she has not conducted major field research in Australia since 1983, her work in Arnhem Land continues to resonate. The escarpment of western Arnhem Land remains linked with the search for human antiquity in Australia, and since the 1980s has regularly been scoured for the oldest sites in Australia. We will return to Arnhem Land and this hunt for the Pleistocene in Chapter 10.

Meehan has continued to work with the Anbarra and has returned to Arnhem Land many times since she and Jones spent their year on the Blyth River in the early 1970s. Many of those she lived with have also travelled south to visit her on the outskirts of Canberra. Two of her main interlocutors, Frank Gurrmanamana and Frank Malkorda, visited Canberra several times as members of the AIAS council. They were transfixed by this place where decisions about their land were made. Jones memorably described Gurrmanamana's reaction on his first visit to Canberra in August 1974:

> Here was a land empty of religious affiliation; there were no wells, no names of the totemic ancestors, no immutable links between land, people and the rest of the natural and supernatural worlds. Here was just a vast *tabula rasa,* cauterised of meaning ... Viewed from this perspective, the Canberra of the geometric streets, and the paddocks of the six-wire fences were places not of domesticated order, but rather a wilderness of primordial chaos.[102]

Both Gurrmanamana and Malkorda were particularly interested in Canberra's role as the national capital: as a place representing the Australian people. So when Meehan and Jones returned to the Blyth River in 1979, Gurrmanamana and Malkorda came to their tent with a proposition: 'They wished to present a *Rom* to the people in Canberra whom they knew, both as an act of reciprocity for hospitality they had received from them and as an extension of friendship to those who had taken an interest in their life and culture.'[103]

A *Rom* is essentially the presentation of a bound and decorated pole to a host community by a visiting group of singers and dancers. The ceremony takes several weeks to prepare and many days to perform. Les Hiatt describes *Rom* as a 'ritual of diplomacy', as it is designed to establish or reaffirm friendly relations between people of different communities, languages and cultures.[104] 'We want that Canberra mob to look at our ceremony because we have been to many meetings there,' they explained to Peter Ucko, director of AIAS and 'big boss in Canberra': 'We have been thinking about this for a long time. We have been thinking about all the men, the big members, all the time we have been attending Institute meetings. We have been thinking we would show all these people our ceremony.'[105] They even specified trees 'near Cooma', and white clay 'from a pit on the Hoskinson/Bungendore road' which they would use to make the ceremonial poles.

Over four days, from 31 October to 3 November 1982, the lawns in front of the AIAS library in Canberra became the ceremonial grounds of dancers and singers from Arnhem Land. All were invited, and thousands of people came to witness the song cycles unfold against the rhythmic sounds of clap sticks and the gravel tones of the didgeridoo.[106] 'It was a gesture of goodwill ... to the people of Canberra,' Stephen Wild later wrote in a book about the performance, 'and since Arnhem Land Aborigines are well aware of the national role of Canberra it was a gesture to Australia as a whole.'[107]

Rom has been performed in Canberra twice since. In 1995 Gurrmanamana and Roy Riwa returned to sing songs from Jambich and Goyulan, while their compatriots leapt and danced in the National Library of Australia, on the lawns of AIATSIS and in Kings Hall in Old Parliament House. In 2001 a new generation of dancers travelled from Arnhem Land to mark the opening of the new building at AIATSIS and reaffirm the long connection with the Anbarra fostered by Les Hiatt and Betty Meehan in the 1950s. On both occasions, the performances were designed 'to make their culture known throughout Australia and, through knowledge, to further reconciliation'.[108]

Recently, Yolngu leader and 1978 Australian of the Year Galarrwuy Yunupingu returned to the philosophy at the heart of the *Rom* ceremony in an essay for *The Monthly*, 'Rom Watangu'. Yunupingu has had interactions with every Australian prime minister since Gough Whitlam, dealing with many of them as one nation's leader to another: 'All the prime ministers I have known have been friendly to me, but I mark them all hard. None of them has done what I asked, or delivered what they promised.' 'What Aboriginal people ask,' Yunipingu wrote from eastern Arnhem Land, is that the modern world now makes the sacrifices necessary to give us a real future. To relax its grip on us. To let us breathe, to let us be free of the determined control exerted on us to make us like you. And you should take that a step further and recognise us for who we are, and not who you want us to be. Let us be who we are – Aboriginal people in a modern world – and be proud of us. Acknowledge that we have survived the worst that the past had thrown at us, and we are here with our songs, our ceremonies, our land, our language and our people – our full identity. What a gift this is that we can give you, if you choose to accept us in a meaningful way.[109]

The full significance of the *Rom* ceremony has yet to be appreciated by the Australian public. At the heart of this symbolic act is a gift – of song and dance and cultural knowledge, but it comes with obligations. The acceptance of such a gift enmeshes the recipients into a continuing process of reciprocity. As a diplomatic ritual, it formalises bonds and establishes an equal footing upon which both communities can build. It is the extension of a hand in friendship, and it is offered in the hope that knowledge will bring understanding, acceptance, rights and recognition.

SEVEN

MARKING COUNTRY

Lesley Maynard and 'the Bob Edwards style'

On 12 September 1940, near the village of Montignac in the Dordogne region of south-western France, an eighteen-year-old apprentice garage mechanic investigated a crevice in a rock wall under Lascaux Manor. Marcel Ravidat followed the narrow passage deep into the rock until it opened out into a vast cave system. The next day he returned with three friends and a grease gun to illuminate their path. As Ravidat held the light up to the walls, the teenagers came face to face with the spectre of charging bulls, leaping stags and galloping horses painted in luminous pigment. They were the first people known to have viewed the vivid, brilliant art in the Cave of Lascaux in around 15,000 years. Archaeologist Abbé Breuil visited soon afterwards, on 21 September, and immediately confirmed the significance of the cavern.[1] The paintings adorning the walls were telecast around the world and celebrated as 'the origins of art', 'the birth of humanity'. The cave art captured the public imagination in a way that other archaeological evidence could not. The people who created these images were unequivocally us: *Homo sapiens*. As Georges Bataille wrote in 1955,

Every beginning supposes what preceded it, but at one point night gave birth to day and the daylight we find at Lascaux illuminates the morning of our immediate species. It is the man who dwelt in this cave of whom for the first time and with certainty we may finally say: he produced works of art; he is of our sort.[2]

As the artist Pablo Picasso supposedly exclaimed on viewing the paintings in 1940, '*Nous n'avons rien inventé*': We have invented nothing.[3]

Although the images from Lascaux, alongside other European cave art, established a connection with Palaeolithic ancestors, Breuil and Bataille were at a loss as to how to interpret them. What did the haunting images mean? Why had they been so carefully painted in the dark caverns of the Dordogne? In search of answers, they turned to the art of Australia. Indigenous Australians were seen as representing a stage in Western evolution, rather than having a past of their own, and the volumes of Australian ethnography that emerged in the early twentieth century were ransacked for insights into 'the primitive mind'. Scholars such as Breuil gleaned the concepts of totemism, sympathetic magic and fertility rites from the Australian literature and applied them wholesale to the Palaeolithic cave art in the Dordogne.[4] It was not until the 1960s that this method of studying rock art was challenged. Annette Laming and André Leroi-Gourhan led the charge, criticising the approach not only for its misplaced evolutionary assumptions, but also for the certainty with which researchers asserted a single, comprehensive hypothesis for the meaning of ancient art. As Peter Ucko and Andrée Rosenfeld reflected in 1967, 'There may as well be one hundred reasons why Palaeolithic men decorated caves.'[5]

When the first European explorers encountered Aboriginal rock paintings and engravings they had mixed reactions. Some dismissed the art as 'crude' and 'rude'; others grudgingly acknowledged that Indigenous people 'possessed some dim notion of the Fine Arts'; while yet others were stunned by the variety and complexity of the images left scattered across the landscape.[6] Ernest Giles described a walk through gullies full of rock art in Central Australia as a visit to 'the aboriginal National Gallery of paintings and hieroglyphics'.[7] Many early explorers struggled to align the rich array of images with their ideas about the 'primitive' nature of Aboriginal culture. The most notorious case was George Grey's refusal to believe that the Wandjina paintings in the Kimberley had been created by Aboriginal people. 'Whatever may be the age of these paintings,' Grey wrote in 1837, 'it is scarcely probable that they could have been executed by the self-taught savage.'[8] Rock art enthusiast Grahame Walsh continued this conjecture into the twenty-first century, arguing – on the basis of aesthetic evaluation – that the luminous human-shaped forms were 'pre-Aboriginal': they represented the art tradition of an earlier race.[9]

The arrival of Europeans can be read on rock surfaces across Australia, as the invaders were absorbed into the existing systems of meaning: boats painted in X-ray style with cargo in the hold; saddled pack horses, pigs and buffalo; whitefellas with broad-brimmed hats, smoking pipes and carrying guns. But with a few exceptions, within a generation or two of the invasion the ancient craft of rock art came to an abrupt halt across Australia. Richard Gould's surprise encounter with two men singing and painting in the Western Desert in 1967 stands as one of the last recorded examples of unprompted rock art creation. And forty years later, the images they made have all but disappeared. Such paintings were not created to be conserved, archaeologist Lesley Maynard reflects. 'They were designed to be repainted.'[10]

The rock art that remains is a beautiful, melancholy evocation of the religious systems and political economy of the first Australians. There are more than 100,000 recorded rock art sites scattered across Australia, from engravings on long-buried rock walls in Cape York to paintings on the eroded gorges, broken massifs and sloping rock shelters of the Arnhem Land escarpment.[11] High-quality pigments have been found at every layer in the oldest sites in the Northern Territory, suggesting that rock art was part of the 'cultural baggage' of the first Australians.[12] In the Dampier Archipelago of Western Australia, Ken Mulvaney has interpreted an Ice Age antiquity for many of the estimated one million engravings at Murujuga (the Burrup Peninsula), based on sea levels and the animals depicted in the art.[13] There have also been a number of claims for the artistic representation of extinct megafauna, which have recently been reviewed and rejected.[14] But the oldest intimation of rock art in Australia – use of pigment on rock – comes from an ochre-stained palette uncovered at Carpenters Gap in the Kimberley and dated to about 40,000 years ago.[15]

The unusual survival of art across the continent brought archaeologist Mike Morwood to declare in 2002 that 'Australia is the rock art capital of the world'.[16] In many instances the pigment used for painting has bonded with the rock, staining the image into landscape, becoming part of the natural features. In some ways, this is how rock art should be viewed: as a fusion of the natural and the cultural. According to the Worora, Wunambal and Ngarinyin peoples, the Wandjina figures which Grey looked upon with disbelief in 1837 came out of the sea and sky, created the features of the landscape and were then absorbed into the walls of rock shelters. It is common for Aboriginal people to attribute the creation of paintings and engravings to supernatural forces instead of people. Many early rock art researchers assumed that this was evidence of an ancient, 'extinct art'. But to describe the art 'as having always been there' is simply an affirmation of the Dreaming, in which the natural and the cultural converge.[17]

Aboriginal rock paintings and engravings are inevitably grounded in place, as they involve the representation of ancestral beings who traversed the country in the Dreaming and transformed the landscape, leaving something of themselves in its topographic features. 'Art provides a sacred charter to the land,' writes anthropologist Howard Morphy, 'and producing art is one of the conditions of existence. It keeps the past alive and maintains its relevance to the present.'[18] Painting, engraving, ritual and ceremony help to focus the power of the Dreaming and reenergise ancestral marks. Charles Mountford observed elders rubbing rock surfaces to release their life essence in the course of ceremonies to maintain and increase natural resources. Dick Kimber has recorded the ways in which Pintupi men greeted their ancestors through art, adding stencils of their hands to decorated rock walls with the words 'hullo old man'. More recently, June Ross has highlighted the cultural significance of the grooves, pits and battered edges around rock art, viewing them as evidence of sensory contact with totemic designs.[19] The old masters who painted and etched the designs found across Australia were not making 'art'; they were *marking country*, curating the Dreaming.

The systematic study of these marks is a relatively new discipline in Australia. The purely aesthetic approach of the early explorers developed into a more descriptive and quantitative craft in the early twentieth century.[20] Most research into the history of Aboriginal rock art was driven by committed individuals, rather than institutions, who were guided by questions of meaning, sequence and chronology. Is it possible to discern purpose and subject matter in rock art? How have styles of rock art changed over time? And when were these pictures created?

The most troublesome of these questions was chronology. Even with the advent of radiocarbon dating, it remains a challenge to date pigment. Thus antiquity must be inferred – from associated archaeology and its place in the landscape, the rate of weathering, discolouration or patination, or the technology and fauna depicted in the art. A range of ingenious dating techniques have been applied, from cation-ratio dating (a technique applied to rock varnish overlying engravings) to optically stimulated luminescence dating (which tests grains of sand in mud-wasp nests overlying or underlying rock paintings). But the most conclusive evidence is when rock art has been buried or detached and then uncovered in the course of an archaeological excavation – or if it depicts elements of known, datable events, such as the winged sails of British ships.

'It is difficult,' John Mulvaney lamented in 1969, 'for a prehistorian to assess Aboriginal art.'[21] Yet within a decade of these words, rock art research had emerged as a vibrant, independent discipline. This chapter touches on some of the main figures and influences in Australian rock art as a distinct but parallel field of study. As John Clegg, the first academic to teach rock art at an Australian university, observed in 1983, while the field of Australian archaeology has become increasingly integrated with ethnography, many rock art specialists have moved in the opposite direction, reducing ancient images to proportions, patterns and statistics.[22] Ironically, at the same time as researchers were moving away from studying art from an aesthetic viewpoint, the beauty and power of Aboriginal art began to be recognised and celebrated around the world. This appreciation of Aboriginal fine art, in turn, stimulated public interest in, and funding for, rock art research.

Although the craft of rock art waned in the twentieth century, it is important to emphasise that the dynamic cultures behind it, and the significance of art within those cultures, did not. As the Indigenous artist Wandjuk Marika wrote in 1976: 'There is no real distinction for us between art and life; art is the expression of our beliefs, it upholds the laws by which we live, and is an important element in the way in which we relate to the physical world around us.'[23] Indeed, art has played a powerful role in Aboriginal political and cultural expression since invasion. Galarrwuy Yunupingu draws particular attention to the 1963 bark petition, through which his people, the Yolngu, opposed the federal government's leasing of their land at Yirrkala on the Gove Peninsula and demanded recognition of their rights to country. The bark painting showed the clan designs of all the areas that were being threatened by the mining company. 'It showed, in ways in which raising a multi-coloured piece of calico could never do, the ancient rights and responsibilities we have towards our country,' Yunupingu wrote. By submitting the bark painting as a legal document, the Yolngu were using art, in another way, to mark their country. 'Our painting,' Yunupingu observed, 'is a political act.'[24]

* * *

Australia's equivalent of the ancient Pleistocene cave art of the Dordogne lies deep below the Nullarbor Plain, an arid expanse bordering the Great Australian Bight in South Australia. Twenty-two kilometres inland, set in open steppe, a crater-like sinkhole plunges into the monotonous plain. The sheer sides drop eight metres and then slope to a depth of 25 metres. Two passages lead off the sunken floor: the Lake Passage, which extends for 600 metres through a series of underground lakes to a depth of 90 metres below the Nullarbor; and the Art Passage, the main chamber, which narrows after 60 metres into a small cavern known as the Squeeze.[25]

The eccentric Hungarian-Australian amateur archaeologist Alexander Gallus was the first to investigate the archaeology of Koonalda Cave, joining a team from the Australian Speleological Federation in 1956. Norman Tindale had earlier identified worked stone tools around the lip of the sinkhole, but it was Gallus, over several field seasons from 1956 to 1973, who uncovered evidence of Aboriginal activity deep within the cave system. He also found clues to what they were doing in the depths of the earth. Scattered throughout the excavation, he found debris from a strong flint-like raw material that had evidently been quarried to make stone tools. Even more strikingly, he recorded a mysterious panel of engravings on the walls of the Art Passage.[26]

Gallus eagerly reported the discovery to his colleagues, claiming to have found Ice Age art alongside evidence of an ancient mining industry under the Nullarbor Plain. The news was received with scepticism.

Gallus was a maverick intellectual with a thick Hungarian accent and a devoted following outside academia. He openly mocked 'Cambridge methods' and instead interpreted the Australian past through a combination of inference, intuition and complex European theory.[27] Amongst the wilder of his 'deductions' was his firmly held belief that people had lived at Bain's Quarry near Keilor in Victoria for 'up to a million years' and that the first Australian was 'naturally a *Homo erectus*'.[28] 'My deductions have always proved right,' Gallus once boasted to a reporter, 'when more technological methods were used.'[29]

In February 1967 the AIAS sent Richard Wright to investigate Gallus' archaeological claims, along with rock art specialists Bob Edwards and Lesley Maynard to conduct a systematic survey of the supposed Ice Age art. The resulting report is an intriguingly contradictory document. Wright's excavation report is delivered alongside, but completely separate from, Gallus' contrary interpretation. They even adopted different terminology to describe raw materials and tool types. 'No hybrid could have been produced,' Wright notes in the preface, 'without mutilating surgery that would have been unacceptable to the authors of both parts.'[30]

Building on Gallus' original trench, Wright dug a six-metre-deep pit and uncovered evidence that the cave had been visited sporadically during the last Ice Age, between 22,000 and 15,000 years ago.[31] People stopped using the site as the sea level began to rise again, bringing the coastline closer and increasing the rainfall in the region. Wright speculated that rising seas would have washed away the nearby coastal dunes and exposed fresh nodules of flint on the surface, leading to the abandonment of Koonalda Cave: why venture into the earth for a material that could be found more easily on the surface? The charcoal Wright and Gallus used to date the site came from the remains of ancient hand-held torches – bundles of burnt twigs, scorched roots and pieces of blackened wood that had once illuminated the dark cavern.

While Wright focused on the flint mines in the Lake Passage, Edwards and Maynard recorded the mesmerising patterns on the walls of the Art Passage. There were a few fresh markings – graffiti from European times – but most were old, heavily eroded grooves. The fine mineral skins that had formed over the markings reinforced the interpretation that the cave had been used frequently in the deep past and then abandoned. The most visually impressive panel was on the southwest wall, where a continuous frieze of entrancing grooved patterns – or 'finger fluting' – had been made by ancient handstrokes: three to four fingers held together, clawing into the soft limestone wall, converging into fan-shaped forms, lattice grids and long, meandering channels. There were some incised markings on walls and boulders, which had been engraved with stone tools, as well as more defined patterns such as concentric circles and a herringbone design. Everything was covered in the powder of limestone dust – or 'moonmilk'.[32]

The Art Passage at Koonalda narrows near the end and slopes sharply into the Squeeze – a five-metre crawl tunnel, barely a foot high at its narrowest point. The darkness in this small cavity is total. Beyond the Squeeze, the passage opens onto a precipitous ledge overlooking an underground lake twenty metres below. Even here, the low ceiling is covered in wall markings and a single worked piece of flint was found. Curiously, the Squeeze – the remotest part of the Art Passage – is the only part of the cave where mining was carried out alongside the wall markings. 'This vein does not seem to be intrinsically superior to flint found in the more accessible outcrops,' Edwards and Maynard mused in their report. 'But was it, in some magical or spiritual way, the better for coming from the deepest, darkest part of the cave?'[33] A small pit excavated at the entrance of the Squeeze yielded a 20,000-year-old date for an upper layer of flaked tools, leading the researchers to conclude that the finger fluting in this part of the cave had indeed been made during the last Ice Age.

There are few ethnographic accounts of Aboriginal people using Koonalda Cave. Anthropologists such as Daisy Bates, who spent time with the Mirning people of the Nullarbor coastal region, recorded stories of how they feared the plain. A 'hideous and gigantic snake' called *Ganba* or *Jeedara* lived in the caves and blowholes on the plain and devoured all intruders. 'Weird hissing noises from the blowholes were the sound of the monstrous snake's breathing,' writes Josephine Flood, 'and in the Dreamtime he had pushed up the steep sea-cliffs so as to swim along beneath them.'[34] Bates described Koonalda as an important stopping place on the 'native highway' that ran roughly parallel to the coast, but few Mirning people were known to have descended into the sinkhole.[35] This history helps explain the archaeological silence in the cave over the last 15,000 years, but it also means that there is no known oral explanation for the patterns on the walls of the Art Passage.

Perhaps, Gallus suggested, they were signposts, indicating where to find nodules of flint.[36] Engravings in other parts of Australia have been similarly interpreted: as maps along Dreaming tracks and between resources and waterholes. Another early theory was that the finger fluting was the 'accidental' consequence of 'people groping their way in the dark' – such was the softness of the limestone. Edwards and Maynard even wondered whether the patterns represented 'an instinctive human impulse to "make marks"', admitting that many members of the 1967 expedition had similar impulses when confronted with a patch of smooth, freshly broken surface. Ultimately, they reasoned, 'none of the pragmatic explanations – mining indicators, accidental marks, bone working or scraping off powder – account for those few definite patterns found among the mass of random markings'.[37] It seemed most likely that the wall markings were deliberately made during ritual activity, as part of the process of marking country.

* * *

Bob Edwards documented the excavations and rock art recording during the 1967 expedition in his film *Flint Miners of the Nullarbor*, using tinfoil reflectors to illuminate the eerie patterns in the dark depths of Koonalda. It was the first of many films on Aboriginal Australia that he directed as the curator of the South Australian Museum (replacing Tindale, who retired in 1965). In another film he paid homage to the mighty canoe trees that lined the Murray River (and unexpectedly triggered a new wave of canoe building in the process); in others he documented archaeological investigations in Arnhem Land and filmed the striking 'archaic faces' engraved in the Cleland Hills in Central Australia.[38]

Edwards' interest in Aboriginal Australia had been kindled at an early age. As a child, he often joined his grandmother, a field naturalist, shell collector and ecologist, on long field trips into the bush around Adelaide, and in the summers he played with Aboriginal people at Goolwa near the mouth of the Murray River, learning how to throw a boomerang.[39] At the age of thirteen he began to attend the Royal Society of South Australia, rubbing shoulders with anthropological luminaries such as Norman Tindale, Charles Mountford, Ted Strehlow, Harold Cooper, TD Campbell, Douglas Mawson and Andrew Abbey. He accompanied them on surface collecting expeditions into the Flinders Ranges and Central Australia, learning about the manufacture of stone tools and their various 'uses and distribution'. Campbell fondly described him as 'one of our local super enthusiasts'.[40] It was not until Edwards worked at Fromm's Landing with John Mulvaney in 1963 that he gained his first formal experience of archaeology.

His main passion, however, was photography, and it was Mountford who taught him to photograph rock art: how to position himself so as not to skew the dimensions of a painting or engraving, and to patiently observe how light and shadows interact with the rock face before taking a photograph. Edwards bought his first camera at the age of thirteen

in Rundle Street for 10 shillings and a sixpence, using all his pocket
money. The Kodak was the first of hundreds he would collect over
his lifetime, most of which followed him into the field. He joined the
camera club at Thebarton Boys Technical High School and even built
his own darkroom in the family home. 'I actually had the audacity to
write a paper on field photography at some stage,' he told me in 2015,
adding: 'I wouldn't write that now.' It is hard to find an early archaeological text in Australia that does not feature his photography.

But despite this passion and his extensive field experience, Edwards
never gained a formal education in archaeology or anthropology. Acute
labour shortages during and following World War II forced him to leave
school to help on the family property at Marion. He continued to visit
and record Aboriginal sites, but during holidays and weekends, alongside family life and his various jobs as a horticulturalist, fruit grower,
winemaker, house decorator, market gardener and marketing director. It was not until he took up the position of curator at the South
Australian Museum in 1965 that he was able to devote himself entirely
to his passion. On learning of the appointment, he wrote to his friend
Dermot Casey: 'There is no doubt I have been extended the greatest
opportunity of my life.'[41]

Although Edwards emerged from an amateur tradition, he saw the
benefits of a systematic approach to Aboriginal art sites. Even on his
earliest expeditions into the bush he was intent on collecting 'statistical data' for computer analysis, by counting, tracing and measuring
rock art motifs.[42] Over several years this patient, quantitative approach
began to yield surprising results.

In 1961 he embarked on a three-year survey in north-east South
Australia with his childhood mentor, Charles Mountford. They jumped
from sheep station to sheep station in pursuit of art sites. One of their
initial survey areas was the series of engraving sites at Panaramitee,
which Mountford had first recorded in 1926. They counted, traced and

photographed over a thousand 'pecked' figures, dominated by animal tracks and circles, as well as crescents, human footprints, radiating lines and a few other nonfigurative designs. The same narrow range of motifs appeared in a number of sites across the station. Some early European explorers believed the engravings to be fossil footprints, or the result of certain algae and lichens eating into the rock. But they were human markings, made by precise pecking with a hand-held stone hammer into hard rock outcrops and covered by a 'desert varnish' or 'patina' – a shiny, dark, rust-coloured accretion that builds up over a long period of time.[43] Mountford, and geologist Herbert Basedow before him, believed the desert varnish to be a sign of great antiquity.[44] When Edwards asked two Aboriginal elders, Jummintjarra and Migenteri, about the origins of such engravings, he was told that they 'have always been there'.[45]

Panaramitee Station was bare and parched from years of drought when Edwards and Mountford roamed across it together, but as they neared the end of their survey a series of spectacular thunderstorms transformed the country, with heavy rain filling rockholes and causing the creeks to flow.[46] The inundation highlighted another curious feature of the engravings: they were all next to some form of water supply. Over the course of the three-year survey, Edwards began to notice the same weathered, track-and-circle engravings at other sites across South Australia and the arid centre, almost all associated with water sources and old camp sites. By carefully recording and measuring the art in each of these locations, he was able to turn broad similarities into statistics, revealing a remarkable consistency in the shape and arrangement of the track-and-circle engravings. He had uncovered a 'stylistic unit': the artistic signature of an ancient, widespread cultural tradition. 'It is significant,' he wrote, 'that the relative frequencies are very similar whether the sites being compared are close to one another, or 1,300 km or more apart.' The homogeneity of this stylistic unit suggested to him that 'these motifs predate the time when tribal boundaries became rigid and separate cultural entities developed'.[47]

In late June 1966 Edwards joined a team led by John Mulvaney to record and photograph sites in the Northern Territory.[48] At Ingaladdi on Willeroo Station, west of Katherine, they dug at the base of a sandstone outcrop covered in pecked tracks and abraded grooves that resembled the Panaramitee engravings. In the lower levels of the pit they were excited to find detached pieces of sandstone bearing pecked engravings of emu and kangaroo tracks. It gave them the first positive date for rock art in Australia, and, at 5000–7000 years old, it confirmed Edwards' belief that the track-and-circle tradition was ancient.[49]

The widespread engraving tradition revealed something intriguing about rock art in ancient Australia, and it was a point of major discussion at a small gathering of rock art specialists and archaeologists at Panaramitee in 1969. For a while the track-and-circle designs were referred to as 'the Bob Edwards style'. After all, Lesley Maynard reflected, 'Edwards made the main contribution of illustrating and describing the range of motifs, environmental setting, archaeological associations, probable age, and vital statistics.' But, she added, 'Godfather Bob never christened his infant.'[50] That task fell to Maynard, who proposed the more general term 'Panaramitee', as the engravings at Panaramitee Station constituted 'a classic assemblage of this type'.[51]

* * *

Lesley Maynard (née McMah) was the first person to take a purely archaeological approach to the study of Australian rock art. She was inspired by international scholars such as Annette Laming and André Leroi-Gourhan, who had demonstrated how an art panel could be studied using a 'punch card' system: a method of recording the distribution, pattern and range of motifs by punching holes in a piece of stiff paper according to predefined categories. Once rock art had been translated into data via punch cards, researchers could use early computers to analyse and compare evidence from hundreds of different sites at one time. It allowed them to move beyond questions about the meaning of motifs to search for social and economic information encoded in the art.[52] Maynard's contemporary, Patricia Vinnicombe, used such analyses in the western Cape of South Africa to reveal that artists were highly selective in their portrayal of animal species: some culturally significant animals, such as the eland and the elephant, were overrepresented in the art, while other dietary staples were completely absent. Far from being a menu or a hunting list, the rock art afforded insights into the cultural worlds of its makers.[53] Maynard was excited by the possibilities of such quantative analyses and in her 1965 honours thesis – the first on rock art in Australia – she began to adapt these techniques to the engravings in the Sydney basin.[54]

Thousands of engravings mark the Hawkesbury sandstone around Sydney. There are outlines of British boats alongside people, spirit creatures, marsupials, birds, fish, weapons and footprints, but there is very little information about what the figures mean or why they were engraved, other than a contemporary Indigenous view that they are 'sacred'. Without direct knowledge of the context in which the images were created or the immediate intentions of the artist, Maynard was forced to rely on visual clues, such as anatomical details and artistic techniques, patterns in the distribution and arrangement of motifs, and the cultural and geographic context. 'My reason for shedding gloom and despair upon the search for meaning in prehistoric Australian rock art is that I believe the study of this material to be basically an archaeological one,' Maynard explained. 'These methods may not tell you why, but they will make a start on who, when, where, and how.'[55]

Following in the footsteps of Frederick McCarthy, Maynard studied the engravings in the Hawkesbury sandstone as if they were stone artefacts, breaking motifs down into their various structural attributes, measuring each element, and then recording the information using a punch card system. She brushed the rock surfaces clean, chalked the grooves to help discern the motifs and laid down a scale or a grid to measure the size and depth of the engraving. It was a slow and mechanical process; Maynard later published a diary of her recording practice with the (half-joking) title 'Day by Dreary Day'.[56] Once a panel was converted into 'data', Maynard was able to analyse recurrent attributes and how they clustered in a site, then compare that information with other motifs and art panels in other sites. Her supervisor, John Clegg, reflected that Maynard's 1965 work was 'a landmark'.[57] It set a new standard for Australian rock art research and tied the young field into parallel debates about 'processual archaeology' in Europe, America and South Africa. She later proposed a new classificatory system for the study of rock art: a common vocabulary with clear definitions of terms to minimise 'value judgements' and 'individual differences' in the recording process.[58]

Maynard continued to work on the Sydney engravings in the late 1960s, but the scope of her study expanded. The work with Edwards at Koonalda Cave in February 1967 had given her a glimpse of what truly ancient art in Australia looked like, while the survey of the Hawkesbury sandstone engravings, on soft exposed material, evidently reflected a more recent art tradition; but how did they fit together in time and space? What was the history of rock art production in Australia, and how had it changed over time? These questions drove her to embark on a continental synthesis of Australian rock art, which in turn led her to Edwards' work on the widespread track-and-circle engravings.

The Koonalda engravings, although ancient, were largely an enigma, as deep cave art was so rare across the continent. The pervasiveness of Panaramitee engravings, on the other hand, became the key to Maynard's sequence. She found less consistency in the tradition than Edwards had claimed, but agreed that they represented a distinct 'cultural unit'. The breadth of her survey also allowed her to consider engravings in Laura in Queensland, Mount Cameron West in northern Tasmania and Ingaladdi in the Northern Territory, which she believed were essentially the same style. The Tasmanian engravings were of particular importance as they presented a means to date the art. If the engravings at Mount Cameron West were indeed part of the same cultural tradition, then the Panaramitee style must predate the formation of Bass Strait around 12,000 years ago.

In 1974 Maynard argued that there were three major identifiable styles in Australian rock art, which she attempted to put into a chronological sequence.[59] There was the ancient deep cave art, such as the finger fluting she and Edwards had recorded at Koonalda; the Panaramitee engravings, a homogenous and widely distributed Pleistocene rock art tradition; and the diverse and regional traditions of the Holocene, represented by 'Simple Figurative styles', such as the clean outlines of creatures engraved in the Hawkesbury sandstone, and 'Complex Figurative styles', such as the luminous Wandjina art in the Kimberley and the intricate X-ray art in Arnhem Land. In many ways her rock art scheme echoed the technological synthesis Mulvaney put forward in *The Prehistory of Australia*. Both theories were simple, continental and presented a view of linear progression, with a relatively homogenous Pleistocene practice that grew and diversified in the mid-Holocene.

Maynard's grand synthesis, and her call for a classificatory system for rock art, reflected the increasing professionalisation of the field. It had come a long way since Edwards' teenage recording escapades with the Royal Society of South Australia. 'Maynard's model was a tour de force,' Flood wrote in 1997, 'and still, twenty years on, forms the basis of our understanding of Australian rock art.'[60] While now 'tattered around the edges', archaeologist Jo McDonald reflected in 2004, 'no one has come up with a better scenario'. Although, she added, 'The days of a simple pan-continental model for rock art in Australia are probably well over.'[61]

By the end of the 1970s, the field of rock art was becoming more integrated with the wider archaeological community. The leadership of Ucko, himself a rock art specialist, also promoted a change in AIAS funding priorities so that rock art was given greater precedence, which in turn attracted more overseas scholars. But the increasing institutionalisation of the field created a divide between researchers working from within universities and those who documented rock art from the periphery. Flood has written about the occasionally internecine politics of these debates: 'a saga of personal feuds, bitter rivalries and competition for "territory" ... Added to this is the explosive mix in the rock art world of so-called "professionals" and "amateurs", all with chips on both shoulders, it seems at times.'[62]

But it is important to recognise the invaluable contributions of individuals from outside the academy. In many cases, extensive site recording programs led directly to more specialist work. For example, Percy Trezise, an Australian pilot, painter, explorer and writer, devoted fifty years to documenting the rock art of the Cape York Peninsula, known for its distinctive representations of ancestral 'Quinkan' spirits. He would fly over the rugged terrain, searching for features that might preserve paintings and later find them on foot, pushing through the scrub in a pith helmet with a pistol on his hip. These forays into the bush laid the foundations for later archaeological work at Mushroom Rock, Early Man rock shelter and on the Koolburra Plateau. His sons Matt and Steven Trezise have taken up his passion for the 'Quinkan' rock art of the Cape York Peninsula.[63]

The study of Arnhem Land rock art was similarly shaped by committed independent researchers, such as Eric Brandl, who migrated to Australia from Germany in 1956. He first encountered the art of Arnhem Land on an epic bicycle trip in the early 1960s from Mount

Isa to Darwin via the East Alligator River. In 1965 he resigned from his job with Carpentaria Exploration, bought a Nissan Patrol with his wife, Maria, and moved to the Northern Territory to pursue his passion for rock art. He had a fierce intelligence and a love of long, solo trips into the bush. He marvelled at the variety and beauty of Arnhem Land art, which he photographed with great care, developing the exposed films each night in his bush camp. His pioneering work on faunal identification in Arnhem Land rock art, in which he described a 'broad zone where metaphysical concept and zoological reality cannot be kept apart', has provided a framework for debates about possible depictions of megafauna in the art. He also produced the first detailed chronology of Arnhem Land rock art styles, a sophisticated regional sequence that has since been expanded by his protégé Darrell Lewis. George Chaloupka, a Czech refugee with a guttural, beard-muffled voice, became enchanted by the art of Arnhem Land around the same time and developed a similar sequence for the region. Through his work at the Northern Territory Museum, Chaloupka formed close bonds with the local communities, especially Badmardi brothers Kapirigi and Namingum, and became a vocal public advocate for the conservation of their rich heritage.[64]

The legacy of a maverick intellectual such as Grahame Walsh is more controversial. He guarded his rock art research closely and was notorious for proposing the existence of pre-Aboriginal civilisations, yet his prodigious recording efforts and popular publications triggered a wave of research into Kimberley art that continues today. Although many of his interpretations have been roundly rejected, he has had an enduring influence. As the chair of the Kimberley Foundation, Maria Myers, reflected after the 2017 rock art survey: 'We couldn't be doing this work without Grahame's archive. We can find the sites from his recordings and take everybody there.'[65]

But as the field of rock art has developed it has become more collaborative and more integrated with other disciplines, such as archaeology, palaeobotany and palaeozoology. There is now less room for the charismatic individual site recorder.

* * *

While Maynard pioneered an archaeological approach to motifs, it was Andrée Rosenfeld's work at Early Man rock shelter that decisively shifted rock art into the archaeological world. She arrived in Australia with her husband, Peter Ucko, in 1972, having already established an international reputation studying European cave art. Working out of the ANU, she was drawn to south-east Cape York Peninsula by reports from Percy Trezise of a large sandstone overhang with paintings and engravings and what appeared to be a rich archaeological deposit. Trezise had found the shelter in 1972 on one of his many surveys with Dick Roughsey and Eddie Oribin. They named it Early Man Shelter after the weathered frieze of 'emu tracks' and circles on the shelter wall that had been 'polished smooth by time'.[66] Rosenfeld saw it as a promising opportunity to test the antiquity of the track-and-circle art style. In August 1974 she opened a series of trenches in the shelter, including up against the back wall. Noting a significant increase in the amount of pigment being deposited in the site and the arrangement of paintings, she suggested a transition from an early rock art tradition of pecked engravings of mostly geometric designs and tracks to a more recent tradition of figurative 'Quinkan' rock painting in the mid-Holocene. The key piece of evidence was a buried panel of deeply weathered, pecked engravings that had begun to get covered by sediment around 14,400 years ago. It was a remarkable discovery. But was it Panaramitee?

Rosenfeld's chronology largely agreed with Maynard's grand scheme, but she argued that there were 'significant differences' between the engraving tradition in Cape York and the Panaramitee style found throughout the arid centre.[67] There were fewer circles, and most were quite irregular in shape, while the 'emu tracks' were ambiguous and abstract, rather than clear representations: Rosenfeld preferred to call them 'tridents'. She believed the Early Man engravings represented a regional art style, distinct from the tradition observed elsewhere in the continent. Maynard, on the other hand, was happy to incorporate the panel – and the dates – into her archaeological sequence as a regional variation of a single tradition. In her mind, the buried engravings confirmed that Panaramitee was a Pleistocene art tradition.

Mike Morwood, then a student at the ANU, followed Rosenfeld's lead, showing the importance of a contextual approach to the study of rock art. In 1976, he began an archaeological study in the central Queensland highlands, involving extensive surveys, four major excavations, and the recording of ninety-two art sites. Over the course of his project, Morwood measured and counted 17,025 motifs, which, once put onto computer coding sheets and statistically analysed by a DEC-10 computer, distinguished 'a total of 87 motif types, fifteen colours and eight techniques'.[68] Significantly, he also believed he had detected a regional variation of the Panaramitee style engravings.

What was truly innovative about Morwood's project was how he linked these designs to both the archaeology of the region and the social and spiritual lives of the Aboriginal groups recorded in local ethnographies. He was particularly interested in the locations of paintings and engravings in the landscape, as these are what 'give them an importance way beyond simple marks on rock'.[69] He found connections, for example, between depictions of 'tortoises' in art sites, the distribution of water sources, and local stories about the paths taken by ancestral beings. He also identified parallels between technological changes uncovered during excavation and variations in art styles. 'It seems no accident,' he argued in his thesis, 'Art and Stone', 'that the appearance of a distinctive Central Queensland rock art coincided with the onset of the Small Tool Tradition in the region.'[70] Both suggested fundamental changes in social networks around 3000 years ago. In this instance, rock art not only enriched the archaeology, it also delivered cultural and social insights that excavation could not yield on its own.

* * *

Lesley Maynard's proposed sequence of Australian rock art dominated the field throughout the 1980s and was hotly debated in the pages of *Rock Art Research* and at the first meeting of the Australian Rock Art Research Association (AURA) in Darwin in 1988. The Panaramitee style, in particular, came under intense scrutiny. The idea of an ancient, homogenous, pan-continental tradition was challenged by growing evidence of regional variability, such as Rosenfeld's work in Cape York and Morwood's survey of the Carnarvon Range. Rosenfeld suggested that the 'unity' of ancient art styles in Australia had been overstated. In 1988 she openly wondered whether the concept of a Panaramitee style was 'dead or alive'.[71] Maynard herself, bemused at the heightened debate, declared that she was 'happy to bury "Panaramitee style"' – but as a name, not necessarily as a cultural unit.[72]

What does this widespread tradition tell us about the social world of the engravers? The battered edges and grooves surrounding the Panaramitee engravings intimate a ritual, not secular production, while the location of the motifs on highly visible pavements around waterholes and near camp sites suggests that they were not secret-sacred. Although it is unwise to project recent ritual practices onto the deep past, ethnography remains a powerful interpretive method. As Finnish scholar Antti Lahelma reflects, 'We simply need to assume that certain core elements of culture, the slow-moving deep-bone structures of the *longue durée*, have remained recognisably similar over extensive periods of time, rather like the basic grammatical structures of a language.'[73] Indeed, archaeologist Bruno David believes that rock art may be the key to understanding the development of those slow-moving deep-bone structures, and in particular, the religious system known as the

Dreaming: 'Like all things cultural, the Dreaming must have a history; it must have arisen out of human practice some time in the deep past.'[74]

The debate over the age of the Panaramitee engravings thus presents two compelling visions of social and religious life in ancient Australia. Scholars such as Natalie Franklin argue that Panaramitee should still be understood as a distinct, pan-continental stylistic entity that began during the last Ice Age.[75] The presence of dingo tracks in some of the art panels suggests that, no matter when the tradition began, it continued until around 4000 years ago. Others, such as June Ross and Mike Smith, believe it is a much more recent graphic tradition, largely restricted to the eastern half of the arid zone, with a major period of production beginning around 8000 years ago.[76] In both instances, the rock art is viewed as a rare archaeological insight into the spiritual life of the first Australians. If the Panaramitee engravings represent the marking out of a cultural landscape, then the increase in distinctive regional rock art styles during the late Holocene would suggest that the Dreaming is a dynamic and emergent culture, rather than an ancient, unchanging system of meaning.

*** ***

The Panaramitee style lives on in contemporary art today. The characteristic track-and-circle motifs are familiar to anyone admiring the stunning acrylic paintings from the Papunya Tula art movement. It is fitting that the man after whom this long graphic tradition was almost named – Bob Edwards – should also have played a significant role in championing its modern incarnation.

In 1965, before taking up the job as curator of the South Australian Museum, Bob Edwards embarked on six months of fieldwork across Arnhem Land and Central Australia with the assistance of John Mulvaney.[77] It was 'a great long 8000 mile journey' that illuminated the challenges and delights of working across cultures. These 'adventures' into remote country, often with little water and limited petrol, and always with few funds, were marked by euphoria and hardship. Edwards was appalled by the negative attitudes towards Aboriginal people in the towns, and he lamented the damage that was being casually – and sometimes deliberately – inflicted on their cultural sites. His heart ached at the loss: 'I have seen Aboriginals stand in these ruined galleries with tears streaming down their faces.'[78] He used the photographs from these expeditions to raise public awareness of the vandalism and to make detailed legislative recommendations for the preservation of 'Aboriginal monuments, antiquities and sites'. To help educate the Australian public about Aboriginal society and rock art, he allowed his diary from a similar expedition to be published by the *Australian* in April 1970 as a six-part feature on 'The Rock Engravers'. His advocacy was anchored in the belief that 'while the Aborigines are the rightful owners of this heritage, all Australians are the beneficiaries of this unique cultural tradition'.[79]

Edwards' main vehicle for change, however, was the Aboriginal Arts Board of the Australia Council, set up by the Whitlam government in 1973 to distribute funds in the field of Aboriginal arts.[80] Edwards had lobbied for its creation and was appointed as the founding director from 1973 until 1980. He saw his role as a means to involve and empower Indigenous voices in national life. The arts, he believed, were the key to changing attitudes towards Indigenous people and their heritage. As director, he was responsible for valuing art as well as collecting artworks to exhibit around Australia and the world. Initially he found it a struggle to even give paintings away to state galleries; such was the resistance to recognising Aboriginal art as 'fine art'. But over the 1970s the board oversaw a renaissance in Aboriginal art. The brilliant acrylic paintings produced at Papunya from 1971 were central to this growing appreciation. While Geoffrey Bardon triggered the developments at Papunya, historian Dick Kimber identifies Edwards as the key 'outsider' who enabled the painting to continue by arranging funds and raising awareness of the works nationally and internationally.[81] This campaign culminated with the inclusion of Aboriginal artworks in the third Biennale of Sydney in 1979 and in the inaugural *Australian Perspecta* in 1981. By the 1980s, the works of Indigenous masters became the central focus of the contemporary art world.

Art historian Ian McLean places great importance on the interaction in this period between Indigenous artists and New Wave artists such as Joseph Kosuth and Marina Abramović. He argues that this contact provided the stimulus for the New Wave generation of artists to move beyond their critique of modernism to a critique of culture. They saw in Indigenous art 'the limits' of their own, Western culture, which enabled a new form of expression. 'In the 1980s Papunya Tula painting revealed to the art world something about itself that had not yet been brought into focus by Western contemporary art,' writes McLean. In a sense, he suggests, 'Aborigines invented the idea of contemporary art.'[82]

Wandjuk Marika, co-founder and later chairman of the Aboriginal Arts Board, celebrated the growing recognition of Indigenous art as fine art:

> Our art is being seen by more and more people. No longer is it hidden in museums, seen only by such people as curators and anthropologists. It is now attracting the interest and attention of the layman, the gallery owner and the collector; and people are learning to appreciate the artistry of my people.[83]

Marika hoped, together with Edwards, that the new, intense interest in Aboriginal art would lead to a more substantial engagement with all aspects of Indigenous history and culture. He urged his fellow Australians 'to learn more about the stories that our paintings recount, to listen to our songs and music, so that gradually there will grow up between us a bond of understanding and respect, to replace the distrust and fear of previous generations'.[84] The development of rock art research, alongside the growth of the contemporary Aboriginal art movement, has allowed a deeper appreciation of the millions of paintings and engravings that mark this country, as well as offering insights into the social worlds of the old masters who created them.

'YOU HAVE ENTERED ABORIGINAL LAND'

The Franklin River Campaign and the Fight for Kutikina

The Franklin River rises in the central highlands of Tasmania and descends into the most remote parts of the south-west rainforest. Its dark, tannin-stained waters, shrouded in mist, course through narrow, winding gorges, rushing over rapids and eddying at confluences and river bends. In 1981 most archaeologists shared the general view that south-west Tasmania was 'a true wilderness': 'the only part of the Australian continent never to be inhabited by Aborigines'.[1] What little archaeology had been uncovered in the region, such as the 'Beginner's Luck' site in the Florentine Valley, suggested that human occupation had been restricted to the margins of the rainforest. The dense heart of south-west Tasmania seemed to be too wild, too remote to have been touched by humankind. 'I thought at that time,' Rhys Jones mused, 'that the canoe journey down the Gordon River in 1958 by Olegas Truchanas was the first crossing of that country from east to west by any human.'[2]

Truchanas, a wilderness photographer and conservationist, had done much to promote this modern view of a 'true wilderness'.[3] Having endured the Russian and the Nazi occupations of Lithuania during World War II, he migrated to Tasmania in 1949 and threw himself into the depths of south-west Tasmania, climbing isolated peaks, rafting

alone along the tumultuous rivers and camping beside the distinctive pink beaches of Lake Pedder.[4] He found peace in photographing
this grand, mysterious landscape, devoid of people. Truchanas' photos
were both a celebration of the natural world and the expression of an
idea: that people could live alongside and protect such a landscape. He
believed that the continued 'wildness' of south-west Tasmania revealed
the best of humankind. It was as much a reflection of humanity as the
horrors of wartime Eastern Europe.

When this vision came under threat in the 1960s with the state
government's plans to dam Lake Pedder, Truchanas led the campaign
against the proposed hydro-electric development. He toured the town
halls of Tasmania broadcasting the landscapes fated to be flooded, pair-
ing his photography with soaring classical music to evoke the subtle
beauty of the remote glacial lake ringed by jagged mountains.[5] These
powerful audio-visual displays instilled outrage and despair in his audiences; their strong reactions reflected the rising ecological consciousness
that was emerging in many places in Australia and around the world
in the 1960s. But despite vigorous protest, the dam went ahead. In July
1972 the Serpentine and Huon rivers were dammed and Lake Pedder
disappeared under steadily rising waters. Truchanas did not live to see
the glacial lake transformed into a hydro-electric impoundment. On
6 January 1972, while hauling his canoe over rapids on the Gordon River,
Truchanas slipped and was sucked into fast-flowing waters.[6]

His body was found three days later by his young protégé, Latvian-
born photographer Peter Dombrovskis. The lives of these two Baltic
photographers were eerily entwined, and both were bound to the idea
of wilderness. Dombrovskis migrated to Tasmania in 1950 at the age of
five. He met Truchanas as a teenager and 'to some extent became his
disciple', hiking and rafting deep into south-west Tasmania and learning
the craft of photography.[7] He, too, used his images to campaign against
the threat of hydro-electric development in the region. And, in a tragic

twist of fate, he also died young in the remote reaches of the landscape he loved, suffering a heart attack on 28 March 1996 while hiking alone near Mount Hayes in the Western Arthurs mountain range. He was found several days later, on his knees, in a remote alpine herbfield. The rucksack on his back, full of camera equipment, had propped up his body in a position of prayer.[8]

These two figures provided the visual underpinnings of the early conservation movement in Tasmania, which developed alongside the first political 'green movement' in the world.[9] Truchanas' influence grew with the posthumous publication of a collection of his photographs in 1975, while Dombrovskis continued to work in the region, picking up where his mentor had left off. His most famous image, 'Morning Mist, Rock Island Bend, Franklin River', was printed in the daily newspapers during the 1983 federal election as a full-page advertisement, under the words: 'Could you vote for a party that would destroy this?' The fact that a remote corner of Australia had become the centre of a national debate reflects what was at stake in the campaigns against hydro-electric development. For many, such as novelist James McQueen, the Franklin was 'not just a river': 'It is the epitome of all the lost forests, all the submerged lakes, all the tamed rivers, all the extinguished species.'[10] As Kevin Kiernan, the first director of the Tasmanian Wilderness Society, wrote in 1976: 'We have to try to sell not the wilderness experience – that is, wilderness as a recreational resource – but the right of wilderness to exist.'[11] 'It is a wild and wondrous thing,' Bob Brown wrote of the Franklin River in May 1978, 'and 175 years after Tasmania's first European settlement, the Franklin remains much as it was before man – black or white – came to its precincts.'[12]

On 1 July 1983, in a dramatic four–three decision, the High Court of Australia ruled to stop the damming of the Franklin River. It brought to an end the protracted campaign, which had helped bring down two state premiers and a prime minister, as well as overseeing the rise of a new figure on the political landscape – the future founder of the Australian Greens, Bob Brown. But it was not only the idea of 'wilderness' – of an ancient, pure, timeless landscape – that saved the Franklin. As two of the judges noted in the immediate aftermath of the case, the archaeological research that took place in the heat of the campaign was at the heart of the High Court decision.[13] It was the revelation that far from being untouched and pristine, south-west Tasmania had a deep human history. What was undoubtedly a natural wonder was also a cultural landscape.[14]

'The battle for the Franklin,' writes historian Frank Bongiorno, 'remains the single greatest environmental struggle in Australian history. It signalled for white Australians a new way of relating to place, a love of country that amounted to something more complex – and attractive – than classical nationalism's appeal to "blood and soil".'[15] But the cultural revelation at the centre of the struggle, which played such a significant role behind the scenes, only figured on the margins of the mainstream campaign. In the early 1980s Australians were still grappling with the implications of having an ancient Indigenous past. The debates the campaign triggered about history and cultural politics, in the public sphere and within the field of Australian archaeology, anticipated the national introspection that accompanied the Bicentenary in 1988.

Nevertheless, the Franklin River campaign thrust archaeology into the centre of national debate in a way that has not been seen before or since. The words of archaeologists were splashed across the front page of newspapers, incremental discoveries made the lead item on nightly radio and television news, and individuals such as John Mulvaney and Rhys Jones argued for cultural heritage in Senate submissions, public lectures and from the back of a truck at rallies outside Parliament House. The campaign was the first time that new heritage legislation, which had accumulated in every state over the preceding two decades, was put to the test in the public arena. It was a symbolic moment in the gradual shift away from the era of university-led research and towards the model of cultural heritage management that dominates Australian archaeology today. But at its heart, the campaign was about the value placed on heritage, both natural and cultural, and who should decide its fate. As Isabel McBryde asked in a landmark symposium in the wake of the campaign: 'Who owns the past?'

* * *

Heritage, as an idea, has been present in Australia since the 1870s, but it re-emerged in the 1960s and '70s alongside the new concern for wilderness.[16] It was a time when Australia was casting around for national symbols, searching for a reservoir of images and stories that would help ease the cultural anxieties that were growing in the new post-imperial world. Britain's retreat into the European Economic Community and its withdrawal of residual military forces east of Suez had symbolically severed familial ties between the two nations and catapulted Australia into a crisis of national identity. The naming of Australia's new decimal currency in 1963 (from the pound to the dollar), the removal of the words 'British Subject' from the cover of Australian passports in 1967, the demise of Empire Day and the upgrading of Australia Day all revealed a consensus within Australia about the need to forge a new national image.[17] But how would Australia define itself without the old certainties of the British world? Native flora and fauna were eagerly seized upon as a match for the cultural grandeur of empire. Areas of wilderness – so rare and foreign to Europeans – were reappraised as sources of national identity, as were distinctive elements of Australian history, including, in a tokenistic manner, Aboriginal heritage. The boomerang joined the koala in the jumbled expressions of 'new nationalism'. And with recognition of worth came responsibility. As zoologist Jock Marshall declared in 1966, 'Our national heritage, be it the Platypus, an old pub or a colonial document, is ours for the skinning, the bulldozing, the burning – or the keeping.'[18]

Between 1965 and 1975 legislation designed to protect Aboriginal sites was passed in every Australian state. The acts were the result of long-term agitation by archaeologists and conservationists, alongside growing public interest in Australia's natural and cultural heritage. Frederick McCarthy and Elsie Brammel of the Australian Museum were early champions of Aboriginal heritage, and in 1938 McCarthy wrote of the 'vital need for legislation for the preservation of prehistoric and aboriginal relics'.[19] They were concerned about the casual vandalism being inflicted upon Aboriginal sites and called for them to be declared 'national monuments' in recognition of their natural and scientific importance. John Mulvaney and Isabel McBryde added their voices to this campaign in the late 1950s and early 1960s, condemning the looting of Aboriginal sites and the destructive culture of collecting. Together, with the likes of McCarthy, Bob Edwards, Laila Haglund and Warwick Dix, they were instrumental in establishing the foundational heritage legislation in every state and territory. Denis Byrne reflects on the intellectual transformation that underwrote these changes: 'While earlier campaigners had argued that Aboriginal sites were the scientifically valuable property of the nation, from the 1960s archaeologists argued that they were the heritage of the nation.'[20]

The establishment in the mid-1960s of the Australian Council of National Trusts and the Australian Conservation Foundation reflected the parallel movement towards the preservation of natural heritage. The Whitlam government brought the two strands of natural and cultural heritage together when it ratified the UNESCO World Heritage Convention in August 1974 and passed the *Australian Heritage Commission Act* the following year, which set up a register of all heritage places in Australia, as well as structures and procedures to facilitate their promotion and protection.[21] But it was not until the Franklin River campaign in the early 1980s that the values and effectiveness of this new heritage legislation were tested on a grand scale.

What worldview did this legislation empower? For whom were the sites protected and why? McBryde was mindful of George Orwell's adage, 'Who controls the past controls the future; who controls the present controls the past.'[22] 'In legislation,' she reflected in 1983, 'there is a consistent assumption: the past in all its physical and elusive forms belongs to all Australians. At a World Heritage level, it belongs to the humans across the globe.'[23] By advocating for the preservation of Indigenous cultural sites and materials, archaeologists and other heritage practitioners across the world had positioned themselves as stewards of this knowledge. They had the power to legitimise – and delegitimise – heritage places and objects, and fight for their protection from within the law. But as Laurajane Smith has explored, the development of these new regulatory processes also coincided with the emergence of increasingly assertive Indigenous groups, who had a much larger stake in how their cultural heritage was managed and understood.[24] The 'balance of power' was rapidly changing, archaeologist Sharon Sullivan observed in 1983: 'Aborigines are moving from a position of abject powerlessness in the community to a position where they feel the power and the ability to express their concern about their own heritage.'[25]

This shift in power, and the contest for knowledge it represents, is encapsulated in the fight to save the archaeological site at the centre of the Franklin River campaign, which for a time was known by two names: Fraser Cave and Kutikina. It is an example of a place that became, in Sullivan's words, 'a sacred site in two cultures: sacred to archaeologists who have a cultural belief in the importance of knowledge; sacred to Aborigines who believe that the strange rituals which archaeologists perform at the site constitute desecration'.[26] To the resurgent Tasmanian Aboriginal community, the site represented their long occupation of the island, and a symbol around which they could forge new meanings about their cultural identity.[27] To archaeologists, it gave an enthralling insight into an ancient world and opened a new chapter in a global story.

* * *

Kevin Kiernan was the first to rediscover Kutikina. He and Greg Middleton came across it on 13 January 1977 as part of a systematic survey of the lower and middle Gordon and Franklin rivers by the Sydney Speleological Society. Kiernan knew the country well: he had been with Olegas Truchanas when he had disappeared into the Gordon River in 1972. Since 1974 he had returned annually with members of the speleological society and local cavers to explore caverns, nooks and crannies in the river gorges. By 1979 these cavers – or speleologists – had described over 100 caves in the region. 'The whole campaign to find caves on the Franklin was entirely politically motivated,' Kiernan later commented. 'The intention was to try and find something . . . maybe a big whiz-bang cave . . . that would help the campaign.'[28] They were acutely aware that the Hydro-Electric Commission (HEC) was considering this landscape for a new dam. But they were looking for a natural wonder: even when confronted with evidence of human occupation they did not immediately recognise its archaeological significance. As part of their attempt to raise awareness of this threatened landscape, they started a tradition of naming rock features 'after the political figures who would decide their fate'.[29] Fraser Cave was thus named after the sitting prime minister, Malcolm Fraser. There was also a Bingham Arch, named after the leader of the state Opposition Max Bingham, a Lowe Cave, named after Tasmanian Premier Doug Lowe, as well as a Whitlam Cave and, after Bill Hayden became leader of the federal Opposition in 1977, a Hayden Cave. When the Tasmanian Nomenclature Board caught wind of this tradition, they accused the members of the Sydney Speleological Society of 'gross impertinence' for naming caves outside their home state. In mid-1982, at the suggestion of the Tasmanian Aboriginal Centre, Fraser

Cave became Kutikina, which means 'spirit' in the oral tradition developed by the dispossessed Tasmanian community on Babel Island in Bass Strait.[30]

A few months after the discovery of Kutikina, in May 1977, the HEC confirmed the rumours and formally proposed a new dam on the Gordon River below its junction with the Franklin River. The HEC was a monolith. As the largest employer in the state it held immense political power. In October 1979 it released the details of the dam project in a nine-volume, $770,300 environmental study of the region, which contained only six sentences on its Aboriginal history. Without conducting any surveys or seeking any contributions from qualified archaeological personnel, its authors concluded: 'There are no known archaeological sites in the project area.'[31] In a particularly misleading use of published information, the authors supported this conclusion with a map drawn from Rhys Jones' 1974 ethnographic survey of Aboriginal Tasmania, in which he had marked the inland mountainous region of south-west Tasmania, including the proposed dam site, as 'unoccupied' between 1802 and 1834. Jones was furious: 'What happened in 1800 or any other arbitrary date is not necessarily what was the case during the prehistoric past.'[32] When Mulvaney read the report in 1981 he was 'disturbed by the cavalier treatment received by cultural heritage in this massive report'.[33]

The archaeological community reacted quickly to the proposed dam, passing a resolution on 25 May 1980 urging the Hydro-Electric Commission to undertake archaeological surveys in the region.[34] AAA president Sandra Bowdler sent word of the resolution to the premier of Tasmania, Doug Lowe, who drew it to the attention of the minister for National Parks and Wildlife, Andrew Lohrey.[35] As a result, two archaeologists, Don Ranson and Rhys Jones, joined the next expedition of cavers up the Franklin River in January 1981.

There was a great sense of drama exploring the wild reaches of the Franklin River. 'It is a mighty stream flowing swiftly in a full river trench,' Jones wrote excitedly in his diary on 8 January 1981. 'It has the greatest flow of any Tasmanian river & must be one of the greatest in Australia.' They passed the site of the proposed dam on their way up the gorge and camped at night in the dense rainforest.[36] Their excavations began in a small limestone cave near Nicholls Range, where they found some flakes but no 'unequivocal evidence for human occupation'. The main discovery on this preliminary expedition came on 11 January 1981, when Ranson, Jones and Barry Blain spotted a tree that had fallen near the confluence of the Denison and Gordon rivers, exposing a clean section of silt on the riverbank. On closer inspection, they found stone tools and charcoal embedded in the earth. Jones even identified a 'conjoin' – a single artefact split in two – suggesting that the riverbank had once been used as a chipping floor and 'a good camp site ... with a commanding view'.[37] It was the first discovery of Aboriginal occupation in the inland south-west rivers region. Intriguingly, the radiocarbon dates of 250–450 years ago showed that the thick rainforest had not been as impenetrable as previously thought.

A few weeks later, Kiernan returned to the lower reaches of the Franklin River with the director of the Tasmanian Wilderness Society, Bob Brown, and its secretary, Bob Burton.[38] Brown was hoping to find the bones of a convict who might have perished in the region after escaping the Macquarie Harbour Penal Station: the story conjured the wildness of the country and would help bring publicity to the campaign against the dam. On 10 February Kiernan returned to Fraser Cave, which he remembered containing a substantial 'bone deposit'. When he climbed into the entrance chamber, he was amazed by the extent of the deposit. There were no convict bones, but: 'Suddenly I found a stone tool in my hand, then another, then the charcoal of an ancient hearth. Whose hand had last held these tools?'[39] The 'two Bobs' joined him in the cave and together they surveyed the artefacts, which were scattered over an area of about 100 square metres, and collected some

charcoal and pollen samples 'and a few surface flakes to convince perhaps armchair ridden bureaucrats back in the city'.[40] Brown was swept
up by the romanticism of the Aboriginal story they had stumbled upon:

> I thought I heard a child laugh in the distance. For a moment I saw
> a group of black people come through the entrance: but it was just
> the play of sun and shadow from the trees outside. It seemed impos-
> sible that centuries had passed since these people left this home. I
> imagined meeting them and learning from them. But they were
> gone, never to return.[41]

Don Ranson, an archaeologist at the Tasmanian National Parks
and Wildlife Service, confirmed that the stones had been worked by
human hands. He dubbed the find 'the Tutankhamen of Tasmanian
cave archaeology'.[42] The news made the front page of the local papers
and was covered by the mainland press, but it was also greeted with
scepticism and cynicism. The hydro-electricity group HEAT criticised
the announcement as a political stunt, while others, such as the chairman of the Tasmanian Legislative Council Select Committee on Power
Development, intimated that the find was too convenient to be believed.
'His tactic of suggesting some people were claiming it a fake was wholly
successful in initiating such claims,' wrote Kiernan, 'although he was
careful to dissociate himself from any such nasty suggestions.'[43]

Three weeks later, a team of archaeologists, cavers and National
Parks officers rafted down the Franklin to investigate the cave. It was
already dark on 9 March 1981 when they tied their boats to the riverbank. They had a deep chill after hours navigating the fast-flowing river,
hauling their aluminium punt and rubber dinghy over successive rapids, journeying deeper into the dense rainforest. The rain picked up
again as they unloaded their gear and stumbled through the thick, wet
scrub to the limestone outcrop perched above the river. 'I had closed
my mind to everything,' Jones later reflected. 'I was just following the

person in front and trying to avoid these wet branches hitting me in the face.'[44] They took shelter in the mouth of the cave, which opened 'like a huge, curved shell'. Some of the team started a small, smoky fire to cook their dinner, while the others, with the light of their torches, ventured further into the cavern. The cave opened out 'like an aircraft hangar' and extended for almost 200 metres into the cliff. But it was not its scale that excited them: it was the idea that this remote cave, buried in thick 'horizontal' rainforest at the southernmost corner of the continent, could have once been home to a thriving human population. As Jones wrote in his journal that night: 'We could see seas of flakes & bones & charcoal in situ.'[45] Too tired to erect their tents, they unrolled their sleeping mats on the disturbed floor at the cave entrance. It later occurred to them that they were probably the first people to sleep there in around 15,000 years.

Over the next two days, as rain poured outside the cave, the team carefully investigated its contents. Greg Middleton mapped the extent of the cavern, Steve Harris documented the surrounding vegetation and Barry Blain searched for a clearing that could be used as a helicopter landing site. The archaeologists, Jones and Don Ranson, surveyed the stone tools and charred animal bones scattered across the surface, and chose a place to open a small trench where the black sediment was covered by a thin layer of soft stalagmite. The stratigraphy was intriguing: a complex of overlapping layers of charcoal, burnt clay, ochre, fragments of charred animal bone, stone tools and occasional 'sterile' layers: sediment without evidence of occupation. They sieved the buckets coming out of the excavation in the river below, watching as the loamy soil 'melted' in the water, 'revealing glistening stone tools of handsome quality, along with huge amounts of broken bone'.[46] By early afternoon the wet-sievers had already filled several plastic bags with artefacts. The test pit only extended to a depth of 1.2 metres before meeting bedrock, but it yielded an extraordinary 75,000 artefacts and 250,000 animal bone fragments, which were counted, analysed and written up very quickly due to the intense political imperatives. The small test pit represented about 1 per cent of the archaeology in the cave, making Kutikina one of the richest sites in Australia. 'In terms of the number of stone tools,' Jones remarked to one journalist, 'much, much richer than Mungo.'[47]

The Kutikina archaeological remains told a remarkable story. The stone tools appeared to be a regional variant of the 'Australian Core Tool and Scraper Tradition', found across the mainland during the Pleistocene, suggesting immense chains of cultural connection before the creation of Bass Strait. Some tools had been knapped out of a material called Darwin glass, from a crater a few days' walk north-west where an ancient meteorite impact had melted the surface rock into a fine natural glass. The bone fragments were also curious. Most had been charred or smashed to extract marrow, and almost all (95 per cent) were wallaby bones, suggesting a finely targeted hunting strategy.[48] But most surprisingly, underneath the upper layer of hearths there were angular fragments of limestone that appeared to have shattered and fallen from the cave roof at a time of extreme cold, forming rubble on the floor. It was one of the main pieces of evidence that led Jones to speculate in his diary: 'Is this the late glacial technology? Are we at say 13k – 15k BP [Before Present]?'[49] Kiernan asked similar questions in his notes as he investigated the limestone cave system: 'The gravels overlying bedrock do represent some sort of higher energy stream environment. Might they be late Last Glacial?'[50]

The possibility of Ice Age dates conjured the image of a dramatically different world. Pollen records in the region revealed that what is now rainforest was once an alpine herbfield like the tundra found in Alaska, northern Russia and northern Canada.[51] At the height of the Last Glacial Maximum the mighty trees of ancient Gondwanaland had retreated to the river gorges, where they were irrigated and sheltered from fire, while wallabies and wombats roamed the high, open plains. The cold blast of

Antarctica, only 1000 kilometres to the south, had dropped temperatures by around 6.5 degrees Celsius.[52] A 65-square-kilometre ice cap presided over the central Tasmanian plateau, feeding a 12-kilometre-long glacier that gripped the upper Franklin valley. Icebergs floated off the Tasmanian coast. After voyaging to Antarctica in 1986, Jones compared the conditions in south-west Tasmania at the Last Glacial Maxiumum to those in Heard Island today.[53]

When the carbon dates came back in December 1981, they confirmed that the cave had been occupied 20,000 years ago. 'I have spent eighteen years looking for archaeological sites in Australia,' Jones declared on his return. 'This is the site I have been looking for.'[54] At the height of the last Ice Age, Kutikina was home to the southernmost humans on earth. In southern Patagonia, the oldest sites of human occupation cluster around 13,000 years ago; in New Zealand, the first voyagers arrived on the southern shores around 1000 years ago; but in south-west Tasmania, 20,000 years ago, people hunted red-necked wallabies on the broad open slopes of Franklin valley, they collected fine stone from glacial melt water gravels and knapped them into tools, and they sheltered in the mouths of deep, limestone caverns, warming themselves beside crackling camp fires. 'They alone,' Jones reflected, 'may have experienced the high latitude, glacier-edge conditions of a southern Ice Age.'[55]

Jones was immediately taken by the similarities between the archaeology in the caves of south-west Tasmania and the celebrated Ice Age sites of the Dordogne. He found similarities between the shape and size of the stone tools, the form of the hearths and the deposit, and the narrowly targeted hunting patterns. Ochre pigment in the deposit even raised the possibility that the walls of Kutikina might once have borne art, like the limestone caverns of southern France. 'Although the sites are nearly twenty thousand kilometres apart, the fundamental thing you can say about them is how similar was the experience of their inhabitants.'[56]

Around 15,000 years ago, the climate warmed, the glaciers began to melt, and, in Europe, the ice retreated to expose ploughed and enriched fertile soils, which became the stage for the human dramas of the agricultural and industrial revolutions. In Tasmania, the rainforest re-emerged from the gorges to invade the slopes above and people seem to have retreated to the region's more hospitable margins. The Bassian Plain became a strait and a thin stalagmite formed over the old hearths upon which they once lived.[57] These 'two paths', Jones mused, so closely aligned during the Ice Age, 'came together again only a hundred and fifty years ago with saddening effects for the descendants of these early men from the Franklin and Gordon Rivers'.[58] When Tasmanian Aboriginal leader Michael Mansell visited Kutikina for the first time in 1982, he described the experience as 'like coming home'.[59]

A political reporter, Hendrik Gout, made a brief documentary of the test excavation and by the time the team returned to Strahan the news of their finds had already been broadcast nationally on television and radio. 'Again the cameras whirled and the presses pressed,' recalled Kiernan.[60] The state Labor government incorporated the new finds into their plans for the region and, on 30 April 1981, Premier Doug Lowe proclaimed the Franklin-Lower Gordon Wild Rivers National Park. He also gained the support of Malcolm Fraser to nominate the region for World Heritage listing on the basis of its natural and cultural values. Nevertheless, these measures were seen by many as largely tokenistic: the Lake Pedder dam had gone ahead in 1972, despite having been designated a national park eighteen years earlier.[61]

Lowe was lukewarm about the HEC's proposal to dam the Franklin, but he was also hesitant to pick a public fight with the largest employer in the state. As a compromise, he suggested a different, less destructive hydro-electricity plan: the Gordon-above-Olga dam, as opposed to the Gordon-below-Franklin. The public would have the chance to decide between the two dams at a referendum called for 12 December 1981.

The compromise made Lowe few friends. The HEC, the Tasmanian Wilderness Society and his own party all opposed it. When he tried to add a 'no dams' option to the ballot, a party coup on 11 November replaced him with Harry Holgate, ensuring that both major parties were in favour of flooding the Franklin.[62]

In the 1981 referendum, 47 per cent of the electorate voted in favour of the Gordon-below-Franklin dam, seemingly sealing the fate of Kutikina. But, remarkably, there was also a 45 per cent informal vote. Tens of thousands of voters had scrawled 'no dams' on their ballot papers.[63] The unprecedented 'write-in' had been organised by the Tasmanian Wilderness Society, led by the tall, plain-speaking medical doctor Bob Brown. Buoyed by the success of the campaign, Brown sought to repeat the result nationally, organising volunteers to protest the dam at local, state and federal elections throughout 1982. In March 1982, 12 per cent of voters wrote 'no dams' on their ballot papers in the federal by-election of Lowe in New South Wales; in June, 40 per cent of voters cast 'no dams' ballots in the ACT House of Assembly election; and in December, 41 per cent of voters registered a 'no dams' protest on their ballots at the federal by-election of Flinders in Victoria. As a sign of the political potency of the issue, Liberal MP Peter Reith won the Flinders by-election by cultivating the 'no dams' vote, and was then voted out at the general election three months later after failing to intervene in the Franklin Dam dispute.[64]

At a state level, the Franklin controversy continued to dog the Labor government. Lowe resigned from the Australian Labor Party, depriving Holgate of his majority and forcing him to an early election in May 1982, which he then lost to Liberal Robin Gray. The new premier immediately passed a bill to proceed with the construction of the dam and (unsuccessfully) called on Fraser to withdraw the pending nomination for World Heritage listing. 'For eleven months of the year,' Gray famously declared, 'the Franklin River is nothing but a brown ditch, leech-ridden, unattractive to the majority of people. You've got to be superbly fit or mentally ill to go rafting down there at any time of the year.'[65] In late July 1982, work on the dam began.

The federal leader of the Australian Democrats, Don Chipp, recognised the mood of the electorate against the dam and in late 1981 initiated an inquiry into 'the federal responsibility in assisting Tasmania to preserve its wilderness areas of national and international importance'.[66] The Tasmanian Aboriginal Centre, Jones, Mulvaney, and the executive of the AAA were amongst the many to make submissions to the new Senate Select Committee on South-West Tasmania. The Tasmanian Aboriginal Centre drew upon the archaeological research in their submission, highlighting especially the comparisons with the Dordogne region of France as a sign of the cave's 'great historical importance'. But they also made a more personal plea: the Franklin River caves 'form part of us – we are of them and they of us. Their destruction represents a part destruction of us.'[67]

In response to these submissions, several members of the Senate Select Committee flew into the Franklin valley on 3 March 1982 to see the ongoing archaeological work for themselves. After the success of the two 1981 expeditions, a larger team had returned to see if there were other sites like Kutikina in the Franklin valley. They found several new sites, including Deena Reena, all of which would be destroyed by the new dam.[68] The chairman of the Senate Select Committee, Liberal senator Brian Archer, was impressed by the work and took detailed notes.

Mulvaney himself visited the site three days later as acting chairman of the Australian Heritage Commission. 'It resembled the set of a horror movie,' he later wrote. 'The floor was littered with bone and stone fragments.'[69] Since he had first read the HEC report on the area in October 1981, he had been vocal in his opposition to the dam. One of the proposals being promoted by state government representatives was to 'salvage' the Franklin sites by impregnating the earth with resin and removing the cave floors completely. It was this suggestion that drove

Mulvaney to commit to the campaign 'boots and all'.[70] When the minister for Home Affairs and Environment, Tom McVeigh, advocated this 'salvage' option in December 1982, Mulvaney resigned in protest from his position on the Interim Council of the National Museum, which was within McVeigh's portfolio. AAA president Ron Lampert wrote a telegram to Fraser, Hayden and Chipp as a measure of support: 'We completely endorse Professor Mulvaney's stand on this issue STOP Cabinet's scheme to preserve caves is utter nonsense and its claim that bulk removal of deposit will preserve heritage is willfully misleading STOP We regard this decision as cowardly and irresponsible.'[71] It was a rare example of the AAA taking an overtly political stance.

Chief HEC geologist SJ Paterson took to the pages of *Nature* and *Quaternary Australasia* in 1983–1984 to accuse the archaeological profession of subordinating science to the promotion of a cause.[72] On the basis of his own, two-week search for archaeological cave sites in the wider region (without a qualified archaeologist), Paterson had concluded that the Franklin valley archaeological sites were neither exceptional nor significant: 'Clearly the Franklin Caves are not unique and the statements made by Prof. Mulvaney, Dr. Jones and Dr. Allen are not scientifically objective.' Moreover, he argued that the obstruction of development under the guise of World Heritage was 'an abomination', especially considering 'the Franklin Caves contain the discards of hunter-gatherers' rather than 'priceless Palaeolithic cave art similar to the Lascaux Cave of the Dordogne'.[73]

In Mulvaney's fiery response he explained that the value of the Tasmanian evidence was that it directly challenged this archaic and 'Europocentric version of prehistory'.[74] As for criticisms about the politicisation of archaeology, 'There are political aspects, but if this area is destroyed, and the scientific world just lets it happen passively because it's not their point to make political interventions, I think they're just abnegating moral duty.'[75]

There were many archaeologists active in the fight to save Kutikina, behind the scenes and on the blockade, but Jones became the other public face of the campaign, communicating the finds to the Senate Select Committee and giving interviews and public talks around the country, including a lecture to the Canberra Archaeological Society titled 'Cavers of the Lost Karst', a nod to the recent release of the first Indiana Jones film. On 4 September 1982 he and Mulvaney arranged for a full-page advertisement to appear in the *Australian*, signed by twenty-five prominent international scholars, with the headline: 'Do people overseas care more about preserving Australia's treasures than our own government?'

Their advocacy had a profound influence. When the Senate Select Committee presented its report, *Future Demand and Supply of Electricity for Tasmania and Other Matters*, on 24 November 1982, archaeology dominated the 'other matters'. The 'expert witnesses' had persuaded them of the international significance of the finds. 'Apart from any other reasons for preserving the area,' they concluded, 'the caves are of such importance that the Franklin River be not inundated.'[76] The next day in the Senate, Susan Ryan singled out Rhys Jones' 'compelling evidence':

> Dr Jones makes it very clear to all of us what our collective responsibility to protect the region really amounts to. We are not talking about an area of parochial interest, we are not talking about a States rights matter, we are not indeed even talking about a national issue; we are talking about an area which is part of the cultural heritage of mankind, as Dr Rhys Jones has so clearly stated ... Of course this means the dam must not be built.[77]

Prime Minister Fraser heeded the conclusions of the report. He did not want the Franklin dam built and was tired of receiving thousands of letters about the affair. Although as a farmer he thought of land 'with economic overtones', his actions in office had earned him the label of 'closet greenie'.[78] He had opposed the inundation of Lake Pedder, stopped sandmining on Fraser Island, banned whaling in Australian waters and prevented the Great Barrier Reef from being drilled for oil – often in the face of great internal criticism. But he was reluctant to intervene in the Franklin River campaign, despite the recommendations of the Senate Select Committee. His hesitancy hinged on a curious point of principle. He considered the decision to be a state matter, and he was eager to uphold what he regarded as one of the main checks of power: the clear divide between states' rights and the federal government. 'If Fraser had not believed this,' Margaret Simons wrote with Fraser in his memoirs, 'he could hardly have advocated the right of the Senate [the states' house] to block supply and bring down Whitlam.'[79] To intervene and stop the dam would be to renege on the principle that had brought him to power. As a compromise, he sought to resolve the issue by offering Tasmania $500 million to fund an alternative electricity scheme. 'The offer is on the table,' he wrote to Gray on 19 January 1983. 'It is for the Tasmanian government to take it up or decline as it sees fit.'[80] Gray did not believe the offer was serious and rejected the money within an hour of hearing of it. Construction on the dam continued.

By that stage the Franklin blockade was already in full swing. On 14 December 1982, the same day the region was formally listed as a World Heritage site for its natural and cultural values, a chain of rubber rafts blocked the main landing sites, protestors occupied the dam site and rallies were held in cities across Australia.[81] According to Jones, when the archaeological team returned in February 1983 the strong police presence and helicopters constantly whirring overhead made the Tasmanian Wilderness Society's camp at Verandah Cliff feel 'like an eco-Viet Nam'.[82] On 24 February they watched police 'evict' protestors from public land: 'a monstrous abuse of powers'.[83] By autumn 1983, 1272 protestors had been arrested, and nearly 450 had done time in Hobart's Risdon Prison, including Tasmanian Aboriginal leaders Michael Mansell and Rosalind Langford, who were charged with trespass on their return from visiting Kutikina and remanded without the offer of bail.[84] On 16 December Bob Brown was also charged with trespass and held in Risdon Prison into the new year. While incarcerated, he received the *Australian*'s nomination for Australian of the Year for displaying 'qualities of sincerity, courage and determination in fighting for what he believes is right'. When he finally signed the bail conditions on 4 January, Brown walked out of the courthouse and into a seat in state parliament, where he continued to campaign against the dam. A week after his release, while walking home in Strahan, he was assaulted by four men, one wielding a wheel brace.[85] It was a violent example of the ways in which the dam dispute divided Tasmanian society and of the heated passions that swirled and eddied around the Franklin River blockade.

While the blockade continued, and with a federal election just around the corner, the ALP made a snap change in its leadership on 3 February 1983. It replaced Bill Hayden, who had voted against Labor's policy to stop the dam at the party's national conference, with the rising, ambitious Bob Hawke, who had voted for it. And in a tumultuous few hours of Australian political history, Fraser called an early election on the same day. 'Fraser had gambled on Labor being unable to effect a clean change of leadership,' wrote Anne Summers in her dissection of the event. 'Labor had gambled by replacing a leader with Ministerial experience with a man who had been in the Parliament a little over two years.'[86] Hawke recognised the symbolism of the Franklin River dispute and harnessed its momentum to make the dam a defining issue in the election campaign.[87] The day after the election was called, on 4 February 1983, 20,000 people rallied at Franklin Square in Hobart, where Langford led the crowd in a chant of 'Land rights to save the sites'.[88]

Neither Fraser nor Hawke believed it was the dispute over the Franklin River dam that decided the 5 March 1983 election, instead citing broader concerns with the economy. But there is a strong case that it swung the result in Hawke's favour. The Wilderness Society placed

3000 volunteers at Save the Franklin polling booths in marginal seats around the country and arranged the widespread publication of Peter Dombrovskis' iconic image of Rock Island Bend.[89] The outgoing deputy prime minister, Doug Anthony, was adamant: 'There is no doubt that the dam was the issue that lost the government the election.'[90] In Tasmania, as a backlash for his 'interventionist' approach to the dam, there was a 4.5 per cent swing against Hawke. But the overall national swing towards Hawke was 4 per cent, which gave him control of the House of Representatives and shared power in the Senate with the Australian Democrats. In his victory speech, just after midnight on 6 March 1983, Hawke declared: 'The dam will not go ahead.'

On 31 March the Hawke government passed regulations under the *National Parks and Wildlife Conservation Act* preventing further construction on the Franklin dam. Premier Gray took the matter to the High Court, challenging the constitutionality of Hawke's 'interventionist' legislation and setting in motion the landmark case 'Commonwealth v. Tasmania'. The legal challenge included claims from counsel that Kutikina could not be of special significance to Aboriginal people because the Tasmanian race was extinct.[91] In response, the members of the Tasmanian Aboriginal Centre signed angry affidavits affirming their cultural identity, while in Canberra, Jones and Mulvaney were called in as archaeological advisors on the case.

On 1 July 1983, by the narrowest of margins, the High Court found in Hawke's favour. The judges in the majority considered that the commonwealth had a clear obligation to use its External Affairs power to stop the proposed dam, as the inundation of 'the Franklin River, including Kutikina Cave and Deena Reena Cave', would breach the *World Heritage Properties Conservation Act* and damage Australia's international standing. They also invoked the commonwealth power to make laws with respect to Aboriginal people. Justice Lionel Murphy stated:

The history of the Aboriginal people of Australia since European settlement is that they have been the subject of unprovoked aggression, conquest, pillage, rape, brutalisation, attempted genocide and systematic and unsystematic deconstruction of their culture. Parliament was entitled to act ... to preserve the material evidence of the history and culture of the Tasmanian Aboriginals.[92]

Although the case is publicly seen as a green victory, behind the scenes it was the Aboriginal story that pushed the decision over the line. The archaeological evidence featured in every report about the judgement, and privately Malcolm Fraser considered it to be the deciding factor.[93]

Within days of the ruling, barges laden with trucks and bulldozers withdrew from the area to Strahan. After over seven years of agitation, the Franklin River campaign had finally come to an end. For the archaeological profession, however, the political ramifications had only just begun.

* * *

During the campaign, archaeologists, conservationists and Tasmanian Aboriginal people converged occasionally at the Tasmanian Wilderness Society's camp at Verandah Cliff. The archaeologists and speleologists shared information with the 'greenies' about how to navigate the region, and protestors such as JE Downie showed the archaeologists stone tools they had found during the blockade.[94] It was a productive, albeit tense alliance. As Mulvaney later reflected, 'We claimed an Ice Age environment of tundra-like grasslands, where their dearly loved primeval forest was supposed to have stood eternally. By discrediting the image of a forest wilderness, we were ruining their image and battle cry!'[95] Even Brown, who was receptive to the views of the different players in the campaign, could not fully accommodate the archaeological insights that emerged from Kutikina. He wrote of his yearning to meet the

Pleistocene inhabitants of Kutikina, remarking, 'We would have so little in common – except the wilderness environment.'[96] The eternal nature of the wilderness ideal clashed with the particularities of archaeological and ecological history, which told a story of transformation.[97]

Added to these tensions was the animosity the Tasmanian Aboriginal community felt towards both the archaeologists, for fossicking on their land, and the conservationists, for suggesting they had never lived there. In late January 1982 Rosalind Langford publicly rebuked the Tasmanian Wilderness Society for their silence on Aboriginal rights.[98] At the AAA meeting in Hobart later that year, she confronted the archaeological profession in a powerful, eloquent and angry speech titled 'Our Heritage – Your Playground'. She invoked the amateur anthropologist William Crowther's grave-robbing at the start of the twentieth century as an example of archaeology's complicity in the colonial project: 'You, as a profession, have a lot of ground to make up.' And on behalf of the Tasmanian Aboriginal community, she asserted her ownership of the sites that had been excavated on the Franklin. 'The issue is control,' she told the audience of archaeologists:

> You seek to say that as scientists you have a right to obtain and study information of our culture. You seek to say that because you are Australians you have a right to study and explore our heritage because it is a heritage to be shared by all Australians, white and black. From our point of view we say – you have come as invaders, you have tried to destroy our culture, you have built your fortunes upon the lands and bodies of our people and now, having said sorry, want a share in picking out the bones of what you regard as a dead past. We say that it is our past, our culture and heritage and forms part of our present life. As such it is ours to control and it is ours to share on our terms … You can either be our guests or our enemies.

But at the end of her address, in what came as a surprise to her audience, Langford extended an olive branch to the archaeological community.

She contrasted Crowther's grave-robbing with a different, more consultative approach: 'We are not hostile to "proper" science and we love our heritage and our culture. But until we can share that knowledge we must be secure with control of our land and our culture.'[99]

As Jim Allen later reported, it was through the grudging recognition of 'proper science' that archaeologists and Aboriginal custodians were able to establish an uneasy truce.[100] To the Australian Archaeological Association, the Tasmanian Aboriginal Centre proposed four motions, all of which were adopted: to acknowledge Aboriginal ownership of their heritage and to seek permission before excavating Aboriginal sites; to consult with the Aboriginal community before accepting private funding for research in south-west Tasmania; to support Aboriginal land rights campaigns 'in acknowledgement of the debt owed to the Aboriginal people by the archaeological profession'; and to support the establishment of a majority-Aboriginal advisory committee that would oversee all further work on Tasmanian Aboriginal sites. The final motion was the only one to pass unanimously. The question of 'Aboriginal ownership of their heritage' fuelled the most discussion, with many taking the philosophical view that no one can own the past, while others – and ultimately the majority – sympathised with Langford's statement: 'If we Aborigines cannot control our own heritage, *what the hell can we control?*'[101]

It was a moment of healing. Through dialogue, a protocol was established for proper consultation, direct lines of communications were opened and Aboriginal people were invited to join all future archaeological investigations in Tasmania.[102] As a result of the meetings, Langford and Mansell travelled to Kutikina Cave in late December 1982. Mansell later wrote of this visit in an essay in *Pugganna News* titled 'That Cave Is Ours'. When they entered, 'The sad dampness of the Cave and the feeling of being close now to my people – the old people – was in the air.' In the back chamber, Langford started to hum and then sing songs familiar to the Tasmanian Aboriginal community. A cool wind and a flicker of sunlight alerted them to an ancestral presence. Near the entrance, she draped an Aboriginal flag across the cave floor as a mark that 'No whites can go there'.[103] Mansell described the rediscovery of the cave as 'the most important cultural thing that's ever happened to us'.[104] And while he and Langford were adamant that no further archaeological work be conducted in this sacred place – 'the most sacred thing in the state' – he also recognised the value of the history that had been uncovered:

> The fact that the Aborigines could survive physically and culturally in adverse conditions and over such a long period of time … helps me counteract the feeling of racial inferiority and enables me to demonstrate within the wider community that I and my people are the equal of other members of the community.[105]

By the start of 1983 the signs of 'No Dams' and 'Think Globally, Act Locally' on the blockade were joined by a new one: 'You Have Entered Aboriginal Land'. It was a statement of time as well as place.

Despite this working rapprochement, some antagonism from the Tasmanian Aboriginal community towards archaeologists remained. Jones in particular was singled out because of his role in the controversial film *The Last Tasmanian*. As he wrote from the 'Greenie's camp' on 19 February 1983, 'Vague rumour about Aborigines slagging us for digging a hole in Fraser Cave – looking for skeletons etc!'[106] In the fallout from the Hobart AAA conference he felt similar hostility from his colleagues.[107] The wound remained raw.

Mulvaney was sympathetic to the connections with the deep past that Mansell and Langford articulated after visiting Kutikina. As he wrote in a letter to Hawke on 24 March 1983, before the government had legislated to stop the damming of the Franklin:

> Unknown two years ago to the 3000 or more Tasmanians who identify as Aboriginal Tasmanians, [the caves in the Franklin valley] have

become places of deep emotional experience. This cannot be dismissed as any cynical or opportunistic 'political' move. It is a fact of their cultural life henceforth, and a major fact in their assertion of cultural identity ... As a person deeply concerned with Aboriginal culture, I urge your government to take this matter very seriously.[108]

But he was also distressed by the Tasmanian Aboriginal community's decision to cease research into the Franklin valley caves and was concerned that a few members of a modern community could exercise the power of exclusive ownership over the deep past. What implications would this have for bringing Aboriginal history into the national and global story? When does a place or an object move from being an individual's heritage – a family matter – to common heritage? Where should one draw the line between the Pleistocene and the present?

These questions came to a head at the end of the decade with the reburial of the Pleistocene skeletal remains from Kow Swamp. In August 1990, acting under an order from the Victorian government, the Museum of Victoria presented the Echuca Aboriginal Cooperative with the bones of some forty individuals who had lived and died at Kow Swamp between 9000 and 15,000 years ago, which palaeoanthropologist Alan Thorne had excavated from an eroding irrigation channel between 1967 and 1972. The remains were subsequently reburied by the Aboriginal community at an undisclosed location. Mulvaney was one of the few archaeologists who spoke publicly about the reburials, which he regarded as a form of vandalism. He saw the decision to rebury the Kow Swamp remains through the same lens as the proposed destruction of the caves of the Franklin valley. Both were examples of irreplaceable, Pleistocene cultural heritage; both spoke to a profound and ancient human story; both were something to treasure and to celebrate. In a frank and passionate essay he questioned our moral duty, as humans, towards the past and the future.[109] The destruction of the

Pleistocene skeletal remains, in his eyes, had deprived future generations of researchers, including Aboriginal scholars, of the opportunity
to learn about their ancestors. His proposed 'middle ground' had fallen
on deaf ears: the creation of a Keeping Place, controlled by scientists and
Aboriginal custodians, where cultural heritage such as the Kow Swamp
remains could be held, untouched, until dialogue had taken full course
and mutual trust and understanding had been reached.

Colin Pardoe, along with Isabel McBryde, represented an alternative view. Although Pardoe was opposed to the reburial of any skeletal
remains as 'the value of these to archaeology and understanding the
past is inestimable', he ultimately concluded that 'it is not my decision':

> By accepting Aboriginal ownership and control of their ancestors'
> bones, I accept their decisions on the disposition of those remains.
> My optimism stems from the hope that by demonstrating the value
> of skeletal studies the day may come when Aboriginal people might
> wish to preserve those remains 'in the name of science'![110]

The key to his optimism was dialogue. For over three decades, Pardoe's
main intellectual output has appeared in the form of plain English
'community reports'. In beautiful, simple prose, he renders his research
on ancient skeletal remains into evocative and information-rich prose-
pictures for the relevant Aboriginal communities, with subheadings
such as 'Who was he?', 'How old?', 'Ancient life' and 'Death by mis-
adventure'. Occasionally, he includes 'A request', in which he outlines
some future work he would like to do, why he is curious, what he might
discover, what he would need to do to uncover that information: for
example, chemically test (and destroy) a small amount of bone. 'I would
like to find out how long ago the Taronga Drive man died,' he writes
in one report. 'Rest assured I won't go ahead without permission. If the
community doesn't want this dating done, it's no big deal. If you do, I
will certainly get the information back when it comes out.'[111]

Pardoe's approach, where possible, empowers custodians whose distant ancestors' lives are being investigated and it delivers the information to those with the greatest stake in that history. 'My concern,' Mulvaney countered, 'is that, despite this seemingly democratic and conciliatory approach, it is wrongly assumed that local communities fully appreciate the future implications of re-burial.' He was particularly alarmed by the actions of the Victorian governor and premier in the Kow Swamp case. Their intervention in favour of reburial had cut short the dialogue between the Museum of Victoria and the Echuca Aboriginal Cooperative. He saw it as a short-term decision based on political imperatives and a sad reflection of the state's lack of interest and investment in Australian and Aboriginal heritage. The Kow Swamp remains, as rare survivals from the millions of burials across the past 15,000 years, were, in his eyes, amongst the Museum of Victoria's 'greatest treasures'. What would the reaction be 'should French nationalist "owners" re-bury the Cro-Magnon human remains or overpaint Lascaux, if Ethiopians cremated "Lucy", or the pyramids became a stone quarry and the Taj Mahal was razed to build apartments'? The decision to repatriate the remains, without investigating all avenues for dialogue or for their preservation in a Keeping Place, represented 'a triumph of bureaucracy and irrationality over prudence and positive, collaborative, racial relations'.[112]

But Mulvaney found himself in an increasingly lonely position challenging claims to exclusive Aboriginal ownership of the deep past. Where did the 'deep past' even begin? In 1984 and 1987 the AAA, in conjunction with the Museum of Victoria, attempted to draw a line between the Pleistocene and the present.[113] Palaeoanthropologist Steve Webb suggested that remains older than 6000–7000 years ago be regarded as common heritage, as that was when Greater Australia shrank to its present size. The National Museum of Australia drew the line at the beginning of what has become known as the Common Era, around 2000 years ago. But after a decade of tense discussion, in 1994, the AAA instituted a code of ethics that made no distinction between the management of a fifty-year-old artefact and a 50,000-year-old arte-fact: both belonged to the custodians of the land upon which they were found. The code reflects the philosophy of the motions passed in the wake of Langford's landmark speech in 1982. It acknowledges the importance of cultural heritage to the survival of Indigenous cultures, and recognises their rights to own, manage and control that heritage.[114]

There were dissenting voices to this unequivocal statement of own-ership. Jim Allen highlighted the complexities of the issue when he pointed out that there might be other claimants to Kutikina, such as mainland Indigenous people, considering Tasmania was connected to Australia while the valley was inhabited.[115] But the most vivid illustration of the debate belonged to Jones. In a complex essay that drew together histories, symbols and folk traditions he made a claim on behalf of his Welsh ancestors to be the legal owner of Stonehenge:

> 'Côr y Cewri' we Welsh call it – 'Court of Giants', that hulking mass of stones that the English call 'Stonehenge'. Our word is old ... There *was* an ancient British past, and its strengths and sinews are the spirits that live in the Welsh culture today. In this way we, the dispossessed, have recovered our history ...[116]

The essay tried to illuminate the ways in which culture and history are appropriated, and the danger of asserting exclusive ownership over the deep past. In the final passages, drawing direct parallels with 'the politics of ethnic identity in Tasmania', he withdrew the land claim on the basis that 'Stonehenge does not "belong" to the Welsh, or to any one else. Rather, it is a thing to be known and held in common by all who regard it. Like the Ice Age occupation caves of the Tasmanian Pleistocene, it forms a part of the common heritage of mankind.'[117]

* * *

Although no further work has been done on Kutikina since 1983, the success of the campaign initially encouraged archaeology in the south-west, outside the Franklin valley. Jones' parallels between the Tasmanian archaeology and northern hemisphere Ice Age communities sparked more than a decade of concentrated fieldwork in south-western Tasmania, producing the most complete regional sequence of late-Pleistocene archaeology in Australia. Jim Allen and Richard Cosgrove directed much of this work under the umbrella of the Southern Forests Archaeological Project, including uncovering a detailed 40,000-year history of occupation at Warreen in the Maxwell River valley, south of Kutikina.[118] In 1987, driven in part by a political struggle to extend the World Heritage area, another intense burst of field research led to the rediscovery of several more occupation sites in the river valleys of south-west Tasmania – the Florentine, Weld and Cracroft rivers. Again archaeology was conducted at the last minute to protect a region from impending development, and through timely fieldwork and public advocacy, archaeologists and conservationists provided the basis for the government to incorporate large tracts of the Southern Forests into the World Heritage listing.

But despite these successes, archaeological work in Tasmania eventually became embroiled in controversy once more. Although excavations continued to be carried out in consultation with the Tasmanian Aboriginal Centre, and with a paid Aboriginal consultant overseeing all work, the Southern Forests Project came to an untimely end. When, as per the *Tasmanian Aboriginal Relics Act* (1975), Allen sought to renew his permits to continue analysis of excavated material, he was flatly refused and was asked to return the materials within the year. Returning the finds without analysis would mean losing the history they held, so he asked the Tasmanian Aboriginal Land Council for more time. His appeal was unsuccessful. The relevant ministers refused to intervene. In July 1995, under the threat of a legal injunction, he and his research partner,

Tim Murray, returned the artefacts with their fate undecided; reburial was the favoured option.[119] In the wake of the 'Tasmanian affair', Allen observed, 'the current view of TALC apparently is that there should be no further excavation in Tasmania. I am sorely tempted to agree with this view on the grounds that sites and assemblages are safest where they are until social attitudes to the values of archaeology change once more.' This is an archaeologist's view of time.[120]

The Franklin River campaign was a rare example of archaeology capturing and holding public attention, with profound political results. Kutikina stopped the Gordon-below-Franklin because of the history it revealed: a history that placed the people of ancient Australia into a global narrative. Aboriginal heritage, by being recognised as part of the world's heritage, could be protected and celebrated as Australian heritage. But despite the success of the campaign, Mulvaney worried about some of the sentiments it had dredged from private depths into the public realm. In his correspondence, he returned often to a comment about Kutikina by the second-most senior official of the Tasmanian Hydro-Electric Commission, Bill Gaskell, in 1982: 'I honestly don't see the point of keeping it. What can old bits of flint and bones tell you? By all means, come and dig it up, photograph it, record it – why keep it? What good does it do anyone?'[121]

Mulvaney was dismayed, after almost three decades working in the field, to find so little interest in the history of ancient Australia and so little understanding of the ways in which archaeological knowledge can contribute to cross-cultural understanding, cultural pride and local, national and global narratives. Would Gaskell have questioned the worth of preserving Phar Lap's heart or Ned Kelly's helmet? The government's intervention in the Kow Swamp reburials and its refusal to intervene in the demise of the Southern Forest Project reflected a similar ambivalence about Aboriginal heritage. Both decisions demonstrated a lack of political will to foster dialogue and protect invaluable chapters of the Australian story. As Jones lamented, 'Politicians sometimes find it easier to give Aboriginal names to national parks, or to grant Heritage rights, than any meaningful land or financial restitution. Giving back the past is easy.'[122] But recognising the multiple meanings of the past, and the responsibilities and possibilities it generates, is hard.

John Mulvaney reads the layered landscape at Fromm's Landing, 1958.

Above: Isabel McBryde surveying
Schnapper Point with her students,
1971.

Right: Rhys Jones dreams of deep
time at Sisters Beach, north-west
Tasmania, c. 1964.

Below: Isabel McBryde at the
University of New England, 1972.

The 1969–1970 excavation team at Puntutjarpa in the Gibson Desert.

Jim Bowler on the desiccated shores of Lake Mungo.

The North Cave at Rocky Cape, Tasmania.

Above: Senior Matuntara man Jack Coulthard watches over Mike Smith's excavations at Illararri Kulpi in Central Australia, 1982.

Below: Isabel McBryde leads the chair of the World Heritage committee, Ralph Slatyer, and NSW Premier Neville Wran on an official tour of the Walls of China, 1983: l-r, Jack Giles, Wran, Slatyer, McBryde, Peter Clarke and David Hurley.

Mutthi Mutthi elder Alice Kelly and Paakantji elder Alice Bugmy on the site where Mungo Lady was found.

Left: Lesley Maynard in a crawl-tunnel known as 'the Squeeze', Koonalda Cave.

Middle: Anbarra women and children gather shellfish at low tide near the mouth of the Blyth River, 1972.

Below: Betty Meehan in camp at Manganama, Arnhem Land, 1972.

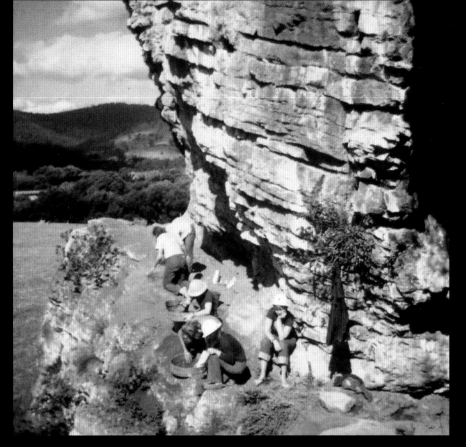

Josephine Flood's team sieve outside Cloggs Cave, near Buchan, 1972.

The excavations at Kutikina played a powerful political role in the Franklin River campaign.

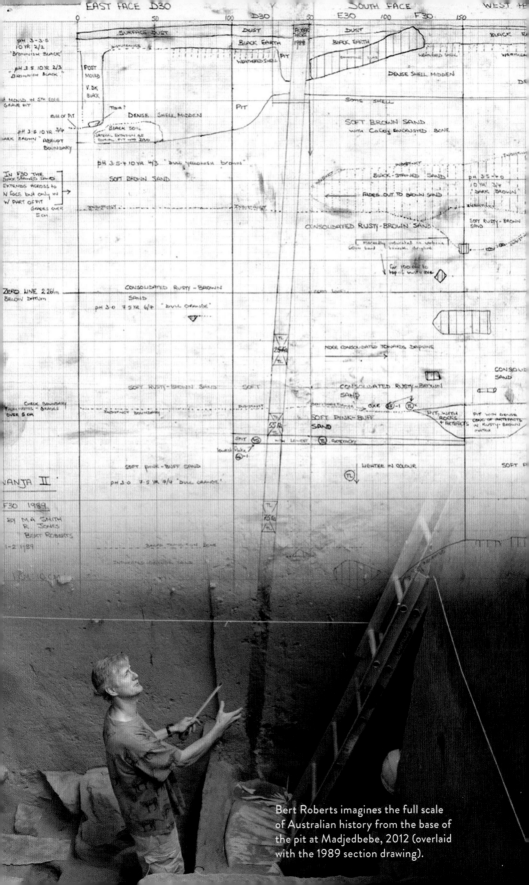

Bert Roberts imagines the full scale of Australian history from the base of the pit at Madjedbebe, 2012 (overlaid with the 1989 section drawing).

Australians to 1988

IT IS EASY TO FORGET, HISTORIAN BAIN ATTWOOD REFLECTS, that as late as 1975 the term 'Aboriginal history', let alone the field it describes, was a novel one.[1] Yet it was adopted quickly in the years that followed and gained new currency in the long lead-up to Australia's Bicentenary. In his portrait of the 1980s, historian Frank Bongiorno brings to life the winding and treacherous road to 1988 and the ideological battles that were fought along the way. The Bicentenary became the subject of a 'history war', waged over questions of national identity, multiculturalism and Aboriginal rights, 'in which contending understandings of the nation's past were upheld or condemned'.[2] Did 26 January – 'Australia Day' – mark the moment of invasion or the birth of a nation? Is it possible to reconcile the past two centuries of Australian history with the tens of millennia that preceded them? These debates sparked a prolonged period of national introspection that increasingly came to revolve around the emerging field of Aboriginal history.

In the public realm, the rise of the idea of Aboriginal history has much to do with the Whitlam government's 'Committee of Inquiry on Museums and National Collections', known as the Pigott Report, which had been commissioned as part of a push to express a new Australian nationalism, removed from the traditional strains of empire. Two of its main authors, John Mulvaney and Geoffrey Blainey, advocated the creation of a new museum for Australia focusing on three interlinking themes: the history of the natural environment; 'the history of Europeans in Australia'; and 'Aboriginal history stretching over some 40,000 years'.[3] The use of the term in this report saw it regularly invoked in parliamentary debates and in newspaper coverage.

Within the academy, Aboriginal history as a historiographical movement emerged alongside the founding in 1977 of the journal bearing its name. Niel Gunson first mooted the idea of *Aboriginal History* in the 1960s, but it was the historian and anthropologist Diane Barwick who guided the journal into being and who became its editor for the first seven years.[4] Barwick, along with her closest colleagues on the editorial board, Isabel McBryde and linguist Luise Hercus, advocated an interdisciplinary approach to the writing of Aboriginal history and emphasised the importance of including Aboriginal perspectives. As Barwick wrote emphatically in December 1976, this journal 'must focus on Aboriginal history not white men's opinions'.[5] The first volume opened with WEH Stanner's detailed account of European dispossession in Sydney, 'The History of Indifference Thus Begins'. The second volume included an article by the young historian Henry Reynolds, who had already begun his campaign to understand and enliven 'the other side of the frontier'.[6]

The impetus for creating the journal in 1977 was sharpened by the political debates over history dredged up by the Aboriginal land rights movement.[7] Over the following decade, from 1979 to 1988, these debates escalated as Australian historians embarked on the ambitious, collaborative enterprise known as the *Australian Bicentennial History Project*. Historian Ken Inglis oversaw the writing of the eleven-volume series, arranging for John Mulvaney and Peter White to edit the archaeological contribution, *Australians to 1788*. On 22 May 1980 Barwick, McBryde and Mulvaney convened a symposium at the Australian Institute of Aboriginal Studies to discuss how to integrate Aboriginal history into

the series. They sought to incorporate oral history alongside documentary sources; to recognise the diversity of Aboriginal experiences in the
wake of invasion, such as their roles on the pastoral frontier and in the
two world wars; and to accommodate a long view of Aboriginal history
that encompassed the story of Pleistocene and Holocene Australia.[8]

In planning and shaping the volume, Mulvaney and White sought
the involvement of many Aboriginal scholars. All invitations to contribute, however, were declined 'because they considered that any
bicentennial enterprise was necessarily a celebration of their people's
dispossession, extermination and degradation'. Some criticised the
very idea of Aboriginal history written by non-Aboriginal people. But
Mulvaney and White believed that the benefits of including Aboriginal
people in this national enterprise outweighed any accusations of appro-
priation or subjugation levelled at them. As editors, they modelled
themselves, and those who contributed to the volume, as 'translators'
of the Indigenous past.[9]

Mulvaney's friend and one-time student Geoffrey Blainey shared
his vision for bringing the humanities into Australian public life, and
the importance of a deep appreciation of Aboriginal history. As we saw
in Chapter 1, Blainey had gained firsthand experience of archaeology as
a field assistant during the excavation of Fromm's Landing in 1956, and
it was at Mulvaney's urging that he wrote about the economic history
of Aboriginal Australia. 'Dear Skipper,' he reported back on 29 May
1972: 'I gave the lectures on Ab history, as ordered. I think they aroused
a fair amount of interest and if I'd prepared them more carefully they
would have been more stimulating.'[10] Three years later, in 1975, these
lectures were published as Blainey's groundbreaking book *Triumph of
the Nomads*, which wove the rapidly emerging archaeological discoveries into an accessible continental narrative. It was the first attempt
to write a popular history of ancient Australia. His 2015 iteration, *The
Rise and Fall of Ancient Australia*, volume one of his two-volume 'Story

of Australia's People', affirms the importance he places on Indigenous history in the national narrative.[11]

In *Triumph of the Nomads* Blainey used colonial sources alongside modern evidence of environmental change to inform his historical imagination and dream of deep time. He described the Pleistocene eruptions of the volcanoes of western Victoria, for example, by transplanting the tremors, fissures, sparks and smoke from volcanic events at Paricutin in Mexico in 1943–1952. He envisaged local inhabitants responding with fright to the explosive events, fleeing the lava that 'glided like a long molten snake across the plains' and watching from afar as the fierce 'red rim of the cone' lit up the night sky: 'The new mountain cones or the rims of craters could not have been meaningless,' he speculated, 'for they towered above their tribal territory and happened in the centre of their world.' The book's most enduring insight was his rendering of the rising seas at the end of the last Ice Age:

> Nothing in the short history of white men in Australia ... can be compared with the ancient rising of the seas, the shaping of thousands of new harbours, the swamping of scores of tribal territories and the wiping out of the evidence of the aboriginal life once lived on those drowned lands.[12]

Blainey's powerful prose captured the drama of these natural and cultural events, and his narrative helped the Australian public populate the immense time span of ancient Australia with moments, images and climatic trends. The story he told challenged the long-held belief that the first Australians were an unchanging people in an unchanging land. 'This assumption can no longer be held,' he declared. 'It is incinerated by the firestick.'[13] But although *Triumph of the Nomads* celebrates the 'impressive achievements' of the first Australians and the 'ingenuity' of their economic life, the book is also filled with coded political language.[14] He refers to the first Australians, for example, as 'the invaders', an odd turn of phrase for an explicitly human history of an as yet unpeopled continent; and the dedication page to *The Rise and Fall of Ancient Australia* bears a similarly veiled sentence: 'Every newcomer to Australia was a discoverer ...' Such statements neutralise the act of dispossession, suggesting that Indigenous people have no greater claim to the continent than those who forged the modern nation. As Blainey wrote in a British paper to mark the Bicentenary, 'Time for Australia to Shed its Guilt Complex': 'The Aboriginals' tragedy is one side of the coin. The shinier side is that in the last two centuries the world's driest continent ... has been turned into a prolific economy which is one of the largest exporters of minerals, fibres and foods.'[15]

As the first historian to write such a vast history, Blainey was refreshingly open about the limitations of his sources. His sentences are filled with speculative words such as 'could', 'might' and 'it is possible', and when faced with the unknown, he fills the gaps in his deep time narrative with rich ethnographic evidence. Tim Murray and Peter White have condemned the book for portraying the history of ancient Australia as simply 50,000 years of nineteenth-century ethnography.[16] But the challenges that Blainey faced remain hard to resolve: how do we write textured histories of people in the deep past without reducing them to an essential version of the societies encountered at the moment of contact?

Archaeologist Josephine Flood confronted these questions in the early 1970s when she sought to understand the Indigenous history of the Australian Alps. In her book *The Moth Hunters*, she paints a vivid picture of Aboriginal life across a vast region, focusing on the massive seasonal gatherings of different clans and family groups to harvest and feast on the region's rich, creamy bogong moths. This cultural phenomenon was recorded in oral histories and primary sources, but was not easily recognisable in the archaeological materials. Moth husks are biodegradable, and the stone tools that survived in the region were not obviously associated with the moths they once crushed and processed.

The story of these cultural events could only be told by combining the archaeology with written and oral sources. As Flood concluded, 'No ethnography, no moth hunters.'[17]

In the 1980s, Flood took on the role of championing the finds and practice of archaeology to the wider public. She wrote explicitly 'for the general reader, for Aborigines interested in learning more of their own heritage, and for secondary and tertiary students'.[18] And unlike Blainey, Flood favoured detailed regional summary over continental narrative synthesis.[19] Her books, written in clear prose with simple, logical structures, helped make Australian archaeology more accessible at a time when it was attracting greater public interest. She wove a sense of excitement into her chapters, and many of the words and phrases she popularised continue to resonate today. 'The longest continuing cultural history in the world', for example, is repeated so often these days that it seems a truism.[20] But what does Flood mean by this, and how does it inform our view of Aboriginal society through time? The question of 'change' in ancient Australia is confronted in Chapter 9.

When the long-anticipated Bicentenary celebrations arrived in 1988, Aboriginal protesters drew on insights thrown up by the recent wave of scholarship. Alongside posters reading 'White Australia has a Black History', was another: 'You have been here for 200 years, we for 40,000'. The comparison magnified the act of dispossession. It was an example, Rhys Jones reflected, of how deep time 'has become a potent symbol for cultural autonomy and emancipation'.[21]

The date of 26 January 1988 was marked by both light-hearted patriotism and quiet mourning. In Australia, tall ships sailed through Sydney Harbour; in England, Aboriginal activist Burnum Burnum 'annexed' the white cliffs of Dover on behalf of the Aboriginal nation. But the most profound result of the Bicentenary was the conversations it opened about Australian history, which continue today. 'As two generations of historians have shown,' Mark McKenna observed in 2016, 'there was no history of Australia that was non-Indigenous. From the moment of first contact, settler history became part of Indigenous history and Indigenous history became part of settler history.'[22] This simple statement reflects a seismic shift in Australian historical consciousness. The field of Aboriginal history has moved from the periphery of the national story to its centre.

NINE

A SOCIAL HISTORY OF THE HOLOCENE

Sylvia Hallam, Harry Lourandos and the
Archaeology of Documents

Fire was a constant presence in early Sydney: from the 'moving lights' on the harbour at night to lone trees burning on the Cumberland Plain, 'the smoke issuing out of the top part as through a chimney'.[1] The Eora used flame to open tracks and to clean country; to drive animals into the paths of hunters and then to cook the kill; to keep warm at night and to carry as a torch the next day; to treat wood, melt resin and crack stone for tools and to gather around and dance and share stories. 'In all the country thro' which I have passed,' wrote Governor Arthur Phillip in May 1788, 'I have seldom gone a quarter of a mile without seeing trees which appear to have been destroyed by fire.'[2] To the newcomers, the Aboriginal people of the Sydney region became known as the 'fire-makers'.[3]

One of my first jobs as a public historian was to trawl through hundreds of early diaries, letters and reports from the wider Sydney region in search of moments when settlers recorded observing an Aboriginal presence in the landscape, such as these descriptions of fire. Whenever I came across a report of a hearth, a canoe or an encounter with a family group I plotted the location on a map, gradually building up a picture of Aboriginal activity at the moment of contact. The map was intended to help identify archaeological sites and to enrich the heritage reports of the archaeology consultancy I was working for.[4] The main challenge I faced was not finding evidence of Aboriginal activity, but capturing the incredible array of cultural imprints left on the landscape.

On a hot dry day in September 1790, John Hunter observed Aboriginal people 'burning the grass on the north shore opposite to Sydney, in order to catch rats and other animals'. Almost exactly twelve months later, on 31 August 1791, they were again 'firing the country' in the same place on a hot day ahead of heavy rains.[5] What the settlers regarded as a 'remarkable coincidence of time' we now recognise as evidence of local burning regimes.[6] The subtle mastery of fire intimates a connection to the land and an understanding of the seasons that the newcomers could not fathom.

I found my journey into these sources to be both a visceral encounter with the moment of invasion and a rich evocation of the societies that called the Sydney region home. There were scenes of violence and retribution, as Aboriginal huts were looted and burnt, graves were opened, and men and women were attacked and killed. There were also vivid accounts of cultural interaction and exchange. The map I created revealed a landscape criss-crossed with Aboriginal paths, many of which later became roads. The Eora made the settlement at Sydney Cove their own, whether eating in the yard of Government House, sharing a table with the governor himself, or gathering at Bennelong's hut, where the Sydney Opera House now stands. Large parties of convicts paid regular visits to an Aboriginal family in Woolloomooloo, 'where they danced and sung with apparent good humour'.[7] A short-lived fish trade sprang up in Parramatta, with Aboriginal people selling fresh bream and mullet for bread and salted meat. As historians Grace Karskens and Paul Irish have shown, early Sydney remained 'an Eora town'.[8]

My spatial approach also highlighted the transformations the landscape underwent in the wake of the invasion, as 'kangaroo grounds'

became suburbs, fishing streams became drains, and early colonial landmarks, such as Mount Prospect, were inverted into quarries and dams
to serve the needs of the growing settler society. Later, through conversations with individuals from local Aboriginal organisations, many
of whom were also archaeological fieldworkers, I added a layer of contemporary cultural reflections to the map, recording memories of where
yams used to grow, where eels could be trapped, and places known for
being 'cold' or 'sacred'. This cultural mapping exercise afforded an insight
into how the landscape was once used and how it remains used today.

Although the map provided flickering insights into Aboriginal social
and economic life in the decades following invasion, it was skewed by
the routes the newcomers used, mostly along rivers and through areas
cleared by Aboriginal burning. But as I worked through the documents,
I found myself considering the limits of what we can learn from the
small window of time they depict. What was the long-term history of
the people who lived in the Sydney region? And how had these societies
changed, not only from the moment of contact, but over the course of
the Holocene – the last 11,700 years – and into the Pleistocene?[9]

These same questions came to drive archaeological research in the
1970s and '80s. As the date for the human colonisation of Australia plateaued around 40,000 years, the search for the oldest sites stalled, and
many archaeologists began to focus their research questions on the more
recent past. This chapter offers a portrait of two archaeologists, Sylvia
Hallam and Harry Lourandos, who worked backwards from the rich
descriptions of Aboriginal life at contact to try to understand how these
societies had developed over time. It explores their innovative attempts
to write a social history of the Holocene.

* * *

Although Aboriginal mastery of fire was clear to many settlers and
explorers in the eighteenth and nineteenth centuries, it was not until the

mid-twentieth century that ecologists, geographers and archaeologists realised the role it had played in creating and maintaining certain vegetation patterns. In 1959 Norman Tindale called for Aboriginal people to be recognised as 'ecological agents'.[10] In 1968, drawing upon the emerging evidence of Aboriginal antiquity, as well as the insights of contemporary burning regimes, Rhys Jones and Western Australian palaeontologist Duncan Merrillees independently suggested that Aboriginal burning had played a profound role in shaping Australia's flora and fauna over millennia. Jones' provocative phrase 'fire-stick farming' endures today.[11]

Sylvia Hallam (née Maycock) was inspired by Jones' and Merrilees' deep time arguments and in 1975 published *Fire and Hearth*, a history of Aboriginal burning in the south-western corner of the continent. The wide-ranging insights she kindled in that regional study have been stoked and tended by many scholars over the decades, including in continental histories such as Stephen Pyne's *Burning Bush* and Bill Gammage's *The Biggest Estate on Earth*.[12] Although written over forty years ago, the ideas in *Fire and Hearth* continue to burn brightly.

Hallam synthesised the emerging evidence of Aboriginal burning and presented a rich portrait of the myriad ways in which Aboriginal people had transformed the country through flame. And unlike Gammage, who telescopes the deep history of Aboriginal Australia into the year 1788, Hallam sought to present 'a long view' of Aboriginal burning. Her archaeological study explored the variety and antiquity of Aboriginal burning traditions, the social, political, spiritual and economic bases of fire, and how burning was integrated into culture through language, art, ritual and law. 'The land the English settled was not as God made it,' Hallam declared in a powerful opening passage. 'It was as the Aborigines made it.'[13]

Hallam grew up in the East Midlands of England and in 1945 won a state scholarship to study natural sciences at Cambridge University. Like Isabel McBryde, she became enamoured of the geographical approaches of OGS Crawford and Cyril Fox, who showed that archaeology had 'as much to do with maps as with museums'.[14] In 1949 she embarked on a decade-long study of settlement patterns in the Fenlands during the Roman occupation of Britain. When her husband and fellow Cambridge graduate, Herbert Hallam, gained a post teaching medieval history at the University of Western Australia in 1961, their young family migrated to Perth. 'Dad's medieval,' their four children were fond of saying, 'but Mum's prehistoric.'[15]

There was no archaeological department in Western Australia when the Hallams arrived in 1961, but Sylvia quickly became a familiar face at UWA, lecturing in the departments of classics and ancient history, geography and anthropology. In 1973 she founded and developed the first department of prehistoric archaeology, within the university's department of anthropology. Although distant from the mainstreams of archaeological research in the east, she fostered her own intellectual community in the west. She formed bonds with the Western Australian Museum and joined the team that excavated at Puntutjarpa rock shelter. It was Richard Gould who passed on the note that led to her most important archaeological site: 'a limestone cave … shaped like an orchestra shell … which I have always suspected of being an aboriginal haven.'[16]

She first visited the dark recesses of Orchestra Shell Cave in April 1970 as part of a vast archaeological survey of the coastal plain around the estuary of the Swan River and the moist, largely forested region to the south-west.[17] In planning the survey, she drew upon her experience studying landscape patterns in Roman Britain to map out the region in a grid-reference system. She gained a grant from the AIAS, trained students in the necessary survey methods and organised a schedule of short and frequent field trips to fit around family commitments. The fact that her region of study encompassed Perth also allowed her to capture information that was being threatened by the ever-encroaching urban sprawl. Alongside stratified excavations at Orchestra Shell Cave, she located and recorded surface scatters and stone arrangements, hunting traps and yam fields, rock art sites and ceremonial grounds, fish weirs and fresh-water wells, open grasslands and cleared paths. Her methods resonated with those whose history she was studying. As Jill Milroy, a Noongar elder and academic from south-west Australia, reflected in 2013:

> My mother and grandmother always taught me ... that it is not people who are the best storytellers: the birds, the animals, the trees, the rocks and the land, our mother, have the most important stories to tell us. These stories exist in place, and by 'mapping' these story systems we fundamentally alter the way in which we can 'know' Country.[18]

By the end of Hallam's methodical survey, she had identified over 120 sites and collected over 10,000 artefacts. She also scoured the local ethnographic literature, searching for documents 'where history intersects with prehistory; where the populations, territories, resources and interactions we wish to elucidate are seen, if fitfully and patchily, in the flickering light of the often unsystematic observations of literate observers'. Resigned to her role as a 'jack-of-all-trades' – a historian and ecologist, as well as an anthropologist and archaeologist – Hallam immersed herself in the published accounts of explorers and early settlers.

She was especially drawn to the diaries of George Grey, who had been shipwrecked in Gantheaume Bay, near Kalbarri, in 1839 and forced to walk some 500 kilometres south to the nearest settlement on the Swan River. She considered him a rare witness to Aboriginal life who allowed himself 'to be persuaded by his own observations', rather than guided by cultural preconceptions.[19] On his trek southwards, he described watching women harvesting and cropping yams in a careful, systematic manner across the alluvial plains. He also came across fertile fields extending 'three and a half consecutive miles' where the ground had been perforated by digging sticks. Grey was impressed by the 'hard manual labour' of these women and described the Aboriginal use of fire to improve these fields as 'a sort of cultivation'. He noticed that the yam fields were connected to other rich areas by 'well-marked roads' and chains of 'deeply sunk wells' and recorded walking through 'villages' of clay-plastered and turf-roofed huts, which seemed to support 'a large and comparatively speaking resident population'.[20]

'What do these descriptions mean?' Hallam wondered. 'What do they imply about Aboriginal landholding, land management and settlement on the west coastal plain? How extensive in space and time, are the phenomena described?'[21] She found answers in the social contract between people and fire. The ways in which the land had been burnt and cropped, she realised, gave insight into 'a close and controlled mesh of usage rights and responsibilities'.[22]

Grey described learning of a 'law that no plant bearing seeds is to be dug up after it has been flowered' and he recorded a system of 'rules' that designated who could burn, where and when.[23] Burning was thus a political and social process, as well as a statement of ownership – a ritual performance, as well as an economic and ecological practice. It was this ceremonial dimension that led Bill Gammage, forty years after Hallam's work, to describe the continent as a single estate, governed by the sacred dictates of the Dreaming.

When the British arrived in 1788, Gammage argues, Aboriginal people were living in a state of harmony with their environment, managing their varied ecological regions as part of one universal system. Drawing on an impressive wealth of historic research, he suggests that the burning regimes settlers unwittingly observed on the northern shores of Sydney Harbour shared the same basic principles as the fire practices recorded on Swan River in Western Australia – and indeed in every other part of Australia. His reason for bringing this array of local evidence into a continental system rests in his understanding of the Dreaming as a constant, governing force. Since 'All Australia obeyed the Dreaming', 'the Dreaming made the continent a single estate'.[24]

Hallam, on the other hand, sought to deepen her understanding of the spiritual role of fire by focusing on specific stories from her region. She investigated the associations between serpent legends and dark caves, such as the site at Orchestra Shell Cave, where fire was 'an essential element in both the myth and the ritual aspects of the tradition'. The 'serpent-fire' theme, she argued, illuminated 'the ancient and essential bond between the ritual and the ecological aspects of the use of fire'.[25]

In 1975 Hallam warned against a homogenous view of Aboriginal burning. She highlighted the ways in which different ecological regions responded to fire, as well as the variety of burning regimes used by the people of the Swan River: 'There is room for a multiplicity of detailed local studies.'[26] In her review of *The Biggest Estate on Earth*, Hallam welcomed 'this important and amazing book', but she issued a similar caution: 'Commonalities and linkages do not cancel local peculiarities and specificities, societal and ecological.'[27] While in some places Aboriginal burning created new and balanced ecosystems, opening up lush grasslands and intricate ecological mosaics, in others it may have exacerbated erosion, caused local faunal extinctions, altered the nutrients in the soil and perhaps increased levels of salinity. She noted that 'Aboriginal legends in southwestern Australia tell of once fresh water becoming salty'.[28] The implications of Aboriginal burning were dramatic, but also varied and complex. 'There was transformation,' archaeologist Peter Hiscock remarks, 'but it was not always Eden that was wrought.'[29]

Perhaps most significantly, Hallam sought to present 'a long view' of the various social and economic phenomena that Grey had observed. She drew upon emerging archaeological evidence and pollen records to argue that Aboriginal burning was ancient, but that it had played an even greater social and economic role over the past 5000 years. 'The increasing, and increasingly regulated, use of fire,' she suggested in *Fire and Hearth*, 'was part of an overall pattern of increasing exploitation and population.'[30]

Hallam was not alone in noticing more intensive and varied forms of archaeology emerging during the Holocene. This was the phenomenon that Mulvaney had described in 1969 as 'the Inventive Phase' of Aboriginal history and he linked it to two external events: the stabilisation of the coastlines around 6000 years ago after millennia of rising seas, and the arrival of the dingo in the north around 4000–5000 years ago. But by the mid-1970s, it was becoming increasingly clear that 'the Inventive Phase' was far more than a technological shift: it appeared to usher in an unprecedented period of cultural and social transformation in ancient Australia. And there were hints that these changes were driven from within.

* * *

In the 1970s, a young Greek-Australian archaeologist by the name of Harry Lourandos sought to understand the changes archaeologists across Australia were observing during the Holocene. Lourandos had been drawn to history, and in particular classical Greek history, from a young age. 'Coming from a Greek-Australian family,' he reflected, 'it empowered me.' But he was also curious about the other half of his heritage: 'I deeply felt that as I lived in Australia, I needed to concentrate on the (pre)history of this region and its Indigenous people.'[31] In 1963, at the age of eighteen, he enrolled in Arts-Law at the University of Sydney, taking a few classes in Near Eastern archaeology. He quickly gravitated towards the prehistory section of the anthropology department, finding inspiration in the seminars of the recently appointed Rhys Jones, who was giving voice to 'a new brand of archaeology'. After joining Jones on his excavation of Rocky Cape in Tasmania in 1964–1965, Lourandos was hooked.

In the late 1960s, together with Jones, Lourandos conducted an extensive survey along the east and south-east coasts of Tasmania, with a few forays inland to the glacial moraine of the central plateau. He published his initial results in 1968, arguing that there were distinct differences in the diets and economies of the societies that lived on the east and west coasts of Tasmania, and that these reflected different social structures: 'A nomadic organisation is interpreted for the Eastern sites, and a semi-sedentary or seasonally-sedentary organisation for the West and North-West coastal sites.'[32] Sandra Bowdler described the paper as 'a Trojan horse dragged into the citadel of his mentors', for it not only challenged elements of Jones' Tasmania-wide interpretation, but explicitly introduced new – and in Australia, relatively unfashionable – theoretical language.[33]

After a short hiatus from archaeology, in which he travelled to his ancestral homeland and briefly considered opening a restaurant in Ithaca selling Vegemite sandwiches, Lourandos returned to the University of Sydney in 1973 and embarked on a survey of the archaeology of Victoria's south-west coast.[34] He recorded limestone shelters by the sea and mapped shell middens eroding out of dunes, but the most important aspect of his archaeological reconnaissance was reading in the Mitchell Library in Sydney. Like Hallam, he found inspiration in the flickering glimpses of Aboriginal society captured in the jottings of early settlers and explorers.[35]

Lourandos was particularly taken with the journals of George Augustus Robinson, who travelled through the western district of Victoria in 1841 as Chief Protector of Aborigines. Robinson's diary included descriptions of durable domed huts of wood and clay, sometimes with stone foundations and walls, which clustered in 'villages' beside lakes and rivers. One hut bordering a swamp near Mount Napier 'measured ten feet in diameter by five feet high, and [was] sufficiently strong for a man on horse back to ride over'.[36] Robinson observed that during times of seasonal abundance these 'villages' were inhabited by up to 1000 people, as family groups and clans converged to trap birds and collect eggs, sow and harvest various cereals, tubers and fruits, and lure whales to shore with flames and feast on their stranded carcasses. The gatherings were also accompanied by ceremonial activities, large-scale hunting drives and increased burning. Fire was used to open up hunting grounds and drive marsupials and emus, to rejuvenate swamp-lands and to clear grasses and expose roots for harvesting. Some of the food gathered during these times of abundance was stored for leaner periods: eels and whale meat were dried and buried, vast quantities of the edible acacia gum were cached and other plants were elaborately processed. 'The root of the bracken fern,' Lourandos drew out as an example, 'was pounded to extract its starch, which was then baked on the ashes as a form of bread.'[37]

Lourandos was most interested in the extensive 'eel traps' that Robinson described. The intricately engineered network of traps in the marshy plains near Mount William, which extended over 60,000 square metres, resembled, to Robinson, 'the work of civilised man but ... on inspection were found to be the work of aboriginal natives'.[38] Over 130 years later, Lourandos found his assumptions similarly challenged: was this evidence consistent with the idea of a 'hunter-gatherer' society?

Groups of Aboriginal people had used digging sticks to create a vast maze of artificial channels that funnelled eels between swamps kilome-tres apart. 'With the coming of the rains and as the swamps overflowed,' Lourandos realised, 'eels (and other fish) would have been flushed out of the swampy ground, and into the drains where an elaborate series of traps would be constructed.'[39] The sheer size of the structure must have left an archaeological footprint.

Over the summer of 1974–1975, with a team of six students, Lourandos followed Robinson's footsteps to the Mount William area, walking the land, talking with landowners and studying aerial photography. He found that few people in the region were aware of the eel traps, and that little visible evidence of these structures remained: the intricate network of channels had been collapsed by hooves and levelled by ploughs. At Toolondo, the team surveyed an eel trap Aldo Massola had recorded in 1962: a 2.5-kilometre drainage channel – or dike – that connected naturally separated ponds.[40] It had survived due to the concerted efforts of one landholder, D McKenry, who had recognised it as an 'Aboriginal fish trap' and preserved it for posterity.[41]

What intrigued Lourandos most about these subtle structures was the possibility that they were more than traps: they seemed to have been designed to control the availability and extend the natural range of eels. As artificial water controls, the channels operated as a form of swamp management, distributing excess water during floods, retaining water in times of drought and directing eels to new parts of the country. And 'since eels flourish in watercourses of this kind', Lourandos observed, 'the drainage ditches might also have increased the local eel population'.[42] The eels, some of which are more nutritious than salmon, were speared year-round, but during their annual migration people from across the district would gather to trap them in elaborate stone, clay and brush weirs built across waterways. It was a finely tuned, sustainable system, which shared much with the practices of contemporary commercial eel fisheries in Europe and Japan. 'The people of south-western Victoria and their neighbours,' Lourandos marvelled in 1987, 'were more numerous, more sedentary and far more ingenious than we ever imagined.'[43]

But when had this eeling economy begun? The traps themselves were difficult to date, as the constant flow of water through the channels had washed away most of the older material. So Lourandos was forced to infer the age of the eel traps from other sites in the region. He found what he was looking for in the deep, stratified limestone caves at Bridgewater near Portland, which had been relatively continuously occupied over the course of the Holocene. The excavation helped Lourandos create a regional chronology, but it also presented him with a conundrum. Around 12,000 years ago, when the sea was 25 kilometres away, the caves were used relatively sporadically by a group of foragers with little interest in eating marine life. As the sea came closer, the surrounding vegetation reacted to the encroaching coast, with banksias and casuarinas giving way to herbfield and shrubland. But although there was a dramatic increase in the range of technology and raw materials in the archaeological deposit, it took people several thousand years to change their eating habits and begin to exploit the nearby marine resources.[44] What had caused this time lag between the changes in the environment and the changes in economic and cultural materials? Perhaps, Lourandos suggested, it was evidence of adaptation driven by internal social factors, rather than external forces of change.

His excavations at Seal Point near the lighthouse at Cape Otway gave him a vivid glimpse of what might have accompanied this late Holocene social change. While excavating the eroding middens, his team found ten large circular depressions which seemed to 'conform to ethnographic descriptions of Aboriginal house pits into which huts were constructed'.[45] The deposit was rich in seal, fish and bird bones, and included some foreign materials, such as a greenstone ground-edge axe, which had been carried or traded from 150 kilometres away. Based on the location and size of the Seal Point site, Lourandos speculated that it had been the principal base camp in the Cape region over the past 1500 years and that this period of intense occupation had changed the ecological balance in the region.[46]

When put alongside other research on south-western Victoria, his excavations seemed to reveal a compelling regional chronology. Although some archaeological sites in western Victoria dated to the end of the last Ice Age, most seemed to cluster around 3000–4000 years ago, with a more intensive phase of occupation over the past

2000 years. He interpreted these archaeological changes as evidence of significant social transformations, with people forming new exchange networks, moving into different environments and living increasingly sedentary lives. This was probably also when the eel traps were built, he concluded.[47]

In a landmark article in 1983, Lourandos gave this range of social and economic transformations a name: 'intensification'. He also proposed an elegant general theory to explain the changes as an internal social development. To illustrate his theory, he drew upon the drainage systems of western Victoria.

Lourandos' central insight, as Marcia Langton observes, was to view the eel traps as social landscapes: 'He regarded the network of manufactured channels and eel-holding ponds as social and political phenomena, not just narrow, economic events.'[48] The maintenance of these vast traps, he reasoned, demanded cooperation and collaboration between different groups. When the eeling season began, people from across the region would have come together, creating new opportunities for trade as well as generating new social and political rivalries. There might even have been peaceful displays of competitiveness, such as friendly bouts of wrestling or football matches using a possum-skin ball (*marngrook*) – the origins of the game of the Australian Football League.[49] 'The survival of these social networks,' Lourandos reasoned,

> thus depended mainly upon eels, as did the prestige of individual clan elders and their following. Everybody involved in these competitive politics had therefore an incentive to work a little harder – in this case by digging ditches and constructing weirs and eel traps – in order to ensure a dependable supply of eels.[50]

In short, he argued that the social politics of eeling encouraged innovation and created more reliable sources of food, which in turn allowed people to live more sedentary lives and conduct more elaborate ceremonies. Significantly, he argued that this process of 'intensification' was occurring at an increasing rate. In the final line of his 1983 paper, in a rhetorical flourish that caused him almost as much grief as Jones' comments about 'doomed' Tasmanians, he concluded: 'Intensification of social and economic relations would appear to have been increasingly taking place during the Holocene period on the Australian mainland, the process being nipped in the bud by the coming of the Europeans.'[51]

This sentence rang alarm bells for many in the field. It seemed to suggest that Aboriginal people were on an evolutionary trajectory towards a more complex, more agricultural way of life, and that they had ceased to change and adapt in the years since the invasion. Lourandos believed that his critics had misunderstood the line, along with the concept of 'complexification' at the heart of his argument.[52] But even those inspired by Lourandos interpreted the intensification model as evidence of cumulative and directional change. Elizabeth Williams, for example, used her work on Victorian cooking mounds to suggest that 'in time, the groups of the Western District would have gone on to develop agriculture. All the preconditions for the development of food production were there.'[53] The use of the language of 'intensification' – a concept first outlined by British archaeologist Barbara Bender in her work on farming societies – inevitably linked Lourandos' arguments to the long-running debates about the origins of agriculture.

Indigenous writer, scholar and storyteller Bruce Pascoe has recently reignited this discussion with the publication of his award-winning 2014 book *Dark Emu: Black Seeds: Agriculture or Accident?* Pascoe draws together the immense ethnographic evidence of Aboriginal land management – burning, tilling, irrigating, harvesting, baking and construction – to argue that Aboriginal societies be viewed through the lens of agriculture: 'Aboriginals did build houses, did cultivate and irrigate crops, did sew clothes and were not hapless wanderers across the soil, mere hunter-gatherers.'[54] In his attempt to contest the negative racial attitudes that remain prevalent in Australian society, and to restore 'Aboriginal pride in the past', he seeks to 're-classify' the first Australians as farmers and horticulturalists. It is a fascinating and provocative argument, building on a long scholarly debate, and it raises important questions about the ways in which Indigenous history is written and perceived. As Pascoe implores his readers after a discussion of the antiquity of seed grinding in Australia: 'Why don't our hearts fill with wonder and pride?'[55]

But what does the language of 'progress' – articulated as the move from foragers to farmers – do to our understanding of change over the last several millennia? Is it necessary to turn to Eurocentric language and ideas to acknowledge the richness and complexity of Indigenous economies? Is it meaningful to define 'agriculture' as a stable category that transcends space and time?

The vexed question of 'why did Aborigines not become farmers?' has long haunted the study of Indigenous society.[56] It is a question bound up in colonial assumptions about evolutionary hierarchies, whereby every society is on a ladder climbing upwards towards the ultimate destination of agriculture and industry. Aboriginal society has long been regarded as residing on one of the lower rungs. The categories of 'hunter-gatherer' and 'agriculturalist', Jones wrote in 1975, 'denote what has been seen as the fundamental division in human history, the watershed which separates savagery from civilization'.[57] It is this division that frames Pascoe's argument for Aboriginal society to be understood through an agricultural lens. But it is important to remember that there is no inherent value to a farming or a foraging way of life. Neither signifies greater sophistication and both are amorphous categories better understood on a spectrum of economic activity. The boundaries between them are blurred.[58] The idea that they still represent a 'fundamental division in human history' is as outdated as the belief that Australia was the last continent to be colonised.

Many of Lourandos' peers were wary of using Western terms to
argue for the significance of Indigenous heritage. Archaeologist John
Beaton bristled at one colleague's suggestion that Aboriginal society at
contact was 'semi-agricultural': 'For me, Aboriginal culture is full-time
Aboriginal culture, and that is its great strength. It need not doff its cap
to Europe's industrial revolution, the Near East's agricultural origins or
Meso-America's evolution of complex societies.'[59] John Mulvaney made
a similar appeal in his second volume of *The Prehistory of Australia*. He
urged the public to seek to understand Aboriginal society on its own
terms and appreciate it for what it is, not for what it may or may not
have become:

> Before posing the 'why no neolithic?' question, therefore, it must be
> observed that an Aboriginal was possibly healthier than a peasant in
> classical Rome and better adjusted than a New York apartment
> dweller. Pharaoh's pyramid testifies to his society's technological
> mastery, but it perished; archaeology hints at an extraordinary con-
> tinuity of social adjustment and spiritual life within Australia.[60]

Part of the reason for Lourandos' despair at the criticism of his
model was that he was trying to use the language of intensification to
move beyond categories such as 'hunter-gatherer' and 'agriculturist',
which create arbitrary boundaries, to discuss the 'grey areas' in between:
'Labels, along with their cultural baggage, only impede our progress.'[61]
In his own research he acknowledged that the term 'hunter-gatherer'
was a colonial artefact, but also worked with it and sought to enlarge
our understanding of the societies it represents. He titled his book-
length history of Aboriginal Australia *Continent of Hunter-Gatherers*.

The intensification model was not an argument for Aboriginal societies to be viewed as agricultural. It was a reminder that cultures have
their own dynamics, and this shapes how they transform over time.
Social factors can play a key role in shaping cultural, technological

and economic patterns in Aboriginal society. 'The main question is no longer "Why or why not agriculture?",' Lourandos argued, 'but "Why change?"'[62]

* * *

In the years since the intensification model was first proposed, it has been enriched and complicated by a new generation of research. A variety of regional histories have challenged the idea of a continent-wide socioeconomic transformation.[63] The intensification model has even been called into question within Lourandos' own region. In 1991 archaeologists Caroline Bird and David Frankel reviewed the western Victorian evidence that Lourandos had drawn upon in the 1970s and struggled to confirm the associations between alliance networks, productivity and settlement patterns that underpinned the idea of intensification.[64] Although they recognised that sites like cooking mounds were a recent phenomenon, they suggested that some of the social transformations Lourandos recorded, such as eeling, may be much older than a few thousand years, and that the proliferation of late-Holocene sites could be a product of preservation, rather than population increase. Archaeology is always biased towards the more recent past, as organic materials decay and disappear over time. By focusing on the particularities of the archaeological sites, Bird and Frankel reframed the questions they were asking of the same evidence. What might seem connected and cumulative under an intensification model could also be interpreted as local, short-term adaptations to specific changes in the immediate environment.[65]

In 2012 one of Lourandos' students, Ian McNiven, in partnership with the Gunditjmara community, led an excavation of the Budj Bim eel traps at Lake Condah in western Victoria. Their findings suggested that the initial channel in the basalt bedrock had been created sometime before 6600 years ago – a time of higher water levels in Lake Condah, which would have probably stimulated the eel population and provided ideal conditions to trap them in such canals. But McNiven's team was cautious not to overstate the antiquity of eeling: 'Despite suggesting a much longer chronology for the trapping systems, our results do not discount the possibility that most traps do indeed date to the past 3000 years.' In particular, they point out that their research provides empirical support for Lourandos' hypothesis that Aboriginal people in south-west Victoria created water controls 'to regularize and stabilize the availability of resources' at a time of late-Holocene drying.[66]

Although there were undoubtedly dramatic changes in the Holocene, the idea of a continental 'Inventive Phase' or a period of socioeconomic intensification over the last 3000–4000 years is less clear-cut than it appeared in the late 1970s and early 1980s.[67] Although internally driven social change was a major factor in the history of ancient Australia, the climatic, ecological and environmental consequences of the end of the last Ice Age, the rising of the seas, and irregular effects of the El Niño–Southern Oscillation also played a role. And, significantly, many of the innovations thought to have emerged during the Holocene appear to have precedents in the Pleistocene.[68] At Wyrie Swamp in South Australia, for example, Roger Luebbers recovered a handful of 10,000-year-old wooden implements, including a boomerang, a spear, digging sticks and a barbed javelin fragment. As Luebbers wrote in 1975, 'We can therefore see the Australian Aborigine emerging from the Pleistocene equipped with a tool kit as vital to the exploitation of the local environment then as it was yesterday, and just as complex.'[69]

There are fewer continental models in Australian archaeology today.[70] And many of the grand narratives proposed in the 1970s and 1980s, such as Lourandos' intensification model and Lesley Maynard's three-part rock art sequence are being challenged by rich regional evidence. Australian archaeology is becoming more local. This emphasis on regionalism does not imply that Aboriginal societies existed in isolation; they were intimately connected to neighbouring groups through trade, marriage and ceremony. But while there remain continental commonalities, the overwhelming insight into the social history of the Holocene resonates with Hallam's understanding of Aboriginal burning regimes: there were different histories of change in every region, as distinct societies responded to their own social, environmental and ecological circumstances.[71]

* * *

In the wake of the intensification debate, Lourandos retreated from the spotlight to work on the archaeology of Aboriginal social landscapes in Queensland. He and Anne Ross believed that the intensification model had 'democratised the discipline', by moving the academic focus from rare Pleistocene sites to more widespread recent phenomena. They also argued that it had taken 'Australian archaeology away from the "cowboy" era of data collection' and linked the field with international theoretical debates.[72] But, as Bernard Huchet reflects, there remains a profound ambiguity in the theoretical methods used in Australia.[73] Instead of approaching the past through international debates, most Australian interpretations – like Lourandos' intensification theory – emerge from deep engagement with documentary sources and patient, systematic fieldwork. 'This is how archaeology actually advances,' Sylvia Hallam observed in 1971, 'not by obsessive introspection on significance, relevance, definitions, aims and methodology', but by 'bringing to bear curiosity, energy, expertise, and experience' on the information gathered through the 'mud, dust and sweat' of fieldwork.[74] A complex view of Aboriginal society has emerged in Australia, but it remains understated.

In the years since her survey of south-western Australia, Hallam has continued to move closer to history. In the late 1970s, she admired an emerging strain of historical scholarship, led by Henry Reynolds, that attempted to understand Aboriginal responses to their conquest and dispossession. The documentary historians she had yearned for when she embarked on her archaeological survey in 1970 had finally arrived on the scene.

In 1983, after falling seriously ill, she redirected her research away from fieldwork and towards the archive. To understand the ways in which populations had changed over time, she started counting the Aboriginal people she found in the sources. This, in turn, led her to write personal stories. It was a different, but just as profound, engagement with the archaeology of documents. Having used these colonial sources to journey back in time, to gain 'a long view' of Aboriginal society throughout the Holocene and into the Pleistocene, she returned to them as a biographer of Indigenous lives, seeking a more subtle, intimate view of the other side of the frontier.[75]

TEN

HUNTING THE PLEISTOCENE

The History and Politics of Jinmium
and Madjedbebe

On 31 May 1992, three days before the landmark *Mabo* decision was handed down in the Australian High Court, a small archaeological team sank a trench beside a weathered sandstone boulder in the far east of the Kimberley region. The site was known as Jinmium. It had been found during a survey of Aboriginal campsites associated with the late nineteenth century pastoral industry.[1] The team leader, Richard Fullagar, was particularly interested in what he could learn about diets and foraging patterns from the stone tools he was uncovering. 'It seems preposterous that stone artefacts have anything significant to tell us about culture,' he reflected in 1994, 'especially in recent Aboriginal Australia, where simple stone chips pale to insignificance alongside the complex social life of Aboriginal people.'[2] But under a microscope he was able to read the history of a stone tool from the wear patterns and residues left behind: plant fibres and seeds, blood and bone. The key, he and his wife and research partner, ecologist and geographer Lesley Head, reflected, is to link the artefacts with the social and economic worlds in which they were crafted. At Jinmium, they hoped to make these connections and, in the process, unravel the deep history of human interaction with the environment in the Keep River region.

Head and Fullagar's team was given permission to excavate by the Aboriginal landowners, the Murinpatha, Jaminjung and Gajerrong peoples, especially senior Gajerrong man Mr Paddy Carlton and Murinpatha woman Mrs Biddy Simon, who explained the significance of the site and told them the story of how Jinmium got its name. Jinmium forms one link in a song cycle that stretches across the Keep River region and connects the locations of important economic and ceremonial resources. The Dreaming track marks the path of a male spirit figure, Djibigun, in pursuit of a female spirit being. Driven by desire, he tracked her across the desert and over creeks, past the red ochre hills and the Bungyala stone quarry, until he caught her at Jinmium. But she eluded him by transforming into the 40-metre-high sandstone monolith that rises above the wooded plains today. While Jinmium towers over the landscape, Djibigun still haunts it in the form of a small quail (*Coturnix australis*). 'According to old people,' Mr Carlton explained, '… that fella [Djibigun] keep walking, keep walking through all of my country, across the river.'[3] Head and Fullagar hoped to investigate the tangible elements of this story through their archaeological excavation. They were trying to understand the Dreaming track within the deep time story, searching for clues that could demonstrate connections between sites on the route followed by Djibigun and Jinmium, such as stone and ochre that could be traced to their source and starchy yam residues on excavated pounding tools that might reveal how people moved through different ecological regions. 'The things that are continuous,' wrote Fullagar and Head, 'are those that can be most closely linked to the story of Djibigun and Jinmium.'[4]

But these fine-grained research goals were sidelined by the preliminary dates that emerged from the 1992 field season. Jinmium, the samples suggested, had been occupied for around 60,000 years, making it possibly the oldest site in Australia. On their return visit, on 19 May 1993, Fullagar reported the dates to Mrs Simon. 'She was very excited,' Fullagar wrote in his journal. 'See,' she told him, 'you come to the right place, you see.'[5] The archaeologists shared her excitement, but they were also suspicious of the date, which lay outside the general pattern of oldest sites in Australia. They were wary of catapulting the site into the most politically charged debate in Australian archaeology: the timing of the arrival of humans on the continent.[6] But under pressure from their main funding source, the Australian Research Council, they made deep time, rather than land use, the central focus of their 1993 excavation.[7]

Thermoluminscence dating expert David Price accompanied the team in 1993 and took new samples from the wall of the pit. Rock art specialist Paul Taçon also joined them to study some circular engravings (or 'pecked cupules') uncovered on the buried rock shelter wall and on a fallen sandstone fragment bearing abraded grooves. Similar engravings were scattered in chains around the region, revealing an intricate web of connections.[8] The dates they uncovered in that field season, both for the evidence of occupation and for the art, were, in Fullagar's words, 'pretty outrageous'.[9] They discussed them with the local community and Fullagar returned to the site in July 1995 with Rhys Jones and another luminescence expert, Bert Roberts, to retest the site.[10] In the meantime, they submitted an initial site report to the prestigious British journal *Antiquity*.[11] The results should have been published in December 1996 in a peer-reviewed academic forum. But after a series of leaks in the months preceding publication, the archaeologists decided to go public and announce the dates via the media. It was a decision made, in part, to include rather than alienate the Indigenous people on whose land they were working.[12]

On 21 September 1996, Australians awoke to news that a 'lost civilisation' had been discovered in the Kimberley, including an 'outback Stonehenge that will rewrite our history'. In a lavish front-page exclusive, Fairfax journalist James Woodford reported that Jinmium had been occupied for as long as 176,000 years – 'possibly tripling the period of occupation of Australia' – and that the rock engravings that Taçon had recorded were 75,000 years old, 'pushing back dramatically the date when humans began to create art'.[13] The feature stretched over many pages and was coordinated with the *New York Times*. It explored the implications of the find for human evolution and how people had colonised the globe, the nature of art and the extinction of the continent's megafauna, as well as profiles of 'the people behind the discoveries' and the reasoning behind publishing the dates in this way.[14] Even the most modest date arising out of the site report – 116,000 years – was still twice the age of the next oldest site in Australia. 'It changes enormously the way we think about Australian prehistory,' Fullagar told the media. 'To suggest that Aborigines have been in Australia for over 100,000 years really does change a lot of things.'[15]

The academic community was divided. 'This is going to cause a huge flutter around the world,' Alan Thorne reflected, 'because there are so many theories (about the evolution and spread of modern humans) tied up in this debate. And one side is wrong.'[16] Kim Ackerman heralded the dates as 'stupendous ... I have no problem contemplating a 100,000 to 200,000 year occupation of Australia', while Peter White, reflecting on the transformations over the previous decades, commented to one reporter that the dates would 'make us rethink some of our models, but there's no reason why not. We're amazed, fairly surprised and rather pleased.'[17] Many Indigenous Australians embraced the new dates. Within weeks of the Jinmium announcement, a group of Aboriginal dancers were promoting their performance as being '176,000 years in the making'.[18]

There were also immediate voices of doubt, especially about the way the story had been broken. 'I would not dream of taking a major discovery to the media first,' Robert Bednarik said. 'They've gone about this the wrong way.'[19] Mike Morwood came forward as one of the referees for the *Antiquity* paper, declaring that he had recommended against publication due to concern with the lack of cross-checks in the dating process used.[20] Rhys Jones also expressed 'serious doubts' about the dating methods, while hastily adding: 'But I'm not a hostile witness. The site is extremely interesting and extremely old – possibly the oldest in Australia. Its implications will challenge contemporary views of modern sapiens. But it has got to be based on believable results.'[21]

The hesitancy to accept the Jinmium dates reflects a suspicion of outliers and a wariness to hastily destabilise a global narrative. If the dates held up, they had implications far beyond the voyages of the first Australians and their possible role in the extinction of native megafauna – they gave fuel to an older theory of human evolution known as the multiregional hypothesis, which suggests that everyone alive today does not have a common modern human ancestor; rather, we have all evolved from different regional populations of *Homo erectus*. Should the history of humanity in Australia be older than 100,000 years, it would dramatically change the global story of human evolution.

The news was magnified by the political context into which the dates were delivered. After the groundswell that followed the *Mabo* decision, the election of the Howard government on 2 March 1996 and the rise of Pauline Hanson's One Nation Party had changed the tenor of debate about native title in Australia. 'I am fed up with being told, "This is our land",' Hanson had declared in her maiden speech. 'Well, where the hell do I go? I was born here, and so were my parents and children.'[22] The *Wik* case, which was being heard in the High Court in 1996, framed the discovery, as the region incorporating the Keep River area was subject to a native title claim by the Miriuwung and Gajerrong peoples.[23] Some journalists latched onto the motivations of the archaeologists in announcing a big date and questioned what the Aboriginal community got out of this find. Maria Ceresa of the *Australian* wrote a series of articles about the money some members of the Aboriginal community were making out of guiding visitors to the site.[24] 'Reinterpreting the past, in a country where native title is at issue, involves contention, and that contention has swept like a whirlwind through this field,' wrote Nicolas Rothwell in an essay on the politicisation of Australian archaeology. 'It would be hard to imagine an archaeologist pursuing a research project that tended to work against Aboriginal interests.'[25]

The credibility of the site suffered from being drawn into the world of media exclusives and newspaper rivalries, and the Jinmium story became as much about the scientific process as it did about the timescale of Australian history. Rothwell criticised the *Sydney Morning Herald*'s coverage in particular: 'The atmospherics, the "spin" surrounding the news was profoundly disquieting. This was, after all, science. Yet the event was tightly managed; splashily presented; given, by the researchers who put it forward, an overtly political context.'[26] The *Australian* editorialised in favour of 'caution and objectivity'.[27]

Within two years, the supposedly 176,000-year-old site was found to be less than 10,000 years old.[28] Quartz grains from a decomposing rock had become mixed with the surrounding sand, giving dates closer to the age of the rock, rather than the human occupation of the site. Fullagar was pilloried by the press and by his colleagues for having 'gone off half-cocked in search of fame' and taking Australian history on 'a chronological roller-coaster ride'.[29] The irony, Fullagar later reflected, was that he had not gone hunting for the Pleistocene at Jinmium: the research stemmed out of a long engagement with a community and an interest in resource use over time. 'We were not out to find the oldest age,' he told journalist Graeme Leech. 'We were not out to create some controversy. It's long-term research which began in 1987. I'll still be there in 20 years, I've no doubt.'[30] Head searched for the positives in the controversy: 'The public response to Jinmium suggests to us that many Australians, and many kinds of Australians, are not only passionate about the prehistory of the continent, but are also looking to archaeology to help them articulate their place in it.'[31]

* * *

In Grahame Clark's 1961 review of *World Prehistory*, he confidently declared that Australia was the last continent to be colonised: 'There is no convincing evidence for the immigration of man into Australia before Neothermal times' – in other words, the Holocene.[32] But by 1975 there were over thirty Pleistocene sites in Australia.[33] The revolution in Australia's timescale since the 1960s has opened the eyes of the Australian public to the antiquity and complexity of Indigenous history, but it has also laid fertile ground for wild claims to take root. There is a 'Gee whiz' element to any dates that transcend our ordinary understanding of time as lived experience.[34] The dates become numbers, and aside from being 'a long time ago' they are hard to grasp imaginatively. The Jinmium controversy is simply one example of dates escaping their context. We need to be able to understand the difference between a history that extends over 40,000, 60,000 or 100,000 years. In context, dates do tell a story.

This chapter follows the quest to uncover the oldest dates for occupation. It focuses on the controversies and possibilities that surround Jinmium and the current oldest site in Australia, Madjedbebe (formerly Malakunanja II), near the border of Arnhem Land and Kakadu National Park.[35] It explores its excavation and re-excavation in 1972, 1989, 2012 and 2015 and attempts to put this key archaeological site in its global context.

Old dates make careers and attract grants. They change history books and, for better or worse, lend a sense of legitimacy to Aboriginal claims to country. They are also fraught with internal politics within the discipline.

'The field of archaeology is full of wild claims,' Rhys Jones reflected to a reporter in 1990. 'And if you get it wrong, you can expect to be knee-capped.'[36] The search for sensational or revolutionary discoveries is also inextricably entwined with questions of gender.[37] While nuanced and humanistic research is often associated with the work of female scientists, Western masculine science is bound to the act of discovery. 'As it is seen in archaeology,' writes Stephanie Moser, 'the Western masculine model of science can be related to a preoccupation with questions of antiquity and origins – discovering the oldest sites, locating the deepest deposits, and finding the most unique sites or data.'[38] Since 1984, this hyper-masculine preoccupation in Australian archaeology has been gently parodied each year with the 'Big Man Award', which is bestowed upon the archaeologist who makes 'the most outrageous statement' at the annual AAA confer-ence.[39] On the tenth anniversary of the award, Elizabeth Williams, the inaugural winner, reflected: 'Given that many of these academics are male and that many have been particularly interested in pursuing "big" things for their research topics (e.g. the oldest site, the coldest site, the hottest site, and so on), I thought it was strange that they hadn't won more Big Man awards.'[40] The same paradox is true of the hunt for the Pleistocene. Although Sharon Sullivan has characterised the search for old dates as an exercise in machismo – 'My Pleistocene sequence is bigger than your Pleistocene sequence' – Australian research into antiquity, origins and routes of colonisation has been led by women as much as men.[41]

At the heart of the hunt for the Pleistocene is a shift in control within the discipline of archaeology, from history to science. 'Why does the world think it is so special?' asked *Antiquity* editor Christopher Chippindale when the peer-reviewed report on Jinmium was finally published. 'Because of the numbers.'[42] The debate came to centre on the means of getting the numbers, and in particular the benefits of various dating methods.[43] It was a mark of how much archaeologists had ceded control to dating specialists, often referred to as 'time lords';

or, in Taçon's words, 'the high priests and sages of science, gowned in white robes and armed with hi-tech and seemingly "magical" instruments capable of counting time down to the nanosecond.'[44]

Gordon Childe foreshadowed this loss of authority in the weeks before his death in 1957, suggesting, in light of the radiocarbon revolution, that 'archaeologists will abandon responsibility for chronology or themselves become nuclear physicists. In any case every prehistorian must master enough mathematics, physics and chemistry to appreciate the limitation of the information [they] can provide.'[45] Rhys Jones suggests that the enormous uncertainty that followed the radiocarbon revolution was part of the reason Childe, the great archaeological synthesiser, took his own life.[46]

Dating techniques can indeed seem magical and mysterious. Even a widely used method like radiocarbon dating is replete with challenges that demand specialised knowledge to overcome. As explored in Chapter 1, the technique measures the decaying isotope, carbon-14, against the steady isotope, carbon-12. The rate of decay and amount of carbon-14 provides the date. But carbon decays frustratingly quickly. After 5700 years, roughly half of the carbon-14 is gone, and after 38,000 years, only 1 per cent of carbon-14 that was present in the living organism survives.[47] And there are further challenges. The proportion of carbon in the atmosphere changes over time and dates need to be calibrated to account for these fluctuations: this process of translating 'radiocarbon years' to 'calendar years' is part of the reason there are so many variations in early dates. But, more significantly, carbon acts like a sponge. It can be contaminated by something as small as a skin cell from a human hand or even organic matter carried in groundwater. If the sample is young, and there is still plenty of carbon-14, then the impact of contamination is minimal. In Tim Flannery's words, 'It is a bit like being one dollar out when counting a thousand.' But when a sample is old, 'the contamination may then be like miscounting by a dollar when there are only two dollars!'[48] It is rare to get a date older than 40,000 years; for a long time this was considered to be the radiocarbon barrier.[49] Even with the latest advances in radiocarbon dating, such as Accelerator Mass Spectrometry (AMS), which uses magnetics to measure carbon atoms directly, and Acid Base Oxidixation and stepwise combustion (ABOX), which uses acid to remove potential micro-layers of contamination, there is an instrumental limit to the technique of 50,000 years, at which point the radiocarbon concentration in a sample becomes one part per thousand trillion.[50]

One of the most significant early sites for dating the antiquity of Australia's human past was Charlie Dortch's work at Devil's Lair, south of Perth in Western Australia.[51] In the 1970s Dortch carefully excavated an extensive five-metre deep trench in the cave, uncovering an intricate local history told in blackened and broken bones, hearths, shells, and stone and bone artefacts. He found a continuous stream of occupation debris in layers of sediment that had built up over 30,000 years. There were also lower artefacts. A flake of opal was uncovered at a 35,000-year-old level and a piece of charcoal was dated to around 38,000 years ago. But there the dates plateaued. Like other sites around the continent, such as the freshwater middens at Lake Mungo and hearths found within clay terraces on the Upper Swan River, the oldest samples were all around the age of 37,000 to 38,000 years.[52]

In 1989 Jim Allen took this cluster of dates at face value. He interpreted them as evidence that the first Australians made landfall no earlier than 40,000 years ago and had spread to every corner of the continent by 35,000 years ago.[53] He was supported by many of his colleagues, such as Sandra Bowdler, who concluded that 'there is no evidence that *Homo sapiens* was present in southeast Asia before 40,000 BP'.[54]

Rhys Jones, on the other hand, thought it was no coincidence that the earliest dates all clustered at around the same time as carbon-14 disappeared from a deposit. He suspected that the oldest dates 'were so close to the theoretical limits of the radiocarbon methods that maybe the "plateau" was really an illusion'.[55] Indeed, he viewed some of these dates as minimum age estimates, owing to sample contamination by modern carbon. As early as 1979 Jones had intuited a date of 50,000 years ('or even more') for initial human settlement.[56] When it came to the state of early Australian archaeology, he liked to fall back on the rather morbid metaphor of a condemned man at the gallows. Every few years, it was as if a trapdoor had opened beneath the field; the dates for human occupation of Australia plunged, only to be jagged to an abrupt halt by the limitations of radiocarbon dating. He called it 'rope-bound theory'.[57]

Jones' search for old dates led him back to Arnhem Land in 1981, to the west of where he had lived in 1972–1973. Over a decade and a half, throughout the 1980s and early 1990s, he embarked on a large-scale survey of deep, stratified rock shelters. He relished the experience of exploring 'very remote country' with Aboriginal men during these surveys, and, in the mode of George Augustus Robinson, constantly plied them with questions, filling his journals with their wide-ranging ecological and geographical knowledge.[58] They also guided him to sites and helped him to dig and sieve them. On his 1981 visit he excavated Nauwalabila I in Deaf Adder Gorge, which was known colloquially as the Lindner site after the crocodile catcher Dave Lindner, who joined many archaeological expeditions in the Top End. Mulvaney regarded him as 'our man in the north'.[59] When I was introduced to him in 2012 his name was preceded by a hushed 'the legendary'.

The shelter at Nauwalabila I had been formed by a massive rock falling off the cliff face and landing at an angle on the valley floor, creating a cool area with deep shade. Jones and Ian Johnson's team dug a narrow three-metre pit straight into the earth: a 'telephone booth' shaft. Jones regarded his time in the bottom of that pit in 1981 as 'one of those turning points in one's life as an archaeologist':

I'm in this section, down at the base, which is three metres high, it's
full of artefacts ... but the problem is that the carbon only goes down
about halfway ... and from then on the artefacts are there, but there's
no carbon. It's all been oxidised. ... and I thought to myself then,
this was in 1981, I will never know the age of the base of that site.[60]

Although these initial field seasons in and around Kakadu turned up a
range of old dates, none could overcome the limitations of the radiocarbon technique.

In early 1987 geochronologist Bert Roberts, who was doing a PhD
on the sand sheets of the Magela Creek catchment, asked Jones whether
he would be interested in returning to Nauwalabila I to resolve the
site's chronology. He suggested comparing the existing radiocarbon
dates with those that could be gained from the relatively new technique of thermoluminescence.[61] Instead of carbon, this method dates
the moment an individual grain of sand last saw sunlight. The general
idea behind luminescence dating is that when a grain of quartz is buried
and protected from light, it is bombarded by background radioactivity from the surrounding sediment. Electrons from this radioactivity
become trapped in the crystal lattice of the quartz, steadily building
up a charge. When the grain of sand is heated (thermoluminescence)
or exposed to light (optically stimulated luminescence), the charge is
released and for a moment the quartz grain luminesces, or glows. The
intensity of this brief glow is proportional to the number of electrons
stored in the grain. And since the rate at which electrons are trapped
is as regular as clockwork, this luminescence process tells us when the
quartz grain was last exposed to sunlight.

The margins of error for this method are still relatively high (5 to
10 per cent), but it is capable of dating anything from a few hundred
years old to several hundred thousand years old. And although it lacks
the symbolic attraction that carbon has of once being alive, there is a
certain romantic quality to the idea that it reveals a surface in time. It

speaks directly to the vision Mike Smith articulates in *The Archaeology of Australia's Deserts* of an archaeological site as a layer cake: a palimpsest of different landscapes, 'stratified in time, stacked one above another'.[62] It allows us to glimpse a world in a grain of sand.

Due to 'sorry business' (Aboriginal funeral rites) in Deaf Adder Gorge, Jones and Roberts could not return to Nauwalabila I, so they instead visited two known sites further to the north, Madjedbebe and Malangangerr. In September 1988, together with Christopher Chippindale, they collected thermoluminescence samples from both sites by twisting an auger – or soil drill – into the earth.[63] The initial dates for the lowest artefacts at Madjedbebe came back between 50,000 and 60,000 years. 'A hush descended on Rhys when I told him the results,' Bert Roberts later wrote, 'a reaction that I now recognise as Rhys in contemplative rapture – and for a while we enjoyed the simple pleasure of being the only two people on the planet to know the age of a momentous event in human prehistory: the time of the arrival of people in Australia.'[64] A third member of the team, an archaeologist known for his 'conservative' interpretive approach, Mike Smith, joined the following year 'to tighten up the credibility' of the preliminary dates.[65] 'And so the three of us – the "cowboy", the conservative, and the chronologist – duly excavated the Malakunanja II [Madjedbebe] deposits in July 1989,' Roberts reflected, 'under the watchful eye of Big Bill [Neidjie], the traditional Aboriginal custodian of the site.'[66] Once more they dug a 'telephone booth' shaft, 4.5 metres into the earth. But while the shaft saved them time and money, by the end of the dig the team was approaching it with 'trepidation'.[67] At the bottom, the light was dim and the scent of dirt and sweat pungent. A long ladder leant against one wall and an enormous rock hung ominously over the edge of the pit, mocking the flimsy plastic hardhats the excavators wore. Four years later, acutely aware of the dangers of trench collapses, each of the three men sought a gravedigger's licence.

The great virtue of the shaft was that it extended well into 'sterile' deposits: from the base of the pit, with torch in hand, they could study the land before human arrival. The oldest dates at the bottom – around 110,000 years ago – told of naturally changing sand aprons, made of different quantities of fluvial sediments and wind-blown sand. At some point on the wall, the sediment began to build up faster and the first signs of human presence appeared in the form of small stone artefacts. This was the most cryptic level of the site. Each scrape of the trowel wiped away around 350 years of history. Organic material had not survived at this depth and there was no carbon to date. Besides, the excavators were well beyond the radiocarbon barrier.

The initial findings, published in *Nature* in 1990, suggested that people had been living in Australia for 55,000 years, plus or minus 5000.[68] Jones often spoke of a human antiquity in Australia of 60,000 years. He revelled in the fact that this was 20,000 years earlier than any modern human site in Europe: it 'really caused people to raise their eyebrows'.[69] A commendation was passed in the Australian Senate noting 'with interest' the discovery of 'art and artefacts in the Malakunanja II [Madjedbebe] rock shelter in Kakadu that have been dated as at least 60,000 years old'.[70]

The importance of these findings cannot be understated. The New World had become the Old. The radiocarbon barrier had been shattered. As American paleoanthropologist Richard Klein remarked, 'If the dates hold up it will force an enormous amount of rethinking.'[71] But there were many who remained sceptical, and when the site was discussed it often carried that same disclaimer: 'if the dates hold up'. As Jones, Roberts and Smith reflected,

> We feel that confirmation of our claims that the human colonization of the Greater Australian continent happened c. 50 [thousand

years] ago can only finally rest with replication at other sites; with the establishment of a pattern of dates of this order of antiquity. Further archaeological applications of TL dating over the next few years should settle the matter.[72]

Dates for Nauwalabila also came in at over 50,000 years, suggesting that Madjedbebe might not be an outlier, but these were also contested. Some criticised Madjedbebe for the use of the relatively new method of luminescence dating; some for the fact that the 1989 dig was never fully written up; others questioned whether 'human treadage' or termite activity might be behind the artefacts in the lowest levels.[73] 'In the small community of Australian archaeologists,' John Mulvaney and Johan Kamminga observed in 1999, 'there is now more disagreement and deeper division over the issue of earliest human settlement than there was a decade ago.'[74]

In 1998 Jim Allen again reviewed the range of claims for early sites in Australia, this time with Jim O'Connell, and concluded 'that initial occupation dates to about 40,000 radiocarbon years ago'.[75] In 2004, incorporating new evidence, they pushed this date back a few thousand years, writing 'that while the continent was probably occupied by 42–45,000 BP, earlier arrival dates are not well-supported'.[76] In their 2014 review they again updated their estimate, concluding that the first Australians arrived shortly after 50,000 years ago – 'on current evidence not earlier than 47–48,000 years ago'.[77] The incremental shifts from 40,000 to 42,000 to 45,000 to 48,000 led anthropologist William F Keegan to remark wryly, 'Archaeologists seem to face far more complications in making the crossing to Sahul than the people who accomplished this feat about 50 [thousand years ago].'[78]

The hestitancy to accept the Madjedbebe and Nauwalabila dates reflects a sensible suspicion of dates that are outside the general pattern of oldest sites: a distrust of discoveries that could quickly join the long list of discredited claims. In a small field like Australian archaeology, personalities and politics have a part to play in this 'long and some-times acrimonious debate'.[79] Jones' long-held belief in an ancient date for Australian occupation, combined with his popular flair and desire to be at the frontiers of archaeological knowledge, caused many of his colleagues to question his objectivity.

Madjedbebe has been re-excavated twice since Jones, Roberts and Smith worked there under the attentive eye of Gaagudju elder Big Bill Neidjie. In 2017, a large interdisciplinary team, led by Chris Clarkson, Zenobia Jacobs, Lynley Wallis, Mike Smith, Ben Marwick and Richard Fullagar, published new dates for the lowest layers of artefacts at Madjedbebe. Their paper in *Nature* addressed earlier criticisms of the site and pushed the baseline date for human occupation back to 65,000 years.[80] It is significant that many who were critics of the 1989 exca-vation, and who were not involved in the recent study, have spoken publicly of the robustness of the find. 'This is the earliest reliable date for human occupation in Australia,' archaeologist Peter Hiscock wrote to one reporter: 'This is indeed a marvellous step forward in our explo-ration of the human past in Australia.'[81]

So what do we do with an outlier that refuses to be dismissed? What does this new number tell us about Australia's deep history? How does it shape our understanding of how humans emerged and moved around the world – and the effect they had on the lands they colonised?

* * *

In 2012 I joined the team of archaeologists that returned to Madjedbebe. I earned my place as the camp manager and cook. The leaders of the dig hoped that recent advances in dating techniques would resolve lingering questions about the antiquity of the site, and, by opening a larger trench, they also sought to verify its structural integrity and better understand the natural processes by which it had formed.[82] In 2015 I reprised my role as camp cook with another team, again led by Clarkson, who was keen

to gain a nuanced picture of the site at its deepest levels. He wanted to
see if he could discern a pattern from the oldest stone tools that might
illuminate the technology used by the colonisers. He had conducted
similar excavations in India, on the route people took from Africa to
Australia. We were hosted by the Mirarr people, who held the right of
veto over all aspects of the work and were involved through a process of
constant and respectful communication. They took pride in having the
oldest Australian site on their land and cautiously supported our curious fascination with the earth. As David Vadiveloo, a lawyer, filmmaker
and consultant to the Gundjeihmi Aboriginal Corporation, put it: 'The
Mirarr did not want this to be a project about them, they wanted this
to be a project that was in partnership with them.'[83]

Madjedbebe is a shelter nestled at the base of a towering sandstone
formation known as Djuwamba: a last remnant of the plateau before
the landscape gives way to wet, scrubby plains. Our drive to work each
day twisted between the luminous Magela floodplain and the jagged
silhouette of the Arnhem Land escarpment, which would blaze red with
the first rays of sun. On site, as the cool mornings gave way to hot,
dry days, dirt mingled with sweat and this quiet corner of Djuwamba
became filled with the scratching of trowels, the rustle of sieves and the
meandering conversations of the excavators.

The site itself is no more than a slight overhang: a long, decorated
rock wall leaning out towards the nearby wetlands. It was only as we
dug that the back wall receded and the full rock shelter was revealed.
The pit had a musty aroma, occasionally sweetened by the scent of
honey wafting in from a nearby hive of feral European bees. The rock
wall is ornamented with over a thousand motifs in reds and yellows and
whites: amidst the array of Dreaming creatures there is a wagon wheel, a
Macassan prau and several guns. There is also a figure rendered in white
kaolin clay, pipe in mouth, broad-brimmed hat and hands on hips:
the familiar whitefella stance. The contact art illustrates the changing

relationship between the newcomers and Aboriginal people, reflecting a growing familiarity with their different cultures and an increasing reliance on each other.[84]

The signs of contact continue below the surface too. In the first week of the 2012 excavation Clarkson cut his foot on some debris left behind from the first time this site was excavated, by Johan Kamminga in 1973. A can of Carlton Draught and a bottle of Scram! insect spray had been backfilled to a 30,000-year-old depth. Another archaeological signature followed us all the way down the length of the pit: a neat scar of black soil from the refilled auger hole that Roberts and Jones twisted into the earth in 1988.

We found hundreds of pieces of ground haematite and crayons of red and yellow ochre scattered through every layer of the site. This pigment was mined from the Cahill Formation, which is now mined for uranium; the crayons were traded or carried to this shelter by thousands of people over thousands of generations; and here they were worn to a recognisable nub. What the haematite was used for is harder to tell. Perhaps it was ground to paint rock and skin, or to preserve food and tools. Perhaps it coloured a ritual object. As Philip Jones reminds us in *Ochre and Rust,* red ochre is the symbolic equivalent of sacred blood. It 'is a medium of transcendence, from sickness to health, death to renewal, ritual uncleanness to cleanness, the secular to the sacred, the present reality to the Dreaming'.[85]

To our surprise, we also encountered human burials. Over several days we watched as a tall, upright stone emerged from the earth. It was surrounded at its base by a ring of evenly spaced large stones. Beneath that was a fully articulated human skeleton. It was one of seventeen individuals who had been buried within the midden several thousand years ago.[86] The discovery brought the excavation to an immediate stop. It was only through a process of quiet, respectful negotiation with the Mirarr board that work was allowed to continue. Although affronted by the idea of disturbing the Old People, the Mirarr also recognised this as an opportunity. They were interested in the genetics of the ancient remains, for these can act as a baseline or a control to compare to contemporary samples. Radium, for example, behaves very similarly to calcium inside the human body. Tooth enamel locks in background radioactivity. If one were to compare the teeth of an individual from pre-mining times to the teeth of someone born and raised beside the Ranger Uranium mine, some compelling results might be found. The deep past can act as a powerful tool in the political present.

* * *

Deep time scholars such as Jared Diamond and Steven Mithen place the birth of history at 50,000 years ago. 'Or thereabouts.'[87] This is the time of Diamond's so-called Great Leap Forward, the moment humans went from being a species no more exceptional than 'beavers, bowerbirds, and army ants' to becoming 'the first species, in the history of life on Earth, capable of destroying all life'.[88] There was no stark anatomical change to mark this shift; rather, it is suggested, this was an inner event – a revolution within the mind.[89] Why did this happen then? Was it, as Tim Flannery argues in *The Future Eaters*, colonisation of the 'new' lands that sparked the change? Was it the development of the modern voice box and thus a more sophisticated manner of communication? Or indeed is this idea of an inner event a misnomer, a 'coming of age' invented by Eurocentric minds obsessed by revolution?[90] Steven Oppenheimer, in his book *Out of Africa's Eden*, argues convincingly that 'Africans were fully modern, singing, dancing, painting humans long before they came out of their home continent'.[91] The debate rages on. And so it should. For at its heart is that most fundamental of questions: what does it mean to be human?

For most of the twentieth century, the prevailing human evolutionary paradigm was the multiregional hypothesis, which suggests that

Homo sapiens evolved from *Homo erectus* simultaneously in different parts of globe. But in the 1980s this was replaced by the rival 'out of Africa' model as strengthening fossil and DNA evidence showed that all people had a shared African ancestry.[92] These competing hypotheses have been central to debates over the origins of the first Australians. Alan Thorne (a multiregionalist) suggested that Australia had been home to two different hominids, one characterised by the robust features of the skeletons uncovered at Kow Swamp and the other with the gracile features of Mungo Lady and Mungo Man. More recently, Colin Pardoe and Peter Brown have revealed these variations to be the result of local climates, gender and head pressing, rather than multiple waves of colonisation. Australia was colonised by one population and they were anatomically modern *Homo sapiens*, like you and me.[93]

It is now clear that *Homo sapiens* emerged in Africa around 200,000 years ago – or perhaps as early as 300,000 years ago.[94] Human evolution, of course, has a far greater antiquity. At least 3.5 billion years have passed since the origin of life, some 7 million years or so since our lineage split from that of the chimpanzee, and around 1.8 million years since our cousins, the wanderlusting *Homo erectus*, first ventured out of the wide plains and rift valleys of Africa to spread around the world.[95] The full name of our species, *Homo sapiens sapiens*, is a kind of taxonomic stutter meaning 'double-wise man'. As science writer James Shreeve points out, 'The redundancy drives home the point that our turbocharged intelligence distinguishes us not only from other animals on earth but also from the other members of the hominid family that came before us.'[96]

The interglacial period around 128,000 years ago created the conditions for *Homo sapiens* to move north out of Africa, but this first journey ended in tragedy with a brief but devastating global freeze. There is an outside possibility that a small relict population survived in a green refuge near Egypt, but this is a matter of heated debate.[97] Most likely, our direct ancestors, modern humans, migrated by foot out of Africa in a single exodus around 70–80,000 years ago. They moved along the river valleys of the Arabian Peninsula and into India, where there was a population expansion. Some groups moved rapidly south into South-East Asia and Australia, others meandered north into Asia and north-west back into Europe. Along the way they met their hominid cousins and slowly came to replace them.[98]

There are two key events for defining this movement out of Africa. The first was the Mount Toba super-eruption in Sumatra around 71–75,000 years ago. It was by far the biggest eruption of the Pleistocene. In the words of Oppenheimer, 'This mega-bang caused a prolonged nuclear winter and released ash in a huge plume that spread to the north-west and covered India, Pakistan, and the Gulf region in a blanket 1–3 metres (3–10 feet) deep.'[99] For six years winter reigned on Earth, and the thousand years that followed were colder on average than the previous glacial maximum. The Toba eruption had dramatic regional implications for people, animals and ecosystems. But for archaeologists, as they try to trace the early movements of our species, it is a blessing. Distinct and datable, Toba ash is found in the Greenland ice record, in submarine cores in the Indian Ocean and as a crisp black stratum in archaeological deposits throughout Asia. It is an invaluable date mark and has inspired a wealth of research questions: are there modern human tools beneath the blanket of Toba ash, or only above it? What effect did the Toba eruption have on modern humans?[100]

The other key event in calibrating the movement of *Homo sapiens* out of Africa was the colonisation of Australia. The endless debates surrounding when modern humans emerged and spread around the world ultimately come to rest on when people arrived at the southernmost extremity of their migration. Archaeologists have long been preoccupied with the question of whether the first Australians were adventurers or castaways.[101] A popular theory in the 1950s suggested that Australia was colonised by 'a boat or raft of castaways from one of the Pacific Islands driven far out of its proper course by stormy conditions'.[102] But recent finds reveal that we have consistently underestimated our ancestors' technological capacities.[103] The colonisation of Australia was no small feat. It required the traverse of a passage of water around 100 kilometres wide to a land where no hominid had roamed before. Based on the array of technical, symbolic and linguistic capabilities such a voyage required, psychologist-archaeologist duo William Noble and Iain Davidson have argued that 'archaeologically, this is the earliest evidence of modern human behaviour'.[104] The construction of boats and the navigation of the deep-sea crossing demanded a level of language and symbolic ability that are not easily discerned elsewhere in the archaeological record, and which appear to be distinctively human expressions. 'When the first footprints of my ancestors touched the northern shoreline of this land,' Stan Grant reflects, 'humanity itself had crossed a threshold.'[105]

The earth was a different place when *Homo sapiens* charged southwards. The ice caps bulged and today's shallow seas were dry. A great plain connected northern Australia and New Guinea; Tasmania was still part of the mainland. This giant land mass is known as Sahul. It was also a period of acute global climate change. Although the regular seasonal cycles of wet and dry continued, a trend towards greater aridity, beginning about 300,000 years ago, began to intensify as people prepared to cross into Sahul around 65,000 years ago. It was a period of global cooling and, in Australia, the dawn of another era of desertification, which created new environmental pressures for Australian flora and fauna, especially the giant marsupials and reptiles known as megafauna.[106]

People would have known about Australia before they saw it. Smoke billowing above the sea spoke of a land that lay beyond the horizon. A dense cloud of birds, following the sun on their annual migrations between northern and southern feeding grounds, may have pointed the way. But the first voyagers were sailing into the unknown.

In 1977 American anthropologist Joseph Birdsell proposed that Australia was colonised by 'a constant if somewhat straggling trickle of small groups of human beings' who took the shortest possible water crossings to Sahul and populated the entire continent within 5000 years.[107] Under this model, there would be no perceivable difference between the earliest colonisation dates for any parts of Australia. Sandra Bowdler, on the other hand, proposed that 'Australia was colonised by people adapted to a coastal way of life' who stayed with what they knew, moving along the coastline and up the major river systems, where their coastal economies were 'transliterated' to freshwater conditions.[108] Her theory of marginal settlement was reinforced by the lack of archaeology in the central deserts in the mid-1970s. With the exception of the finds on the desiccated shores of the Willandra Lakes region, archaeological activities tended to hug the coast. Even Richard Gould's excavation at Puntutjarpa had not produced an early Pleistocene date.

A range of finds in the arid zone in the 1980s began to destabilise the 'coastal colonisation' model. Mike Smith's discovery at Puritjarra in Central Australia of a few stone tools at 45,000 years ago and a continuous stream of artefacts from 35,000 years ago demonstrated that people moved into the arid zone early and stayed in well-watered locales throughout the dramatic climatic changes of the Last Glacial Maximum.[109] In 1989 Peter Veth explained human movements across the interior as being between 'refuges', where fresh water was always available; 'corridors', which might have been occupied or abandoned depending on climatic conditions; and 'barriers', like the harsh desert dunefields, which were only occupied after people learnt to tap groundwater.[110] Peter Hiscock and Lynley Wallis have added another layer to this model, suggesting that people colonised the arid interior during a favourable period of higher rainfall and then adapted to the changing conditions as the desert transformed around them.[111]

Recent genetic studies indicate that Australia had a single, large and diverse founding population. The DNA also suggests that after exploring the continent around 50,000 years ago, many of these groups may have retained distinct regional identities over tens of millennia.[112] Powerful examples of this kind of regionalism emerge in the Dampier archipelago – the Franklin of the north-west – and the Kimberley, which have been a focus of archaeological activity since the 1960s. Archaeologists have brought together evidence of rock art, occupation debris and stone arrangements to paint a vivid picture of the Indigenous societies that lived in the north-west of the continent, where the desert meets the sea. Ken Mulvaney has interpreted the vast body of rock engravings from the north-west as evidence for 'differentiation in the symbolic structuring of people's lives relatively early after colonisation'.[113] This supports the idea that innovation and regionalism are also Pleistocene expressions.

In 1968 paleontologist Duncan Merrilees argued that the arrival of humans had a destructive effect on Australian fauna.[114] Through fossilised remains found eroding from riverbanks and beach dunes, in ancient swampy peat bogs and dried-up salt lakes, archaeologists had long been aware that megafauna had once roamed the continent. These large, now extinct animals included a marsupial lion (*Thylacoleo*), a two-metre-tall flightless bird (*Genyornis*), a giant short-faced kangaroo (*Procoptodon*), a seven-metre-long goanna (*Megalania*) and the largest known marsupial ever to have lived, *Diprotodon*, sometimes described as a rhinoceros wombat. Perhaps, Merrilees mused, people drove the megafauna to extinction through their burning. Jones also pursued the idea, wondering aloud: 'If man had *not* managed to cross the last water channel of Wallacea those distant tens of millennia ago ... would at least some large beasts, lumbering down to the water's edge, have graced the sketchbooks of a Joseph Banks or a Charles Lesueur?'[115]

This question was at the heart of Tim Flannery's elegant and provocative work, *The Future Eaters*, in which he argued that the first

Australians hunted the megafauna to extinction. In a new land, he reasoned, released from the grip of coevolution, 'every hunt would have been successful': 'Without predators and surrounded by naive prey, people would have become, in a sense, gods. For they were now all-powerful beings in a land of plenty.'[116] As part of a large-scale inter-disciplinary dating effort in 2001, Flannery and Bert Roberts concluded that most species of megafauna died out in a continental extinction around 46,000 years ago.[117] Flannery also suggested that this extinction led to widespread ecological disruptions, as what was once food for herbivores became fuel for wildfire. These destructive fires transformed the landscape, changed the nutrients in the soil and may have stimulated the first Aboriginal burning regimes.[118] Perhaps inevitably, such arguments about the deep past became mired in the politics of contemporary Indigenous land management.[119]

There were international precedents for the 'overkill' hypothesis.[120] As Chris Johnson observes, wherever people have exploited their environment, large, slow-breeding and slow maturing species have been the most likely to disappear, especially on islands.[121] But Lesley Head cautions against pointing to specific causes for the extinction of the megafauna. A continent is not comparable to an island, and people relate to their environments in myriad ways. 'I have come to the conclusion that the term "impact" should be reserved for meteorites,' she reflects, 'and that the concept of "interaction" is more useful.'[122]

Although Flannery's book has been criticised for promoting the controversial 'overkill' hypothesis, its great insight was in highlighting the ecological sensitivity of the continent before the arrival of people. As environmental historians Libby Robin and Tom Griffiths write, 'The Future Eaters confronted Australians with truths about their land that they have not yet fully assimilated: that Australia has the poorest soils in the world, a stressful, unreliable climate, a fragile and heavily interdependent ecology, and great biodiversity.'[123] Australia's delicate and capricious environment may have had a greater role in the extinction of the megafauna than any human activities. After all, megafauna had been dying out for millennia before the arrival of humans, and many smaller species also died out. In a sense, David Horton argues,

> Australia's design is such that it has always been a close call, the megafauna teetering on the edge of the table … Just a little bit drier on the margins, the desert just a bit bigger, just a few less active rivers and waterholes, and there are massive impacts on a few species that had survived hundreds of thousands of years of smaller fluctuations previously. And the presence of humans is of no more significance than that there was an audience for the losses.[124]

The megafauna debate rolls on. And there are important deep time insights embedded in the arguments. In particular, the range of evidence warns us against using blanket categories when writing histories of people, animals or the environment. 'Continental' extinction was simply the end point of a series of smaller local extinctions. Every glacial cycle had its own character, triggering different climatic and ecological changes in each region, which animals and people responded to in a variety of ways. The megafauna, too, were diverse, with different diets and reproductive cycles. Their extinction and their size define them, but it is worth remembering that some 'megafauna' survived to live alongside us today, such as the red kangaroo, the emu and the saltwater crocodile. The most intriguing development in recent years has been the increasing evidence of coexistence between people and megafauna in ancient Australia, as the idea of an 'extinction event' around 46,000 years ago fades. In 2017, for example, Michael Westaway's team published evidence that suggests that the large, lumbering wombat-like marsupial, *Zygomaturus trilobus*, survived for some 17,000 years after people moved into the Willandra Lakes district.[125] In the wake of the latest Madjedbebe dates, Chris Clarkson was emphatic: 'It puts to bed the whole idea that humans wiped them out. We're talking 20,000 to 25,000 years of coexistence.'[126]

* * *

When people first started visiting Madjedbebe 65,000 years ago, the climate was mild and stable. They camped in a wooded valley with a river nearby. Around 35,000 years ago, Australia entered an age of extreme aridity. Global temperatures cooled, and the sea receded as more and more water became locked in the polar ice caps. The vegetation in the region became shorter and sparser, and fresh water became scarce. Temperatures dropped by between 6 and 10 degrees Celsius.[127] The monsoon failed for perhaps 20,000 years in the tropical north.[128] 21,000 years ago marked the peak of the Last Glacial Maximum. The sea had retreated, leaving the shelter 300 kilometres inland.

Then came the flood. Between 17,000 and 7000 years ago the extended polar ice caps melted and the sea level rose by around 125 metres.[129] At its most rapid rate, between 13,000 to 11,000 years ago, the ocean submerged the poorly vegetated Arafura plain at the rate of one metre per week (110 kilometres in 2000 years).[130] With every tide, the sea advanced further.

Around 6000 years ago, the sea level stabilised. Mainland Australia looked much as it does today. Close to three million square kilometres of land around the margins of the continent had been flooded. The loss for those who survived it must have been immense. Vast territories, invaluable resources and sacred features would have been submerged in the flood. The advancing coastline pushed people inland, forcing local crowding, the mixing of cultures, and, most likely, causing conflict. Paul Taçon and Christopher Chippindale believe this to be the cause of 'great battle scenes' they claim entered the rock art of Arnhem Land at around this time. These would be amongst the earliest depictions of

warfare in any world art tradition.[131] Darrell Lewis offers a more peaceful perspective. Rising seas increased social tension, he suggests, but this
is linked with the appearance in the rock art of the Rainbow Serpent.
Instead of warfare, a more conciliatory philosophy emerged amongst
these more crowded communities: 'The Rainbow snake symbolises the
possibilities of alliance among clan groups.'[132]

The sea drowned the wooded river valleys of the South Alligator
and East Alligator Rivers, bringing mangroves and tidal conditions up
to the edge of the shelter. Then, as recently as 1400–1000 years ago,
the estuarine conditions retreated. Sedimentation behind the intertidal
zone had gradually built up levees, which protected the coastal plains
from saltwater inundation and allowed the formation of the freshwater
wetlands and lagoons we see today. For the past thousand years, people
have gathered at Madjedbebe in the dry season to harvest fish, turtles,
crabs, goannas and freshwater mussels from the rich surrounds.[133]

This is the history as is it told in stones and bones, in coastal maps
and shoreline graphs, in oral history and Dreaming stories. But data can
only take us so far. As Carmel Schrire reminds us in *Digging Through
Darkness*, 'Only imagination fleshes out the sound and taste of time
past, anchoring the flavour of lost moments in the welter of objects
left behind.'[134]

*** ***

Dating the arrival of the first Australians to 65,000 years ago is a dramatic step, and it throws up questions that are not easily resolved. But
it is not, as one journalist declared in the week of the discovery, 'so old it
[will] rewrite everything about the continent's human history', nor is it,
as dozens of reports asserted in their headlines, 'evidence of Aboriginal
habitation up to 80,000 years ago'.[135] Such overstatements come from an
unhelpful view that older is better; they diminish the site by emphasising
numbers and dates rather than the long and varied history they reveal.

In the weeks that followed the publication of the Madjedbebe dates, another sensational discovery emerged: Kira Westaway dated a modern human tooth in Sumatra to 73,000 to 63,000 years ago.[136] The tooth, found on the route to Australia, seemed to reinforce the idea that people were migrating south earlier than previously thought.

It is important to stress that the history uncovered at Madjedbebe enriches, rather than eclipses, archaeological understandings of other regions. The new, older date doesn't necessarily destabilise the strong pattern of settlement that has been established by archaeologists across Australia from 50,000 years ago; rather, it reveals how little we know about the 15,000 years that preceded it. Around 65,000 years ago, the first Australians were probably swept to the Sahul Rise: a low-lying, fan-like formation of skeletal limestone, riddled with tidal channels.[137] The landing site, along with many signs of early occupation, now lies submerged on the Arafura Sea shelf. It is only though the lowest layers at Madjedbebe, at the margins of this vast inundated region, that we can glimpse the earliest chapter of Australia's human history. 'It's not exactly Atlantis,' Mike Smith and Chris Clarkson remarked to me, 'but it's pretty bloody close.'

The full implications of the Madjedbebe finds will take time to absorb. They speak to a remarkable story of resilience, adaptation and survival. But let us not be dazzled by old dates – nor become numb to their power. The history of Jinmium, at 10,000 years old, remains ancient. It is twice as old as Stonehenge and tells a rich local story of economic innovation and the creation of a cultural landscape. 'Changes in the numbers rewrite a certain kind of history,' Head reminds us, 'but it is not the only interesting or important one.'[138]

While Pleistocene dates may dominate headlines, the archaeological story of Aboriginal Australia continues today. Some of the most exciting contemporary archaeology focuses on recent histories, such as the enduring cultural significance of sea country: land that was flooded but not forgotten at the end of the last Ice Age. There is also a vibrant thread of research in the field of historical archaeology, which engages with Australia's material record in the wake of invasion. 'The enduring perception of timeless territoriality has imagined Aboriginal culture as a sheet of glass, strong and cohesive in isolation but highly vulnerable to the hammer blow of colonial impact,' writes historian and archaeologist Paul Irish. 'The reality could not be more different.'[140] Since the 1960s, led by Judy Birmingham's work at Wybalenna mission and Jim Allen's excavation of the Port Essington settlement, the field of historical archaeology has chronicled the myriad ways in which Aboriginal people shaped colonial Australia.

An archaeological eye not only allows us to dream of deep time, it adds a palpability to our understanding of the more recent past. It gives agency to those who exist on the margins of the documentary record and often destabilises established historical narratives. Over the past three generations, archaeologists and historians have worked together to illuminate the profound roles played by Indigenous individuals in the pastoral and whaling industries, on the colonial frontiers and in the world wars, on the Victorian goldfields and in the heart of early Sydney.[141] These histories of cultural entanglement are just as wondrous as the global story told in the lowest layers at Madjedbebe. They link the deep past more immediately with the present, enlivening our understanding of the social, economic and spiritual worlds of the people who thrived on these shores at the moment of invasion, and who continue to shape Australian society today.

EPILOGUE

Australia's Classical Culture

On the drive back to Mildura, after a few days exploring the shores of Lake Mungo, I dream of deep time. As the ethereal expanse of the Willandra region fades behind me, my mind lingers on the scattered shells, kitchen hearths and ancient footprints that mark the desiccated lakes system. I strive to imagine the lives of the people who left these traces: the ancestors of the Mutthi Mutthi, Ngyiampaa and Paakantji peoples who fished, hunted, cooked, sang, laughed, danced, loved and died beside the lakeshores at the height of the last Ice Age. While the texture of their lives may forever elude us, the last few decades of research in the region has opened a small window on the world they inhabited. It is a radical insight.

As I approach the outskirts of town, my reverie is broken by a different vision of the deep past. Looming high above the road, a nine-metre pharaoh sits imperiously in the car park of Tutankhamen's Bistro, his plaster arms clutching his knees, his light-bulb eyes staring emptily across a vast Aboriginal landscape. It is a striking image, and a jarring reminder of the dissonance at the heart of Australian cultural life. The monument encapsulates the anxieties of a settler nation still struggling to come to terms with its deep Indigenous history, fumbling for foreign symbols to fill an unfamiliar land.

The chapters of this book challenge the pharaoh's hollow gaze. They echo art historian Bernard Smith's appeal for Australians to seek 'a more balanced, a more archaeological, a more humanist view of our history'.[1] Smith sought a historical inquiry that drew upon words, but also moved beyond them to embrace the sensuous materiality of Australian history, encompassing the arts as well as artefacts. Such an approach opens our eyes to archaeological stories held in stone and sand, ochre and ink, lore and local knowledge. It helps bring the long and varied history of Aboriginal and Torres Strait Islander peoples into Australian consciousness. 'It is this culture that is the Iliad and Odyssey of Australia,' Noel Pearson wrote of the song cycles of the women of central Australia. 'It is these mythic stories that are Australia's Book of Genesis.'[2]

In 1986, while archaeologists explored his land in northern Kakadu, Gaagudju elder Big Bill Neidjie wondered about the antiquity of the Dreaming:

> *When that law started?*
> *I don't know how many thousand years.*
> *European say 40,000 years,*
> *but I reckon myself probably was more because ...*
> *it is sacred.*[3]

In these words, we can appreciate the differences between the two world views invoked in my title: the deep time history, which is bound to notions of linear time, and the active, continuous time of the Dreaming, which is a self-referencing and self-affirming system of meaning. Yet despite these differences, historian David Christian observes, both world views are foundational: 'They speak to our deep spiritual, psychic, and social need for a sense of place and a sense of belonging.' In his landmark work, *Maps of Time*, Christian brings together insights from the fields of physics, geology, biology and archaeology to create a 'modern creation myth', 'a map of time that embraces the past at all scales', from the big bang to the present. Such a project, he acknowledges, constitutes 'what indigenous Australians might call a modern "Dreaming" – a coherent account of how we were created and how we fit into the scheme of things'. In writing 'big history', Christian is also taking up Bernard Smith's appeal, moving beyond the traditional bounds of the historian to tell a 'story that attempts to grasp reality whole'.[4]

Through the lens of big history, the Australian nation quickly becomes a shallow stratum in a richly layered Indigenous place. While such a rendering could be perceived as a threat to the legitimacy of the society that has formed here since 1788, it also holds promise. It is only through a long view of Australian history that we can come to understand the Australian landscape, which is as much cultural as it is natural. It helps us grasp the immensity of human experience on this continent and learn lessons about resilience, adaptability and connections to country. It is a scale that allows us to view ourselves as a species – a vital insight in a warming world. A deep time perspective also presents an opportunity for us to recognise cultures and histories that for so long have gone unrecognised.

'My expectation of a good Australia,' Aboriginal activist Charles Perkins told historian Peter Read in 1989,

> is when White people would be proud to speak an Aboriginal language, when they realise that Aboriginal culture and all that goes with it, philosophy, art, language, morality, kinship, is all part of their heritage. And that's the most unbelievable thing of all, that it's all there waiting for us all. White people can inherit 40,000 or 60,000 years of culture, and all they have to do is reach out and ask for it.[5]

Perkins' plea places Indigenous culture and the archaeological story of ancient Australia at the heart of Australian identity. But these words were uttered in despair. At fifty-three years of age, Perkins felt that his attempts to share his history, to bring his culture into national life, were falling on deaf ears. When he walked the streets of Sydney, he felt like a foreigner in his own land. He, too, struggled with the vexed question of belonging in Australia. 'We know we cannot live in the past,' he reflected in an Australia Day address, 'but the past lives with us.'[6]

In the generation since Perkins talked with Read about the promise of reconciliation, the landmark *Mabo* and *Wik* judgements have been handed down by the High Court, acknowledging Indigenous rights to country; the injustices of the Stolen Generations have been the subject of a prime ministerial apology; and the campaign to recognise Indigenous Australians in the Constitution has now been accompanied by calls for a treaty – or Makarrata – as well as a truth and reconciliation commission and an Indigenous voice to parliament. Archaeological insights have featured in each of these national conversations, as Australians gradually respond to Perkins' invitation and seek to understand and celebrate all that Indigenous histories and cultures have to offer. 'With substantive constitutional change and structural reform,' the Indigenous leaders at the 2017 National Constitutional Convention at Uluru announced, 'we believe this ancient sovereignty can shine through as a fuller expression of Australia's nationhood ... When we have power over our destiny our children will flourish. They will walk in two worlds and their culture will be a gift to their country.'[7]

Over the past sixty years, Australian archaeology has grown from the efforts of a few isolated scholars into a thriving, multi-dimensional discipline. Within a generation of the first attempts to establish an overview of the continent's human history, archaeologists were engaging with complex questions of cultural exchange, the creation of social landscapes, and theories of change over time. Large-scale continental models have gradually been replaced by an appreciation of the distinctive regional and temporal character of Indigenous societies.

As the field has expanded it has also diversified, opening new areas of specialisation, incorporating a dazzling array of chemical, ecological and mathematical techniques, and becoming increasingly integrated with heritage legislation. Although technological advances have pushed the field towards the laboratory, archaeology remains a discipline that straddles the border between the humanities and the sciences. As historian Greg Dening observes, 'The history in places, especially in places of cross-cultural encounters, will take as much imagination as science to see.'[8] There has been no dominant theoretical force within Australian Aboriginal archaeology, as with the 'new archaeologists' in America and the 'post-processualists' in the United Kingdom. Rather, Australian research is distinctive for its close engagement with the culture and politics of the first Australians and their histories of invasion, dispossession, adaptation and self-determination. Archaeological questions and conclusions are shaped as much by the use of ethnography, history and dialogue with Indigenous custodians as they are by categorising stone tools, weighing shells and measuring motifs.

The enduring question asked in the wake of the Franklin River campaign – 'Who owns the past?' – continues to haunt archaeology in Australia. There remains conflict between those who approach the past from a critical, deep time perspective and those who view it as a living heritage, an affirmation of cultural identity. This is the central tension within the discipline today. But, as two generations of scholarship have shown, it can be a creative tension. There are dozens of collaborative investigations currently underway in Australia, with archaeologists working in partnership with traditional custodians. There is also a growing number of Indigenous archaeologists, harnessing Western techniques to investigate their own past through excavation and survey.

Archaeology will perhaps always face political challenges, not only for the cultural sensitivities of its subject matter, but also because it cannot help but interact with great human stories and symbolic narratives that readily translate into icons, dates and slogans. Like history, it beck-ons when we search for origins and understanding, and since at least the 1970s it has been inextricably bound to questions of national identity. This is a radical shift, Denis Byrne observes, because 'until the 1960s Australian national identity had been constructed partly in *opposition* to Aborigines'.[9] But like Byrne, I am sceptical of nationalistic attempts, in Harry Allen's words, to graft 'white culture directly onto an Aboriginal root'.[10] It is a project that has gained traction through the creation of a 'detached' and tokenistic version of Aboriginal culture: a timeless and traditional foundation upon which the contemporary nation can build. As Byrne laments, 'Australia's embracing of Aboriginal heritage as part of national heritage has not, unfortunately, meant an end to treating Aboriginal culture as the Other of white Australian culture.'[11]

Perkins' hope that all Australians would come to identify with this deep history as their own, as a source of wisdom and pride, was not an open invitation. It carried obligations, too. The act of 'inheriting' demands the respectful acknowledgement of all that has happened – and still is happening – in the confluence of cultures and histories. It asks that we not only engage with the deep past as a dynamic human history, but also reflect upon the tumultuous road of the past two cen-turies. It calls for us to adopt a more archaeological, a more humanist approach to the past. It is only then that we can appreciate the ancient voyages of the first Australians as the opening chapters of Australian history, and the songs, paintings and traditions of their descendants as the classical culture of this continent.

Acknowledgements

A dear friend once told me that a book is a gift, given to its author by all the people who made it possible. This book has grown out of hundreds of conversations over many years. I am particularly grateful to the Australian archaeological community for their advice, encouragement and intellectual generosity.

I thank Jim and Joan Bowler, Bob Edwards, Isabel McBryde, Betty Meehan, Carmel Schrire, Liz Morrison and the late John Mulvaney for reading and commenting on words I wrote about their lives. Mike Smith has helped this project grow from a flicker of curiosity into the full flames of obsession. Iain McCalman and Mark McKenna have been enduring sources of scholarly support and literary inspiration.

I have sought to visit the sites I write about in this book and in some cases I have had the privilege of working on them in later excavations. This would not have been possible without the assistance of many people. I thank Fenella Atkinson, Ramiro Barberena, Barry Cain, Chris Clarkson, Bob Faulkner, Guy Fitzhardinge, Richard Fullagar, Darrell Lewis, Tiina Manne, Mandy Martin, Ben Marwick, Daryl Pappin, June Ross, Mike Smith, Lynley Wallis, Jim Wheeler, Alan Williams and the team at Extent Heritage, all of whom created opportunities for me to visit archaeological sites.

My time in libraries and archives has been as important as my experiences in the field. I would like to acknowledge the help of staff at the Australian Institute of Aboriginal and Torres Strait Islander Studies (AIATSIS), the Department of Manuscripts and University Archives (University of Cambridge), the Mitchell Library, the National Archives of Australia, the National Film and Sound Archive, the National Library of Australia, the National Museum of Australia Library, the University of Sydney Archives and the State Library of Victoria. I have also benefited from the work of librarians and archivists who have made vast collections of papers, newspapers and publications available through digitisation.

The early chapters of this book were first workshopped in a writing group led by the late John Hirst, who was a great mentor of young historians. John read every word I wrote during the formative stages of this project and it was he who first suggested the interlude structure I have adopted. I owe him an immense debt and I am grateful to everyone who engaged with my words and ideas in this group, as well as outside of it.

This book has been enriched through a rigorous process of peer review. I thank David Christian, David Frankel, Peter Hobbins, Grace Karskens, Emma Kowal, Darrell Lewis, Iain McCalman, Mark McKenna, Mike Smith and Mick Warren for carefully reading versions of this text as a whole. I am also grateful to everyone who commented on single chapters, including Malcolm Allbrook, Sam Balaton-Chrimes, David Brooks, Xavier Carah, Chris Clarkson, Rose Cullen, Emilie Dotte-Sarout, Jamie Dunk, Ebbe Hayes, James Findlay, Kate Fullagar, Richard Fullagar, Jarrod Hore, Julia Horne, Alex Knight, Kelsey Lowe, Anna Georgia Mackay, Tiina Manne, Ben Marwick, Jacq Matthews, Cameron Muir, Tim Neale, Justin O'Brien, Bert Roberts, June Ross, Matthew Spriggs, Victoria Stead and Lynley Wallis.

Julianne Schultz at *Griffith Review* published the essay that grew into this book, and Peter Browne, Suzy Freeman-Greene, Nathan

Hollier and Peter Rose have encouraged my writing during the course of this research. My research has also benefited from conversations with Craig Barker, Jane Carruthers, Vincent Carruthers, Manik Datar, Liz Foley, Hannah Forsyth, Marg Friedel, Zenobia Jacobs, Dick Kimber, Antonio Gonzalez Zarandona, Debbie Miller, Richard Nelson, Tamson Pietsch, Matt Poll, Lynette Russell, Tom Sapienza, Rebe Taylor, Sam Vincent, Kelly Wiltshire and Katie Woo.

I am grateful to the staff at the Department of History at the University of Sydney for their encouragement over many years and I thank the team at the Alfred Deakin Institute for Citizenship and Globalisation for their warm support. Roy MacLeod and Julia Kindt gave me time off work to pursue early fieldwork opportunities and Vicki Huang fostered a positive writing environment for me to write the final chapters. Jim Bowler, Bob Edwards, Darrell Lewis, Isabel McBryde, Ingereth Macfarlane, Mary-Jane Mountain, Justin O'Brien, Rob Paton, Mike Smith, David Vadiveloo and Alan Williams kindly helped me with the images for this book. Bob Edwards, Jon Sterenberg and John Tunn also shared with me papers from their archives.

It has been a truly rewarding experience working with the team at Black Inc. Chris Feik had faith in this book from its beginnings and has greatly enriched it with his discerning editorial eye. Jo Rosenberg worked closely and sympathetically with the manuscript over several months and Dion Kagan guided it during its final stages.

Writing and research can be an isolating process, and I am fortunate to have had the support of a wide circle of friends and family. I thank Tom, Libby, Kate and Brent, for always being open to talk about ideas (or football), and my partner, Emily, for her love and companionship throughout this whole adventure.

I thank you all. It is a great gift you have given me.

Picture Credits

John Mulvaney at Fromm's Landing, 1958 (Dermot Casey), courtesy of the National Library of Australia (PIC P11128/10).

Isabel McBryde surveying Schnapper Point, 1971 (Fairfax), courtesy of Isabel McBryde.

Rhys Jones at Sisters Beach, c. 1964, courtesy of the Tasmanian Archive and Heritage Office and the Jack Thwaites Collection (NS3195/1/4269).

Isabel McBryde at the University of New England, 1972 (Armidale Newspaper Ltd.), courtesy of Isabel McBryde.

The team at Puntutjarpa, 1970 (Bruce Wright), courtesy of the Australian Institute of Aboriginal and Torres Strait Islander Studies (WRIGHT.B09.CS-000140709).

The North Cave at Rocky Cape, 2014 (Billy Griffiths).

Jim Bowler at Lake Mungo, courtesy of Jim Bowler.

Jack Coulthard and Mike Smith at Illararri Kulpi, 1982, courtesy of Mike Smith.

Isabel McBryde leads an official tour of Lake Mungo, 1983 (Australian Information Service), courtesy of Isabel McBryde.

Alice Kelly and Alice Bugmy on the Joulni lunette, Lake Mungo, courtesy of Jim Bowler.

Anbarra women and children collecting shell fish at Madangadjira, 1972 (Betty Meehan), courtesy of the Australian Institute of Aboriginal and Torres Strait Islander Studies (MEEHAN.B04.BW-N08565_13).

Lesley Maynard in the Squeeze, 1967 (Robert Edwards), courtesy of the Australian Institute of Aboriginal and Torres Strait Islander Studies (EDWARDS.R08.BW-N07701_02).

Betty Meehan at Manganama, 1972 (Rhys Jones), courtesy of the Australian Institute of Aboriginal and Torres Strait Islander Studies (MEEHAN_JONES.005.CS-000152305).

Josephine Flood's team at Cloggs Cave, 1972, courtesy of Darrell Lewis.

Excavations at Kutikina, 1981 (Rhys Jones), courtesy of the Australian Institute of Aboriginal and Torres Strait Islander Studies (JONES.R09.CS-000142949).

Section drawing from the 1989 excavations at Madjedbebe (Malakunanja II), courtesy of Mike Smith.

Bert Roberts in the pit at Madjedbebe, 2012 (Billy Griffiths).

Endnotes

INTRODUCTION: THE OLD WORLD

1   Rachel Perkins, *A Rightful Place: Correspondence*, Quarterly Essay 56 (Melbourne: Black Inc., 2014), 82–86, 82.

2   Robert Pulleine, 'The Tasmanians and Their Stone-Culture', *Australasian Association for the Advancement of Science* 19 (1928), 294–314, 310.

3   John McPhee, *Annals of the Former World* (New York: Farrar, Straus and Giroux, 1998), 90.

4   Alistair Paterson, *A Millennium of Cultural Contact* (Walnut Creek: Left Coast, 2011).

5   This sentence paraphrases David Frankel's words in *Remains to Be Seen: Archaeological Insights into Australian Prehistory* (Melbourne: Longman Cheshire, 1991), vii.

6   This is the first overview of Australian Aboriginal archaeology that has been written by someone outside the field, which makes it an explicitly cross-disciplinary endeavour. There has been a range of bigger-picture studies on the history of Aboriginal archaeology, such as David Horton's edited collection of documents, Tim Murray's work on the changing philosophies and methodologies in archaeology and Stephanie Moser's research on the field's disciplinary culture. More recently, Sarah Colley, Hilary Du Cros and Laurajane Smith have explored the practice, politics and ethics of Australian archaeology, teasing out the questions and ideas that have arisen from heritage debates and the struggles of Indigenous peoples for ownership and control of their land, cultural materials and ancestral remains. See, for example, David Horton, *Recovering the Tracks: The Story of Australian Archaeology* (Canberra: Aboriginal Studies Press, 1991); Tim Murray (ed.), *Archaeology from Australia* (Melbourne: Australian Scholarly Publishing, 2004); Stephanie Moser, 'The Aboriginalisation of Archaeology: The Contribution of the Australian Institute of Aboriginal Studies to the Indigenous Transformation of the Discipline', in Peter J Ucko (ed.),

Theory in Archaeology: A World Perspective (London: Routledge, 1995), 150–177; Sarah Colley, *Uncovering Australia: Archaeology, Indigenous People and the Public* (Crows Nest, NSW: Allen & Unwin, 2002); Hilary du Cros, *Much More Than Stones and Bones: Australian Archaeology in the Late Twentieth Century* (Melbourne: Melbourne University Press, 2002) and Laurajane Smith, *The Uses of Heritage* (London: Routledge, 2006).

7   Hilary du Cros, 'Popular Notions of Australian Archaeology', *Journal of Australian Studies* 23(62) (1999), 190–97, 192.

8   Nicholas Jose, *The Custodians* (Sydney: Macmillan, 1997), 354.

9   Rosalind in William Shakespeare, *As You Like It* (New York: Penguin Books, 2000), 4:1:83–4; James Ussher, *The Annals of the World* (London: E Tyler, 1658), 12. The discovery of deep time is explored in Martin JS Rudwick, *Earth's Deep History: How It Was Discovered and Why It Matters* (Chicago: University of Chicago Press, 2014); Clive Gamble and Theodora Moutsiou, 'The Time Revolution of 1859 and the Stratification of the Primeval Mind', *Notes and Records of The Royal Society* 65(1) (2011), 43–63.

10 McPhee coined the term in *Basin and Range*, the first book in his five-volume geological history of North America, which was published as *Annals of the Former World* (New York: Farrar, Straus and Giroux, 1998).

11 Paul Crutzen and Will Steffen, 'How Long Have We Been in the Anthropocene Era?', *Climatic Change* 61(3) (2003), 251–57; Alison Bashford, 'The Anthropocene is Modern History: Reflections on Climate and Australian Deep Time', *Australian Historical Studies* 44(3) (2013), 341–49.

12 John Mulvaney, 'Archaeological Retrospect 9', *Antiquity* 60(229) (1986), 96–107, 104.

13 Tim Winton, *Island Home: A Landscape Memoir* (Melbourne: Hamish Hamilton, 2015), 28–29.

14 Jim Bowler, 'Perceptions of Australia: Towards Cultural Integration', 27 Oct 1992, John Mulvaney Papers, National Library of Australia, MS 9615/1/40, Box 5.

15 Emphasis in original. WEH Stanner, 'The Dreaming (1953)', *The Dreaming & Other Essays* (Melbourne: Black Inc. Agenda, 2009), 57–72, 58.

16 Bill Gammage, *The Biggest Estate on Earth: How Aborigines Made Australia* (Crows Nest, NSW: Allen & Unwin, 2011), 123.

17 Patrick Wolfe, 'On Being Woken Up: The Dreamtime in Anthropology and in Australian Settler Culture', *Comparative Studies in Society and History* 33(2) (Apr 1991), 197–224, 199.

18 Howard Morphy, 'Empiricism to Metaphysics: In Defence of the Concept of the Dreamtime', in Tim Bonyhady and Tom Griffiths (eds), *Prehistory to Politics: John Mulvaney, the Humanities and the Public Intellectual* (Melbourne: Melbourne University Press, 1996), 163–89, 187.

19 These are the words used by Prime Minister Kevin Rudd in his apology to the Stolen Generations in 2008. Kevin Rudd, 'Apology to Australia's Indigenous Peoples', Parliament of Australia, House of Representatives, 13 Feb 2008.

20 See Ian J McNiven and Lynette Russell, *Appropriated Pasts: Indigenous Peoples and the Colonial Culture of Archaeology* (Lanham, MD: AltaMira Press, 2005).

ONE Explorers in an Ancient Land: John Mulvaney at Fromm's Landing

1   Newstead, as quoted in Martin Thomas, *The Artificial Horizon: Imagining the Blue Mountains* (Melbourne: Melbourne University Press, 2003), 224.

2   This account benefits from Peter C Rickwood's careful analysis of the location, details and cause of Childe's death in 'Forensic History: Professor Childe's Death Near Govetts Leap – Revisited', *Blue Mountains Historical Journal* 3 (2012), 35–51.

3   Glyn Daniel, 'Editorial', *Antiquity* 53(208) (Jul 1979), 85–92, 87.

4   Vere Gordon Childe to Grahame Clark, 1 Oct 1957, Sir Grahame Clark: archaelogical papers, Cambridge University Library, Department of Manuscripts and University Archives, Cambridge, GBR/0012/MS Add.9409/35.

5   Childe to Grimes, dated 20 October 1957 (inaccurate), published in Glyn Daniel, 'Editorial', *Antiquity* 54(210) (Mar 1980), 1–3, 3.

6   John Mulvaney, 'V.G. Childe 1892–1957', *Historical Studies: Australia and New Zealand* 8(29) (Nov 1957), 93–94, 93.

7   Childe to Grimes in Daniel, 'Editorial (1980)', 2.

8   Jim Allen also makes this observation in 'Perspectives of a Sentimental Journey: V. Gordon Childe in Australia 1917–1921', *Australian Archaeology* 12 (1981), 1–12, 10.

9   Sally Green, *Prehistorian: A Biography of V. Gordon Childe* (Bradford-on-Avon: Moonraker Press, 1981), 149.

10   Childe to Crawford, 6 Aug 1957, cited in Rhys Jones, 'Dating the Human Colonization of Australia: Radiocarbon and Luminescence Revolutions', *Proceedings of the British Academy* 99 (1999), 37–65, 39.

11   Laila Haglund, letter to Antiquity, published in Daniel, 'Editorial (1979)', 86–87; Laila Haglund, 'Memories of Gordon Childe', *Australian Archaeology* 30 (Jun 1990), 33–35, 34.

12   Vere Gordon Childe, 'Australian Broadcasting Commission, Guest of Honour, Broadcast Sunday, 13 October 1957 (7.15 p.m. 2FC)', *Australian Archaeology* 30 (1990), 26–28, 26–27.

13   Mulvaney, 'V.G. Childe 1892–1957', 94.

14   Vere Gordon Childe to John Mulvaney, 16 Sept 1957, John Mulvaney Papers, National Library of Australia, MS 9615/1/64, Box 8.

15   John Mulvaney, 'From "The Dawn" to Sunset: Gordon Childe in Melbourne, 1957', *Australian Archaeology* 30 (Jun 1990), 29–32, 30.

16   Childe, as quoted in Tim Murray, 'Aboriginal (Pre)History and Australian Archaeology: The Discourse of Australian Prehistoric Archaeology', *Journal of Australian Studies* 16(35) (1992), 1–19, 4.

17   John Mulvaney, *Digging Up a Past* (Sydney: UNSW Press, 2011), 13.

18   Mulvaney, *Digging Up a Past*, 20.

19   Mulvaney, *Digging Up a Past*, 40; Tom Griffiths, *The Art of Time Travel: Historians and Their Craft* (Melbourne: Black Inc., 2016), 61–73.

20   Mulvaney, *Digging Up a Past*, 56; John Mulvaney, 'A Note Taker at Manning's 1948 Lectures', in *Manning Clark by Some of his Students* (Canberra: Manning Clark House, 2002), 22–25.

21   Clark, as quoted in Mark McKenna, *An Eye for Eternity: The Life of Manning Clark* (Melbourne: The Miegunyah Press, 2011), 619.

22   Isabel McBryde, 'Australia's Once and Future Archaeology', *Archaeology in Oceania*, 21(1) (1986), 13–28, 17.

23   Mulvaney, *Digging Up a Past*, 53–54.

24   Ken Inglis, 'John Mulvaney's Universities', in Tim Bonyhady and Tom Griffiths (eds), *Prehistory to Politics: John Mulvaney, the Humanities and the Public Intellectual* (Melbourne: Melbourne University Press, 1996), 20–41, 27.

25   Tom Griffiths, *Hunters and Collectors: The Antiquarian Imagination in Australia* (Cambridge: Cambridge University Press, 1996), 19–20, 55–85.

26   Mulvaney, *Digging Up a Past*, 69. The book was: Stanley Robert Mitchell, *Stone-Age Craftsmen: Stone Tools and Camping Places of the Australian Aborigines* (Melbourne: Tait Book Co., 1949).

27   James R Arnold interviewed by Rhys Jones and Mike Smith, ANU, 28 Sept 1993, Transcript, Rhys Jones Papers, National Library of Australia, MS ACC 03/250, Folder 112, Box 23, 10.

28   John Mulvaney, 'A New Time Machine', *Twentieth Century* 8 (Spring 1952), 16–23, 16.

29   F Johnson, 'Radiocarbon Dating Mem 8, Society of American Archaeology', Supplement to *American Antiquity* 17 (1951).

30   Mulvaney received a PhD in 1970 on the strength of his published work. Mulvaney, *Digging Up a Past*, 71.

31   John Mulvaney, 'The Australian Aborigines 1606–1929: Opinion and Fieldwork', *Australian Historical Studies* 8 (1958), 131–51, 297–314, 297.

32   John Mulvaney, 'Archaeological Retrospect 9', *Antiquity* 60(229) (1986), 96–107, 98.

33   Jack Golson, 'Old Guards and New Waves: Reflections on Antipodean Archaeology 1954–1975', *Archaeology in Oceania*, 21(1) (1986), 2–12, 4.

34   LM Groube, '"Dig Up Those Moa Bones, Dig": Golson in New Zealand, 1954–1961', in M Spriggs et al. (eds), *A Community of Culture: The People and Prehistory of the Pacific* (Canberra: Department of Prehistory, Research School of Pacific Studies, Australian National University, 1993), 6–17.

35   John Mulvaney, 'Grahame Clark in the Antipodes', in Arkadiusz Marciniak and John Coles (eds), *Grahame Clark and His Legacy* (Newcastle upon Tyne: Cambridge Scholars Publishing, 2010), 27–46, 32.

36   John Mulvaney and Johan Kamminga, *Prehistory of Australia* (St Leonards, NSW: Allen & Unwin, 1999), 303–6.

37   Denis Byrne, 'Deep Nation: Australia's Acquisition of an Indigenous Past', *Aboriginal History* 20 (1998), 82–107, 92.

38   Greg Dening, 'The History in Things and Places', in Bonyhady and Griffiths, *Prehistory to Politics*, 85–97, 88.

39   Herbert M Hale and Norman B Tindale, 'Notes on Some Human Remains in the Lower Murray Valley', *Records of the South Australian Museum* 4 (1930), 145–218.

40   John Mulvaney, 'The Stone Age of Australia', *Proceedings of the Prehistoric Society* 27 (1961), 56–107, 65.

41   Charles Barrett, 'Ancient Man in Australia', *Melbourne Herald*, 18 Jul 1930.

42   The most systematic of the excavations conducted over the following decades were led by Frederick McCarthy of the Australian Museum. His analysis of the stone tool technology from Lapstone Cave at Emu Plains in 1935–36, published in 1948, was

the first observation of cultural change over time. In David Horton's words, 'Today's archaeologists are the heirs of McCarthy, not Tindale.' But even this pioneering fieldwork was marked by varying degrees of rigour. Amateur anthropologist CC Towle wrote disapprovingly of the 'rough and ready methods' used by his stone tool collector friends at Emu Plains, yet his own methods would alarm a contemporary archaeologist: he 'carefully' excavated a 4.5 metre trench in a day, recording the finds by the 'shovelful'. David Horton, *Recovering the Tracks: The Story of Australian Archaeology* (Canberra: Aboriginal Studies Press, 1991), 154; CC Towle to AS Kenyon, 9 Dec 1935, Dermot Casey Papers, AIATSIS Library, MS 1326/A/f/1/I, Box 1; Frederick D McCarthy, 'The Lapstone Creek Excavation: Two Culture Periods Revealed in Eastern New South Wales', *Records of the Australian Museum* 22(1) (1948), 1–34.

43 Norman B Tindale, 'A South Australian Looks at Some Beginnings of Archaeological Research in Australia', *Aboriginal History* 6 (1982), 92–110, 93.

44 Norman B Tindale, 'Ecology of Primitive Aboriginal Man in Australia', in A Keast, RL Crocker and CS Christian (eds), *Biogeography and Ecology in Australia* (Den Haag, Netherlands: W Junk, 1959), 36–51, 39; Norman B Tindale, 'Culture Succession in South-Eastern Australia', *Records of the South Australian Museum* 13 (1957), 1–49.

45 Archibald Grenfell Price, 'St Mark's College Scientific Work at Fromm's Landing', *Proceedings of the Royal Geographical Society Australasia, South Australian Branch* 53 (1952), 25–27.

46 Mulvaney, *Digging Up a Past*, 96.

47 John Mulvaney, 'Fromm's Notebook I, 1956', Mulvaney Papers, NLA, MS 9615/8.1/2, Box 61.

48 In his autobiography, Mulvaney described this trip as lasting three years; he later revised this to two (pers. comm. 2016); Mulvaney, *Digging Up a Past*, 76.

49 John Mulvaney to Herbert Hale, Director of the South Australian Museum, undated, in 'Fromm's 6, 1963', Mulvaney Papers, NLA, MS 9615/8.1/6, Box 61.

50 Mulvaney, 'Fromm's Notebook I, 1956', 19 Jan 1956.

51 Dening, 'The History in Things and Places', 87.

52 Mulvaney, *Digging Up a Past*, 83–84.

53 Mulvaney, 'Fromm's Notebook I, 1956', 13–15 Jan 1956.

54 Mulvaney, 'Fromm's Notebook I, 1956', 19 Jan 1956; John Mulvaney, 'Archaeological Excavations at Fromm's Landing on Lower Murray River, South Australia', *Proceedings of the Royal Society of Victoria* 72(2) (1960), 53–85, 58–59.

55 Mulvaney, 'Fromm's Notebook I, 1956', 1–4 Feb 1956.

56 Griffiths, *Hunters and Collectors*, 78.

57 David Frankel, 'The Archaeologist as Tribal Elder: John Mulvaney 1925–2016', *Australian Archaeology* 82(3) (2016), 286–89, 88.

58 John Mulvaney, 'ANU: Proposal for Honorary Degrees: F.D. McCarthy and N.B. Tindale, 1979–1980', Mulvaney Papers, NLA, MS 9615/7/25, Box 60.

59 Norman Tindale to Herbert Hale, 1 Feb 1956, in John Mulvaney, 'Digging in the Archaeology Archives', *Australian Archaeology* 50 (2000), 1–6, 4.

60 See, for example, Mulvaney, 'Fromm's Notebook I, 1956', 23 Jan 1956, 1 Feb 1956; John Mulvaney, 'Fromm's 2 Notebook, 1958', Mulvaney Papers, NLA, MS 9615/8.1/3, Box 61, 18 Feb 1958.

61 Emily O'Gorman, *Flood Country: An Environmental History of the Murray-Darling Basin* (Melbourne: CSIRO Publishing, 2012), 135–36.

62 Mulvaney, *Digging Up a Past*, 100–1, 322–23.

63 Mulvaney, *Digging Up a Past*, 114.

64 John Mulvaney, 'The Stone Age of Australia'.

65 Rhys Jones, 'Rocky Cape and the Problem of the Tasmanians', PhD thesis, Australian National University, 1971, 52.

66 John Mulvaney, 'Prehistory from Antipodean Perspectives', *Proceedings of the Prehistoric Society* 37(2) (1971), 228–52, 229.

67 John Mulvaney, 'Research into the Prehistory of Victoria: A Criticism and a Report on a Field Survey', *Historical Studies: Australia and New Zealand* 8(29) (1957), 32–43; John Mulvaney, 'Archaeological Excavations on the Aire River, Otway Peninsula, Victoria', *Proceedings of the Royal Society of Victoria* 75(1) (1962), 427–32; John Mulvaney, 'Prehistory of the Basalt Plains', *Proceedings of the Royal Society of Victoria* 77(2) (1964), 1–15.

68 John Mulvaney and EB Joyce, 'Archaeological and Geomorphological Investigations on Mt Moffat Station, Queensland, Australia,' *Proceedings of the Prehistoric Society* 31 (1965), 147–212, 149.

69 Edmund Gill, *Rivers of History* (Sydney: Australian Broadcasting Commission, 1970), 12.

70 Mulvaney, *Digging Up a Past*, 109; Inglis, 'John Mulvaney's Universities', 38.

71 Mulvaney, *Digging Up a Past*, 109.

72 Mulvaney and Joyce, 'Investigations on Mt Moffat Station', 195, 204; John Mulvaney, 'Kenniff/Tombs Notebook, 1960', Mulvaney Papers, NLA, MS 9615/8.4/2, Box 62, 10 Aug 1960.

73 John Mulvaney, 'Foreword: Archaeology in Queensland', *Queensland Archaeological Research* 1 (1984), 4–7, 5.

74 Mulvaney and Joyce, 'Investigations on Mt Moffat Station', 147.

75 John Callow to John Mulvaney, 20 Jul 1962, Mulvaney Papers, NLA, MS 9615/8.4/8, Box 62.

76 John Mulvaney to John Callow, 5 Dec 1962, Mulvaney Papers, NLA, MS 9615/8.4/8, Box 62.

77 John Mulvaney, pers. comm., 2014.

78 Mulvaney and Joyce, 'Investigations on Mt Moffat Station', 176.

79 John Mulvaney, *The Prehistory of Australia* (New York: Praeger, 1969), 107.

80 Richard A Gould, 'Puntutjarpa Rockshelter: A Reply to Messrs Glover and Lampert', *Archaeology and Physical Anthropology in Oceania* 4 (1969), 229–37.

81 JM Bowler, R Jones, H Allen and AG Thorne, 'Pleistocene Human Remains from Australia: A Living Site and Human Cremation from Lake Mungo, Western New South Wales', *World Archaeology* 2(1) (1970), 39–60, 48.

82 Mulvaney, *The Prehistory of Australia*, 12.

83 Peter J Ucko, 'Jack Golson: A Personal Appreciation of his Institutional Role', in M Spriggs et al., *A Community of Culture*, 32–34; Tom Griffiths, 'In Search of Australian Antiquity', in Bonyhady and Griffiths, *Prehistory to Politics*, 42–62, 56.

84   Frankel, 'The Archaeologist as Tribal Elder', 288.

85   John Mulvaney interviewed by Bronwyn Hanna, 18 Sept 2012, National Library of Australia, sound recording, ORAL TRC 6265/15.

86   This sentence echoes Mulvaney's obituary of Childe. Mulvaney, 'V.G. Childe 1892–1957', 94.

TWO   Haunted Country: Isabel McBryde in New England

1   Isabel McBryde, 'Archaeological Field Survey Work in Northern New South Wales', *Oceania* 33(1) (Sept 1962), 12–17, 14.

2   Jack Golson, 'The Personality of New England: Isabel McBryde and the Dimensions of her Regional Archaeology', in I Macfarlane, MJ Mountain and R Paton (eds), *Many Exchanges: Archaeology, History, Community and the Work of Isabel McBryde* (Canberra: Aboriginal History Inc., 2005), 13–34.

3   Judith Wright, 'The Broken Links', in *Born of the Conquerors: Selected Essays* (Canberra: Aboriginal Studies Press, 1991), 29–30, 29.

4   Judith Wright, 'Nigger's Leap: New England', *Meanjin* 4(2) (Winter, 1945), 85. Historian Georgina Arnott cautions against the tendency of postcolonial scholars to merge Wright's early, passive laments with her later work, which recognised the complicity of her forebears in land-taking and the destruction of Aboriginal lives. Poems like 'Nigger's Leap' and 'Bora Ring', Arnott argues, are as much about meeting the stylistic demands of the Victorian Gothic as they are about confronting dispossession. While Wright was a progressive thinker, she was also a product of her historical context. Georgina Arnott, *The Unknown Judith Wright* (Perth: UWA Publishing, 2016), 160–68.

5   Judith Wright, 'Bora Ring', in *The Moving Image* (Melbourne: Meanjin Press, 1946), 12.

6   WEH Stanner, 'The Aborigines (1938)', in *The Dreaming & Other Essays* (Melbourne: Black Inc. Agenda, 2009), 123–45, 124.

7   WEH Stanner, 'The Boyer Lectures: After the Dreaming (1968)', in *The Dreaming & Other Essays*, 172–224, 189.

8   Stanner argued that the 'great Australian silence' began with the establishment of a colony in Sydney in 1788. Henry Reynolds, amongst others, has argued persuasively that colonial Australia was not as captive to this 'silence' as the Australian nation has been. See, for example, Reynolds, *Why Weren't We Told?* (Ringwood, Vic: Penguin, 1999), 92.

9   Isabel McBryde interviewed by Martin Thomas, 17–19 Aug 2004, National Library of Australia, sound recording, ORAL TRC 5194/2.

10   Isabel McBryde, 'Introduction', in Isabel McBryde (ed.), *Records of Times Past: Ethnohistorical Essays on the Culture and Ecology of the New England Tribes* (Canberra: Australian Institute of Aboriginal Studies, 1978), 1–4, 3.

11   McBryde interviewed by Thomas, ORAL TRC 5194/3.

12   Sharon Sullivan, 'Out of the Box: Isabel McBryde's Radical Contribution to the Shaping of Australian Archaeological Practice', in Macfarlane, Mountain and Paton, *Many Exchanges*, 83–94, 87, 92.

13   McBryde interviewed by Thomas, ORAL TRC 5194/1.

14   McBryde interviewed by Thomas, ORAL TRC 5194/1; Isabel McBryde,
      'Imperium et Libertas: The Roman Opposition under the Flavian Principate
      69–96 A.D.', MA thesis, University of Melbourne, 1959.

15   Frederick D McCarthy, 'Methods and Scope of Australian Archaeology', *Mankind*
      5(7) (Apr 1959), 297–316, 297.

16   McBryde interviewed by Thomas, ORAL TRC 5194/2.

17   A version of this map appears in Grahame Clark, *Prehistory at Cambridge and
      Beyond* (Cambridge: Cambridge University Press, 1989), 100. See also Grahame
      Clark, *World Prehistory: An Outline* (Cambridge: Cambridge University Press,
      1961), 260; Brian Fagan, *Grahame Clark: An Intellectual Biography of an
      Archaeologist* (Boulder, CO: Westview Press, 2001).

18   In 1981, Tim Murray and Peter White characterised the field of Australian
      archaeology as 'Cambridge in the Bush', sparking a vigorous debate about what is
      distinctive about the discipline. I have pursued some of these discussions in Billy
      Griffiths, '"The Dawn" of Australian Archaeology: John Mulvaney at Fromm's
      Landing', *Journal of Pacific Archaeology* 8(1) (2017), 100–11. See also Tim Murray
      and Peter White, 'Cambridge in the Bush? Archaeology in Australia and New
      Guinea', *World Archaeology* 13(2) (1981), 255–63, 257.

19   Isabel McBryde, 'Australia's Once and Future Archaeology', *Archaeology in Oceania*
      21(1) (Apr 1986), 13–28, 16.

20   Jack Golson, 'Old Guards and New Waves: Reflections on Antipodean
      Archaeology 1954–1975', *Archaeology in Oceania* 21(1) (Apr 1986), 2–12, 2.

21   Grahame Clark, *Aspects of Prehistory* (Berkeley: University of California Press,
      1970), 52.

22   McBryde, 'Australia's Once and Future Archaeology', 17.

23   OGS Crawford, *Archaeology in the Field* (London: Phoenix House Ltd., 1953), 36.

24   Crawford, *Archaeology in the Field*, 51–52.

25   Cyril Fox, *The Personality of Britain* (Cardiff: National Museum of Wales, 1938), 9.

26   Mulvaney, 'Antiquity of Man in Australia', 37.

27   McBryde interviewed by Thomas, ORAL TRC 5194/2.

28   Iain Davidson, Isabel McBryde and Graham Connah, 'Archaeology and
      Palaeoanthropology at U.N.E.: Prehistory and History, 1959–1999', in JS Ryan
      (ed.), *The Arts from New England: University Provision and Outreach 1928 to 1998*
      (Armidale: University of New England, 1999), 194–207, 194, 196; John Mulvaney,
      'Isabel McBryde: From Regional Research to National Reconciliation and Global
      Heritage', in Macfarlane, Mountain and Paton, *Many Exchanges*, 3–12, 4.

29   Isabel McBryde, 'Archaeology in Australia – Some Recent Developments', *The
      Record* 6(1) (Mar 1964), 5–7, 7.

30   Isabel McBryde, '"Worth a Thousand Words"?: Words, Images and Material Culture',
      in P McConvell and N Evans (eds), *Archaeology and Linguistics: Aboriginal Australia
      in Global Perspective* (Melbourne: Oxford University Press, 1997), 311–40, 313.

31   McBryde, 'Australia's Once and Future Archaeology', 26.

32   Isabel McBryde, 'Past and Present Indivisible? Archaeology and Society,
      Archaeology in Society', in Tim Bonyhady and Tom Griffiths (eds), *Prehistory to
      Politics: John Mulvaney, the Humanities and the Public Intellectual* (Melbourne:
      Melbourne University Press, 1996), 65–84, 84.

33   Sandra Bowdler, 'Hook, Line and Dilly Bag: An Interpretation of an Australian
      Coastal Shell Midden', *Mankind* 10(4) (1976), 248–58, 256.
34   Isabel McBryde, 'An Archaeological Survey of the New England Region, New
      South Wales', PhD thesis, University of New England, 1966, 245–46; Isabel
      McBryde, *Aboriginal Prehistory in New England: An Archaeological Survey of
      Northeastern New South Wales* (Sydney: Sydney University Press, 1974), 91–3,
      168–71; Isabel McBryde, 'Report on Archaeological Work Carried Out in the
      New England Area of New South Wales', 1963, AIATSIS Library, PMS 2279,
      Doc. 63/76; 'Report on Archaeological Work in New England District of N.S.W.
      Jul.–Dec. 1964', 1964, AIATSIS Library, PMS 2282, Doc. 65/224; 'Report on
      Archaeological Work Northeastern N.S.W.', 1965, AIATSIS Library, PMS 2283,
      Doc. no.66/412.
35   Attrib. McBryde in Davidson et al., 'Archaeology and Palaeoanthropology at
      U.N.E.', 197. Fieldwork was an intensely cross-disciplinary affair, involving
      zoologist David Horton, geologist Ray Binns, geographer Ellis Thorpe, sociologist
      Mary Jackes and English professor John Ryan.
36   Sullivan, 'Out of the Box', 87.
37   Ingereth Macfarlane, 'Preface: Connections, Complexity and Diversity', in
      Macfarlane, Mountain and Paton, *Many Exchanges*, xix–xxxv, xxii.
38   McBryde, 'Introduction', 3.
39   McBryde, 'Australia's Once and Future Archaeology', 14.
40   Isabel McBryde, 'Determinants of Assemblage Variation in New England
      Prehistory', in RVS Wright (ed.), *Stone Tools as Cultural Markers: Change,
      Evolution and Complexity* (Canberra: Australian Institute of Aboriginal Studies,
      1977), 225–50, 229, 249.
41   Ray Binns and Isabel McBryde, *A Petrological Analysis of Ground-Edge Artefacts
      from Northern New South Wales* (Canberra: Australian Institute of Aboriginal
      Studies, 1972), 5, 63–65.
42   Mulvaney, 'Isabel McBryde', 6.
43   Isabel McBryde, 'Kulin Greenstone Quarries: The Social Contexts of Production
      and Distribution for the Mt William Site', *World Archaeology* 16 (1984), 267–85.
      McBryde records the distribution network as extending over 1000 kilometres in:
      'Continuity and Discontinuity: Wurundjeri Custodianship of the Mt William
      Quarry', in S Kleinert and M Neale (eds), *The Oxford Companion to Aboriginal Art
      and Culture* (Oxford: Oxford University Press, 2000), 247–51, 247. See also Colin
      Renfrew, JR Cann and JE Dixon, 'Obsidian in the Aegean', *The Annual of the
      British School at Athens* 60 (1965), 225–47.
44   John Mulvaney, '"The Chain of Connection": The Material Evidence', in Nicolas
      Peterson (ed.), *Tribes and Boundaries in Australia* (Canberra: Australian Institute of
      Aboriginal Studies, 1976), 72–94, 80.
45   Isabel McBryde, 'Goods from Another Country: Exchange Networks and the
      People of the Lake Eyre Basin', in John Mulvaney and J Peter White (eds),
      Australians to 1788 (Sydney: Fairfax, Syme & Weldon Associates, 1987),
      253–73, 268.
46   Vincent Megaw, 'Australian Archaeology – How Far Have We Progressed?',
      Mankind 6(7) (Jun 1966), 306–12, 311.

47   John Mulvaney, 'Australian Archaeology, 1929–1964: Problems and Policies',
     Australian Journal of Science 27(2) (1964), 39–44, 42.

48   McBryde, *Aboriginal Prehistory in New England*, 14; McBryde, 'Australia's Once
     and Future Archaeology', 20.

49   Joan Gero, 'Gender Bias in Archaeology: Here, Then, and Now', in S Rosser (ed.),
     Feminism Within the Science and Health Care Professions: Overcoming Resistance
     (Oxford: Pergamon Press, 1988), 33–43; Alison Wylie, 'Gender Theory and the
     Archaeological Record: Why Is There No Archaeology of Gender?', in Joan Gero
     and Margaret Conkey (eds), *Engendering Archaeology* (Oxford: Basil Blackwell,
     1991), 31–54, 34–35. For further discussion of this see: Sandra Bowdler and
     Genevieve Clune, 'That Shadowy Band: The Role of Women in the Development
     of Australian Archaeology', *Australian Archaeology* 50 (Jun 2000), 27–35; Wendy
     Beck and Lesley Head, 'Women in Australian Prehistory', *Australian Feminist
     Studies* 5(11) (1990), 29–48.

50   Stephanie Moser, 'Science, Stratigraphy and the Deep Sequence: Excavation versus
     Regional Survey and the Question of Gendered Practice in Archaeology', *Antiquity*
     70(270) (Dec 1996), 813–23.

51   Sylvia Hallam, 'Review of The Moth Hunters: Aboriginal Prehistory of the
     Australian Alps by Josephine Flood', *Aboriginal History* 6 (1982), 154–59, 154.

52   Peter Read, 'Many Exchanges, Many Ripples: The Work of Isabel McBryde',
     Aboriginal History 29 (2005), 138–41, 140.

53   Macfarlane, 'Preface', xxiv.

54   Isabel McBryde, 'Miss Mary, Ethnography and the Inheritance of Concern',
     in Julie Marcus (ed.), *First in Their Field: Women and Australian Anthropology*
     (Melbourne: Melbourne University Press, 1993), 15–45, 160–67, 15, 29, 45.

INTERLUDE I   Before It Is Too Late, 1961

1   WEH Stanner, 'Introduction', in H Sheils (ed.), *Australian Aboriginal Studies:
     Conference on Aboriginal Studies, May 1961* (Melbourne: Oxford University Press,
     1963), xi–xviii, xiii.

2   John Mulvaney, 'Section III', in *Prehistory and Heritage: The Writings of John
     Mulvaney* (Canberra: Department of Prehistory, Australian National University,
     1990), 149–50, 149; Vincent Megaw, 'Australian Archaeology – How Far Have
     We Progressed?', *Mankind* 6(7) (Jun 1966), 306–12, 306.

3   Hilary du Cros, *Much More Than Stones and Bones: Australian Archaeology in the Late
     Twentieth Century* (Melbourne: Melbourne University Press, 2002), 22; Ron Lampert,
     'Trends in Australian Prehistoric Research', *Antiquity* 49 (1975), 197–206, 197; David
     Horton, 'The 1961 Conference', *Australian Aboriginal Studies* 1 (1986), 83–84.

4   Isabel McBryde interviewed by Martin Thomas, 17–19 Aug 2004, National
     Library of Australia, sound recording, ORAL TRC 5194/3.

5   McBryde interviewed by Thomas, ORAL TRC 5194/3.

6   WC Wentworth, 'Revised Proposals for an Australian Institute for Aboriginal Studies',
     Cabinet submission 700/38, 1960, National Archives of Australia, A452, 1961/7988.

7   WC Wentworth, 'An Australian Institute for Aboriginal Studies', undated, WEH
     Stanner Papers, AIATSIS Library, MS 3752 19/1(c), 2–3.

8   Wentworth, 'Revised Proposals for an Australian Institute for Aboriginal Studies'.
9   Nicolas Peterson, '"Studying Man and Man's Nature": The History of the
     Institutionalisation of Aboriginal Anthropology', *Australian Aboriginal Studies* 2
     (1990), 3–19, 16.
10   John McEwen, Acting Prime Minister, 'For Cabinet: Proposed Australian Institute
     of Aboriginal Studies', 24 May 1960, Cabinet submission 700/38, National
     Archives of Australia, A452, 1961/7988.
11   WEH Stanner to EJ Bunting, Secretary, Prime Minister's Department, 23 May
     1961, in 'Establishment of Australian Institute of Aboriginal Studies, 1961–1963',
     National Archives of Australia, A452, 1960/2944; WEH Stanner, 'Report on the
     Conference on Aboriginal Studies, 23 May 1961', National Archives of Australia,
     A452, 1960/2944, 1, 7.
12   Item 6 in WC Wentworth, 'Minutes of the Interim Council', 10 Mar 1962, as
     quoted in John Mulvaney, 'WEH Stanner and the Foundation of the Australian
     Institute for Aboriginal Studies, 1959–1964', in Melinda Hinkson and Jeremy
     Beckett (eds), *An Appreciation of Difference: WEH Stanner and Aboriginal Australia*
     (Canberra: Aboriginal Studies Press, 2008), 58–75, 67–68.
13   McEwen, 'For Cabinet: Proposed Australian Institute of Aboriginal Studies';
     Jaqueline Ann Lambert, 'A History of the Australian Institute of Aboriginal
     Studies 1959–1989: An Analysis of How Aboriginal and Torres Strait Islander
     People Achieved Control of a National Research Institute', PhD thesis, Australian
     National University, 2011, 54.
14   Robert G Menzies, 1 Jun 1963, 'For Cabinet: Australian Institute of Aboriginal
     Studies', Cabinet submission 711/37, National Archives of Australia, A452,
     1961/7988.
15   Kim Beazley, Commonwealth of Australia, *Parliamentary Debates (Hansard)
     Session 1964*, 1st Session of the 25th Parliament, Vol. H. or R. 42 (new series),
     21 Apr 1964 – 20 May 1964, 2161.
16   Megaw, 'Australian Archaeology', 306.
17   Stephanie Moser, 'Archaeology and its Disciplinary Culture: The
     Professionalisation of Australian Prehistoric Archaeology', PhD thesis, University
     of Sydney, 1995, 73.
18   Frederick D McCarthy, 'A Coat of Paint', *Australian Aboriginal Studies* 2 (1984),
     72–81, 80–81, 79.
19   Stephanie Moser, 'The Aboriginalisation of Archaeology: The Contribution of the
     Australian Institute of Aboriginal Studies to the Indigenous Transformation of
     the Discipline', in Peter J Ucko (ed.), *Theory in Archaeology: A World Perspective*
     (London: Routledge, 1995), 150–77.

THREE   The First Tasmanians: Rhys Jones at Rocky Cape

1   Rhys Jones to Robert Sessions, 21 Oct 1980, Rhys Jones Papers, National Library
     of Australia, MS ACC 03/250, Folder 72, Box 14.
2   Rhys Jones, 'The Tasmanian Paradox', in RVS Wright (ed.), *Stone Tools as Cultural
     Markers: Change, Evolution and Complexity* (Canberra: Australian Institute of
     Aboriginal Studies, 1977), 189–204, 189.

3   Rhys Jones interviewed by Mike Smith, 12 Apr 1991, National Library of
    Australia, sound recording, ORAL TRC 2677/1.

4   Jones to Sessions, 21 Oct 1980.

5   Artis Film Productions, 'Information: The Last Tasmanian', Rhys Jones Papers,
    NLA, MS ACC 03/250, Folder 75, Box 15, 6.

6   Bernard Smith, *The Spectre of Truganini: The 1980 Boyer Lectures* (Sydney: ABC,
    1980), 10. Ann Curthoys, James Boyce and Lyndall Ryan also argue that the
    Tasmanians suffered genocide. Henry Reynolds has illuminated the process of
    Indigenous erasure with deliberate intent in Tasmania, but he questions the broad
    assumptions of genocide. See Ann Curthoys, 'Genocide in Tasmania: The History of
    an Idea', in Dirk Moses (ed.), *Empire, Colony, Genocide: Conquest, Occupation, and
    Subaltern Resistance in World History* (New York: Berghahn Books, 2008), 292–352;
    James Boyce, *Van Diemen's Land* (Melbourne: Black Inc., 2008), 259–313; Lyndall
    Ryan, *Tasmanian Aborigines: A History Since 1803* (Sydney: Allen & Unwin, 2012),
    215; Henry Reynolds, *An Indelible Stain? The Question of Genocide in Australia's
    History* (Ringwood, Vic: Viking, 2001), 29–85.

7   Rhys Jones to Robert Sessions, Mar 1980, 'Progress Report on the Last
    Tasmanian', Rhys Jones Papers, NLA, MS ACC 03/250, Folder 72, Box 14.

8   Rhys Jones, 'Gondwana Supercontinent and the Southern Rain Forest', undated
    manuscript, Rhys Jones Papers, NLA, MS ACC 03/250, Folder 72, Box 14.

9   Jones to Sessions, 21 Oct 1980.

10 John Mulvaney, 'Reflections', *Antiquity* 80(308) (Jun 2006), 425–34, 433.

11 Mulvaney, 'Reflections', 433.

12 Rhys Jones is the clear inspiration for Ralph Kincaid in Nicholas Jose, *The
    Custodians* (Sydney: Macmillan, 1997) and Janos Belcredi in Keith Thomas,
    Idlers in the Land (London: Hutchinson, 1979); Russell Deiley, 'The First
    Australians', *Australian Playboy* (Sept 1979), 50–56; Cheryl Jones, 'Australiana
    Jones and the Last Crusade', *The Bulletin* (19 Jun 2001), 36–37; Lenore Nicklin,
    'The Prehistory Cowboy Strikes Again', *The Bulletin*, 12 Jun 1990, 94–95; Mick
    Barnes, 'He Digs Up the Past … and Stirs Up the Present', *Women's Day*, 8 Jan
    1979, 16–17.

13 Rebe Taylor, 'Reliable Mr Robinson and the Controversial Dr Jones', in Anna
    Johnston and Mitchell Rolls (eds), *Reading Robinson: Companion Essays to Friendly
    Mission* (Hobart: Quintus, 2008), 111–28. See also Rebe Taylor, 'The Polemics of
    Eating Fish in Tasmania: The Historical Evidence Revisited', *Aboriginal History*
    31 (2007), 1–26; Rebe Taylor, 'The Polemics of Making Fire in Tasmania: The
    Historical Evidence Revisited', *Aboriginal History* 32 (2008), 1–26; Rebe Taylor,
    'Archaeology and Aboriginal Protest: The Influence of Rhys Jones's Tasmanian
    Work on Australian Historiography', *Australian Historical Studies* 45(3) (2014),
    331–49. This work has been consolidated in Taylor's recent book *Into the Heart
    of Tasmania: A Search for Human Antiquity* (Melbourne: Melbourne University
    Press, 2017).

14 Rhys Jones, '*Sylwadau Cynfrodor Ar Gôr Y Cewri*; or a British Aboriginal's Land
    Claim to Stonehenge', in Christopher Chippindale et al. (eds), *Who Owns
    Stonehenge?* (London: BT Batsford Ltd, 1990), 62–87, 66.

15 Jones, '*Sylwadau Cynfrodor Ar Gôr Y Cewri*', 86.

16 Carmel Schrire, 'Betrayal as a Universal Element in the Sundering of Bass Strait', in Atholl Anderson, Ian Lilley and Sue O'Connor (eds), *Histories of Old Ages: Essays in Honour of Rhys Jones* (Canberra: Pandanus Books, 2001), 25–33, 30.

17 The film was titled *Y Tasmaniad Olaf.* See Patrick Robertson, *The Guinness Book of Film Facts and Feats* (Enfield: Guiness Books, 1985), 146. Jones also narrated a French-language version of the film: *Les Derniers Tasmaniens*. He published his first article in Welsh in 1965 with help from Alice Powell: Rhys Jones, 'Pwy oedd y Tasmaniad? Ymchwiliadau archaeolegol', *Y Gwyddonydd* 3 (1965), 30–36.

18 Betty Meehan, 'The Early Life of a New Chum, 1941–1969', in Anderson, Lilley and O'Connor, *Histories of Old Ages*, 1–16, 4.

19 Jones interviewed by Smith, ORAL TRC 2677/1.

20 Jones interviewed by Smith, ORAL TRC 2677/1. See also Rhys Jones and Vincent Megaw, 'Confessions of a Wild Colonial Boy: Rhys Jones in conversation with Vincent Megaw', *Australian Archaeology* 50 (2000), 12–26; Meehan, 'The Early Life of a New Chum', 4.

21 Jones in Meehan, 'The Early Life of a New Chum', 4.

22 Rhys Jones, 'Geography: Form III A' (1954), Rhys Jones Papers, NLA, MS ACC 08/042, Item 1, Box 1.

23 Jones interviewed by Smith, ORAL TRC 2677/1.

24 There was a fourteen-day delay between letters. Grahame Clark to Rhys Jones, 26 May 1961, Rhys Jones Papers, NLA, MS ACC 05/191, Item 74, Box 11.

25 Jack Golson, 'Old Guards and New Waves: Reflections on Antipodean Archaeology 1954–1975', *Archaeology in Oceania* 21(1) (1986), 2–12.

26 Gordon Willey and Philip Phillips, *Method and Theory in American Archaeology* (Chicago: University of Chicago Press, 1958); Sally R Binford and Lewis R Binford (eds), *New Perspectives in Archeology* (Chicago: Aldine Pub. Co., 1968).

27 Don Brothwell and Eric Higgs (eds), *Science in Archaeology: A Comprehensive Survey of Progress and Research* (Bristol: Thames and Hudson, 1963), 15.

28 Rhys Jones, 'Journals and Diaries, 1960–1962', Rhys Jones Papers, NLA, MS ACC 08/42, Box 1.

29 Meehan, 'The Early Life of a New Chum', 6.

30 Rhys Jones, 'The Coming of the Aborigines', in John Hardy and Alan Frost (eds), *Studies from Terra Australis to Australia*, Occasional Paper No. 6 (Canberra: Australian Academy of the Humanities and Highland Press, 1989), 10–24, 23.

31 Rhys Jones, 'Diary and Notes, Feb 6–Jun 16, 1963', Rhys Jones Papers, NLA, MS ACC 08/042, Item 10–17, Box 1.

32 Jones interviewed by Smith, ORAL TRC 2677/1.

33 Golson, 'Old Guards and New Waves', 2.

34 Golson, 'Old Guards and New Waves', 5.

35 Rhys Jones and Jim Allen, 'Caveat Excavator: A Sea Bird Midden on Steep Head Island, North West Tasmania', *Australian Archaeology* 8 (1978), 142–45, 144.

36 This scene is recreated from: Meehan, 'The Early Life of a New Chum', 9; Jones and Megaw, 'Confessions of a Wild Colonial Boy', 14; Jones interviewed by Smith, ORAL TRC 2677/1.

37 Rhys Jones, 'Archaeological Reconnaissance in Tasmania, 1963/64', Rhys Jones Papers, NLA, MS ACC 03/250, Folder 57, Box 11, 3.

38   Jones interviewed by Smith, ORAL TRC 2677/1.

39   John Mulvaney, *Digging Up a Past* (Sydney: UNSW Press, 2011), 116–17.

40   Rhys Jones, 'Second Archaeological Report for Field Season in Tasmania, Summer
      1964–65', Report to AIAS, Oct 1965, Rhys Jones Papers, NLA, MS ACC 03/250,
      Folder 115, Box 24, 3.

41   Jim Allen, 'Hunter Gatherers as Colonisers: The First Humans East of the Wallace
      Line', The Mulvaney Lecture, Australian National University, 24 Mar 1999.

42   JL Davies to Rhys Jones, 29 Nov 1963, Rhys Jones Papers, NLA, MS ACC
      03/250, Folder 61, Box 12.

43   Rhys Jones, 'Rocky Cape and the Problem of the Tasmanians', PhD thesis,
      Australian National University, 1971, 58.

44   Robert Pulleine, 'The Tasmanians and Their Stone-Culture', *Australasian
      Association for the Advancement of Science* 19 (1928), 294–314, 310.

45   Jones, 'Second Archaeological Report for Field Season in Tasmania, Summer
      1964–65', 8.

46   Jones, 'Rocky Cape and the Problem of the Tasmanians', 57, 59.

47   Rhys Jones, torn note page, dated 21st [Dec 1963], Rhys Jones Papers, NLA,
      MS ACC 05/191, Item 55, Box 5.

48   Jones, 'Second Archaeological Report for Field Season in Tasmania, Summer
      1964–65', 5; Jones, 'Archaeological Reconnaissance in Tasmania, 1963/64',
      1, 4, 9.

49   Rhys Jones, 'Excavations on a Stone Arrangement in Tasmania', *Man* 62
      (May–Jun, 1965), 78–79.

50   Rhys Jones, 'West Point I, Book 1', Dec 1964–Jan 1965, Field Journals, AIATSIS
      Library, MS 5040/1/6; Rhys Jones, 'West Point I, Book 2', 1965, Field Journals,
      AIATSIS Library, MS 5040/1/7.

51   NWG Macintosh and BCW Barker, *The Osteology of Aboriginal Man in Tasmania*
      (Sydney: Australasian Medical Publishing Co., Oceania Monographs No. 12,
      1965), 56–68; Alan Thorne, 'The Racial Affinities of Tasmanian Aborigines: Some
      New Skeletal Evidence', MA thesis, University of Sydney, 1967.

52   Meehan, 'The Early Life of a New Chum', 10–11.

53   Jones interviewed by Smith, ORAL TRC 2677/1.

54   Rhys Jones and Betty Meehan, 'A Crucible of Australian Prehistory: The 1965
      Hobart ANZAAS Conference' in Atholl Anderson and Tim Murray (eds),
      Australian Archaeologist: Collected Papers in Honour of Jim Allen (Canberra:
      Coombs Academic Publishing, 2000), 40–61, 55.

55   Rhys Jones, 'Rocky Cape Book A', 5 Jun–14 Jul 1967, Field Journals, AIATSIS
      Library, MS 5040/1/17; Jones, 'Second Archaeological Report for Field Season in
      Tasmania, Summer 1964–65', 1.

56   Jones interviewed by Smith, ORAL TRC 2677/1.

57   Jones interviewed by Smith, ORAL TRC 2677/1.

58   Rhys Jones vividly describes the image in: 'Hunting Forbears', in M Roe (ed.),
      The Flow of Culture: Tasmania Studies (Canberra: Australian Academy of the
      Humanities, 1987), 14–49, 31–32.

59   Rhys Jones, 'Rocky Cape South Cave', Feb 1965, Field Journals, AIATSIS Library,
      MS 5040/1/11.

60   Jones, 'Second Archaeological Report for Field Season in Tasmania, Summer 1964–65', 1.

61   Rhys Jones, 'A Speculative Archaeological Sequence for North-West Tasmania', *Records of the Queen Victoria Museum* 25 (Dec 1966), 1–12.

62   Rhys Jones, 'Man as an Element in a Continental Fauna: The Case of the Sundering of the Bassian Bridge', in Jim Allen, Jack Golson and Rhys Jones (eds), *Sunda and Sahul* (London: Academic Press, 1977), 318–86, 345.

63   Jones, 'Rocky Cape and the Problem of the Tasmanians', 603.

64   Jones, 'Rocky Cape and the Problem of the Tasmanians', 607.

65   Jones, 'A Speculative Archaeological Sequence for North-West Tasmania', 9.

66   Jones, 'The Tasmanian Paradox', 203.

67   Tim Murray, 'Tasmania and the Constitution of "The Dawn of Humanity"', *Antiquity*, 66 (1992), 730–43.

68   Sandra Bowdler, 'Hunter Hill, Hunter Island', PhD thesis, Australian National University, 1979; Harry Allen, 'Left out in the Cold: Why the Tasmanians Stopped Eating Fish', *The Artefact* 4 (1979), 1–10; Harry Lourandos, '10,000 Years in the Tasmanian Highlands', *Australian Archaeology* 16 (1983), 39–44; Ron Vanderwal, 'Adaptive Technology in Southwest Tasmania', *Australian Archaeology* 8 (1978), 107–27; David Horton, 'Tasmanian Adaptation', *Mankind* 12 (1979), 28–34; Taylor, 'The Polemics of Eating Fish in Tasmania', 1–26; Attrib. Wright, 1982, in David Horton, 'Here be Dragons: A View of Australian Archaeology', in MA Smith, M Spriggs and B Fankhauser (eds), *Sahul in Review: Pleistocene Archaeology in Australia, New Guinea and Island Melanesia* (Canberra: Department of Prehistory, ANU, 1993), 11–16, 13.

69   Jones and Meehan, 'A Crucible of Australian Prehistory', 52–53; NJB Plomley, *Friendly Mission: That Tasmanian Journals and Papers of George Augustus Robinson 1829–1834* (Hobart: Tasmanian Historical Research Association, 1966).

70   Jones, 'Rocky Cape and the Problem of the Tasmanians', 13, 16; Rhys Jones, 'Tasmanian Aborigines and Dogs', *Mankind* 7 (1970), 256–71.

71   Rhys Jones, 'Middens and Man in Tasmania', *Australian Natural History* (Sept 1967), 359–64, 359.

72   WD Jackson, 'Vegetation', in JL Davies (ed.), *Atlas of Tasmania* (Hobart: Lands and Surveys Department, 1965), 30–35, 30, 33. See also David Harris, 'People, Land, Fire and Food: Comments on Two Jonesian Themes', in Anderson, Lilley and O'Connor, *Histories of Old Ages*, 55–59, 56.

73   Jones, 'Second Archaeological Report for Field Season in Tasmania, Summer 1964–65', 4.

74   Rhys Jones, 'The Geographical Background to the Arrival of Man in Australia and Tasmania', *Archaeology and Physical Anthropology in Oceania* 3(3) (Oct 1968), 186–215, 206.

75   Jones, 'Rocky Cape and the Problem of the Tasmanians', 77.

76   Rhys Jones, 'Fire-Stick Farming', *Australian Natural History* 16 (1969), 224–28, 227.

77   See WK Hancock, *Discovering Monaro: A Study of Man's Impact on his Environment* (Cambridge: Cambridge University Press, 1972), 25–26; Sylvia Hallam, *Fire and Hearth: A Study of Aboriginal Usage and European Usurpation in South-Western Australia* (Canberra: Australian Institute of Aboriginal Studies, 1975).

78   Rhys Jones, 'A Trip to Mirrngadja, NE Arnhem Land with Nic Peterson', 15–27
     May 1970, Field Journals, AIATSIS Library, MS 5040/1/29.
79   Rhys Jones quoted in Cheryl Jones, 'Australiana Jones and the Last Crusade', 36.
80   Rhys Jones, 'The Neolithic, Palaeolithic and the Hunting Gardeners: Man and
     Land in the Antipodes', in RP Suggate and M Cresswell (eds), *Quaternary Studies*
     (Wellington: Royal Society of New Zealand, 1975), 21–34.
81   Jones, 'The Tasmanian Paradox', 196.
82   Beth Gott, 'Fire-Making in Tasmania: Absence of Evidence Is Not Evidence of
     Absence', *Current Anthropology* 43(4) (Aug–Oct 2002), 650–56, 655.
83   Jones, 'Rocky Cape and the Problem of the Tasmanians', 16, 17.
84   Schrire, 'Betrayal as a Universal Element in the Sundering of Bass Strait', 30.
85   Taylor, 'Reliable Mr Robinson and the Controversial Dr Jones'.
86   Rhys Jones, 'Appendix: Tasmanian Tribes', in Norman B Tindale, *Aboriginal Tribes
     of Australia* 1 (Berkeley: University of California Press, 1974), 319–54.
87   Jones, 'Rocky Cape and the Problem of the Tasmanians', 9.
88   Tom Haydon (dir.), *The Last Tasmanian* (1978), Sydney: Artis Film Productions.
89   Tom Haydon, 'Interview with I. Stocks', *Cinema Papers* 12 (1977), 304–6, 372,
     377; Rhys Jones, 'Obituaries: Tom Haydon (1938–1991): Film Interpreter of
     Australian Archaeology', *Australian Archaeology* 35 (1992), 51–64, 63; Artis Film
     Productions, 'Information: The Last Tasmanian', 10.
90   Jones, 'The Tasmanian Paradox', 203. In the film Jones used similar words:
     'Tasmanian history ... ends in catastrophe ... in a sense their doom was sealed by
     that event.' Haydon, *The Last Tasmanian*.
91   The press responses were collated in Artis Film Productions, 'The Impact of The
     Last Tasmanian', Rhys Jones Papers, NLA, MS ACC 03/250, Folder 75, Box 15.
     These representative quotes come from Bev Tivey, *Daily Telegraph*, 6 Oct 1978;
     Penny Valentine, *Time Out*, 19–25 May 1978 and *ANU Reporter*, 12 May 1978.
     Film and television historian James Findlay argues that *The Last Tasmanian* played
     a pivotal role in generating public awareness of colonial frontier violence and its
     legacy for contemporary race relations. See James Findlay, 'Caught on Screen:
     Representations of the Convict Experience in Film and Television', PhD thesis,
     University of Sydney, 2017.
92   These are Beryl Phillips' words in letter to the *Age* on behalf of Aboriginal Action,
     29 March 1977, in Artis Film Productions, 'Cuttings etc re the Controversy', Rhys
     Jones Papers, NLA, MS ACC 04/142, Item 252, Box 19.
93   Michael Mansell, State Secretary of the Aboriginal Information Service in
     Survival International, Oct 1977, in Artis Film Productions, 'Cuttings etc re the
     Controversy'.
94   Rosalind F Langford, 'Our Heritage – Your Playground', *Australian Archaeology* 16
     (Jun 1983), 1–6, 5.
95   Bickford linked the film with '19th century racist ideology', while Bowdler
     compared its theoretical basis to social Darwinism. Rebe Taylor records the details
     of Bickford's protest. Anne Bickford, 'The Last Tasmanian: Superb Documentary
     or Racist Fantasy?', *Filmnews* (Jan 1979), 11–14; Sandra Bowdler, 'Fish and
     Culture, a Tasmanian Polemic', *Mankind* 12(4) (1980), 334–40, 335; Taylor, *Into
     the Heart of Tasmania*, 198.

96   Bickford, 'The Last Tasmanian: Superb Documentary or Racist Fantasy?', 13.

97   Keith Windschuttle, *The Fabrication of Aboriginal History. Vol. 1, Van Dieman's Land 1803–1847* (Sydney: Macleay Press, 2002), 378; Shayne Breen, 'Reinventing Social Evolution', in Robert Manne (ed.), *Whitewash: On Keith Windschuttle's Fabrication of Aboriginal History* (Melbourne: Black Inc. Agenda, 2003), 139–59, 142–3.

98   Tom Haydon, 'The Last Tasmanian: A Witness to History', *Film News* (Apr 1979), 12–14.

99   Annette Mansell, as in Haydon, *The Last Tasmanian*.

100 Rhys Jones, 'Obituaries: Tom Haydon (1938–1991)', 57.

101 Taylor, *Into the Heart of Tasmania*, 195.

102 Tom Haydon to Rhys Jones, 11 Mar 1975, Rhys Jones Papers, NLA, MS ACC 03/250, Folder 75, Box 15; Tom Haydon to Rhys Jones, 24 Jun 1976; Rhys Jones to Tom Haydon, 25 Jul 1976, Rhys Jones Papers, NLA, MS ACC 03/250, Folder 74, Box 14; Taylor, *Into the Heart of Tasmania*, 195.

103 Lyndall Ryan, *The Aboriginal Tasmanians* (St Lucia: University of Queensland Press, 1981), 257.

104 John Mulvaney, 'Peopled Landscapes: From Prehistoric Tasmania to Contemporary Arnhem Land', in Anderson, Lilley and O'Connor, *Histories of Old Ages*, 19–22, 21.

105 Tim Flannery, 'Obituary: Brief Life of Clarity and Compassion: Rhys Maengwyn Jones', *Australian Archaeology* 53 (2001), 39–40, 40.

106 Noel Pearson, *A Rightful Place: Race, Recognition and a More Complete Commonwealth*, Quarterly Essay 55 (Melbourne: Black Inc., 2014), 11–12.

107 Pearson, *A Rightful Place*, 16–17.

108 The children were Jo Anne and Dooley Burke and Theresa and Seamus Campbell. Margery Godfrey, 'Digging Through Time at Rocky Cape', *Advocate*, 8 Jul 1967; 'Cave Inhabited About 8000 Years Ago: Expert Claims', *Advocate*, 22 May 1967; 'Cave Find 8,000 Years Old', *Canberra Times*, 22 May 1967.

109 Jones, 'Rocky Cape and the Problem of the Tasmanians', 164, 558–64.

110 Jones interviewed by Smith, ORAL TRC 2677/1.

111 Sandra Bowdler, *Hunter Hill, Hunter Island: Archaeological Investigations of a Prehistoric Tasmanian Site* (Canberra: Australian National University, Research School of Pacific Studies, Department of Prehistory, 1984).

112 Richard Cosgrove, 'Forty-Two Degrees South: The Archaeology of Late Pleistocene Tasmania', *Journal of World Prehistory* 13(4) (Dec 1999), 357–402, 359; Robin Sim, 'Why the Tasmanians Stopped Eating Fish: Evidence for Late Holocene Expansion in Resource Exploitation Strategies', in J Hall and I McNiven (eds), *Australian Coastal Archaeology* (Canberra: ANU, 1999), 263–69.

113 Tim Flannery, *The Future Eaters: An Ecological History of the Australasian Lands and People* (Sydney: Reed New Holland, 1994), 270. See also Jared Diamond, 'Ten Thousand Years of Solitude', *Discover* 14(3) (1993), 48–57.

114 Greg Dening, 'Living in and with Deep Time', *Journal of Historical Sociology* 18(4) (2005), 269–81, 270.

FOUR   Tracks in the Desert: Richard and Betsy Gould at Puntutjarpa

1   Richard A Gould, *Yiwara: Foragers of the Australian Desert* (New York: Scribner, 1969), 5.

2   Peter Hiscock and Lynley Wallis, 'Pleistocene Settlement of Deserts from an Australian Perspective', in Peter Veth, Mike Smith and Peter Hiscock (eds), *Desert Peoples: Archaeological Perspectives* (Oxford: Blackwell Publishers, 2005), 34–57, 42. This summary also draws upon Mike Smith, *The Archaeology of Australia's Deserts* (Cambridge: Cambridge University Press, 2013), 89; Peter Veth, *Islands in the Interior: The Dynamics of Prehistoric Adaptations within the Arid Zone of Australia* (Ann Arbor, Michigan: International Monographs in Prehistory, 1993); Peter Hiscock, *Archaeology of Ancient Australia* (London: Routledge, 2008), 56–57.

3   Mike Smith, 'Reading Puritjarra', in Mandy Martin, Libby Robin and Mike Smith, *Strata: Deserts Past, Present and Future* (Mandurama, NSW: Mandy Martin, 2005), 19–24, 19.

4   Mike Smith, Alan N Williams and June Ross, 'Puntutjarpa Rockshelter Revisited: A Chronological and Stratigraphic Reappraisal of a Key Archaeological Sequence for the Western Desert, Australia', *Australian Archaeology* 83(1–2) (2017), 20–31.

5   Mike Smith, '"The Compleat Archaeologist": Mike Smith, Desert Archaeology and Museums', National Museum of Australia, Canberra, 8 Feb 2013.

6   Richard A Gould, 'An Introduction to Tolowa Prehistory: Archaeology and Ethnology Along the Northwestern California Coast', PhD thesis, University of California, Berkeley, 1966.

7   David L Conlin, 'Gould, Richard A.', in Claire Smith (ed.), *Encyclopedia of Global Archaeology* (New York: Springer-Verlag, 2014), 3100–02, 3100.

8   AP Elkin to Richard Gould, 23 Nov 1965, in AP Elkin Papers, University of Sydney Archives, 5/4/38, Box 220.

9   Ronald M Berndt, 'Groups with Minimal European Associations' in H Shiels (ed.), *Australian Aboriginal Studies: A Symposium of Papers Presented at the 1961 Research Conference* (Oxford: Oxford University Press, 1963), 385–408.

10   Richard B Lee and Irven Devore (eds), *Man the Hunter* (Chicago: Aldine, 1968).

11   Tom Griffiths, *Hunters and Collectors: The Antiquarian Imagination in Australia* (Cambridge: Cambridge University Press, 1996), 86–87, 94.

12   Richard B Lee and Irven Devore, 'Problems in the Study of Hunters and Gatherers', in Richard B Lee and Irven Devore (eds), *Man the Hunter*, 3–12, 3.

13   Frances Dahlberg (ed.), *Woman the Gatherer* (New Haven: Yale University Press, 1981).

14   Irven DeVore and Richard B Lee to AP Elkin, 7 Mar 1966, in AP Elkin Papers, University of Sydney Archives, 5/2/38, Box 221.

15   See, for example, Lewis R Binford, 'Archaeology as Anthropology', *American Antiquity* 28 (2) (Oct 1962), 217–25.

16   Norman B Tindale, 'Stone Implement Making among the Nakako, Ngadadjara and Pitjandjara of the Great Western Desert', *Records of the South Australian Museum* 15 (1) (1965), 131–64, 162–63; Richard A Gould, *Living Archaeology* (Cambridge: Cambridge University Press, 1980). Since Donald Thomson's ethno-archaeological

work in Cape York in the 1920s, only a few Australian scholars, such as Peter White and Jack Golson, had studied the material culture of contemporary foraging societies. Donald Thompson, 'The Seasonal Factor in Human Culture', *The Proceedings of the Prehistoric Society* 5 (1939), 209–21; J Peter White, 'Ethno-Archaeology in New Guinea: Two Examples', *Mankind* 6 (1967), 409–14.

17   Gould, *Yiwara*, 4.

18   Richard Gould, 'Research Proposal', sent to AP Elkin, 28 Oct 1965, in AP Elkin Papers, University of Sydney Archives, 5/4/38, Box 220, 2.

19   Gould, 'Living Archaeology', 120

20   Gould, *Yiwara*, 137.

21   Gould, *Yiwara*, 171–72.

22   Kim Mahood, 'Kartiya are like Toyotas: White Workers on Australia's Cultural Frontier', *Griffith Review* 36 (2012), 43–59.

23   RG Kimber, 'Reflections on "Living Archaeology"', *Australian Archaeology* 13 (Dec 1981), 12–15, 14.

24   Peter Morton, *Fire Across the Desert: Woomera and the Anglo-Australian Joint Project 1946–1980* (Canberra: AGPS Press, 1989), 3.

25   Sue Davenport, Peter Johnson and Yuwali, *Cleared Out: First Contact in the Western Desert* (Canberra: Aboriginal Studies Press, 2005), 143–53; Shannyn Palmer, '(Un)making Angas Downs: A Spatial History of a Central Australian Pastoral Station 1930–1980', PhD thesis, Australian National University, 2016, 41–82.

26   Gould, *Yiwara*, 192, 167. The Ngaanyatjarra people did not leave the Gibson Desert 'forever'; many returned to their homelands during the outstation movement. See David Brooks and Vikki Plant, 'Out of Sight, Out of Mind, But Making the Best of It: How Outstations Have Worked in the Ngaanyatjarra Lands', in Nicolas Peterson and Fred Myers (eds), *Experiments in Self-Determination: Histories of the Outstation Movement in Australia* (Canberra: ANU Press, 2015), 121–34.

27   Richard Gould to John Mulvaney, 5 Jun 1970, Mulvaney Papers, NLA, MS 9615/1/108, Box 14.

28   Gould, *Yiwara*, 191.

29   Richard A Gould, *Recovering the Past* (Albuquerque: University of New Mexico Press, 1990), 28.

30   Richard A Gould, Dorothy A Koster and Ann HL Sontz, 'The Lithic Assemblage of the Western Desert Aborigines of Australia', *American Antiquity* 36(2) (Apr 1971), 149–69, 165.

31   Philip Jones, *Ochre and Rust: Artefacts and Encounters on Australian Frontiers* (Kent Town, SA: Wakefield Press, 2007), 1.

32   Gould, *Yiwara*, 103–04.

33   Gould, *Yiwara*, 108.

34   Gould, *Yiwara*, 181.

35   Richard A Gould, 'Puntutjarpa Rockshelter and the Australian Desert Culture', *Anthropological Papers of the American Museum of Natural History* 54 (1) (1977), 1–187, 49–50.

36   Richard A Gould, 'Summary Report of Field Activities, November 1966–June 1967', AIATSIS Library, PMS 671, Doc. 68/686.

37   Ian Glover and Ron Lampert, 'Puntutjarpa Rockshelter Excavations by RA Gould: A Critical Review', *Archaeology and Physical Anthropology in Oceania* 4 (1968), 223–28, 222–23. He was criticised for similar practices in his excavation of Point St George in 1963–65. See FJ Allen, 'Archaeology of the Point St George Site and Tolowa Prehistory by Richard A Gould (Book Review)', *Archaeology & Physical Anthropology in Oceania* 3(3) (Oct 1968), 236–37, 236.

38   Gould, 'Puntutjarpa Rockshelter and the Australian Desert Culture', 182; Richard A Gould, 'The Archaeologist as Ethnographer: A Case from the Western Desert of Australia', *World Archaeology* 3 (2) (Oct 1971), 143–77, 175.

39   The interpretations at Danger Cave in Utah were eventually rejected for similar reasons. Smith, *The Archaeology of Australia's Deserts*, 157–58; Peter Hiscock and Peter Veth, 'Change in the Australian Desert Culture: A Reanalysis of Tulas from Puntutjarpa', *World Archaeology* 22 (1991), 332–45.

40   Smith, Williams and Ross, 'Puntutjarpa Rockshelter Revisited', 20.

41   Richard A Gould, 'Australian Institute of Aboriginal Studies: Fieldwork Report', 1970, AIATSIS Library, PMS 668, Doc. 70/1017.

42   Ian Dunlop, 'Technical and Production Problems of Ethnographic Films: Some Aspects of Filming in Australia's Western Desert', Round Table on Ethnographic Film in the Pacific Area (Sydney: Australian National Advisory Committee for UNESCO, 1966), 34–45, 40.

43   Richard A Gould to Frank Gare, Commissioner Department of Native Welfare, 7 Dec 1970, 'Gould R.A. – Yiwara', AIATSIS Library, File 65/19(a).

44   Gould, *Yiwara*, vii.

45   Fred Myers 'We Are Not Alone: Anthropology in a World of Others', *Ethnos: Journal of Anthropology* 71 (2) (2006), 233–64. There were a number of contemporaneous books which published secret-sacred images, including: Ronald M Berndt (ed.), *Australian Aboriginal Art* (Sydney: Ure Smith, 1964); Ronald M Berndt and Catherine H Berndt, *The World of the First Australians* (Sydney: Ure Smith, 1964); AP Elkin, *The Australian Aborigines: How to Understand Them* (Sydney: Angus & Robertson, 1964); Walter Gill, *Petermann Journey* (Adelaide: Rigby, 1968); Charles P Mountford, *Winbaraku and the Myth of Jarapiri* (Adelaide: Rigby, 1968); Charles P Mountford, *The Aborigines and Their Country* (Adelaide: Rigby, 1969); Norman B Tindale and HA Lindsay, *Aboriginal Australians* (Brisbane: Jacaranda Press, 1963).

46   My account of the incident draws on archival sources from AIATSIS as well as the following secondary sources: RMW Dixon, *Searching for Aboriginal Languages: Memoirs of a Field Worker* (Cambridge: Cambridge University Press, 2011), 38–39; Leith Duncan, 'Book Review: Diprotodon to Detribalization: Studies in Change Among Australian Aborigines by Arnold R Pilling and Richard A Waterman', *The Journal of the Polynesian Society* 83 (1) (Mar 1974), 112–14, 113; Barry Hill, *Broken Song: TGH Strehlow and Aboriginal Possession* (Milsons Point, NSW: Vintage Books, 2003), 741–49; Jaqueline Ann Lambert, 'A History of the Australian Institute of Aboriginal Studies 1959–1989: An Analysis of How Aboriginal and Torres Strait Islander People Achieved Control of a National Research Institute', PhD thesis, Australian National University, 2011, 108–26; Pamela Faye McGrath, 'The "Gould Controversy": A Cautionary Tale about

Photography and Consent', 2010, AIATSIS Library, PMS 6397, 1–14; John Mulvaney, 'Reflections', *Antiquity* 80 (308) (Jun 2006), 425–34, 426; John Mulvaney, *Digging Up a Past* (Sydney: UNSW Press, 2011), 173–74.; Myers 'We Are Not Alone', 249; Nicolas Peterson, 'The Changing Photographic Contract: Aborigines and Image Ethics', in Christopher Pinney and Nicolas Peterson (eds), *Photography's Other Histories* (Durham: Duke University Press, 2003), 119–45, 135. This direct quote comes from George Marcus, 'Censorship in the Heart of Difference', in Robert Post (ed.), *Censorship and Silencing: Practices of Cultural Regulation* (Los Angeles: Getty Publications, 1998), 221–42, 230.

47   Australian Institute of Aboriginal Studies, 'Conference on the Aborigines and the Anthropologist: Problems of Field Access', Canberra, 9–10 Aug 1971, Transcript of proceedings, Vol. 1 (Canberra, ACT: Australian Institute of Aboriginal Studies, 1971), 14.

48   AIAS, 'Problems of Field Access', 144; Noel Wallace, 'Field Report, May–August 1971', AIATSIS Library, PMS 2431, Doc. 71/1146.

49   Ian Crawford reporting on the observations of Mr Lock and Mr Warwick Deitch in AIAS, 'Problems of Field Access', 119; John Mulvaney, Acting AIAS Principal, to Peter Howson, Minister for the Environment, Aborigines and the Arts, 12 Aug 1971, AIATSIS File 65/19(a).

50   Pamela Faye McGrath and David Brooks, 'Their Darkest Hour: The Films and Photographs of William Grayden and the History of the "Warburton Range Controversy" of 1957', *Aboriginal History* 34 (2010), 115–41, 134.

51   Crawford in AIAS, 'Problems of Field Access', 81.

52   Bruce Gouldthorp, Headmaster of the WA Government School at Warburton, to Richard A Gould, 29 Aug 1971 in AIATSIS File 65/19(a); Don Lipscombe, 'Tribal Threat to Spear School Girl', *Sunday Australian*, 4 Jul 1971.

53   Mulvaney, *Digging Up a Past*, 173; John Mulvaney to Richard A Gould, 21 Jul 1971, AIATSIS File 65/19(a).

54   Macintosh and Crawford in AIAS, 'Problems of Field Access', 51, 54.

55   Peterson in AIAS, 'Problems of Field Access', 128.

56   John Mulvaney, 'Archaeological Retrospect 9', *Antiquity* 60 (229) (1986), 96–107, 105; Stephanie Moser, 'The Aboriginalisation of Archaeology: The Contribution of the Australian Institute of Aboriginal Studies to the Indigenous Transformation of the Discipline', in Peter J Ucko (ed.), *Theory in Archaeology: A World Perspective* (London: Routledge, 1995), 150–77, 152.

57   As quoted in Peterson, 'The Changing Photographic Contract', 137.

58   Lambert, 'A History of the Australian Institute of Aboriginal Studies 1959–1989', 111–12.

59   Sharon Sullivan, 'The Custodianship of Aboriginal Sites in Southeastern Australia' in Isabel McBryde (ed.), *Who Owns the Past?: Papers from the Annual Symposium of the Australian Academy of the Humanities* (Melbourne: Oxford University Press, 1985), 139–56, 139.

60   Richard Gould to Ronald Berndt, 29 Sept 1971; Gouldthorp to Gould, 29 Aug 1971; Malcolm Griffiths, 'Report on Gould Case for AIAS', 1971, 9–18; Ronald Berndt to Bruce A McLarty, A/Commissioner of Native Welfare, 24 Feb 1971, in AIATSIS File 65/19(a).

61   Richard Gould to John Mulvaney, 19 Nov 1971, Mulvaney Papers, NLA, MS 9615/1/108, Box 14.

62   Richard A Gould to NGW Macintosh, 8 Mar 1972; John Mulvaney to Ian Crawford, 15 Aug 1972; Gould to Heuer, 14 Jul 1971; Richard A Gould to Frank Gare, 22 Feb 1972; Richard A Gould to John Mulvaney, 26 Jul 1971, in AIATSIS File 65/19(a).

63   McGrath, 'The "Gould Controversy"', 4. There is a growing movement to repatriate of images from this era. See: Jane Lydon, 'Introduction: The Photographic Encounter' in Jane Lydon (ed.), *Calling the Shots: Aboriginal Photographies* (Canberra: Aboriginal Studies Press, 2014) 1–18, 7–8.

64   McGrath, 'The "Gould Controversy"', 7; Kim Akerman, 'John Tregenza and Ushma Scales Burning Copies of Dick Gould's Records', 7 Mar 1979, Wingellina, Central Reserve, WA, AIATSIS Library, Photo 3615.

65   Richard Wright and Peter White to Richard Gould, 15 Jun 1972, Mulvaney Papers, NLA, MS 9615/1/108, Box 14.

66   Richard Gould to Richard Wright, 21 Jun 1972, Mulvaney Papers, NLA, MS 9615/1/108, Box 14.

67   Hill, *Broken Song*, 743.

68   Hill, *Broken Song*, 741–49.

69   Christoph Antons, 'Foster v Mountford: Cultural Confidentiality in a Changing Australia', in Sam Ricketson (ed.), *Landmarks in Australian Intellectual Property Law* (Melbourne: Cambridge University Press, 2009), 110–25, 118; Christopher Anderson, 'The Economics of Sacred Art: The Uses of a Secret Collection in the South Australian Museum', in Christopher Anderson, *Politics of the Secret*, Oceania Monograph 45 (Sydney: Oceania Publications, University of Sydney, 1995), 97–107, 99.

70   Michael Davis, 'Law, Anthropology, and the Recognition of Indigenous Cultural Systems', in R Kuppe and R Potz (eds), *Law and Anthropology: International Yearbook for Legal Anthropology*, Volume 11 (The Hague: Brill, 2001), 298–320, 311.

71   Davis, 'Law, Anthropology, and the Recognition of Indigenous Cultural Systems', 311.

72   Richard A Gould to NWG Macintosh, 8 Mar 1972, AIATSIS File 65/19(a).

73   Gould, *Yiwara*, 75.

74   Gould, as quoted in McGrath, 'The "Gould Controversy"', 7.

75   Peterson, 'The Changing Photographic Contract', 129.

76   Rhys Jones, 'Different Strokes for Different Folks: Sites, Scale and Strategy', in Ian Johnson (ed.), *Holier than Thou: Proceedings of the 1978 Kiola Conference on Australian Prehistory* (Canberra: Department of Prehistory, Research School of Pacific Studies, Australian National University, 1980), 151–71.

77   Gould to Gare, 7 Dec 1970, AIATSIS File 65/19(a).

78   Conlin, 'Gould', 3101.

79   Gould, 'Puntutjarpa Rockshelter and the Australian Desert Culture', 6.

80   Gould, 'Puntutjarpa Rockshelter and the Australian Desert Culture', 182.

81   Eugene Stockton's work at Kurringke, near Santa Teresa, in 1968 was the only other early excavation in the central deserts. Eugene Stockton, 'Investigations at Santa Teresa, Central Australia', *Archaeology and Physical Anthropology in Oceania* 6 (1971), 44–61.

82   Richard A Gould, 'Islands in the Interior: The Dynamics of Prehistoric
      Adaptations within the Arid Zone of Australia by Peter Marius Veth (Book
      Review)', *American Antiquity* 60 (3) (Jul 1995), 562–63.
83   Smith, *The Archaeology of Australia's Deserts*, 208.
84   Sue O'Connor, Peter Veth and Colin Campbell, 'Serpent's Glen Rockshelter:
      Report of the First Pleistocene-aged Occupation Sequence from the Western
      Desert', *Australian Archaeology* 46 (1998), 12–22.
85   Mike Smith, 'Desert Archaeology, Linguistic Stratigraphy and the Spread of the
      Western Desert Language', in Peter Veth, Mike Smith and Peter Hiscock (eds),
      Desert Peoples: Archaeological Perspectives (Oxford: Blackwell Publishers, 2005),
      222–242; Smith, *The Archaeology of Australia's Deserts*, 203–11.
86   Smith, *The Archaeology of Australia's Deserts*, 211.

FIVE   A Desiccated Garden of Eden: Jim Bowler at Lake Mungo

1   Kirsty Douglas, *Pictures of Time Beneath: Science, Heritage and the Uses of the Deep
      Past* (Collingwood, Vic: CSIRO Publishing, 2010), 128.
2   Keith Newman, 'An Artist's Journey into Australia's "Lost World": Western
      Inferno', *Sydney Morning Herald*, 16 Dec 1944, 5.
3   As in Martin Butler and Bentley Dean (dir.), *First Footprints* (2013), Sydney: Contact
      Films; Steve Webb, 'Further Research of the Willandra Lakes Fossil Footprint Site,
      Southeastern Australia', *Journal of Human Evolution* 52 (2007), 711–15.
4   Lou Klepac, *The Life and Work of Russell Drysdale* (Sydney: Bay Books, 1983), 81–82.
5   Keith Newman, 'Riddle of the Sands: Erosion Solution May Be Buried There:
      Urgent Need for Scientific Assault', *Sydney Morning Herald*, 19 Dec 1944, 5.
6   Newman, 'An Artist's Journey into Australia's "Lost World"'.
7   Jim Bowler interviewed by Billy Griffiths, 12–14 Oct 2015, National Library of
      Australia, sound recording and timed summary available for public use, ORAL
      TRC 6680/1.
8   Jim Bowler, 'Water and Sand: Climate in Ancient Australia', in John Mulvaney
      and Peter White (eds), *Australians to 1788* (Sydney: Fairfax, Syme & Weldon
      Associates, 1987) 24–45, 25.
9   Jim Bowler, 'Port Phillip Survey 1957–1963: Geology and Geomorphology',
      Memoirs of the National Museum of Victoria 27 (Nov 1966), 19–67, 20–21; Jim
      Bowler and Tatsuji Hamada, 'Late Quaternary Stratigraphy and Radiocarbon
      Chronology of Water Level Fluctuations in Lake Keilambete, Victoria', *Nature*
      232(5309) (1971), 330–32; RW Galloway, 'Evidence for Late Quaternary
      Climates', in John Mulvaney and Jack Golson (ed.), *Aboriginal Man and
      Environment in Australia* (Canberra: ANU Press, 1971), 14–25, 15.
10   Jenny Bowler, 'Mungo Memories', *Griffith Review* 19 (2008), 180–85.
11   Nicholas Jose, 'The Mungo Excursion', in Donata Carrazza and Paul Kane (eds),
      Vintage: Celebrating Ten Years of the Mildura Writers' Festival (Melbourne: Hardie
      Grant Books, 2004), 25–37, 30–33.
12   Jim Bowler, 'Aridity in Australia: Age, Origins and Expression in Aeolian
      Landforms and Sediments', *Earth-Science Reviews* 12 (1976), 279–310, 289–93;
      Douglas, *Pictures of Time Beneath*, 141.

13   Jim Bowler, 'Clay Dunes: Their Occurrence, Formation and Environmental Significance', *Earth-Science Reviews* 9 (1973), 315–38.

14   Jim Bowler, 'Recent Developments in Reconstructing Late Quaternary Environments in Australia', in RL Kirk and AG Thorne (eds), *The Origin of the Australians* (Canberra: Australian Institute of Aboriginal Studies, 1976), 55–77, 67.

15   Bowler interviewed by Griffiths, ORAL TRC 6680/3.

16   George Seddon, 'Thinking like a Geologist: The Culture of Geology', Mawson Lecture, *Australian Journal of Earth Sciences* 43 (1996), 487–95, 495.

17   Rhys Jones, 'Editorial', *Mankind* 6 (1968), 535–36, 535.

18   Bowler interviewed by Griffiths, ORAL TRC 6680/3.

19   Jim Bowler in JM Bowler, R Jones, H Allen and AG Thorne, 'Pleistocene Human Remains from Australia: A Living Site and Human Cremation from Lake Mungo, Western New South Wales', *World Archaeology* 2(1) (1970), 39–60, 43; Bowler interviewed by Griffiths, ORAL TRC 6680/3.

20   Jim Bowler, as quoted in Helen Lawrence (ed.), *Mungo over Millennia: The Willandra Landscape and its People* (Sorell, TAS: Maygog Publishing, 2006), 17; Claudio Tuniz, Richard Gillespie and Cheryl Jones, *The Bone Readers: Atoms, Genes and the Politics of Australia's Deep Past* (Crows Nest, NSW: Allen & Unwin, 2009), 29.

21   Rhys Jones and Harry Allen in Bowler et al., 'Pleistocene Human Remains from Australia', 47.

22   John Mulvaney, comment in Andrew Pike and Ann McGrath (dir.), *Message from Mungo* (2014), Canberra: Ronin Films.

23   Harry Allen, comment in Pike and McGrath, *Message from Mungo*.

24   Rhys Jones, 'Mungo Man, 2nd Trip', 23 Mar–14 Apr 1969, Field Journals, AIATSIS Library, MS 5040/1/28.

25   JM Bowler, AG Thorne, and HA Polach, 'Pleistocene Man in Australia: Age and Significance of the Mungo Skeleton', *Nature* 240(5375) (1972), 48–50.

26   Alan Thorne, comment in Pike and McGrath, *Message from Mungo*.

27   Alan Thorne, 'Kow Swamp and Lake Mungo: Towards an Osteology of Early Man in Australia', PhD thesis, University of Sydney, 1975; Peter Brown, 'Artificial Cranial Deformation: A Component in the Variation in Pleistocene Australian Aboriginal Crania', *Archaeology in Oceania* 16 (1981), 156–67, 165–66; Peter Brown, 'Nacurrie 1: Mark of Ancient Java, or a Caring Mother's Hands, in Terminal Pleistocene Australia?' *Journal of Human Evolution* 59(2) (Aug 2010), 168–87. For a succinct overview of the field, see: Colin Pardoe, 'Australian Biological Anthropology for Archaeologists', in Tim Murray (ed.), *Archaeology from Australia* (Melbourne: Australian Scholarly Publishing, 2004), 131–50, 132–36.

28   Dorothy Lawson, comment in Pike and McGrath, *Message from Mungo*.

29   Mary Pappin, 'Working Together', in Lawrence, *Mungo over Millennia*, 50–51.

30   Bowler interviewed by Griffiths, ORAL TRC 6680/3.

31   Tanya Charles, comment in Pike and McGrath, *Message from Mungo*.

32   Dorothy Lawson, comment in Jim Bowler (prod.), *Lake Mungo: Window to Australia's Past* (2002), CD–ROM, Melbourne: School of Earth Sciences, University of Melbourne.

33 Ronnie Mitchell, comment in Bowler, *Lake Mungo*.

34 Harry Allen, comment in Pike and McGrath, *Message from Mungo*; Harry Allen, 'Where the Crow Flies Backwards: Man and Land in the Darling Basin', PhD thesis, Australian National University, 1972, 133.

35 AW Howitt, 'Dieri and Other Kindred Tribes of Central Australia', *Journal of the Anthropological Institute of Great Britain and Ireland* 20 (1891), 30–104, 40; as quoted in Allen, 'Where the Crow Flies Backwards', 29.

36 Alice Kelly interviewed by Judy Atkinson, 1990, as quoted in Judy Atkinson, *Trauma Trails, Recreating Song Lines: The Transgenerational Effects of Trauma in Indigenous Australia* (Melbourne: Spinifex Press, 2002), 64.

37 Olga Gostin, *Accessing the Dreaming: Heritage, Conservation and Tourism at Mungo National Park* (Underdale, SA: University of South Australia, 1995), 34.

38 Betty Meehan and Rhys Jones (eds), *Archaeology with Ethnography: An Australian Perspective* (Canberra: Department of Prehistory, Research School of Pacific Studies, Australian National University, 1988), viii.

39 See, for example, J Peter White and James F O'Connell, *A Prehistory of Australia, New Guinea and Sahul* (Sydney: Academic Press, 1982), 39.

40 Allen, 'Where the Crow Flies Backwards', 20, 133.

41 Allen, 'Where the Crow Flies Backwards', 96.

42 Allen, 'Where the Crow Flies Backwards', 356.

43 Allen, 'Where the Crow Flies Backwards', 327, 350.

44 Harry Allen, 'Reinterpreting the 1969–1972 Willandra Lakes Archaeological Surveys', *Archaeology in Oceania* 33(3) (Oct 1998), 207–20, 207; Jane Balme, '30,000 Years of Fishery in Western New South Wales', *Archaeology in Oceania* 30 (1995), 1–21, 18–19; Allen enriches this discussion in his recent critique of the concepts of 'progress' and 'essentialism' as applied to history and culture. See Harry Allen, 'The Past in the Present? Archaeological Narratives and Aboriginal History', in Ann McGrath and Mary Anne Jebb (eds), *Long History, Deep Time: Deepening Histories of Place* (Canberra: ANU Press, 2015), 171–202.

45 Gavin Souter, 'Adam and Eve in Australia … Part One: The Young Woman at Lake Mungo', *Sydney Morning Herald*, 10 Aug 1974, 13.

46 Graham Williams, 'The Dawn of Man', *Australian*, 22 Mar 1975, 19.

47 Jacqueline Rees, 'Traces of Ancient Australians', *Canberra Times*, 10 Aug 1974, 9.

48 *Sydney Morning Herald*, 15 Jul 1974, 42–43.

49 Michael Westaway, 'Caring for the Willandra', in Lawrence, *Mungo over Millennia*, 45–49; Australian Heritage Commission, 'Nomination of The Willandra Lakes Region for inclusion in the World Heritage List', Oct 1980, Mulvaney Papers, NLA, MS 9615/15/4, Box 122.

50 Jim Bowler, as quoted in Douglas, *Pictures of Time Beneath*, 131.

51 Mulvaney to Barnes, 'Field Work', 20 Feb 1969 in John Mulvaney, 'Digging in the Archaeology Archives', *Australian Archaeology* 50 (2000), 1–6, 6.

52 John Mulvaney, 'Research Application to Australian Institute of Aboriginal Studies', 29 Jun 1972, Mulvaney Papers, NLA, MS 9615/8.10/1, Box 70.

53 DA Johnstone to John Mulvaney, 3 Aug 1973, Mulvaney Papers, NLA, MS 9615/8.10/5, Box 70.

54 Marcia Langton, comment in Pike and McGrath, *Message from Mungo*.

55   Harvey Johnston and Peter Clark, 'Willandra Lakes Archaeological Investigations 1968–98', *Archaeology in Oceania* 33(3) (Oct 1998), 105–19; Bowler interviewed by Griffiths, ORAL TRC 6680/3.

56   Jim Bowler, 'Mungo Man is a Physical Reminder of the Need for Indigenous Recognition', *Guardian*, 25 Feb 2014.

57   In 2000, Peter Brown questioned the sex of Mungo 3, arguing that the skeleton lacks the most diagnostic areas of the skull and pelvis. A reexamination of the remains published in 2009 reached the conclusion that Mungo 3 was male. Peter Brown, 'Australian Pleistocene Variation and the Sex of Lake Mungo 3', *Journal of Human Evolution* 38 (2000) 743–47; Arthur C Durband, Daniel RT Rayner and Michael Westaway, 'A New Test of the Sex of the Lake Mungo 3 Skeleton', *Archaeology in Oceania* 44(2) (Jul 2009), 77–83.

58   Jim Bowler and Alan Thorne, 'Human Remains from Lake Mungo: Discovery and Excavation of Lake Mungo III', in Kirk and Thorne, *The Origin of the Australians*, 127–38, 136. In 1999, a team of scientists led by Thorne used new techniques to date the remains of Mungo 3 to around 62,000 years old. Bowler and Magee were immediately sceptical of the dates and cast doubt upon their validity. In 2003 another team of researchers, led by Bowler, published a paper arguing that Mungo I and Mungo 3 were both buried around 40,000 years ago and that humans were present at Lake Mungo by 50,000–46,000 years ago. A Thorne et al., 'Australia's Oldest Human Remains: Age of the Lake Mungo 3 Skeleton', *Journal of Human Evolution* 36 (1999), 591–612, 605; JM Bowler and JW Magee, 'Redating Australia's Oldest Humans Remains: A Sceptic's View', *Journal of Human Evolution* 38 (2000), 719–26; JM Bowler et al., 'New Ages for Human Occupation and Climatic Change at Lake Mungo, Australia', *Nature* 421 (2003), 837–40.

59   Bowler, 'Mungo Man is a Physical Reminder of the Need for Indigenous Recognition'.

60   Steve Webb, 'The Pathology and Ecology of Ice Age Willandra People', in Lawrence, *Mungo over Millennia*, 41–44, 43.

61   Tanya Charles, interview by Ann McGrath, Oct 2011, as quoted in Malcolm Allbrook and Ann McGrath, 'Collaborative Histories of the Willandra Lakes: Deepening Histories and the Deep Past', in McGrath and Jebb, *Long History, Deep Time*, 241–52, 246.

62   Bowler interviewed by Griffiths, ORAL TRC 6680/5.

63   Jim Bowler, 'Willandra Lakes Revisited: Environmental Framework for Human Occupation', *Archaeology in Oceania* 33(3) (Oct 1998), 120–55, 120.

64   Jim Bowler, 'Mungo Man Needs Help – To Come Home', *Inside Story*, 9 Feb 2016.

65   Wilfred Shawcross, comment in Pike and McGrath, *Message from Mungo*.

66   By the time the Black collection arrived in Melbourne, silverfish had eaten the labels describing the context of the bones, rendering the collection useless to the Department of Anatomy. The bones were dispatched to the Institute of Anatomy in Canberra, where they remained until they were repatriated in the early 1990s. Jim Bowler conducted an interview with Black in his eighties in which he told this sorry tale. Jim Bowler, 'Reading the Australian Landscape: European and Aboriginal Perspectives', *Cappuccino Papers* 1 (1995), 9–14.

67   Alice Kelly's letter, as quoted in Isabel McBryde to John Mulvaney, undated [1973], Mulvaney Papers, NLA, MS 9615/8.10/4, Box 70.

68   McBryde to Mulvaney, undated, 'Mungo 1973–1974'.

69   Tanya Charles, comment in Pike and McGrath, *Message from Mungo*.

70   Jim Bowler, '"Tribal Loyalties": Reconnecting with the Land: A Tribute to Mrs Alice Kelly, 1919–2003', *Aboriginal History* 27 (2003), 247–48, 247.

71   Jean Charles, comment in Pike and McGrath, *Message from Mungo*.

72   Isabel McBryde, 'Alice (Ally) Ellen Kelly: 26 June 1919 – 30 June 2003', *Australian Aboriginal Studies* 2 (2003), 140–143, 141; Allbrook and McGrath, 'Collaborative Histories of the Willandra Lakes', 247–48.

73   Isabel McBryde, comment in Pike and McGrath, *Message from Mungo*.

74   Christopher Chippindale, 'Skeletons Rattle Down Under', *New Scientist* 1447 (14 Mar 1985), 10–11, 11.

75   Olga Gostin carefully navigates these overlapping legislative realms in her chapter on 'Managing the Dreaming' in *Accessing the Dreaming*, 32–50, 69.

76   'The Mungo Statement: Towards a Reconciliation; A record of discussion at the Willandra Research Publication Workshop, Thursday 22 June 1989', Mulvaney Papers, NLA, MS 9615/8.10/14, Box 71.

77   Mark McKenna, *This Country: A Reconciled Republic?* (Sydney: UNSW Press, 2004), 23–25.

78   Bates, as quoted in Rhys Jones and Vincent Megaw, 'Confessions of a Wild Colonial Boy: Rhys Jones in Conversation with Vincent Megaw', *Australian Archaeology* 50 (2000), 12–26, 23.

79   Lottie Williams, comment in Pike and McGrath, *Message from Mungo*.

80   Allbrook and McGrath, 'Collaborative Histories of the Willandra Lakes', 247.

81   Junette Mitchell in 2006, as quoted in Tuniz et al., *The Bone Readers*, 1, 3.

82   Mary Pappin in 2006, as quoted in Tuniz et al., *The Bone Readers*, 5–6.

83   Kelly, as quoted in Gostin, *Accessing the Dreaming*, 77.

84   Simon Schama, *Landscape and Memory* (New York: Vintage Books, 1996), 14–15.

85   Douglas, *Pictures of Time Beneath*, 148.

86   AP Elkin, *The Australian Aborigines* (Sydney: Angus & Robertson, 1974), 373, 384.

87   Bowler, 'Mungo Memories', 181.

88   Bowler, 'Mungo Man is a Physical Reminder of the Need for Indigenous Recognition'.

89   Bowler interviewed by Griffiths, ORAL TRC 6680/8.

90   Bowler, 'Mungo Man is a Physical Reminder of the Need for Indigenous Recognition'.

91   Bowler, 'Mungo Memories', 185.

92   Mary Pappin, speaking at the Willandra Seminar, 5 Nov 2015, Australian National University. The seminar was recorded and parts of it were televised on SBS and ABC.

93   Nicola Stern, Steve Webb and Jim Bowler, speaking at a publicly recorded event as part of the Willandra Seminar, 5 Nov 2015, Australian National University.

INTERLUDE II   Eaglehawk and Crow, 1974

1   Gough Whitlam, 'Foreword', in Mary White (ed.), *The Art of the Aboriginal Australian* (Canberra: Australian Department of Aboriginal Affairs, 1974), 1.

2   Gough Whitlam, Policy Speech, 13 Nov 1972, as quoted in *The Whitlam Government 1972–1975* (Ringwood, Vic: Viking, 1985), 466.

3   John Mulvaney, 'Conflict and the Rituals of Diplomacy: Les Hiatt and the AIAS', in Francesca Merlan, John Morton and Alan Rumsey (eds), *Scholar and Sceptic: Australian Aboriginal Studies in Honour of LR Hiatt* (Canberra: Aboriginal Studies Press, 1997), 29–38, 34–35.

4   Ucko, as quoted in Neal Ascherson, 'Peter Ucko (1938–2007)', *Australian Archaeology* 65 (Dec 2007), 73–74, 73.

5   Peter J Ucko, 'Review of AIAS activities, 1973', *AIAS Newsletter* I (1974), 5–15, 13. See also Stephanie Moser, 'The Aboriginalisation of Archaeology: The Contribution of the Australian Institute of Aboriginal Studies to the Indigenous Transformation of the Discipline', in Peter J Ucko (ed.), *Theory in Archaeology: A World Perspective* (London: Routledge, 1995), 150–77.

6   RJ Lampert, 'Retrospective', *Australian Archaeology* 39 (1994), v–vii, v.

7   Marjorie Sullivan, 'The Australian Association of Consulting Archaeologists', *Australian Archaeology* 10 (Jun 1980), 117–18.

8   RJ Lampert, 'Editorial', *Australian Archaeology* 2 (Apr 1975), 1–2, 1.

9   Ian M Crawford, 'The Role of the Australian Archaeological Association', *Australian Archaeology* 2 (Apr 1975), 3–4, 3.

10   John Mathew, *Eaglehawk and Crow: A Study of the Australian Aborigines Including an Inquiry into their Origin and a Survey of Australian Languages* (Melbourne: Melville, Mullen and Slade, 1899).

11   Terry Widders, Peter Thompson, Gary Williams, Lyn Thompson, Bob Bellear and Len Watson, 'Eaglehawk and Crow: Open Letter Concerning the Australian Institute of Aboriginal Studies', 29 Mar 1974, AIATSIS Library, File 73/119, 1, 4.

12   Jaqueline Ann Lambert, 'A History of the Australian Institute of Aboriginal Studies 1959 –1989: An Analysis of How Aboriginal and Torres Strait Islander People Achieved Control of a National Research Institute', PhD thesis, Australian National University, 2011, 135–37.

13   David R Moore, 'Archaeologists and Aborigines', *Australian Archaeology* 2 (Apr 1975), 8–9, 9.

14   John Mulvaney, 'What Future for Our Past', *Australian Archaeology* 13 (1981), 16–27, 21.

15   Jack Golson, 'Archaeology in a Changing Society', *Australian Archaeology* 2 (Apr 1975), 5–8, 8.

16   Ray Kelly, 'From the "Keeparra" to the "Cultural Bind": An Analysis of the Aboriginal Situation', *Australian Archaeology* 2 (Apr 1975), 13–17, 16.

17   Sandra Onus, 'Archaeologists and Aborigines', *Australian Archaeology* 3 (1975), 2.

18   Peter J Ucko, 'Australian Academic Archaeology: Aboriginal Transformations of its Aims and Practices', *Australian Archaeology* 16 (1983), 11–26, 15.

19   Stan Grant, *Talking to My Country* (Sydney: HarperCollins, 2016), 59.

20   Grant, *Talking to My Country*, 65–67.

21   Marcia Langton, 'A Fireside Chat', in Tim Bonyhady and Tom Griffiths (eds), *Prehistory to Politics: John Mulvaney, the Humanities and the Public Intellectual* (Melbourne: Melbourne University Press, 1996), 134–43, 142.

SIX   **Landscapes of the Mind: Carmel Schrire and Betty Meehan in Arnhem Land**

1   The title of this chapter draws from a strong tradition in Australian archaeology. Rhys Jones used the phrase as a title in his essay: 'Landscapes of the Mind: Aboriginal Perceptions of the Natural World', in John Mulvaney (ed.), *The Humanities and the Australian Environment* (Canberra: Australian Academy of the Humanities, 1991), 21–48; Isabel McBryde wrote of 'numinous landscapes of the mind, peopled by beings from an ever-present Dreaming whose actions were marked by the features of the created landscape … a landscape "mapped by stories".' Isabel McBryde, 'Travellers in Storied Landscapes', *Aboriginal History* 24 (2000), 152–74, 156. Bruno David and Harry Lourandos have also argued that 'History, like geography, is about tracing the landscapes of the mind', in: 'Landscape as Mind: Land Use, Cultural Space and Change in North Queensland Prehistory', *Quaternary International* 59 (1999), 107–23, 107.

2   Rhys Jones and Tia Negerevich, 'A Review of Previous Archaeological Work', in Rhys Jones (ed.), *Archaeological Research in Kakadu National Park* (Canberra: Australian National Parks and Wildlife Service, 1985), 1–16, 1, 15.

3   Ernestine Hill, 'Arnhem Land: Deals, Death and Defiance', *Northern Standard*, 21 Jul 1933, 5.

4   Rhys Jones and Betty Meehan, 'The Arnhem Salient', in Desmond Ball (ed.), *Aborigines in the Defence of Australia* (Canberra: Australian National University Press, 1991), 100–62, 100.

5   John Mulvaney, 'Bêche-de-mer, Aborigines and Australian History', *Proceedings of the Royal Society of Victoria* 79(2) (Sept 1966), 449–57, 449.

6   Campbell Macknight, *The Voyage to Marege': Macassan Trepangers in Northern Australia* (Melbourne: Melbourne University Press, 1976), 97–99.

7   Macknight found 'anomalous' older dates in his early excavations, which he discounted in favour of the written record. Darrell Lewis, *The Rock Paintings of Arnhem Land, Australia: Social, Ecological and Material Culture Change in the Post-Glacial Period* (Oxford: British Archaeological Reports International Series 415, 1988), 102–04; Anne Fiona Clarke, 'Winds of Change: An Archaeology of Contact in the Groote Eylandt Archipelago, Northern Australia', PhD thesis, Australian National University, 1994, 470.

8   Henry Reynolds, *North of Capricorn: The Untold Story of Australia's North* (Sydney: Allen & Unwin, 2003), 13–14.

9   Bernard Smith, *European Vision and the South Pacific, 1768–1850: A Study in the History of Art and Idea* (Oxford: Clarendon Press, 1960).

10   Howard Morphy, *Aboriginal Art* (London: Phaidon Press, 1998), 14.

11   Jim Allen, 'Archaeology and the History of Port Essington', PhD thesis, Australian National University, 1969. There were earlier failed settlements at nearby Fort Dundas (1824–29) and Raffles Bay (1827–29), see: Mark McKenna,

From the Edge: Australia's Lost Histories (Melbourne: The Miegunyah Press, 2016), 65; Peter G Spillett, *Forsaken Settlement: An Illustrated History of the Settlement of Victoria, Port Essington, North Australia 1838–1849* (Melbourne: Lansdowne Press, 1972).

12   John Woinarski and Freya Dawson, 'Limitless Lands and Limited Knowledge: Coping with Uncertainty and Ignorance in Northern Australia', in JW Handmer, TW Norton and SR Dovers (eds), *Ecology, Uncertainty and Policy: Managing Ecosystems for Sustainability* (New York: Prentice-Hall, 2002), 83–115, 89–95.

13   Rhys Jones, 'Ordering the Landscape', in I Donaldson and T Donaldson (eds), *Seeing the First Australians* (Sydney: Allen & Unwin, 1985), 181–209, 185.

14   Paul Keating, 'Redfern Speech (Year for the World's Indigenous People)', Delivered in Redfern Park, 10 Dec 1992.

15   Carmel Schrire, 'Exploring the Legacy of the 1948 Arnhem Land Expedition (Book Review)', *Archaeology in Oceania* 47(2) (Jul 2012), 108–11, 108.

16   Carmel Schrire, *Digging Through Darkness: Chronicles of an Archaeologist* (Charlottesville: University Press of Virginia, 1995), 44–45.

17   Bain Attwood, *Possession: Batman's Treaty and the Matter of History* (Melbourne: Melbourne University Press, 2009), 262–63.

18   Prime Minister Gough Whitlam returned part of the land of the Gurindji people in the Northern Territory (albeit in the form of a lease rather than a title of ownership) in a ceremony at Daguragu in August 1975. Charlie Ward, *A Handful of Sand: The Gurindji Struggle, After the Walk-off* (Melbourne: Monash University Publishing, 2016), esp. 27–44, 175–94.

19   See Bain Attwood and Andrew Markus, *The 1967 Referendum: Race, Power and the Australian Constitution* (Canberra: Aboriginal Studies Press, 2007).

20   Carmel Schrire, *The Alligator Rivers: Pre-history and Ecology in Western Arnhem Land* (Canberra: Department of Prehistory, Research School of Pacific Studies, Australian National University, 1982), 30.

21   Sally K May, *Collecting Cultures: Myth, Politics, and Collaboration in the 1948 Arnhem Land Expedition* (Lanham, Maryland: AltaMira Press, 2010), 2. See also Martin Thomas, 'A Short History of the Arnhem Land Expedition', *Aboriginal History* 34 (2010), 143–70.

22   Charles P Mountford, *Records of the American-Australian Scientific Expedition to Arnhem Land, Volume 1: Art, Myth and Symbolism* (Melbourne: Melbourne University Press, 1956), xxviii–xxix.

23   Frederick D McCarthy and Frank M Setzler, 'The Archaeology of Arnhem Land', in Charles P Mountford (ed.), *Records of the American-Australian Scientific Expedition to Arnhem Land, Volume 2: Anthropology and Nutrition* (Melbourne: Melbourne University Press, 1960), 215–96, 215.

24   May, *Collecting Cultures*, 85–86.

25   Les Eyzies, in the heart of the Vezere Valley, is the centre of archaeological research in the Dordogne in France. Carmel Schrire, 'Interactions of Past and Present in Arnhem Land, North Australia', in Carmel Schrire (ed.), *Past and Present in Hunter Gatherer Studies* (Orlando: Academic Press, 1984), 67–93, 79.

26   Schrire, 'Exploring the Legacy of the 1948 Arnhem Land Expedition', 109.

27   Anne Clarke and Ursula Frederick, 'Making a Sea Change: Rock Art, Archaeology
      and the Enduring Legacy of Frederick McCarthy's Research on Groote Eylandt',
      in Martin Thomas and Margo Neale (eds), *Exploring the Legacy of the 1948 Arnhem
      Land Expedition* (Canberra: ANU E Press, 2011), 135–55.

28   Jack Golson, 'Australia', *COWA Surveys and Bibliographies* III (1964), 1–11, 5.

29   Carmel White, 'Plateau and Plain: Prehistoric Investigations in Arnhem
      Land, Northern Territory', PhD thesis, Australian National University, 1967,
      471–75.

30   Martin Thomas, '"Because It's Your Country": Bringing Back the Bones to
      West Arnhem Land', *Australian Book Review* 350 (Apr 2013), 26–37, 30; May,
      Collecting Cultures, 184–88.

31   Schrire, *Digging Through Darkness*, 45.

32   Schrire, *Digging Through Darkness*, 148.

33   Schrire, *Digging Through Darkness*, x.

34   Dening, as quoted in Schrire, *Digging Through Darkness*, 10.

35   Schrire, *The Alligator Rivers*, 30.

36   Schrire, 'Exploring the Legacy of the 1948 Arnhem Land Expedition', 108.

37   Schrire, *Digging Through Darkness*, 202–04.

38   John Mulvaney, 'Arnhem Land Prehistory', *Australian Archaeology* 16 (Jun 1983),
      160–62, 160; Carmel Schrire to John Mulvaney, 14 Jul 1983, Mulvaney Papers,
      NLA, MS 9615/1/206, Box 25.

39   Carmel White, 'The Prehistory of the Kakadu People', *Mankind* 6 (1967),
      426–31, 426.

40   White, 'Plateau and Plain', 377–78.

41   White, 'Plateau and Plain', dedication, vii.

42   This is a different site to Malakunanja II (Madjedbebe). Schrire, *The Alligator
      Rivers*, 31.

43   Schrire, *Digging Through Darkness*, 205.

44   Schrire, *Digging Through Darkness*, 1, 51.

45   Schrire, *Digging Through Darkness*, 20–25.

46   Schrire, *Digging Through Darkness*, 25–26.

47   Schrire, *Digging Through Darkness*, 33–41.

48   Schrire, *Digging Through Darkness*, 40.

49   Schrire, *Digging Through Darkness*, 43.

50   Claire Smith and Emer O'Donnell, 'Gender and the Disciplinary Culture of
      Australian Archaeology', in Sarah Nelson (ed.), *Handbook of Gender in Archaeology*
      (Berkeley, USA: AltaMira Press, 2006), 691–732.

51   Isabel McBryde, 'In Her Right Place ...'? Women in Archaeology, Past and
      Present', in Hilary du Cros and Laurajane Smith (eds), *Women in Archaeology: A
      Feminist Critique* (Canberra: Department of Prehistory, Research School of Pacific
      Studies, Australian National University, 1993), xi–xv, xi.

52   Sandra Bowdler and Genevieve Clune, 'That Shadowy Band: The Role of Women
      in the Development of Australian Archaeology', *Australian Archaeology* 50 (Jun
      2000), 27–35, 32.

53   Val Attenbrow and Betty Meehan, 'Editorial', *Australian Archaeology* 32 (1991), 1.

54   Schrire, *The Alligator Rivers*, 31.

55   Grahame Clark, *World Prehistory: An Outline* (Cambridge: Cambridge University Press, 1961), 253.

56   Peter Hiscock, Sue O'Connor, Jane Balme and Tim Maloney, 'World's Earliest Ground-Edge Axe Production Coincides with Human Colonisation of Australia', *Australian Archaeology* 82(1) (2016), 2–11; Chris Clarkson et al., 'Human Occupation of Northern Australia by 65,000 Years Ago', *Nature* 547 (20 Jul 2017), 306–10.

57   White, 'Plateau and Plain', 1; White, 'The Prehistory of the Kakadu People', 431.

58   Carmel White and Nicolas Peterson, 'Ethnographic Interpretations of the Prehistory of Western Arnhem Land', *Southwestern Journal of Anthropology* 25(1) (1969), 45–67, 61–63.

59   Richard A Gould, *Living Archaeology* (Cambridge: Cambridge University Press, 1980), 34–35; J Peter White and James F O'Connell, *A Prehistory of Australia, New Guinea and Sahul* (Sydney: Academic Press, 1982), 42.

60   Schrire, 'Interactions of Past and Present in Arnhem Land', 88.

61   Robert Ross, 'Historical Archaeology in South Africa (Book Review)', *South African Archaeological Bulletin* 71(203) (2016), 104.

62   Schrire, 'Interactions of Past and Present in Arnhem Land', 68.

63   Carmel White, 'Report on Field Trip to Caledon Bay, Northern Territory Dec./ Jan. 1968–69', 1969, AIATSIS Library, PMS 2004, Doc. 69/816, 2.

64   Betty Meehan, 'Irreverent Recollections of the Making of an Anthropologist', in Francesca Merlan, John Morton and Alan Rumsey (eds), *Scholar and Sceptic: Australian Aboriginal Studies in Honour of LR Hiatt* (Canberra: Aboriginal Studies Press, 1997), 11–28, 11–13, 15–17.

65   Syd Kyle-Little, a patrol officer of the Native Affairs Branch in Darwin, chose the site of Maningrida as a 'trading post' on 9 June 1949, but it was abandoned a few months later after a devastating outbreak of disease. The government settlement was created in 1957. See Billy Griffiths, 'Caring for Country: The Place Where the Dreaming Changed Shape', *Griffith Review* 56 (2017), 232–45, 236–37.

66   Betty Meehan, *Shell Bed to Shell Midden* (Canberra: Australian Institute of Aboriginal Studies, 1982), 19.

67   Ingrid Drysdale, *The End of Dreaming* (Adelaide: Rigby, 1974), 194.

68   Helen Bond-Sharp, *Maningrida: A History of the Aboriginal Township in Arnhem Land* (Howard Springs: Helen Bond-Sharp, 2013), 67.

69   Betty Meehan and Rhys Jones, 'The Outstation Movement and Hints of a White Backlash', in Rhys Jones (ed.), *Northern Australia: Options and Implications* (Canberra: Research School of Pacific Studies, 1980), 131–57, 135.

70   Meehan, *Shell Bed to Shell Midden*, 20.

71   John Hunter to Betty Hiatt, 7 Aug 1970, National Archives of Australia, E460, 1974/380, Doc. 70/1029; Betty Hiatt, 'Application for Research Grant, Australian Institute of Aboriginal Studies', National Archives of Australia, E460, 1974/380, Doc. 69/828; Betty Hiatt, 'Report on Reconnaissance, August – September 1970', National Archives of Australia, E460, 1974/380, Doc. 70/1029.

72   Betty Meehan, 'Anbara Project', 1970–74, National Archives of Australia, E460, 1974/380, 3.

73 Frederick D McCarthy and Margaret McArthur, 'The Food Quest and the Time Factor in Aboriginal Economic Life', in Mountford, *Records of the American-Australian Scientific Expedition to Arnhem Land, Volume 2*, 145–94.

74 Meehan, *Shell Bed to Shell Midden*, 47.

75 Meehan, *Shell Bed to Shell Midden*, 7.

76 This approach was also pursued by Sandra Bowdler in the 1970s at Balls Head and Bass Point, see: Sandra Bowdler, 'Balls Head: The Excavation of a Port Jackson Rockshelter', *Records of the Australian Museum* 28 (1971), 117–28, 126; Sandra Bowdler, 'Hook, Line, and Dilly Bag: An Interpretation of an Australian Coastal Shell Midden', *Mankind* 10 (1976), 248–58.

77 Meehan, *Shell Bed to Shell Midden*, 160, 167–68.

78 Meehan, *Shell Bed to Shell Midden*, 171–72.

79 Meehan, 'Anbara Project', 6.

80 Meehan, *Shell Bed to Shell Midden*, 46–47, 162.

81 Betty Meehan, Rhys Jones and Annie Vincent, 'Gulu-kula: Dogs in Anbarra Society, Arnhem Land', *Aboriginal History* 23 (1999), 83–106, 91.

82 Meehan, *Shell Bed to Shell Midden*, 46.

83 Betty Meehan, 'Bandeiyama: She Keeps Going', in Isobel White, Diane Barwick and Betty Meehan (eds), *Fighters and Singers: The Lives of Some Australian Aboriginal Women* (Sydney: Allen & Unwin, 1985), 200–13, 205.

84 Betty Meehan, 'The Dinnertime Camp', in Betty Meehan and Rhys Jones (eds), *Archaeology with Ethnography* (Canberra; Deptartment of Prehistory, Research School of Pacific Studies, Australian National University, 1988), 171–81, 179–80; Jane Balme, 'Prehistoric Fishing in the Lower Darling, Western New South Wales', in C Grigson and J Clutton-Brock (eds), *Animals and Archaeology: Vol. 2: Shell Middens, Fishes and Birds* (Oxford: BAR International Series 183, 1983), 19–32, 23; Josephine Flood, *Archaeology of the Dreamtime: The Story of Prehistoric Australia and its People* (Sydney: Angus & Robertson, 1983), 50; Roger A Luebbers, 'Meals and Menus: A Study of Change in Prehistoric Coastal Settlements in South Australia, PhD thesis, Australian National University, 1978, 302; Jim Stockton, 'The Prehistoric Geography of Northwest Tasmania', PhD thesis, Australian National University, 1982, 202.

85 Rhys Jones, 'The Tasmanian Paradox', in RVS Wright (ed.), *Stone Tools as Cultural Markers: Change, Evolution and Complexity* (Canberra: Australian Institute of Aboriginal Studies, 1977), 189–204, 201.

86 Jones, 'Ordering the Landscape', 203.

87 Bond-Sharp, *Maningrida*, 148.

88 Hiatt, 'Report on Reconnaissance, August–September 1970'.

89 Bond-Sharp, *Maningrida*, 152–53.

90 Schrire, *Digging Through Darkness*, 206.

91 David Lawrence, *Kakadu: The Making of a National Park* (Melbourne: Melbourne University Press, 2000), 52–64.

92 Allen to Mulvaney, 28 Oct 1972 (from Arnhem Land), Mulvaney Papers, NLA, MS 9615/1/5, Box 1.

93 Allen to Mulvaney, 15 Nov 1972 (Oenpelli), Mulvaney Papers, NLA, MS 9615/1/5, Box 1.

94 John Mulvaney to Harry Allen, 27 Jun 1973, Mulvaney Papers, NLA, MS 9615/1/5, Box 1.

95 Johan Kamminga and Harry Allen, *Alligator Rivers Environmental Fact-Finding Study: Report of the Archaeological Survey* (unpublished report, Canberra, Aug 1973), 108.

96 Lawrence, *Kakadu*, 103.

97 Lawrence, *Kakadu*, 103, 78.

98 Justin O'Brien, 'Canberra Yellowcake: The Politics of Uranium and How Aboriginal Land Rights Failed the Mirrar People', *Journal of Northern Territory History* 14 (2003), 79–92, 79.

99 See Marcia Langton, *The Quiet Revolution: Indigenous People and the Resources Boom*, Boyer Lectures 2012 (Sydney: Harper Collins, 2013), 31–58.

100 Mike Smith interviewed by Tom Griffiths, 8 Jun 2012, National Library of Australia, sound recording, ORAL TRC 6429/3.

101 Schrire, *Digging Through Darkness*, 46. This work culiminated with her recent book: Carmel Schrire (ed.), *Historical Archaeology in South Africa: Material Culture of the Dutch East India Company at the Cape* (Walnut Creek: Left Coast Press, 2014).

102 Jones, 'Ordering the Landscape', 205–07.

103 Betty Meehan and Rhys Jones, 'From Anadjerramiya to Canberra', in Stephen A Wild (ed.), *Rom, an Aboriginal Ritual of Diplomacy* (Canberra: Australian Institute of Aboriginal Studies, 1986), 15–31, 25.

104 Les Hiatt, 'Rom in Arnhem Land', in Wild, *Rom, an Aboriginal Ritual of Diplomacy*, 3–13, 10–11.

105 Meehan and Jones, 'From Anadjerramiya to Canberra', 25–26.

106 Margaret Clunies Ross, 'Rom in Canberra', in Wild, *Rom, an Aboriginal Ritual of Diplomacy*, 33–53.

107 Stephen Wild, 'Introduction', in Wild, *Rom, an Aboriginal Ritual of Diplomacy*, xi–xiii, xii–xiii.

108 Andy Greenslade, 'A Report on the Rom Ceremony Performances January 5th to 7th 1995', AIATSIS Library, PMS 5643, 8, 15.

109 Galarrwuy Yunupingu, 'Rom Watangu: The Law of the Land', *Monthly*, Jul 2016, 18–29, 28–29.

SEVEN Marking Country: Lesley Maynard and the 'Bob Edwards style'

1 Abbé H Breuil (trans. Mary E Boyle), *Four Hundred Centuries of Cave Art* (Montignac, Dordogne: Centre d'Etudes et Documentation Prehistoriques, 1952), 107.

2 Georges Bataille (trans. Austryn Wainhouse), *Lascaux, or The Birth of Art* (Switzerland: Skira, 1955), 11.

3 The factual basis of this story has been questioned by Paul Bahn, in 'A Lot of Bull? Pablo Picasso and Ice Age Cave Art', *Munibe (Antropologia-Arkeologia)* 57 (2005), 217–23.

4 See Eduardo Palacio-Perez, 'Cave Art and the Theory of Art: The Origins of the Religious Interpretation of Palaeolithic Graphics Expression', *Oxford Journal of Archaeology* 29(1) (Feb 2010), 1–14; Salomon Reinach, *The Story of Art Throughout the Ages: An Illustrated Record* (London: William Heinemann, 1904), 2–3.

5   Peter J Ucko and Andrée Rosenfeld, *Palaeolithic Cave Art* (London: Weidnenfeld and Nicolson, 1967), 7; André Leroi-Gourhan (trans. Norbert Guterman), *The Art of Prehistoric Man in Western Europe* (London: Thames & Hudson, 1967), 34.

6   Susan Lowish, 'Setting the Scene: Early Writing on Australian Aboriginal Art', *Journal of Art Historiography* 4 (Jun 2011), 1–12, 4–5.

7   Ernest Giles, *Australia Twice Traversed*, vol. 1 (London: S Low, Marston, Searle & Rivington, Limited, 1889), 101.

8   George Grey, *Journals of Two Expeditions of Discovery in North-West and Western Australia During the Years 1837, 38 and 39* (London: T and W Boone, 1841), 263.

9   Grahame L Walsh, *Bradshaws: Ancient Rock Paintings of North-West Australia* (Carouge-Geneva, Switzerland: published for the Bradshaw Foundation by Edition Limitée, 1994), 56–66.

10 Lesley Maynard, 'Restoration of Aboriginal Rock Art: The Moral Problem', *Australian Archaeology* 3 (Oct 1975), 54–60, 58.

11 June Ross, 'Australian Rock Art', in Claire Smith (ed.), *Encyclopedia of Global Archaeology* (New York: Springer, 2014), 686–97, 688.

12 Jo McDonald and Peter Veth, 'Information Exchange Amongst Hunter-Gatherers of the Western Desert of Australia', in Robert Whallon, William A Lovis and Robert K Hitchcock (eds), *Information and Its Role in Hunter-Gatherer Bands: Ideas, Debates, and Perspectives* (Los Angeles: Cotsen Institute of Archaeology Press), 221–33.

13 Ken Mulvaney, *Murujuga Marni: Rock Art of the Macropod Hunters and Mollusc Harvesters* (Perth: UWAP Scholarly, 2015).

14 Darrell Lewis, 'Megafauna Identification for Dummies: Arnhem Land and Kimberley "Megafauna" Paintings', *Rock Art Research* 34(1) (2017), 82–99; Robert G Bednarik, 'Megafauna Depictions in Australian Rock Art', *Rock Art Research* 30(2) (2013), 197–215.

15 Sue O'Connor and Barry Fankhauser, 'Art at 40,000BP? One Step Closer: An Ochre Covered Rock from Carpenters Gap Shelter 1, Kimberley Region, Western Australia', in Atholl Anderson, Ian Lilley and Sue O'Connor (eds), *Histories of Old Ages: Essays in Honour of Rhys Jones* (Canberra: Pandanus Books, 2001), 287–301.

16 Michael J Morwood, *Visions from the Past: The Archaeology of Australian Aboriginal Art* (Crows Nest, NSW: Allen & Unwin, 2002), 37.

17 Robert Layton, *Australian Rock Art: A New Synthesis* (Cambridge: Cambridge University Press, 1992), 33–47; Mike Smith, *The Archaeology of Australia's Deserts* (Cambridge: Cambridge University Press, 2013), 221.

18 Howard Morphy, *Aboriginal Art* (London: Phaidon Press, 1998), 5.

19 Charles P Mountford, *Nomads of the Australian Desert* (Adelaide: Rigby, 1976), 543; Kimber, as quoted in Smith, *The Archaeology of Australia's Deserts*, 220; June Ross, 'Rock Art, Ritual and Relationships: An Archaeological Analysis of Rock Art from the Central Australian Arid Zone', PhD thesis, University of New England, 2003, 150.

20 Michael J Morwood and Claire Smith, 'Rock Art Research in Australia 1974–94', *Australian Archaeology* 39 (Dec 1994), 19–38, 23.

21 John Mulvaney, *The Prehistory of Australia* (New York: Praeger, 1969), 174.

22 John Clegg, 'From the Study of Aboriginal Art to the Archaeology of Prehistoric Pictures', *Australian Archaeology* 16 (Jun 1983), 87–91, 87.

23   Wandjuk Marika, 'Introduction', in Robert Edwards (ed.), *Aboriginal Art in Australia* (Sydney: Ure Smith, 1978), 6–9, 6.

24   Galarrwuy Yunupingu, 'The Black/White Conflict', in Wally Caruana (ed.), *Windows on the Dreaming* (Canberra: Australian National Gallery, 1989), 13–17, 13–14.

25   RVS Wright, 'Preface', in RVS Wright (ed.), *Archaeology of the Gallus Site, Koonalda Cave* (Canberra: Australian Institute of Aboriginal Studies, 1971), iii.

26   Alexander Gallus, 'Results of the Exploration of Koonalda Cave, 1956–1968', in Wright, *Archaeology of the Gallus Site, Koonalda Cave*, 87–133, 87.

27   John Mulvaney, 'Dr Gallus and Australian Archaeology', *The Artefact* 21 (1998), 4–8.

28   Alexander Gallus, 'A Summary of the Results of Excavations at Keilor', *The Artefact* 33 (1974), 1–9, 1, 5.

29   C Forbes, 'Keilor: The Key to Australia's Past?' *Age*, 29 Jul 1978.

30   Wright, 'Preface', iii.

31   RVS Wright, 'The Cave', in Wright, *Archaeology of the Gallus Site, Koonalda Cave*, 22–29, 24–26.

32   Lesley Maynard and Robert Edwards, 'Wall Markings', in Wright, *Archaeology of the Gallus Site, Koonalda Cave*, 59–80, 70.

33   Maynard and Edwards, 'Wall Markings', 76.

34   Josephine Flood, *Rock Art of the Dreamtime: Images of Ancient Australia* (Sydney: Angus & Robertson, 1997), 27; Maynard and Edwards, 'Wall Markings', 76.

35   Daisy Bates (1938), as quoted in RVS Wright, 'An Ethnographic Background to Koonalda Cave Prehistory', in Wright, *Archaeology of the Gallus Site, Koonalda Cave*, 1–16, 13.

36   Gallus, 'Results of the Exploration of Koonalda Cave', 128.

37   Maynard and Edwards, 'Wall Markings', 79.

38   Edwards, *Flint Miners of the Nullarbor*; Robert Edwards (dir.), *Aboriginal Canoe Trees of the Murray* (1968), Adelaide: South Australian Museum in cooperation with AIAS; Robert Edwards (dir.), *Aboriginal Arnhem Land* (1969), Adelaide: South Australian Museum in cooperation with AIAS. Robert Edwards (dir.), *Prehistoric Rock Art of the Cleland Hills* (1968), Adelaide: South Australian Museum in cooperation with AIAS.

39   Dick Richards, 'Bob Edwards: From Orchardist to Ethnographer', Transcript, National Musuem of Australia, 'Bob Edwards: A Tribute', 22 Mar 2011.

40   TD Campbell to Dermot Casey, 27 Sept 1963, Dermot Casey Papers, AIATSIS Library, MS 1326/A/h/1-3, Box 1.

41   Robert Edwards to Dermot Casey, 10 May 1965, Casey Papers, AIATSIS Library, MS 1326/B/b/i, Box 2.

42   Robert Edwards to WP Crowcroft, Director of the South Australian Museum, 'Application for Curator of Anthropology', 12 Nov 1964, courtesy of Bob Edwards; in possession of the author.

43   They were originally thought to have been made with the indirect percussion of a stone hammer and chisel, but experimental archaeology suggests otherwise. Flood, *Rock Art of the Dreamtime*, 103.

44   Norman B Tindale, Herbert M Hale and Charles P Mountford, 'A Unique Example of Aboriginal Rock Carving at Panaramitee North', *Transactions of the Royal Society of South Australia* 53 (1929), 245–48; Herbert Basedow, 'Aboriginal

Rock Carvings of Great Antiquity in South Australia', *Journal of the Royal Anthropological Institute of Great Britain and Ireland* 44 (1914), 195–211.

45   Robert Edwards, 'Comparative Study of Rock Engravings in South and Central Australia', *Transactions of the Royal Society of South Australia* 90 (1966), 33–38, 36.

46   Charles P Mountford and Robert Edwards, 'Rock Engravings of Panaramitee Station, North-Eastern South Australia', *Transactions of the Royal Society of South Australia* 86 (1963), 131–46, 132.

47   Robert Edwards, 'Art and Aboriginal Prehistory', in John Mulvaney and Jack Golson (eds), *Aboriginal Man and Environment in Australia* (Canberra: ANU Press, 1971), 356–67, 362–63.

48   Robert Edwards, 'Preliminary Fieldwork Report on Recording of Cave Paintings and Rock Engraving Sites, Northern Territory', Sept 1966, AIATSIS Library, PMS 540, Doc. 66/456.

49   Robert Edwards, 'Application for Research Grant: The Australian Institute of Aboriginal Studies', 1970, courtesy of Bob Edwards; in possession of the author.

50   Lesley Maynard, 'Comment on Frederick D. McCarthy's "Rock Art Sequences: A Matter of Clarification"', *Rock Art Research* 5(1) (May 1988), 30–31, 30.

51   Leslie Maynard, 'The Archaeology of Australian Aboriginal Art', in SM Mead (ed.), *Exploring the Visual Art of Oceania* (Honolulu: University Press of Hawaii, 1979), 83–110, 92.

52   Leroi-Gourhan, *The Art of Prehistoric Man in Western Europe*, 35.

53   Patricia Vinnicombe, *People of the Eland: Rock Paintings of the Drakensberg Bushmen as a Reflection of Their Life and Thought* (Pietermaritzburg: University of Natal Press, 1976), 151.

54   Lesley McMah, 'A Quantitative Analysis of the Aboriginal Rock Carvings in the District of Sydney and the Hawkesbury River', BA honours thesis, University of Sydney, 1965.

55   Maynard, 'The Archaeology of Australian Aboriginal Art', 84–87.

56   Lesley Maynard, 'Day by Dreary Day: A Few Jottings from the Aboriginal Relics Diary', *Napawi* 2 (1973), 6–8.

57   Clegg, 'From the Study of Aboriginal Art to the Archaeology of Prehistoric Pictures', 88.

58   Lesley Maynard, 'Classification and Terminology in Australian Rock Art', in Peter J Ucko (ed.), *Form in Indigenous Art: Schematisation in the Art of Aboriginal Australia and Prehistoric Europe* (Canberra: Australian Institute of Aboriginal Studies, 1977), 387–402, 393.

59   Maynard, 'The Archaeology of Australian Aboriginal Art', 91. There had been earlier attempts to synthesise rock art into a pan-Australia sequence. See, for example, Daniel Sutherland Davidson, *A Preliminary Consideration of Aboriginal Australian Decorative Art* (Philadelphia: University of Pennsylvania Press, 1937); Frederick D McCarthy, *Australian Aboriginal Rock Art* (Sydney: Trustees of the Australian Museum, 1958); Charles P Mountford, *Aboriginal Art* (Longmans, 1961); Andreas Lommel, 'The Rock Art of Australia', in Hans-Georg Bandi et al., *The Art of the Stone Age: Forty Thousand Years of Rock Art* (London: Methuen, 1961), 205–37.

60   Flood, *Rock Art of the Dreamtime*, 194.

61   Josephine McDonald, 'Australia: "Rock Art Capital of the World"', in Tim Murray (ed.), *Archaeology from Australia* (Melbourne: Australian Scholarly Publishing, 2004), 96–115, 106.

62   Flood, *Rock Art of the Dreamtime*, xi.

63   Layton, *Australian Rock Art*, 131–34.

64   Eric Brandl, 'Some Notes on Faunal Identification and Arnhem Land Rock Paintings', *Australian Institute of Aboriginal Studies Newsletter*, New Series 14 (1980), 6–13, 13; Eric Brandl, *Australian Aboriginal Paintings in Western and Central Arnhem Land* (Canberra: Australian Institute of Aboriginal Studies, 1973); Darrell Lewis, *The Rock Paintings of Arnhem Land, Australia: Social, Ecological and Material Culture Change in the Post-Glacial Period* (Oxford: BAR International Series 415, 1988); George Chaloupka, *Journey in Time: The World's Longest Continuing Art Tradition: The 50,000 Year Story of the Australian Aboriginal Rock Art of Arnhem Land* (Chatswood, NSW: Reed, 1993). See also Maria Brandl, 'Biographical Note', in Eric J Brandl Papers, 1958–1974, AIATSIS Library, MS 1348; Nicolas Rothwell, 'L Marks the Spot', *Australian*, 17 Aug 2013; Nicolas Rothwell, 'Rock Art Pioneer in Exile', *Australian*, 20 Oct 2011.

65   Victoria Laurie, 'Rock Art Researcher Grahame Walsh Got It Wrong', *Australian*, 25 Sept 2017. See also Nicolas Rothwell, 'Lone Wolf Discovered Art for Ages', *Australian*, 24 Aug 2007.

66   Percy Trezise, *Last Days of a Wilderness* (Sydney: Collins, 1973), 193; Andrée Rosenfeld, 'Excavations at the Early Man Shelter', in Andrée Rosenfeld, David Horton and John Winter, *Early Man in North Queensland: Art and Archaeology in the Laura Area*, Terra Australis 6 (Canberra: Australian National University, 1981), 5–34, 5.

67   Andrée Rosenfeld, 'Rock Engravings in the Laura District', in Rosenfeld, Horton and Winter, *Early Man in North Queensland*, 50–89, 89.

68   Morwood, *Visions from the Past*, 212.

69   Morwood, *Visions from the Past*, 306.

70   Michael J Morwood, 'Art and Stone: Towards a Prehistory of Central-Western Queensland', PhD thesis, Australian National University, 1979, 410.

71   Andrée Rosenfeld, 'Panaramitee: Dead or Alive?', in P Bahn and A Rosenfeld (eds), *Rock Art and Prehistory: Papers Presented to Symposium G of the AURA Congress, Darwin 1988* (Oxford: Oxbow, 1991), 136–44; Rosenfeld, 'Rock Engravings in the Laura District', 89.

72   Maynard, 'Comment on Frederick D. McCarthy's "Rock Art Sequences"', 30.

73   Antti Lahelma, 'Politics, Ethnography and Prehistory: In Search of an "Informed" Approach to Finnish and Karelian Rock Art', in David Morris, Benjamin Smith and Knut Arne Helskog (eds), *Working with Rock Art: Recording, Presenting and Understanding Rock Art Using Indigenous Knowledge* (Johannesburg: Wits University Press, 2012), 113–34, 117.

74   Bruno David, *Landscapes, Rock-Art and the Dreaming: An Archaeology of Preunderstanding* (London: Leicester University Press, 2002), 1.

75   Natalie R Franklin, *Explorations of Variability in Australian Prehistoric Rock Engravings* (Oxford: BAR International Series, 2004), 41; Morwood, *Visions from the Past*, 40, 57–58.

76   Ross, 'Rock Art, Ritual and Relationships', 197; Smith, *The Archaeology of Australia's Deserts*, 228–29, 240.

77   Robert Edwards, 'Survey of Cave Paintings in Arnhem Land and Central Australia', Australian Institute of Aboriginal Studies, General Meeting, 19 May 1966, AIATSIS Library, PMS 539.

78   Robert Edwards, 'Clues in Quartzite', *Australian*, 15 Apr 1970.

79   Robert Edwards, 'Deterioration and Preservation of Rock Art', in Edwards, *Aboriginal Art in Australia*, 54–57, 57.

80   Dick Roughsey, 'The Aboriginal Arts Board', in Edwards, *Aboriginal Art in Australia*, 58–65, 62.

81   RG Kimber, 'Recollections of Papunya Tula 1971–1980', in Hetti Perkins and Hannah Fink (eds), *Papunya Tula: Genesis and Genius* (Sydney: Art Gallery of New South Wales in association with Papunya Tula Artists, 2000), 205–15, 205–6.

82   Ian McLean, 'How Aborigines Invented the Idea of Contemporary Art', in Ian McLean (ed.), *How Aborigines Invented the Idea of Contemporary Art* (Sydney: Institute of Modern Art and Power Publications, 2011), 333–40, 340; Ian McLean, *Rattling Spears: A History of Indigenous Australian Art* (London: Reaktion Books, 2016), 135–38.

83   Marika, 'Introduction', 7.

84   Marika, 'Introduction', 9.

EIGHT   'You Have Entered Aboriginal Land': The Franklin River campaign and the fight for Kutikina

1   Rhys Jones, 'Hunters and History: A Case Study from Western Tasmania', in Carmel Schrire (ed.), *Past and Present in Hunter Gatherer Studies* (Orlando, Florida; Academic Press, 1984), 27–65, 50.

2   Jones, 'Hunters and History', 50.

3   Truchanas was also following the footsteps of earlier wilderness photographers in Tasmania such as John Watt Beattie. Jarrod Hore, '"Beautiful Tasmania": Environmental Consciousness in John Watt Beattie's Romantic Wilderness', *History Australia* 12(1) (2017), 48–66.

4   Natasha Cica, *Pedder Dreaming: Olegas Truchanas and a Lost Tasmanian Wilderness* (St Lucia, Qld: University of Queensland Press, 2011), 15–20.

5   Max Angus, *The World of Olegas Truchanas* (Hobart: Olegas Truchanas Publishing Committee, 1975), 37–38.

6   Kevin Kiernan, 'Discovering the Franklin', in Roger Green (ed.), *Battle for the Franklin: Conversations with the Combatants in the Struggle for South West Tasmania* (Sydney: Fontana/Australian Conservation Foundation, 1984), 82–99, 95.

7   Peter Dombrovskis, 'Discovering the Franklin', in Green, *Battle for the Franklin*, 100–4, 101

8   Richard Flanagan, 'It's Peter Dom', in *And What Do You Do, Mr Gable?* (Sydney: Random House, 2011), 23–31, 31.

9   In 1972, the United Tasmania Group became the first green party in the world. Libby Robin, 'Biological Diversity as a Political Force in Australia', in Marco Armiero and Lise Sedrez (eds), *A History of Environmentalism: Local Struggles, Global Histories* (London: Bloomsbury, 2014), 39–56, 41.

10 James McQueen, *The Franklin: Not Just a River* (Ringwood, Vic: Penguin, 1983), 2.

11 Drew Hutton and Libby Connors, *A History of the Australian Environment Movement* (Cambridge: Cambridge University Press, 1999), 161.

12 Brown, as quoted in Peter Thompson, *Bob Brown of the Franklin River* (Sydney: Allen & Unwin, 1984), 94.

13 Verge Blunden, 'What the High Court Justices Had to Say', *Sydney Morning Herald*, 2 Jul 1983, 7, 19.

14 Tom Griffiths, 'History and Natural History: Conservation Movements in Conflict?', *Australian Historical Studies* 24(96) (1991), 16–32.

15 Frank Bongiorno, *The Eighties: The Decade that Transformed Australia* (Melbourne: Black Inc., 2015), 87.

16 Tim Bonyhady, 'The Stuff of Heritage', in Tim Bonyhady and Tom Griffiths (eds), *Prehistory to Politics: John Mulvaney, the Humanities and the Public Intellectual* (Melbourne: Melbourne University Press, 1996), 144–62, 144.

17 Robert Menzies' initial choice for the new currency – 'the royal' – was almost unanimously criticised for its antiquated imperial origins. The 'Australian dollar' eventually won out over suggestions such as the tasman, the regal, the austral, the koala, the matilda, the austbrit, as well as some more tongue-in-cheek names: the dinkum, the sheepsback and the bobmenz. There were also a range of stylised Aboriginal words canvassed in a public naming competition, such as the mayee, the woogoo, the nulla and the aborroo. James Curran and Stuart Ward, *The Unknown Nation: Australia After Empire* (Melbourne: Melbourne University Press, 2010), 91–96, 131.

18 AJ Marshall, 'The World of Hopkins Sibthorpe', in AJ Marshall (ed.), *The Great Extermination: A Guide to Anglo-Australian Cupidity, Wickedness and Waste* (London: Heinemann, 1966), 1–8, 8.

19 Frederick D McCarthy, 'Aboriginal Relics and Their Preservation', *Mankind* 2(5) (1938), 120–26, 120. Hilary du Cros highlights Elsie Brammel's role in this campaign at the Australian Museum in: *Much More Than Stones and Bones: Australian Archaeology in the Late Twentieth Century* (Melbourne: Melbourne University Press, 2002), 25.

20 Denis Byrne, 'Deep Nation: Australia's Acquisition of an Indigenous Past', *Aboriginal History* 20 (1998), 82–107, 98.

21 Sarah Colley, *Uncovering Australia: Archaeology, Indigenous People and the Public* (Crows Nest, NSW: Allen & Unwin, 2002), 27.

22 George Orwell, *Nineteen Eighty-Four* (New York: Buccaneer Books, 1949), 251.

23 Isabel McBryde, 'Introduction', in Isabel McBryde (ed.), *Who Owns the Past?: Papers from the Annual Symposium of the Australian Academy of the Humanities* (Melbourne: Oxford University Press, 1985), 1–10, 1.

24 Laurajane Smith, *The Uses of Heritage* (London: Routledge, 2006), 298.

25 Sharon Sullivan, 'The Custodianship of Aboriginal Sites in Southeastern Australia', in McBryde, *Who Owns the Past?*, 139–56, 150.

26 Sharon Sullivan, 'The State, People and Archaeologists', *Australian Archaeology* 2 (Apr 1975), 23–31, 30.

27 Tasmanian Aboriginal Centre, 'Submission to the Senate Select Committee on South West Tasmania, 8 February 1982', *Pugganna News* 12 (Mar 1982), [no page numbers].

28   Kiernan, 'Discovering the Franklin', 93.

29   Kevin Kiernan, 'Days in a Wilderness', *Southern Caver* 12(4) (May 1981),
     72–78, 77.

30   Tim Bonyhady, '"So Much for a Name"' in Tim Bonyhady and Tom Griffiths
     (eds), *Words for Country: Landscape & Language in Australia* (Sydney: University of
     New South Wales Press, 2001), 140–61.

31   Hydro-Electric Commission, Tasmania, *Report on the Gordon River Power
     Development Stage Two* (Hobart: The Commission, 1979), 80.

32   Rhys Jones, 'Submission to the Senate Select Committee on South West
     Tasmania', Commonwealth Hansard, 19 Mar 1982, 1715–64, as reprinted in
     Australian Archaeology 14 (1982) 96–106, 97.

33   John Mulvaney, 'Submission to the Senate Select Committee on Southwest
     Tasmania, 7 December 1981', in *Prehistory and Heritage: The Writings of John
     Mulvaney* (Canberra: Department of Prehistory, Research School of Pacific
     Studies, Australian National University, 1990), 319–24, 319.

34   J Hall, 'Annual General Meeting of the Australian Archaeological Association:
     The Minutes in Brief', *Australian Archaeology* 10 (Jun 1980), 112–14, 113.

35   Sandra Bowdler, 'Communication Breakthrough', *Australian Archaeology* 12
     (Jun 1981), 16.

36   Rhys Jones, 'Gordon River, Tasmania, January 1981', Field Journals, AIATSIS
     Library, MS 5040/1/47, 8 Jan 1981.

37   Jones, 'Gordon River, Tasmania, January 1981', 11 Jan 1981.

38   Greg Middleton, 'S.S.S. Franklin River Expedition 1977: South-West Tasmania:
     8th–21st January 1977', *Journal of the Sydney Speleological Society* 23(3) (1979),
     51–91, 75.

39   Kiernan, 'Days in a Wilderness', 75.

40   Kiernan, 'Days in a Wilderness', 75.

41   Bob Brown (with Peter Dombrovskis), *Wild Rivers* (Hobart: P Dombrovskis,
     1983), 6.

42   Don Ranson, as quoted in Bonyhady, '"So Much for a Name"', 147.

43   Kiernan, 'Days in a Wilderness', 76; SJ Paterson, 'Comments on Archaeological
     Investigations in the Andrew River Valley, Acheron River Valley and at Precipitous
     Bluff', *Australian Archaeology* 21 (Dec 1985), 148–50.

44   Rhys Jones and Kenneth Russell Henderson, 'The Extreme Climatic Place? An
     Interview with Rhys Jones', *Hemisphere* 26(1) (Jul/Aug 1981), 54–59, 56.

45   Rhys Jones, 'Trip to Franklin River', Field Journals, AIATSIS Library, MS
     5040/1/50, 9 Mar 1981.

46   Stephen Harris, 'A Narrative of an Archaeological Expedition to the Franklin
     River', *Southern Caver* 12(4) (May 1981), 79–84, 81.

47   Jones and Henderson, 'The Extreme Climatic Place?', 55.

48   Jones, 'Submission to the Senate Select Committee on South West Tasmania', 101.

49   Jones, 'Trip to Franklin River', 12 Mar 1981.

50   Kevin Kiernan, 'An Alternative Chronology for the Cave Deposits', 13 Mar 1981,
     in Jones, 'Trip to Franklin River'.

51   MK Macphail, 'Vegetation and Climates in Southern Tasmania Since the Last
     Glaciation', *Quaternary Research* 11 (1979), 306–41.

52   Rhys Jones, 'From Kakadu to Kutikina: The Southern Continent at 18,000 Years Ago', in Olga Soffer and Clive Gamble (eds), *The World at 18,000 BP* (London: Unwin Hyman, 1990), 264–95, 278–9.

53   Rhys Jones, 'Voyage 6 Anare, Jan–Feb, 1987', Rhys Jones Papers, NLA, Acc 04/142, Box 2.

54   Rhys Jones as quoted in McQueen, *The Franklin*, 41.

55   Jones, 'From Kakadu to Kutikina', 290–91.

56   Jones and Henderson, 'The Extreme Climatic Place?', 59.

57   Jones, 'Submission to the Senate Select Committee on South West Tasmania', 100–1.

58   Jones and Henderson, 'The Extreme Climatic Place?', 59.

59   McQueen, *The Franklin*, 43.

60   Kiernan, 'Days in a Wilderness', 76–77.

61   Greg Buckman, *Tasmania's Wilderness Battles: A History* (Crows Nest, NSW: Allen & Unwin/Jacana Books, 2008), 14–29, 45.

62   Patrick Weller, 'The Anatomy of a Grievous Miscalculation: 3 February, 1983', in Howard R Penniman (ed.), *Australia at the Polls: The National Elections of 1980 and 1983* (Sydney: Allen & Unwin, 1983), 248–80, 264.

63   Hutton and Connors, *A History of the Australian Environment Movement*, 161–62.

64   Weller, 'The Anatomy of a Grievous Miscalculation', 264–70; Hutton and Connors, *A History of the Australian Environment Movement*, 161–62.

65   Gray, as quoted in Thompson, *Bob Brown of the Franklin River*, 160.

66   Don Chipp, 'Select Committee on South West Tasmania', *Senate Hansard*, 19 Aug 1981, 44.

67   Tasmanian Aboriginal Centre, 'Submission to the Senate Select Committee'.

68   Rhys Jones, Don Ranson, Jim Allen and Kevin Kiernan, 'The Australian National University: Tasmanian National Parks and Wildlife Service Archaeological Expedition to the Franklin River, 1982: A Summary of Results', *Australian Archaeology* 16 (1983), 57–70, 69.

69   John Mulvaney, *Digging Up a Past* (Sydney: UNSW Press, 2011), 234–35.

70   John Mulvaney, 'The World Stage', in Green, *Battle for the Franklin*, 218–27, 218.

71   Mulvaney felt that the archaeological community had been slow to support his interventions. RJ Lampert, telegram to Malcolm Fraser, Bill Hayden and Don Chipp, in Rhys Jones Papers, NLA, MS ACC 05/191, Item 41, Box 4.

72   SJ Paterson, R Underwood, RK Tarvydas, DR Wilson and FJ Baynes, 'Geological Report No. 644-94-23', in Hydro-Electric Commission, Tasmania, *Report on the Gordon River Power Development Stage Two, Cave Survey* (Hobart: The Commission, 1983), 12; SJ Paterson, 'Franklin Valley Not So Special?', *Nature* 305 (29 Sept 1983), 354; John Mulvaney, 'Franklin Valley Defended', *Nature* 306 (15 Dec 1983), 636; Rhys Jones, 'Franklin Valley Sites', *Nature* 306 (22/29 Dec 1983), 726; SJ Paterson, 'The Lesson of Franklin Valley', *Nature* 309 (10 May 1984), 108; Paterson, 'Comments on Archaeological Investigations'.

73   SJ Paterson, 'Quaternarists in Confrontation: The Franklin Controversy – A Rebuttal', *Quaternary Australasia* 2 (1–2) (May 1984), 1–7, 2–3.

74   Mulvaney, 'Franklin Valley Defended', 636.

75   Mulvaney, 'The World Stage', 225.

76   Senate Select Committee on South West Tasmania, *Future Demand and Supply*

of Electricity for Tasmania and Other Matters (Canberra: Australian Government Publishing Service, Nov 1982), 204.

77 Susan Ryan, Second Reading of the 'World Heritage Properties Protection Bill 1982', *Hansard*, 25 Nov 1982, 2857–61, 2858.

78 Malcolm Fraser and Margaret Simons, *Malcolm Fraser: The Political Memoirs* (Melbourne: Melbourne University Press, 2015), 555–57, 580.

79 Fraser and Simons, *Malcolm Fraser*, 556.

80 Fraser to Gray, 19 Jan 1983, as quoted in Fraser and Simons, *Malcolm Fraser*, 581.

81 Thompson, *Bob Brown of the Franklin River*, 162–66.

82 Rhys Jones, 'Expedition to the Lower Franklin and Gordon Rivers, Feb–Mar 1983', Field Journals, AIATSIS Library, MS 5040/1/66, 18 Feb 1983.

83 Jones, 'Expedition to the Lower Franklin and Gordon Rivers', 24 Feb 1983.

84 McQueen, *The Franklin*, 43.

85 Thompson, *Bob Brown of the Franklin River*, 168–71.

86 Anne Summers, *Gamble for Power: How Bob Hawke Beat Malcolm Fraser: The 1983 Federal Election* (Melbourne: T Nelson Australia, 1983), 12.

87 Phillip Toyne and Simon Balderstone, 'The Environment', in Susan Ryan and Troy Bramston (eds), *The Hawke Government: A Critical Retrospective* (Melbourne: Pluto Press, 2003), 170–83.

88 Geoff Law, *The River Runs Free: Exploring and Defending Tasmania's Wilderness* (Camberwell, Vic: Penguin, 2008), 189.

89 Thompson, *Bob Brown of the Franklin River*, 177.

90 Anthony, as quoted in Thompson, *Bob Brown of the Franklin River*, 178.

91 Lyndall Ryan, *Tasmanian Aborigines: A History Since 1803* (Sydney: Allen & Unwin, 2012), 319.

92 Blunden, 'What the High Court Justices Had to Say', 7, 19.

93 Robyn Williams, 'Down the Franklin by Lawn Mower', *Australian Archaeology* 20 (1985), 151.

94 JE Downie, 'Vehicles Churn Up Evidence of Prehistoric Tasmanians', *Australian Archaeology* 16 (1983), 84–86.

95 Mulvaney, *Digging Up a Past*, 238.

96 Brown, *Wild Rivers*, 7.

97 Richard Flanagan, *A Terrible Beauty: History of the Gordon River Country* (Melbourne: Greenhouse, 1985), 3.

98 Bonyhady, '"So Much for a Name"', 152.

99 Rosalind F Langford, 'Our Heritage – Your Playground', *Australian Archaeology* 16 (Jun 1983), 1–6, 2, 5, 6.

100 Jim Allen, 'Aborigines and Archaeologists in Tasmania, 1983', *Australian Archaeology* 16 (Jun 1983), 7–10, 7.

101 Emphasis in the original. Langford, 'Our Heritage – Your Playground', 4.

102 Allen, 'Aborigines and Archaeologists in Tasmania, 1983', 9.

103 Michael Mansell, 'That Cave is Ours', *Pugganna News* 15 (Sept 1983).

104 McQueen, *The Franklin*, 43.

105 Mansell as quoted in Ryan, *Tasmanian Aborigines*, 319.

106 Jones, 'Expedition to the Lower Franklin and Gordon Rivers', 19 Feb 1983.

107 Jones, 'Expedition to the Lower Franklin and Gordon Rivers', 18 Mar 1983.

108 John Mulvaney to RJ Hawke, 24 Mar 1983, Rhys Jones Papers, NLA, MS ACC 05/191, Item 41, Box 4.

109 John Mulvaney, 'Past Regained, Future Lost: The Kow Swamp Pleistocene Burials', *Antiquity* 65(246) (Mar 1991), 12–21.

110 Colin Pardoe, 'Sharing the Past: Aboriginal Influence on Archaeological Practice, a Case Study from New South Wales', *Aboriginal History* 14 (1990), 208–23, 222.

111 Pardoe, 'Sharing the Past', 220.

112 Mulvaney, 'Past Regained, Future Lost', 12, 17, 18, 21.

113 Betty Meehan, 'Aboriginal Skeletal Remains', *Australian Archaeology* 19 (1984), 122–47, 127.

114 Australian Archaeological Association, 'Code of Ethics', *Australian Archaeology* 39 (1994), 129.

115 Jim Allen, 'The Politics of the Past', *Australian Archaeology* 49 (1999), 34–43, 41.

116 Rhys Jones, '*Sylwadau Cynfrodor Ar Gôr Y Cewri*; or a British Aboriginal's Land Claim to Stonehenge', in Christopher Chippendale et al. (eds), *Who Owns Stonehenge?* (London: B.T. Batsford Ltd, 1990), 62–87, 62, 87.

117 Jones, '*Sylwadau Cynfrodor Ar Gôr Y Cewri*', 87.

118 Jim Allen and Richard Cosgrove, 'Background History of the Southern Forests Archaeological Project', in Jim Allen (ed.), *Report of the Southern Forests Archaeological Project, Volume 1, Site Descriptions, Stratigraphies and Chronologies* (Melbourne: La Trobe University, 1996), 3–19, 9.

119 Tim Murray and Jim Allen, 'The Forced Repatriation of Cultural Properties to Tasmania', *Antiquity* 69 (1995), 871–74.

120 Jim Allen, 'A Short History of the Tasmanian Affair', *Australian Archaeology* 41 (Dec 1995), 42–48, 48.

121 Gaskell spoke these words to a public meeting of the Victorian branch of the Royal Australian Planning Institute in November 1982. John Mulvaney and Rhys Jones quote the passage at length in an unaddressed letter dated 4 January 1983 in Rhys Jones Papers, NLA, MS ACC 05/191, Item 41, Box 4. Josephine Flood provides the context for Gaskell's words in: Josephine Flood, 'Letter to the Editor: Philistines in Tasmania', *Canberra Times*, 19 Nov 1982, 2.

122 Rhys Jones, 'Landscapes of the Mind: Aboriginal Perceptions of the Natural World', in John Mulvaney (ed.), *The Humanities and the Australian Environment* (Canberra: Australian Academy of the Humanities, 1991), 21–48, 43.

INTERLUDE III Australians to 1988

1 This sentence closely paraphrases Bain Attwood's words in 'The Founding of *Aboriginal History* and the Forming of Aboriginal History', *Aboriginal History* 36 (2012), 119–71, 119.

2 Frank Bongiorno, *The Eighties: The Decade that Transformed Australia* (Melbourne: Black Inc., 2015), 241.

3 PH Pigott, *Museums in Australia 1975: Report of the Committee of Inquiry on Museums and National Collections Including the Report of the Planning Committee on the Gallery of Aboriginal Australia* (Canberra: Australian Government Publishing Service, 1975), 71.

4   Attwood, 'The Founding of *Aboriginal History*', 119.

5   Barwick, as quoted in Attwood, 'The Founding of *Aboriginal History*', 139.

6   WEH Stanner, 'The History of Indifference Thus Begins', *Aboriginal History* 1 (1977), 3–26; Henry Reynolds, '"Before the Instant of Contact": Some Evidence from Nineteenth-Century Queensland', *Aboriginal History* 2 (1978) 63–69. See also Henry Reynolds, 'The Other Side of the Frontier: Early Aboriginal Reactions to Pastoral Settlement in Queensland and Northern New South Wales', *Historical Studies* 17(66) (1976), 50–63.

7   Isabel McBryde, 'Perspectives of the Past: An Introduction', in Valerie Chapman and Peter Read (eds), *Terrible Hard Biscuits: A Reader in Aboriginal History* (St Leonards: Journal of Aboriginal History and Allen & Unwin, 1996), 1–15, 3.

8   John Mulvaney and J Peter White, 'Aboriginal Australians and the Bicentennial History: A Progress Report', *Australian Archaeology* 11 (Dec 1980), 53–64, 59.

9   John Mulvaney and J Peter White, 'Introduction', *Australians to 1788* (Sydney: Fairfax, Syme & Weldon Associates, 1987), xv–xvi, xvi. See also Marcia Langton, 'Preparing Black History: Report on Working Party of Aboriginal Historians for Bicentennial History', *Identity* 4(5) (1981), 7–8.

10   Geoffrey Blainey to John Mulvaney, 29 May 1972, John Mulvaney Papers, National Library of Australia, MS 9615/1/34, Box 5.

11   Geoffrey Blainey, *The Triumph of the Nomads: A History of Ancient Australia* (South Melbourne: Macmillan, 1975); Geoffrey Blainey, *The Story of Australia's People: The Rise and Fall of Ancient Australia* (Melbourne: Penguin Books, 2015), xi.

12   Blainey, *Triumph of the Nomads*, 10–14.

13   Blainey, *Triumph of the Nomads*, 83.

14   See Mark McKenna, 'Different Perspectives on Black Armband History', *Research Paper* 5 (Canberra: Department of the Parliamentary Library, 1997).

15   Geoffrey Blainey, 'Time for Australia to Shed its Guilt Complex', *Sunday Telegraph*, 31 Jan 1988, reprinted in Bob Layton and Elizabeth Williams, 'Salute from the Poms? One View of Aborigines and the Bicentenary', *Australian Archaeology* 28 (1989), 111–14, 114.

16   Tim Murray and J Peter White, 'Cambridge in the Bush? Archaeology in Australia and New Guinea', *World Archaeology* 13(2) (1981), 255–63, 258.

17   Josephine Flood, *The Moth Hunters: Aboriginal Prehistory of the Australian Alps* (Canberra: Australian Institute of Aboriginal Studies, 1980); Josephine Flood, 'No Ethnography, No Moth Hunters', in Betty Meehan and Rhys Jones (eds), *Archaeology with Ethnography* (Canberra; Department of Prehistory, Research School of Pacific Studies, Australian National University, 1988), 270–76.

18   Josephine Flood, *Archaeology of the Dreamtime: The Story of Prehistoric Australia and Its People* (Sydney: Collins, 1983), 12.

19   Flood, *Archaeology of the Dreamtime*, revised in 1989, 1992, 1995, 1999, 2004, 2010; Josephine Flood, *The Riches of Ancient Australia: A Journey into Prehistory* (St Lucia, Qld: University of Queensland Press, 1990), revised in 1993, 1999; Josephine Flood, *Rock Art of the Dreamtime: Images of Ancient Australia* (Sydney: Angus and Robertson, 1997); Josephine Flood, *The Original Australians: Story of the Aboriginal People* (Sydney: Allen & Unwin, 2006).

20   Flood, *Archaeology of the Dreamtime*, 16.

21   Rhys Jones, 'Dating the Human Colonization of Australia: Radiocarbon and Luminescence Revolutions', *Proceedings of the British Academy* 99 (1999), 37–65, 57.

22   Mark McKenna, *From the Edge: Australia's Lost Histories* (Melbourne: Melbourne University Publishing, 2016), xviii.

NINE   A Social History of the Holocene: Sylvia Hallam, Harry Lourandos and the Archaeology of Documents

1   Joseph Banks, *The Endeavour Journal of Joseph Banks, 25 Aug 1768 – 12 Jul 1771*, 2, arranged by BP Sandford (Sydney: State Library of New South Wales, 1998), 243; John White, *Journal of a Voyage to New South Wales* (London: J Debrett, 1790), 163.

2   Arthur Phillip to Lord Sydney, 15 May 1788, *Historical Records of Australia* 1(1) (Sydney: William Applegate Guillick, Government Printer, 1914).

3   William Cox, *Journal*, 7 Jul 1814 – 6 Jan 1815, SLNSW, Manuscript, C 708/1-2, filed at Safe 1/264-265, 15 Sept 1814.

4   The author developed these resources for Extent Heritage between 2013 and 2017 under the titles 'Mapping Sydney's Aboriginal Past' and 'Mapping Melbourne's Aboriginal Past'.

5   John Hunter, *An Historical Journal of the Transactions at Port Jackson and Norfolk Island* (London: Printed for John Stockdale, 1793), 469, 545.

6   David Collins, *An Account of the English Colony in New South Wales* (London: T Cadell Jun and W Davies, 1798), 563.

7   Collins, *An Account of the English Colony in New South Wales*, 35.

8   Grace Karskens, *The Colony: A History of Early Sydney* (Crows Nest, NSW: Allen & Unwin, 2009), 351; Paul Irish, *Hidden in Plain View: The Aboriginal People of Coastal Sydney* (Sydney: New South Publishing, 2017).

9   For some answers to these big questions, see: Val Attenbrow, *Sydney's Aboriginal Past: Investigating the Archaeological and Historical Records* (Sydney: University of New South Wales Press, 2010); James Kohen, *The Darug and their Neighbours: The Traditional Aboriginal Owners of the Sydney Region* (Blacktown, NSW: Darug Link in association with Blacktown and District Historical Society, 1993); Karskens, *The Colony*.

10   Norman B Tindale, 'Ecology of Primitive Aboriginal Man in Australia', in A Keast, RL Crocker and CS Christian (eds), *Biogeography and Ecology in Australia* (Den Haag, Netherlands: W Junk, 1959), 36–51. For early ecological studies on Aboriginal burning see, for example, CA Gardner, 'The Fire Factor in Relation to the Vegetation of Western Australia', *Western Australian Naturalist* 5 (1957), 166–73; JL Davies, 'A Vegetation Map of Tasmania', *Geography Review* 54 (1964), 249–53; and WD Jackson, 'Vegetation', in JL Davies (ed.), *Atlas of Tasmania* (Hobart: Lands and Surveys Department, 1965), 30–35.

11   Rhys Jones, 'The Geographical Background to the Arrival of Man in Australia', *Archaeology and Physical Anthropology in Oceania* 3 (1968), 186–215; Duncan Merrilees, 'Man the Destroyer: Late Quaternary Changes in the Australian Marsupial Fauna', *Journal of the Royal Society of Western Australia* 51 (1968), 1–24; Rhys Jones, 'Fire-stick Farming', *Australian Natural History* 16 (1969), 224–28.

12   Stephen J Pyne, *Burning Bush: A Fire History of Australia* (New York: Holt, 1991);
      Bill Gammage, *The Biggest Estate on Earth: How Aborigines Made Australia* (Crows
      Nest, NSW: Allen & Unwin, 2011).

13   Sylvia Hallam, *Fire and Hearth: A Study of Aboriginal Usage and European
      Usurpation in South-Western Australia* (Canberra: Australian Institute of Aboriginal
      Studies, 1975), vii.

14   Sylvia J Hallam, 'Review of A Matter of Time', *The Agricultural History Review*
      9(2) (1961), 120–22, 120.

15   Caroline Bird, 'Preface', in Caroline Bird and R Esmée Webb (eds), *Fire and
      Hearth Forty Years On: Essays in Honour of Sylvia J. Hallam* (Perth: Western
      Australian Museum, 2011), x–xi, x.

16   The note was written by Ian Murray, who drew the cave to Gould's attention on
      13 February 1970. Sylvia J Hallam, 'Excavations in the Orchestra Shell Cave,
      Wanneroo, Western Australia: Part II. Archaeology (Continued)', *Archaeology and
      Physical Anthropology in Oceania* 9(2) (Jul 1974), 134–55, 134.

17   Sylvia J Hallam, 'An Archaeological Survey of the Perth Area, Western Australia: A
      Progress Report on Art and Artefacts, Dates and Demography', *Australian Institute
      of Aboriginal Studies Newsletter* 3(5) (1972), 11–19.

18   Jill Milroy and Grant Revell, 'Aboriginal Story Systems: Remapping the West,
      Knowing Country, Sharing Space', *Occasion: Interdisciplinary Studies in the
      Humanities* 5 (2013), 1–24, 2.

19   Hallam, *Fire and Hearth*, 13.

20   George Grey, *Journals of Two Expeditions of Discovery in North-West and Western
      Australia, During the Years 1837, 1838 and 1839, Volume II* (London: T and W
      Boone, 1841), 20.

21   Sylvia Hallam, 'Yams, Alluvium and "Villages" on the West Coastal Plain', in GK
      Ward (ed.), *Archaeology at ANZAAS 1984* (Canberra: Canberra Archaeological
      Society: 1986), 116–32, 116.

22   Hallam, *Fire and Hearth*, 42.

23   Grey, *Journals of Two Expeditions of Discovery*, 292, 270.

24   Gammage, *The Biggest Estate on Earth*, 125, xix.

25   Hallam, *Fire and Hearth*, 84.

26   Hallam, *Fire and Hearth*, 46.

27   Sylvia J Hallam, 'Review of The Biggest Estate on Earth', *Australian Aboriginal
      Studies* (2011/2), 123–26, 126.

28   Hallam, 'Topographic Archaeology and Artifactual Evidence', 175.

29   Hiscock, 'Creators or Destroyers?: The Burning Questions of Human
      Impact in Ancient Aboriginal Australia', *Humanities Australia* 5 (2014),
      40–52.

30   Hallam, *Fire and Hearth*, 105.

31   Harry Lourandos, Bruno David, Bryce Barker and Ian J McNiven, 'An Interview
      with Harry Lourandos', in Bruno David, Bryce Barker and Ian J McNiven (eds),
      The Social Archaeology of Australian Indigenous Societies (Canberra: Aboriginal
      Studies Press, 2006), 20–39, 20–21.

32   Harry Lourandos, 'Dispersal of Activities: The East Tasmanian Sites', *Papers and
      Proceedings of the Royal Society of Tasmania* 102 (1968), 41–46.

33   As a student, Lourandos was particularly drawn to the cultural theory of Lewis
     Binford, but later found more comfortable grounding in the neo-Marxist and
     post-processualist schools of thought that were gaining momentum in the United
     Kingdom, which privileged social and political explanations for change over
     environmental or economic determinants. Sandra Bowdler, 'Harry Lourandos'
     Life and Work: an Australian Archaeological Odyssey', in David, Barker and
     McNiven, *The Social Archaeology of Australian Indigenous Societies*, 40–49, 41.

34   Bowdler, 'Harry Lourandos' Life and Work', 43.

35   Harry Lourandos, 'Forces of Change: Aboriginal Technology and Population in
     South Western Victoria', PhD thesis, University of Sydney, 1980, 16.

36   Robinson as in AS Kenyon, 'The Aboriginal Protectorate of Port Phillip', *Victorian
     History Magazine* 12 (1928), 134–72, 150.

37   Harry Lourandos, 'Swamp Managers of South-Western Victoria', in John
     Mulvaney and J Peter White (eds), *Australians to 1788* (Sydney: Fairfax, Syme &
     Weldon, 1987), 292–307, 298.

38   Robinson's observation was made on 7 July 1841, as quoted in Harry Lourandos,
     'Interim Report on Archaeological Field Work in South-Western Victoria,
     1974/75', 1975, AIATSIS Library, PMS 1040/12058, 3.

39   Harry Lourandos, 'Change or Stability?: Hydraulics, Hunter-Gatherers and
     Population in Temperate Australia', *World Archaeology* 11 (1980), 245–64, 253.

40   Aldo Massola, 'The Native Fish Trap at Toolondo, in the Wimmera', *Victorian
     Naturalist* 79 (1962), 162–66.

41   Lourandos, 'Interim Report', 6.

42   Lourandos, 'Swamp Managers of South-Western Victoria', 306–7.

43   Lourandos, 'Swamp Managers of South-Western Victoria', 307.

44   Lesley Head, 'Pollen Analysis of Sediments from the Bridgewater Caves
     Archaeological Site, Southwestern Victoria', *Australian Archaeology* 20 (Jun 1985),
     1–15, 12–13.

45   Lourandos, 'Forces of Change', 220–24.

46   Harry Lourandos, 'Intensification: A Late-Pleistocene–Holocene Archaeological
     Sequence from South-Western Victoria', *Archaeology in Oceania* 18 (1983), 81–94, 85.

47   Lourandos, 'Intensification'; Lourandos, 'Forces of Change', 422.

48   Marcia Langton, 'Earth, Wind, Fire and Water: The Social and Spiritual
     Construction of Water in Aboriginal Societies', in David, Barker and McNiven,
     The Social Archaeology of Australian Indigenous Societies, 139–60, 159.

49   Lourandos, 'Swamp Managers of South-Western Victoria', 296; Jenny Hocking
     and Nell Reidy, 'Marngrook, Tom Wills and the Continuing Denial of Indigenous
     History: On the Origins of Australian Football', *Meanjin* 75(2) (Jun 2016), 83–93.

50   Lourandos, 'Swamp Managers of South-Western Victoria', 307.

51   Lourandos, 'Intensification', 92.

52   Lourandos et al., 'An Interview with Harry Lourandos', 28.

53   Elizabeth Williams, *Complex Hunter-Gatherers: A Late-Holocene Example from
     Temperate Australia* (Oxford: British Archaeological Reports, 1988), 222.

54   Bruce Pascoe, *Dark Emu: Black Seeds: Agriculture or Accident?* (Broome: Magabala
     Books, 2014), 156.

55   Pascoe, *Dark Emu*, 156.

56   This has been a key preoccupation of Geoffrey Blainey's, for whom isolation and distance are part of the answer. For a recent iteration see the first chapter of John Hirst, *Australian History in 7 Questions* (Melbourne: Black Inc., 2014). See also J Peter White, 'New Guinea and Australian Prehistory: The "Neolithic Problem"', in John Mulvaney and Jack Golson (eds), *Aboriginal Man and Environment in Australia* (Canberra: ANU Press, 1971), 182–95; J Peter White, 'Revisiting the "Neolithic Problem" in Australia', *Records of the Western Australian Museum* 79 (2011), 86–92, 86.

57   Rhys Jones, 'The Neolithic, Palaeolithic and the Hunting Gardeners: Man and Land in the Antipodes', in RP Suggate and M Cresswell (eds), *Quaternary Studies* (Wellington: Royal Society of New Zealand, 1975), 21–34.

58   Alistair Paterson, 'Once Were Foragers: The Archaeology of Agrarian Australia and the Fate of Aboriginal Land Management', *Quaternary International* (In Press, Mar 2017), 1–13, 11.

59   John M Beaton, 'The Riches of Ancient Australia: An Indispensable Guide for Exploring Prehistoric Australia (Book Review)', *Australian Aboriginal Studies* (2) (1993), 101–03, 103. The original quote comes from Josephine Flood, *The Riches of Ancient Australia: An Indispensable Guide for Exploring Prehistoric Australia* (St Lucia: University of Queensland Press, 1993), 26.

60   John Mulvaney, *The Prehistory of Australia* (Ringwood, Vic: Penguin Books, 1975), 239.

61   Harry Lourandos, 'Australia and the Origins of Agriculture (Book Review)', *Australian Archaeology* 70 (Jun 2010), 75–77, 76–77.

62   Harry Lourandos, 'Comment on B Hayden, "Research and Development in the Stone Age: Technological Transitions among Hunter-Gatherers"', *Current Anthropology* 22(5) (1981), 536–37, 536; Harry Lourandos, *Continent of Hunter-Gatherers: New Perspectives in Australian Prehistory* (Melbourne: Cambridge University Press, 1997).

63   The discovery of Pleistocene dates for occupation in the heart of the arid zone, for example, undermined a core tenet of the intensification model: that these were marginal landscapes, only occupied during the last few thousand years. The chronology and mechanism of intensification was also hotly contested on the banks of the Murray River: the most populated part of Australia in the Holocene. Mike Smith, *The Archaeology of Australia's Deserts* (Cambridge: Cambridge University Press, 2013), 273; Stephen Webb, *Palaeopathology of Aboriginal Australians: Health and Disease across a Hunter-Gatherer Population* (Cambridge: Cambridge University Press, 1995), 279; Colin Pardoe, 'The Pleistocene Is Still with Us: Analytical Constraints and Possibilities for the Study of Ancient Human Remains in Archaeology', in Smith, Spriggs and Fankhauser, *Sahul in Review*, 81–94.

64   Caroline Bird and David Frankel, 'Chronology and Explanation in Western Victoria and South-East South Australia', *Archaeology in Oceania* 26(1) (Apr 1991), 1–16, 10.

65   This sentence paraphrases David Frankel, 'The Australian Transition: Real and Perceived Boundaries', *Antiquity* 69(265) (1995), 649–55, 653. See also Caroline Bird and David Frankel, *An Archaeology of Gariwerd: From Pleistocene to Holocene in Western Victoria* (St Lucia, Qld: Tempus 8, University of Queensland, 2005), esp. 27–36.

66   Ian J McNiven et al, 'Dating Aboriginal Stone-Walled Fishtraps at Lake Condah, Southeast Australia', *Journal of Archaeological Science* 39(2) (2012), 268–86, 284.

67   Alan N Williams, 'A New Population Curve for Prehistoric Australia', *Proceedings: Biological Sciences* 280 (1761) (22 Jun 2013), 1–9, 1.

68   Peter Hiscock, *Archaeology of Ancient Australia* (London: Routledge, 2008), 120; Pardoe, 'The Pleistocene Is Still with Us'.

69   Roger Luebbers, 'Ancient Boomerangs Discovered in South Australia', *Nature* 253 (1975), 39.

70   Those that have been put forward, such as Alan Williams' population curve, are promoted as 'first-order frameworks' to be used alongside detailed regional research. See Alan N Williams et al., 'A Continental Narrative: Human Settlement Patterns and Australian Climate Change Over the Last 35,000 years', *Quaternary Science Reviews* 123 (2015), 91–112, 106.

71   Sean Ulm, '"Complexity" and the Australian Continental Narrative: Themes in the Archaeology of Holocene Australia', *Quaternary International* 285 (Feb 2013), 182–92, 189.

72   Lourandos and Ross, 'The Great "Intensification Debate"', 59.

73   Bernard MJ Huchet, 'Theories and Australian Prehistory: The Last Three Decades', *Australian Archaeology* 33 (Dec 1991), 44–51, 49. Mulvaney did not consider this pragmatic use of theory a bad thing. 'Australians may not theorise in the American manner,' he reflected in 2012, 'but their "theory" lies in the application of ethnographic or written ethno-historic evidence that is unavailable elsewhere in such complexity for hunter-gatherer studies.' John Mulvaney, *Digging Up a Past* (Sydney: UNSW Press, 2011), 329.

74   Sylvia J Hallam, 'Reflections on Burrill Lake: Archaeologist as Ecologist', *Anthropological Forum* 3(2) (1972), 197–204, 200.

75   She collaborated with Neville Green as a biographer for the Aboriginal volumes of the *Bicentennial Dictionary of Western Australia*. Bird, 'Preface', x; Sylvia J Hallam, 'A View from the Other Side of the Western Frontier: Or "I Met a Man Who Wasn't There ..."', *Aboriginal History* 7 (1983), 134–56.

TEN   Hunting the Pleistocene: The History and Politics of Jinmium and Madjedbebe

1   Richard Fullagar, David Price and Lesley Head, 'Early Human Occupation of Northern Australia: Archaeology and Thermoluminescence Dating of Jinmium Rock-Shelter, Northern Territory', *Antiquity* 70(270) (Dec 1996), 751–73.

2   Richard Fullagar, 'Traces of Times Past: Stone Artefacts into Prehistory', *Australian Archaeology* 39 (1994), 63–73, 64.

3   Paddy Carlton, in Geoffrey Burchfield (prod.), *The Sands of the Dreamtime: Burden of Proof* (1997), Sydney: ABC TV, Quantum.

4   Richard Fullagar and Lesley Head, 'Exploring the Prehistory of Hunter-Gatherer Attachment to Place: An Example from the Keep River Area, Northern Territory, Australia', in Peter Ucko and Robert Layton (eds), *The Archaeology and Anthropology of Landscape* (London: Routledge, 1999), 322–35, 333.

5   Fullagar and Simon, as quoted in James Woodford, 'Unearthed: Australia's Lost
     Civilisation', *Sydney Morning Herald*, 21 Sept 1996, 29, 32.

6   Graeme Leech, 'Experts at Odds over Archaeological Dating', *Australian*, 23 Sept
     1996, 5.

7   Woodford, 'Unearthed', 32; 'We Believe It Is Better to Present the Evidence',
     Sydney Morning Herald, 21 Sept 1996, 33.

8   Stephen Brook, 'Carvings May Mark a Pathway for Nomads', *Australian*, 23 Sept
     1996, 4.

9   As quoted in Ann Gibbons, 'Doubts Over Spectacular Dates', *Science*, New Series
     278(5336) (10 Oct 1997), 220–22, 220.

10   Richard G Roberts et al., 'Optical and Radiocarbon Dating at Jinmium Rock
     Shelter in Northern Australia', *Nature* 393 (28 May 1998), 358–62.

11   Fullagar et al., 'Early Human Occupation of Northern Australia'. See also Paul SC
     Taçon, Richard Fullagar, Sven Ouzman and Ken Mulvaney, 'Cupule Engravings
     from Jinmium-Granilpi (Northern Australia) and Beyond: Exploration of a
     Widespread and Enigmatic Class of Rock Markings', *Antiquity* 71(274) (Dec
     1997), 942–65.

12   Paul SC Taçon and Richard Fullagar, 'Living with the Past', *Sydney Morning
     Herald*, 24 Sept 1996, 13; James Woodford, 'The Dating Game', *Sydney Morning
     Herald*, 28 Sept 1996, 33; Lesley Head, 'Headlines and Songlines', *Meanjin* 55(4)
     (1996), 736–43, 737.

13   James Woodford, 'Unveiled: Outback Stonehenge that Will Rewrite our History',
     Sydney Morning Herald, 21 Sept 1996, 1.

14   John Noble Wilford, 'In Australia, Signs of Artists Who Predate Homo Sapiens',
     New York Times, 21 Sept 1996; James Woodford, 'The Arrival of Man and Nature
     of Art', *Sydney Morning Herald*, 21 Sept 1996, 33; 'We Believe it Is Better to
     Present the Evidence'; 'The People Behind the Discoveries', *Sydney Morning
     Herald*, 21 Sept 1996, 33.

15   Fullagar, as quoted in Woodford, 'Unveiled', 1.

16   Graeme Leech, 'Scientists Split over Rock Find's Implications for Evolution',
     Australian, 23 Sept 1996, 1.

17   Ackerman, as quoted in Woodford, 'Unveiled', 1; White, as quoted in Woodford,
     'The Dating Game', 33.

18   Paul Willis, 'Jinmium Revisited', *The Slab*, 25 Mar 1999.

19   Nicolas Rothwell, 'Politics Etched in Stone', *Australian*, 23 Sept 1996, 1, 4.

20   Mike Morwood, 'Jinmium and the Dilemmas of Dating', *Australian*, 24 Sept
     1996, 13.

21   Graeme Leech, 'Scientists Query Dating Methods in Historic Rock Find',
     Australian, 24 Sept 1996, 1, 4.

22   Hanson, as quoted in Ann Curthoys, 'Expulsion, Exodus and Exile in White
     Australian Mythology', *Journal of Australian Studies* 23(61) (1999), 1–19,
     17–18.

23   The case, *Ben Ward and Others v. The State of Western Australia and Others*, is
     explored in Libby Riches, 'Exploring Encounter: A New Relationship Between
     Archaeologists and Indigenous People?', in Tim Murray (ed.), *Archaeology from
     Australia* (Melbourne: Australian Scholarly Publishing, 2004), 151–67, 157.

24 Maria Ceresa, 'Territory Will Extend Park to Protect Site', *Australian*, 23 Sept 1996, 5; Maria Ceresa, 'Rock that Holds Fingerprints of Life', *Australian*, 25 Sept 1996, 1.

25 Rothwell, 'Politics Etched in Stone', 4.

26 Rothwell, 'Politics Etched in Stone', 1.

27 Editorial, 'Jinmium Find Call for Caution', *Australian*, 24 Sept 1996, 12.

28 Roberts et al., 'Optical and Radiocarbon Dating at Jinmium Rock Shelter in Northern Australia'; Alan Watchman, Paul Taçon, Richard Fullagar and Lesley Head, 'Minimum Ages for Pecked Rock Markings from Jinmium, North Western Australia', *Archaeology in Oceania* 35(1) (Apr 2000), 1–10.

29 Graeme Leech, 'Our Origins on Rocky Ground', *Australian*, 28–29 Sept 1996, 27; Bruce Bower, 'Australian Site Jumps Forward in Time', *Science News* 153(22) (1998), 343.

30 Graeme Leech, 'Dates for the Rock Art Site at Jinmium (NT) May Have Been Miscalculated', *Australian*, 21 Feb 1997, 13.

31 Lesley Head, 'Risky Representations: The "Seduction of Wholeness" and the Public Face of Australian Archaeology', *Australian Archaeology* 46 (Jun 1998), 1–4, 1.

32 Grahame Clark, *World Prehistory: An Outline* (Cambridge: Cambridge University Press, 1961), 243.

33 Rhys Jones, 'Australia Felix – The Discovery of a Pleistocene Prehistory', *Journal of Human Evolution* 6(4) (1977), 353–61, 357.

34 George Seddon, as quoted in Kirsty Douglas, *Pictures of Time Beneath: Science, Heritage and the Uses of the Deep Past* (Collingwood, Vic: CSIRO Publishing, 2010), 11.

35 The name was formally changed in 2013 by the Mirarr people to better reflect its location on their country.

36 Lenore Nicklin, 'The Prehistory Cowboy Strikes Again', *Bulletin*, 12 Jun 1990, 92–93, 93.

37 Evelyn Fox Keller, *Reflections on Gender and Science* (New Haven: Yale University Press, 1985).

38 Stephanie Moser, 'Science, Stratigraphy and the Deep Sequence: Excavation versus Regional Survey and the Question of Gendered Practice in Archaeology', *Antiquity* 70(270) (Dec 1996), 813–23, 818.

39 RJ Lampert and Betty Meehan, 'The Big Man Award', *Australian Archaeology* 25 (1987), 113–14.

40 Elizabeth Williams, 'AAA Big Man Award', *Australian Archaeology* 39 (1994), 134.

41 Sharon Sullivan, comment in Andrew Pike and Ann McGrath (dir.), *Message from Mungo* (2014), Canberra: Ronin Films. This interpretation does not contradict Laurajane Smith and Hilary du Cros' observation in 1993 that, statistically, 'the majority of work done on the Pleistocene is done by men'. Hilary du Cros and Laurajane Smith, 'Introduction', in Hilary du Cros and Laurajane Smith (eds), *Women in Archaeology: A Feminist Critique* (Canberra: Department of Prehistory, Research School of the Pacific and Asian Studies, Australian National University, 1993), xvii–xx, xviii.

42 Christopher Chippindale, 'In Science, Publication Is Always Provisional', *Australian*, 6 Dec 1996, 11.

43 Nigel Spooner, 'Human Occupation at Jinmium, Northern Australia: 116,000 Years Ago or Much Less?', *Antiquity* 72(275) (1998), 173–78; RF Galbraith et al., 'Optical Dating of Single and Multiple Grains of Quartz from Jinmium Rock Shelter, Northern Australia, Part I, Experimental Design and Statistical Models', *Archaeometry* 41 (1999), 339–64; RG Roberts et al., 'Optical Dating of Single and Multiple Grains of Quartz from Jinmium Rock Shelter, Northern Australia, Part II, Results and Implications', *Archaeometry* 41 (1999), 365–95.

44 Paul SC Taçon, 'Tracking Time: The Story of a Human Concern', *The Slab*, 30 Sept 1999.

45 As quoted in Sally Green, *Prehistorian: A Biography of V. Gordon Childe* (Bradford-on-Avon: Moonraker Press, 1981), 167.

46 Rhys Jones, 'Dating the Human Colonization of Australia: Radiocarbon and Luminescence Revolutions', *Proceedings of the British Academy* 99 (1999), 37–65. See also James R Arnold interviewed by Rhys Jones and Mike Smith, ANU, 28 Sept 1993, Transcript, Rhys Jones Papers, National Library of Australia, MS ACC 03/250, Folder 112, Box 23, 7.

47 Martin Aitken, *Science-Based Dating in Archaeology* (London: Longman, 1990).

48 Tim Flannery, *The Future Eaters: An Ecological History of the Australasian Lands and People* (Sydney: Reed New Holland, 1994), 151.

49 Rhys Jones, Richard G Roberts and Michael A Smith, 'Beyond the Radiocarbon Barrier in Australian Prehistory', *Antiquity* 68 (Sept 1994), 611.

50 Henry Polach has demonstrated that AMS is capable of dating extremely high-quality samples to around 65,000 years, but such large samples are rarely preserved in the upper layers of archaeological sites, let alone near the bottom. Claudio Tuniz, Richard Gillespie and Cheryl Jones, *The Bone Readers: Atoms, Genes and the Politics of Australia's Deep Past* (Crows Nest, NSW: Allen & Unwin, 2009), 33.

51 Charles Dortch, *Devils Lair: A Study in Prehistory* (Perth: Western Australian Museum, 1984).

52 Richard G Roberts, 'Luminescence Dating in Archaeology: From Origins to Optical', *Radiation Measurements* 27(5/6) (1997), 819–892, 853; Jones, 'Dating Australian Colonisation', 45.

53 Jim Allen, 'When Did Humans First Colonize Australia?', *Search* 20(5) (1989), 149–154.

54 Sandra Bowdler, 'Sunda and Sahul: A 30 kyr BP Culture Area?', in M Spriggs *et al* (eds), *A Community of Culture: The People and Prehistory of the Pacific* (Canberra: Department of Prehistory, Research School of Pacific Studies, Australian National University, 1993), 60–70, 65.

55 Jones, 'Dating the Human Colonization of Australia', 45–46; Rhys Jones, 'Ions and Eons: Some Thoughts on Archaeological Science and Scientific Archaeology', in WR Ambrose and P Duerden (eds), *Archaeometry: An Australasian Perspective* (Canberra: Australian National University, Research School of Pacific Studies, Department of Prehistory, 1982), 22–35, 30.

56   Rhys Jones, 'The Fifth Continent: Problems Concerning the Human Colonisation of Australia', *Annual Review of Anthropology* 8 (1979), 445–66, 460.

57   Rhys Jones, 'Different Strokes for Different Folks: Sites, Scale and Strategy', in Ian Johnson (ed.), *Holier than Thou: Proceedings of the 1978 Kiola Conference on Australian Prehistory* (Canberra: Department of Prehistory, Research School of Pacific Studies, Australian National University, 1980), 151–71.

58   Rhys Jones, 'Kakadu. Archaeological Expedition to the Kakadu National Park, Book 1', 27 May–4 Aug 1981, Field Journals, AIATSIS Library, MS 5040/1/55, 42.

59   John Mulvaney to Dave Lindner, 10 Sept 1969, John Mulvaney Papers, National Library of Australia, MS 9615/1/6, Box 1.

60   Jones, comment in Burchfield, *The Sands of the Dreamtime*; Rhys Jones and Ian Johnson, 'Deaf Adder Gorge: Lindner Site, Nauwalabila 1', in Rhys Jones (ed.), *Archaeological Research in Kakadu National Park* (Canberra: Australian National Parks and Wildlife Service, 1985), 165–228.

61   Richard G Roberts, 'Sediment Budgets and Quaternary History of the Magela Creek Catchment, Tropical Northern Australia', PhD thesis, University of Wollongong, 1991.

62   Mike Smith, *The Archaeology of Australia's Deserts* (Melbourne: Cambridge University Press, 2013), iv.

63   Richard G Roberts, Rhys Jones and Michael A Smith, 'Optical Dating at Deaf Adder Gorge, Northern Territory, Indicates Human Occupation between 53,000 and 60,000 Years Ago', *Australian Archaeology* 37 (Dec 1993), 58–59.

64   Richard G Roberts, 'The Celtic Chronologist: Rhys Jones and the Dating of the Human Colonisation of Australia', in Atholl Anderson, Ian Lilley and Sue O'Connor (eds), *Histories of Old Ages: Essays in Honour of Rhys Jones* (Canberra: Pandanus Books, 2001), 89–93, 90.

65   Nicklin, 'The Prehistory Cowboy Strikes Again', 93.

66   Roberts, 'The Celtic Chronologist', 91.

67   Mike Smith, 'Field Notes: Archaeological Excavations at Malakunanja II: July–August 1989', 1989, Field Journals, AIATSIS Library, Canberra.

68   Roberts et al., 'Thermoluminescence Dating of a 50,000 year-old Site'.

69   Virginia Morell, 'The Earliest Art Becomes Older – And More Common', *Science* 267 (Mar 31 1995), 1908.

70   Irina Dunn, Notices of Motion to the Senate, *Hansard*, 16 May 1990, 425.

71   Klein, as quoted in Morell, 'The Earliest Art Becomes Older', 1908.

72   Richard G Roberts, Rhys Jones and Michael A Smith, 'Early Dates at Malakunanja II: a Reply to Bowdler, *Australian Archaeology* 31 (Dec 1990), 94–97.

73   Peter Hiscock gives an overview of these criticisms in *Archaeology of Ancient Australia*, 34–37, 42–44. The 1989 excavation has recently been written up with a full site report. See Chris Clarkson et al., 'The Archaeology, Chronology and Stratigraphy of Madjedbebe (Malakunanja II): A Site in Northern Australia with Early Occupation', *Journal of Human Evolution* 83 (2015), 46–64

74   John Mulvaney and Johan Kamminga, *Prehistory of Australia* (St Leonards, NSW: Allen & Unwin, 1999), 138.

75   James F O'Connell and Jim Allen, 'When Did Humans First Arrive in Greater

Australia, and Why Is it Important to Know?', *Evolutionary Anthropology* 6 (1998) 132–46, 142.

76 James F O'Connell and Jim Allen, 'Dating the Colonization of Sahul (Pleistocene Australia-New Guinea): A Review of Recent Research', *Journal of Archaeological Science* 31(6) (Jun 2004), 835–53.

77 Jim Allen and James F O'Connell, 'Both Half Right: Updating the Evidence for Dating First Human Arrivals in Sahul', *Australian Archaeology*, 79 (Dec 2014), 86–108, 103.

78 William F Keegan, 'Now Bring Me That Horizon', comment on JF O'Connell and J Allen, 'The Restaurant at the End of the Universe: Modelling the Colonisation of Sahul', *Australian Archaeology* 74 (2012), 5–31, 22.

79 Allen and O'Connell, 'Both Half Right', 86.

80 Chris Clarkson et al., 'Human Occupation of Northern Australia by 65,000 Years Ago', *Nature* 547 (20 Jul 2017), 306–10.

81 Nicholas St Fleur, 'Humans First Arrived in Australia 65,000 Years Ago, Study Suggests', *New York Times*, 19 Jul 2017.

82 Clarkson et al., 'The Archaeology, Chronology and Stratigraphy of Madjedbebe'; Billy Griffiths, 'A World in a Grain of Sand: The Malakunanja II Diaries', *Griffith Review* 41 (2013), 162–77.

83 As quoted in Helen Davidson and Calla Wahlquist, 'Australian Dig Finds Evidence of Aboriginal Habitation up to 80,000 Years Ago', *Guardian Australia*, 20 Jul 2017.

84 Sally K May et al., 'Symbols of Power: The Firearm Paintings of Madjedbebe (Malakunanja II)', *International Journal of Historical Archaeology* (2017), 1–18, 15.

85 Philip Jones, *Ochre and Rust: Artefacts and Encounters on Australian Frontiers* (Kent Town: Wakefield Press, 2007), 349.

86 Kelsey M Lowe et al., 'Ground-Penetrating Radar and Burial Practices in Western Arnhem Land, Australia: GPR and Burials in Arnhem Land, Australia', *Archaeology in Oceania* 49 (2014), 148–57.

87 Steven Mithen, *After the Ice: A Global Human History 20,000–5000 BC* (London: Phoenix, 2004), 3; Jared Diamond, *Guns, Germs and Steel: A Short History of Everybody for the Last 13,000 years* (London: Vintage, 1998), 39.

88 Jared Diamond, *The Rise and Fall of the Third Chimpanzee* (London: Radius, 1991), 48.

89 Lydia V Pyne and Stephen J Pyne, *The Last Lost World: Ice Ages, Human Origins, and the Invention of the Pleistocene* (New York: Viking, 2012), 195.

90 This so-called revolution is often referred to as 'The Upper Palaeolithic Mirage'. Sally McBrearty and Alison S Brooks, 'The Revolution That Wasn't: A New Interpretation of the Origin of Modern Human Behavior', *Journal of Human Evolution* 39 (2000), 453–563.

91 Steven Oppenheimer, *Out of Africa's Eden: The Peopling of the World* (Jeppestown: Jonathan Ball Publishers, 2003), 55.

92 The key article for the ascendancy of the 'out of Africa' hypothesis was: Rebecca L Cann, Mark Stoneking and Allan C Wilson, 'Mitochondrial DNA and Human Evolution,' *Nature* 325(6099) (1987), 31–36.

93 Peter Brown, 'Pleistocene Homogeneity and Holocene Size Reduction: The Australian Human Skeletal Evidence', *Archaeology in Oceania* 22(2) (Jul 1987),

41–67; Colin Pardoe, 'Australian Biological Anthropology for Archaeologists', in Murray, *Archaeology from Australia*, 131–50, 132–36.

94 Jean-Jacques Hublin et al., 'New Fossils from Jebel Irhoud, Morocco and the Pan-African Origin of *Homo Sapiens*', *Nature* 546 (8 Jun 2017), 289–92.

95 Mithen, *After the Ice*, 3.

96 James Shreeve, *The Neanderthal Enigma: Solving the Mystery of Modern Human Origins* (New York: William Morrow and Company Inc, 1995), 8–9.

97 P Vermeersch et al., 'A Middle Palaeolithic Burial of a Modern Human at Taramsa Hill, Egypt', *Antiquity* 72(277) (Sept 1998), 475–84; Oppenheimer, *Out of Africa's Eden*, 54–63.

98 Quentin D Atkinson, Russell D Gray and Alexei J Drummond, 'mtDNA Variation Predicts Population Size in Humans and Reveals a Major Southern Asian Chapter in Human Prehistory', *Molecular Biology and Evolution* 25(2) (Mar 2008), 468–74; Vincent Macaulay et al., 'Single, Rapid Coastal Settlement of Asia Revealed by Analysis of Complete Mitochondrial Genomes', *Science* (13 May 2005), 1034–36.

99 Stephen Oppenheimer, *The Real Eve: Modern Man's Journey Out of Africa* (New York: Carroll & Graf Publishers, 2004), 82.

100 There is a suggestion that people had reached India before the Toba eruption and strong evidence that its effects were regional. See Chris Clarkson, Sacha Jones and Clair Harris, 'Continuity and Change in the Lithic Industries of the Jurreru Valley, India, Before and After the Toba Eruption', *Quaternary International* 258 (May 2012), 165–79.

101 This was the subject of the First Mariners Project, in which a team of archaeologists constructed and tested a variety of watercrafts to ascertain the navigational skills and cognitive and technological capabilities required to cross into Australia. Robert G Bednarik, 'Replicating the First Known Sea Travel by Humans: The Lower Pleistocene Crossing of Lombok Strait', *Human Evolution* 16(3–4) (Jul–Dec 2001), 229–42.

102 Jane Ada Fletcher, *The Stone Age Man of Tasmania: A Brief Account of His Life and Conditions* (Hobart: Tasmanian Education, 1956), 1.

103 Tools dated at 840,000 years old found beneath lava flows in Flores show that *Homo erectus* did cross the treacherous Lombok Strait and, in doing so, Wallace's Line. Adam Brumm et al., 'Early Stone Technology on Flores and its Implications for Homo Floresiensis', *Nature* 441(7093) (2006), 624–28.

104 William Noble and Iain Davidson, *Human Evolution, Language and Mind: A Psychological and Archaeological Inquiry* (Hong Kong: Cambridge University Press, 1996), 217.

105 Stan Grant, *Talking to My Country* (Sydney: HarperCollins, 2016), 10.

106 Mike Smith, 'Genyornis: Last of the Dromornithids', in Libby Robin, Robert Heinsohn and Leo Joseph (eds), *Boom and Bust: Bird Stories for a Dry Country* (Melbourne: CSIRO Publishing, 2009), 147–83, 163, 180–81.

107 Joseph B Birdsell, 'The Recalibration of a Paradigm for the First Peopling of Greater Australia', in Jim Allen, Jack Golson and Rhys Jones (eds), *Sunda and Sahul: Prehistoric Studies in Southeast Asia, Melanesia and Australia* (London: Academic Press, 1977), 113–67, 123.

108 Sandra Bowdler, 'The Coastal Colonisation of Australia', in Allen, Jones and
     Golson, *Sunda and Sahul*, 205–46, 205, 213.
109 Smith, *The Archaeology of Australia's Deserts*, 89.
110 Veth put these ideas forward in his PhD, later published as: Peter Veth, *Islands
     in the Interior: The Dynamics of Prehistoric Adaptations within the Arid Zone of
     Australia* (Ann Arbor, Michigan: International Monographs in Prehistory, 1993).
111 Peter Hiscock and Lynley Wallis, 'Pleistocene Settlement of Deserts from an
     Australian Perspective', in Peter Veth, Mike Smith and Peter Hiscock (eds), *Desert
     Peoples: Archaeological Perspectives* (Oxford: Blackwell Publishers, 2005), 34–57.
112 K Huopenen, TG Schurr, Y-S Chen, and D Wallace, 'Mitochondrial DNA
     Variation in an Aboriginal Australian Population: Evidence for Genetic Isolation
     and Regional Differentiation', *Human Immunology* 62 (2001), 954–69; Ray Tobler
     et al., 'Aboriginal Mitogenomes Reveal 50,000 Years of Regionalism in Australia',
     Nature 544 (13 Apr 2017), 180–84; Anna-Sapfo Malaspinas et al., 'A Genomic
     History of Aboriginal Australia', *Nature* 538 (13 Oct 2016), 207–14.
113 Ken Mulvaney, 'Iconic Imagery: Pleistocene Rock Art Development Across
     Northern Australia', *Quaternary International* 285 (Feb 2013), 99–110, 99.
114 Duncan Merrilees, 'Man the Destroyer: Late Quaternary Changes in the
     Australian Marsupial Fauna', *Journal of the Royal Society of Western Australia* 51
     (1968), 1–24.
115 Rhys Jones, 'The Neolithic, Palaeolithic and the Hunting Gardeners: Man and
     Land in the Antipodes', in RP Suggate and M Cresswell (eds), *Quaternary Studies*
     (Wellington: Royal Society of New Zealand, 1975), 21–34, 29–30.
116 Flannery, *The Future Eaters*, 160.
117 Richard G Roberts et al., 'New Ages for the Last Australian Megafauna: Continent-
     Wide Extinction About 46,000 Years Ago', *Science* 292(5523) (2001), 1888–92.
118 Tim Flannery, 'Pleistocene Faunal Loss: Implications of the Aftershock for
     Australia's Past and Future', *Archaeology in Oceania* 25 (1990), 45–67.
119 Marcia Langton, *The Quiet Revolution: Indigenous People and the Resources Boom*,
     Boyer Lectures 2012 (Sydney: Harper Collins, 2013), 24–27; Tuniz et al., *The
     Bone Readers*, 64, 130; Lesley Head, 'Meganesian Barbecue: Reply to Seddon',
     Meanjin, 54 (1995), 702–09.
120 See, for example, Paul S Martin, 'The Discovery of America', *Science* 179 (4077)
     (9 Mar 1973), 969–74, 969.
121 Chris Johnson, *Australia's Mammal Extinctions: A 50,000 Year History* (Melbourne:
     Cambridge University Press, 2006), 114.
122 Lesley Head, 'The (Aboriginal) Face of the (Australian) Earth', The Jack Golson
     Lecture series, Centre for Archaeological Research, Australian National University,
     2006, 15.
123 Libby Robin and Tom Griffiths, 'Environmental History in Australasia',
     Environment and History 10(4) (Nov 2004), 439–74, 458.
124 David Horton, *The Pure State of Nature: Sacred Cows, Destructive Myths and the
     Environment* (St Leonards, NSW: Allen & Unwin, 2000), 122.
125 Michael C Westaway, Jon Olley and Rainer Grün, 'At Least 17,000 Years of
     Coexistence: Modern Humans and Megafauna at the Willandra Lakes, South-
     Eastern Australia', *Quaternary Science Reviews* 157 (Feb 2017), 206–11. See also

Giles Hamm et al., 'Cultural Innovation and Megafauna Interaction in the Early Settlement of Arid Australia', *Nature* 539(7628) (2016), 280–83.

126 St Fleur, 'Humans First Arrived in Australia 65,000 Years Ago'.

127 Hiscock, *Archaeology of Ancient Australia*, 56–57.

128 See David MJS Bowman, 'The Australian Summer Monsoon: A Biogeographic Perspective', *Australian Geographical Studies* 40 (2002), 261–77, 267.

129 Stephen E Lewis et al., 'Post-Glacial Sea-Level Changes Around the Australian Margin: A Review', *Quaternary Science Reviews* 74 (2013), 115–38, 124.

130 There are differences between the rate of flooding and the rate of sea-level rise, due to contours in the Sunda Shelf. During an earlier pulse, between 14,300 and 14,600 years ago, the sea level rose about 16 metres in only 300 years. TJJ Hanebuth, K Stattegger and PM Grootes, 'Rapid Flooding of the Sunda Shelf: A Late-Glacial Sea-Level Record', *Science* 288 (2000), 1033–35, 1034.

131 Paul Taçon and Christopher Chippindale, 'Australia's Ancient Warriors: Changing Depictions of Fighting in the Rock Art of Arnhem Land, N.T.', *Cambridge Archaeological Journal* 4 (1994), 211–48.

132 Darrell Lewis, *The Rock Paintings of Arnhem Land, Australia: Social, Ecological and Material Culture Change in the Post-Glacial Period* (Oxford: BAR International Series 415, 1988), 90–91.

133 Rhys Jones, 'Recommendations for Archaeological Site Management in Kakadu National Park', in Jones, *Archaeological Research in Kakadu National Park*, 305–06.

134 Carmel Schrire, *Digging Through Darkness: Chronicles of an Archaeologist* (Charlottesville: University Press of Virginia, 1995), 11.

135 Tony Wright, 'Australia's Oldest Human Technology Emerges From 65,000 Hidden Years', *Sydney Morning Herald*, 20 Jul 2017; Davidson and Wahlquist, 'Australian Dig Finds Evidence of Aboriginal Habitation up to 80,000 Years Ago'.

136 Kira E Westaway, 'An Early Modern Human Presence in Sumatra 73,000–63,000 Years Ago', *Nature* 548 (17 Aug 2017), 322–25.

137 Mulvaney and Kamminga, *Prehistory of Australia*, 111.

138 Head, 'Headlines and Songlines', 743.

139 Paul Irish, *Hidden in Plain View: The Aboriginal People of Coastal Sydney* (Sydney: New South Publishing, 2017), 18–19.

140 Susan Lawrence and Peter Davies, *An Archaeology of Australia Since 1788* (New York: Springer, 2010).

EPILOGUE   **Australia's Classical Culture**

1 Bernard Smith, 'History and the Collector (1974)', in *The Death of the Artist as Hero: Essays in History and Culture* (Melbourne: Oxford University Press, 1988), 97–98.

2 Noel Pearson, 'A Rightful Place: Race, Recognition and a More Complete Commonwealth', Quarterly Essay 55 (Melbourne: Black Inc., 2014), 36.

3 Bill Neidjie, Stephen Davis and Allan Fox, *Kakadu Man ... Bill Neidjie* (Darwin: Mybrood, 1986), 48.

4 David Christian, *Maps of Time: An Introduction to Big History* (Berkeley: University of California Press, 2004), 2, 3.

5   Perkins, as quoted in Peter Read, *Charles Perkins: A Biography* (Melbourne: Viking, 1990), 315.

6   Perkins' 1984 Australia Day address in Melbourne, as quoted in Read, *Charles Perkins*, ix.

7   First Nations National Constitutional Convention, 'Uluru Statement from the Heart', Press Release, 26 May 2017.

8   Greg Dening, 'The History in Things and Places', in Tim Bonyhady and Tom Griffiths (eds), *Prehistory to Politics: John Mulvaney, the Humanities and the Public Intellectual* (Melbourne: Melbourne University Press, 1996), 85–97, 97.

9   Emphasis in original. Denis Byrne, 'Deep Nation: Australia's Acquisition of an Indigenous Past', *Aboriginal History* 20 (1998), 82–107, 99.

10   Harry Allen, 'History Matters: A Commentary on Divergent Interpretations of Australian History', *Australian Aboriginal Studies* 2 (1988), 79–89, 83.

11   Byrne, 'Deep Nation', 99.

Index